BLUE

SIMON AND SCHUSTER

NEW YORK   LONDON   TORONTO   SYDNEY   TOKYO   SINGAPORE

THUNDER

**How the Mafia Owned
and Finally Murdered
Cigarette Boat King
Donald Aronow**

THOMAS BURDICK
AND CHARLENE MITCHELL

Simon and Schuster
Simon & Schuster Building
Rockefeller Center
1230 Avenue of the Americas
New York, New York 10020

Copyright © 1990 by Thomas Burdick

Designed by Levavi & Levavi
Manufactured in the United States of America

10   9   8   7   6   5   4   3   2   1

Library of Congress Cataloging in Publication Data
Burdick, Thomas, date.
   Blue Thunder: how the Mafia owned and finally murdered Cigarette boat king
Donald Aronow/Thomas Burdick and Charlene Mitchell
      p. cm.
      1. Murder—Florida—Miami—Case studies.   2. Aronow, Donald Joel,
d. 1987. 3. Drug traffic—Florida—Miami—Case studies.   4. Mafia—Florida—
Miami—Case studies.   5. Murder victims—Florida—Biography.   6. Naval
architects—Florida—Biography.   7. Boating industry—Florida.   I. Title.
HV6534.M6B87   1990
364.1'523'09759381—dc20   90-41373
                                                                                      CIP

ISBN 0-671-66321-6

CONTENTS

Author's Note

It is rare for an author to be part of the story he is researching and writing. When I arrived in Miami on assignment for *Playboy* magazine within months after Don Aronow was murdered, I never expected to spend the next three years delving full-time into the Cigarette Boat King's life and death. In doing so, I inevitably became entwined in the story. My efforts to investigate the murder eventually affected the outcome.

My coauthor, Charlene Mitchell, who shared fully in the writing of the book, was not involved in the investigative aspects of its preparation. Because of this, and because of my role in the investigation, I am the "I" of the story in the latter two-thirds of the book.

Over the last thirty-six months, hundreds of people have been interviewed and thousands of documents examined, all in an effort to unravel the complex life and violent death of Don Aronow. Precise methods of recording conversations were used, so that the dialogue in this book is, as much as possible, exact. Where such methods were not possible, as in certain undercover situations, notes were made immediately after the meetings.

I am obliged to the many people who were willing to go on the record for this book. In some limited instances, where sources requested that their names not be used, their wishes of course have been respected. Because of the nature of this book and the very dangerous aspects it probes, there are those individuals who could suffer physical retribution or lose their jobs for participating in this project. For that reason, descriptions of three individuals in particular have been altered to give them "plausible deniability" should they be jeopardized for their cooperation with me. I am equally appreciative of their participation as well. Other than this, all the people named in *Blue Thunder* are real, and all events described are as reported to me. I have rendered descriptions as accurately as I could.

Both authors are grateful to our editor Marie Arana-Ward and attorney Eric Rayman of Simon and Schuster; attorney Lettie Bien; and Edna Buchanan of the *Miami Herald* for their support, encouragement, and enthusiasm.

—T. B.
August 1, 1990

THE WAR ON DRUGS

November 18, 1982

PRESIDENT RONALD REAGAN REMARKING ON THE EFFORTS OF VICE PRESIDENT GEORGE BUSH AND HIS VICE PRESIDENTIAL SOUTH FLORIDA JOINT DRUG TASK GROUP:

"Here at Homestead Base we see visible evidence of the Federal commitment to the war on criminal drug smuggling in south Florida. Under the leadership of Vice President George Bush . . . we have brought together the resources of many agencies of the Federal government from Customs to the DEA to the FBI and many others to assist you in a coordinated and concentrated attack on the powerful, highly organized crime rings that deal in the illegal drug trade. . . .

"Our goal is to break the power of the mob in America and nothing short of that. We mean to end their profits, imprison their members, and cripple their organization. And if anyone doubts what Federal, state, and local authorities working with the support of the people can achieve, let them come to south Florida, to Dade County, and to Miami and see what we have done here today."

PROLOGUE

Islamorada, the Florida Keys
January 4, 1984

It was, despite all the preparations, the manpower, and the expense, an unremarkable event. But like so many things that begin innocuously, it would have far from innocent results. George Bush wanted to test-ride a boat developed by his friend Don Aronow, the legendary "king of high-performance powerboating." Because Bush was the vice president of the United States, the planning for the trip required several months.

Bush was scheduled to give a luncheon speech at the Omni International Hotel in Miami, Florida, on January 4, 1984. A good part of his talk would focus on the Reagan administration's much-vocalized "War on Drugs." The drug issue was one of Bush's key assignments —he was head of the Vice Presidential South Florida Joint Drug Task Group—and in that role he had so far focused on a high-profile publicity campaign.

The Vice President saw his trip to Miami as the perfect opportunity to get together with Aronow, a man he had long admired. They had known each other for almost ten years, the relationship initiated by Bush, who had seen newspaper accounts of Aronow, his international racing exploits, and his world-renowned powerboats.

Donald Joel Aronow epitomized the classic rags-to-riches story that Americans love. The son of impoverished immigrants, he rose to the top in three different fields. He built a construction empire in New Jersey, then retired at the age of thirty-three to Miami in 1961. There he turned to powerboat racing and became an international legend—considered by many to be the greatest offshore powerboat racer ever. He won racing titles throughout the world and set one record after another. All in boats that he designed.

On Florida's Gold Coast, he created the modern powerboat industry. His ideas and designs gave birth to internationally recognized names—Formula, Donzi, Magnum—and the most famous powerboat ever: the Cigarette. Nicknamed "the Ferrari of the open seas," it became the boat desired by the famous as well as the infamous throughout the world, from former presidents Nixon and Johnson to the Shah of Iran to fugitive financier Robert Vesco.

Aronow was handsome in a rugged way. He was six foot four, powerfully built, with thick, black, wavy hair, eyebrows that almost overwhelmed his dark brown eyes, and a roguish grin. Fresh out of college after World War II, he was spotted on a New York street and offered an audition for the lead in a Tarzan movie. He turned it down, saying he had other plans. From his teenage years as a lifeguard on Coney Island to the end of his life, he exuded a masculine charm that was singularly fascinating to both men and women.

George Bush joined a long list of noteworthy people all over the world who sought Aronow out. "The rich and famous cottoned on to him," says Willie Meyers, a powerboat racer and former underwater stunt man. "They put him on a pedestal. People like Lord Lucan, Billy Shand-Kydd—he's related to Princess Di's mother—and Sir Max Aitken, the son of Lord Beaverbrook." He was friends with Spain's King Juan Carlos; King Hussein of Jordan; Prince Rainier and Princess Grace; Frank Borman, the former astronaut; Jim Kimberly, the Kimberly-Clark heir; Mark Donahue, the Indy "500" winner; Alvin Malnik, Miami's jetsetting multimillionaire attorney; and Charles Keating, later a central figure in the savings & loan scandal. People who seemed to have little in common with each other or with Aronow.

Most of them were attracted by Aronow's daredevil escapades, the promise of adventure and the titillation of danger, the feeling that something, anything, could happen when you were in his company. He was fondly viewed as the enfant terrible of the ocean—and his exploits both on and off the waters were followed with delight.

So it was with George Herbert Walker Bush, a man born and

raised to assume a role in the running of the country. Bush, a boating enthusiast, wanted to meet Aronow and it was arranged. They were introduced at a boat show in 1974 where Bush, an ambassador at the time, bought one of Aronow's Cigarettes. Bush named his boat *Fidelity*, and he can still be seen cutting across the waters by his Kennebunkport home in it.

Their friendship grew, despite their contrasting personalities. George Bush was Ronald Reagan's yes-man; few people dared to tell Aronow what to do. Bush was a patrician, born to a life of privilege, raised in the upper classes, an Ivy League WASP; Aronow was born to Jewish immigrants from Russia, a street-smart Brooklyn kid who became a multimillionaire by thirty. Bush was always in danger of fading into the background; Aronow was always the center of attention. Bush had too little sex appeal, Aronow had too much. Bush was hounded by the "wimp" factor; Aronow, as the world's greatest powerboat racer, had earned the nickname The Animal.

Yet for all these differences each man derived satisfaction from the relationship. Aronow enjoyed having upper-class friends; according to Meyers, "he liked the idea that he knew all these people. And it was especially important to him that they came to him." It affirmed to the kid from Coney Island that he had not only become wealthy and famous, but he had elevated his social status as well. The association with Bush brought the added bonus of a powerful contact in Washington, and eventually the cachet of being friends with the vice president of the United States.

For Bush, there were other rewards. His friend Aronow, the macho racer, the builder of the fastest boats in the world, had the charisma, reputation, and lifestyle that seemed to fascinate the preppie politician. Perhaps Bush, who could only dream of breaking out of the confinements dictated by his too proper background, lived vicariously through Aronow's exploits.

Over the years, the men kept in contact through letters and phone calls. When Bush became vice president, the exigencies of the office demanded most of his time. Aronow, retired from the racing circuit, was entrenched in his business—designing and producing the fastest offshore powerboats in the world. The two men drifted apart.

But in 1983, Bush renewed the association. He had worn out a pair of engines on the *Fidelity* and he immediately called Aronow. "During this period he wouldn't do anything about his boat without first consulting with Don," Meyers recalls. "After he'd talked to Don about his boat, lots of times he'd say, 'Hey, Don, I'll be down there fishing,' and they'd get together."

During one of their conversations in late 1983, Aronow told Bush about a boat that his new company, USA Racing Team, was developing. "The Vice President had great respect for Don and his boats," Randy Riggs, Aronow's private helicopter pilot, recalls. When he sold Cigarette Racing Team, Aronow had signed a noncompete clause. To get back into the boat design business he had to develop something radically different from the sleek and powerful Cigarette design. He came up with a 39-foot catamaran.

Bush was eager to try out the new "cat." The January Omni appearance was already scheduled, another in a series of speeches that he made in Miami after assuming the role of interdiction chief. It hadn't gone unobserved by Floridians that Bush almost always decided to give one of his "drug war pep talks" when Washington was suffering the harsh winter weather—since he had become vice president he had given eleven speeches in Miami, only one of which took place during the summer.

Bush thought this trip to Miami would be the perfect opportunity to test-drive the new boat. He was going bonefishing over New Year's with his friend, former senator Nicholas Brady, chairman of the investment banking firm Dillon, Reed. (Later, Brady would become Treasury secretary.) Then they would both get together with Aronow Wednesday morning for a test drive.

There were numerous arrangements that had to be made. The Vice President's assistant and Secret Service agents scurried back and forth from Miami coordinating the meeting location, checking out possible boat routes, trying to determine just how much time would be needed for the trip, and reviewing the necessary security details. Islamorada, one of the lesser-known Florida keys, was selected as the meeting site. There was a Coast Guard base that offered both security for the Vice President and a landing pad for Aronow's helicopter.

The fact that the test drive would be a perfect photo opportunity for the administration's War on Drugs was not overlooked—the Vice President navigating the same southeastern Florida coastline used by drug smugglers. Arrangements were made for a White House photographer to follow Bush in a helicopter, ensuring pictorial highlights of "Bush against the sea."

Early in the morning of January 4, Randy Riggs landed Don's helicopter on the roof of USA Racing Team. Aronow, who had owned a succession of helicopters, had built a special makeshift wooden landing pad to keep them from crushing the asphalt roof. The White House photographer and Aronow hopped in and they flew off to Islamorada. When they arrived at the Coast Guard station, security agents with specially trained dogs dashed to the helicopter. They ran hand-held buzzers over the three men and then proceeded to inspect the aircraft for bombs and weapons.

Twenty minutes later the Bush convoy arrived. Barbara Bush was there along with her driver and security guards. Mrs. Bush was not making the boat trip. She would be driven by limousine to Miami from Islamorada along Route One, the lone highway that links the Keys with the mainland.

Bush and Aronow greeted each other warmly. They spoke privately for about twenty minutes by the dock and then proceeded to the boat where Bush introduced Aronow to Brady. "I had heard of him, of course," says Brady of the racing legend. "He was a very colorful fellow." Also going along for the ride was a Secret Service agent equipped with special emergency communications gear and Willie Meyers, included to assist in case anything went wrong.

Meyers, with his British accent and air of continental sophistication, often served as "ambassador at large" for Aronow with various dignitaries. This was particularly so in recent years when Don's other interests, especially his stables—he owned a Kentucky Derby contender—took him away from the boating company. Meyers was also an underwater expert. In the early sixties he assisted the Navy in the recovery of an H-bomb that was lost in the waters off Spain when a B-52 crashed, and more recently in retrieving a top-secret Cobra helicopter that went down in the Gulf of Mexico.

The procession began. Ready to push off behind them were six chase boats, mostly Cigarettes, manned by Customs agents and the Secret Service. At this time Customs had no official boats to use in the War on Drugs; they had to rely completely on boats seized from smugglers. Since the Cigarette, a boat that has won more racing records than any other powerboat in the world, was equally revered by smugglers and agents, the plan had worked well enough. But the agency was looking forward to the day when it could purchase its own boats—expecting naturally that they would be Cigarettes. As the saying went among Customs officials, "It takes a Cigarette to catch a Cigarette."

The Coast Guard also followed in their own boats. Overhead two helicopters hovered, one flown by Riggs for the White House photographer, another a Huey attack helicopter from nearby Homestead Air Force Base carrying more Secret Service agents. Altogether, there were at least forty Secret Service and other security personnel involved in the trip.

Bush, steering the boat, was genuinely thrilled by the adventure, according to Riggs. His crooked boyish smile was a constant slash across his thin-featured face. He wore black-rimmed racing goggles and leather racing gloves. He gripped the wheel and hunched over to cut down on wind resistance as if he were competing in a race.

It was a clear day and there were slight waves as they began. Aronow, in an unusual position for him, was a passenger. Meyers was at the throttle. As they proceeded, Meyers used the tabs on the engine to adjust the angle of the propellers—it helped to keep the ride as smooth as possible. After a time, Bush noticed Meyers pushing on the buttons at the side of the controls for the two 440-horsepower engines and finally his curiosity got the better of him.

"What'cha doin', Willie?" the Vice President asked, puzzled by the actions.

"Trimming the boat."

Bush paused, confused, and then said, "I have those buttons on my boat. I thought they were for raising the propellers when the boat's on the trailer."

The men on the cat looked at Bush in surprise. Trimming the props for a smoother ride was an elementary boating concept, and Bush had owned a powerboat for at least ten years. It seemed incredible that he would be unaware of this. They burst out laughing. Even though it was at his expense, Bush joined in, delighted to be part of the male camaraderie.

The atmosphere of the boat was jovial, the men were all in good humor. As they reached the halfway point of the two-hour trip, they turned toward the Atlantic side of the Keys. The winds became stronger, churning up the sea. The boat smashed into the waves, each hit sending powerful body blows to the men. Aronow had seen worse, and in fact had won races because he was able to withstand the beating that broke other men. Meyers had also endured similar conditions. For Bush it was an opportunity to demonstrate his toughness and he relished the chance.

But former senator Brady was not accustomed to the speeds or the conditions that powerboat racers accept as typical. Nor was he interested in maintaining or projecting a macho image. He grew increasingly anxious and uncomfortable. "It got rougher and rougher," Brady recalls. "I don't know how big the seas got, eight feet or something. It was terrifying, the boat would absolutely disappear into those enormous caverns. It was at least forty-five minutes on those bloody waves, and I was hanging on for dear life." To add to Brady's problems, each time the boat hit a wave especially hard, his Bermuda shorts would fall down.

By the time they arrived in Miami, there was a throng of press people from the local papers and television stations waiting. William von Raab, the director of Customs, who would later implement the immensely unpopular "zero tolerance" strategy—the right to search and seize any boat bearing even a trace of drugs—was also eager for the glare of publicity.

As he stepped off the boat, Bush's expression was one of pure delight. "He was very happy, thrilled, to say the least," Randy Riggs remembers. "Like a kid the first time on an airplane ride." Riggs says Bush told the audience that "he hadn't been out on rough seas like that in a long time and he really enjoyed getting out there and going that fast and beating the waves. He said the cat was a great boat." The Vice President then went on to the Omni Hotel where he met with Edwin Meese, then White House counselor. Aronow flew off in his helicopter.

On the flight back, Aronow chatted with Riggs. "Don said he was real glad to see the Vice President again, that he had handled the boat well," Riggs recalls. "We talked about all the money the government had spent for Bush to take this short boat trip. Don was very much aware of the great expense—the Secret Service that was involved, the limousines, the security—all to protect one man."

Aronow asked Riggs how the boat looked in the water. "He was always very conscious of how his boats looked," Riggs explains. "Then he said he'd like to sell boats to the government." Riggs says Aronow didn't suggest that idea to Bush that day. "He wouldn't have been that forward. Don wasn't that kind. He would do it through the back door . . . like offering the Vice President a ride in the boat, and all the Customs people would see the Vice President in Don's boat."

That same day, while Bush was posing in Miami for photos, and addressing the news cameras, he launched into the rhetoric that was now familiar to Miamians. He told the press that the battle against drugs was not yet won, and that there would be no truce in the Reagan administration's war against "drug-financed hoodlums" and the "gangsterism" they spawned in south Florida. He noted that Customs could use a few boats like Aronow's catamaran—that "boats like that would help in the drug war."

A week later Bush took the time to personally type a letter to Aronow on the vice presidential stationery:

THE VICE PRESIDENT

Washington

January 14, 1984

Dear Don,

Here are some pretty shots which I hope will bring back some pretty good memories. I included one signed shot in your packet for Randy. Also am enclosing a set of picture [sic] for Willie not having his address or knowing how he spells Myers? Will you please give them to him and thank him for his part in our wonderful outing. He is quite a guy and I learned a lot from him on the way up to Miami from the keys.

Again Don this day was one of the greatest of my life. I love boats, always have. But ever since knowing you that private side of my life has become ever more exciting and fulfilling. Incidentally, I didn't get to tell you but my reliable 28 footer Cigarette that is, is still doing just fine . . . no trouble at all and the new last year engines.

All the best to you and all your exciting ventures. May all your boats bee [sic] number one and may the hosres [sic] be not far behind.

He then added in his own handwriting "My typing stinks" and signed it.

For both men it had been a day to remember. For Bush it had been an exciting adventure that had spurred an idea for the government's War on Drugs. For Aronow, it had strengthened his relationship with the Vice President and led to a lucrative contract to build interceptor boats for the government. The catamarans would become known as Blue Thunders and would serve as the cornerstone of the "Blue Lightning" drug-interdiction program.

Their renewed relationship would add considerably to Aronow's prestige, and he would become a conduit for Miamians who wanted to get Bush's attention on various matters. "When Don called the Vice President, Bush would take his call immediately," says Ken Whittaker, former head of the FBI in Miami. With time, the two men would become so close that Aronow would seriously contemplate the possibility of an ambassadorial appointment in a Bush administration.

But neither man realized that their brief boat trip would have other, more sinister results. It would set into motion a series of events that would lead to conspiracy, a government cover-up, and a link between organized crime, drug smugglers, and the highest levels of the United States government. It would culminate in Don Aronow's murder.

BOOK ONE

ONE

Don Aronow knew he was going to be murdered. Or more precisely, he thought there was a good possibility. But he was an optimist, always had been. And besides, luck had been such an integral part of his incredible life. Why should it desert him now?

So he tried to ride it out, facing the prospect of death in much the same way he had faced it so many times on the ocean—a broad grin and confident eyes that belied the pain. Occasionally the mask would fall, and his fears slipped out. But no one realized it at the time. It only became apparent with hindsight. It was only after Aronow was killed that those around him began to recall strange incidents. Curious phone calls. Melancholic reminiscences.

The first sign to his wife, Lillian, that something was wrong was three weeks before the murder, soon after New Year's in January 1987. There were a number of phone calls placed to the Aronow home on Sunset Isle, a private island off Miami Beach. Each time she answered, the caller hung up. She thought the calls might be from people trying to determine the family's schedule so that they could rob them.

A week after the mysterious hang-ups began, Don suggested that he and Lillian take a short walk from their home on Biscayne Bay to the beach on the ocean side. He was pensive, reflective, and he wanted to talk to her about the future. He discussed things that he had never spoken about with her. She needed to know what to do, he told her, if anything should happen to him. He had a complicated tangle of businesses and financial dealings. At thirty-five, Lillian was almost twenty-five years younger than Aronow, and he had managed their finances for all of their eight-year marriage. It was an arrangement that had suited them both.

But now, he said, it was important to him to know that she would take care of his children and that she understood what he wanted for them. He warned her that two of his three children by his previous marriage, David and Claudia, were "money hungry." He emphasized that she "stay strong and don't let them push you around." He asked her to take special care of Michael, his thirty-six-year-old son who was a paraplegic from injuries he'd suffered in an automobile accident years earlier.

He also told her that he wanted to be cremated rather than buried. That he didn't want any memorial service or even a eulogy. Everything should be taken care of quickly and quietly. Most importantly, he emphasized, if anything did happen to him and she had any problems, she was to call Vice President George Bush immediately.

Lillian was puzzled by the uncharacteristic talk. "Don was different those last few weeks," she recalls. "He didn't want to sit still. He was always moving around. We went to tons of movies in those few weeks—even in the daytime—more than we have since I've known him." But most of all, Lillian noticed "a tenderness in him" that she had never seen before toward his children, especially Michael, from whom he had been estranged for a time.

A few days after their walk on the beach, Aronow bought his wife a diamond-studded, solid-gold watch from Bulgari jewelers in New York. It cost $18,000 and he had it delivered in an armored car.

In the week before his murder, Aronow was talking with Mike Kandrovicz, an employee who had been with him for years. "Old Mike," as he was fondly called by the men in the North Miami powerboat industry, was seventy years old and Don's self-proclaimed "right-hand man." Kandrovicz says that "Don was always jolly, always upbeat, except those last weeks, when he seemed kind of nervous and fidgety."

Aronow brought up the subject of Kandrovicz's heart attack. During the days when Aronow owned the Cigarette Racing Team, Kandrovicz had suffered a severe heart attack while driving the company truck. He lost consciousness at the wheel. The truck smashed through a wall and plunged into a swimming pool. When the paramedics got to him, his heart had stopped.

"What did it feel like to have a heart attack?" Aronow asked. The question surprised Old Mike—Aronow was never one to dwell on illness or dying, he was always too busy pursuing life with a vengeance.

"Nothing." Kandrovicz is a blunt, sometimes feisty man who, like many men connected with powerboating, wastes no words.

Aronow paused for a second, lost in thought. Then he said, "That's the way I'd like to go." He hesitated again, and then looking directly at Old Mike, asked, "What does it feel like to almost die?"

"It just hits you," Kandrovicz replied. Aronow nodded thoughtfully and repeated, "Yeah, that's the way I want to go."

A little later Aronow called Dick Genth, a highly regarded man in the powerboat industry. Genth is known as one of the top troubleshooters in the business. "Dick takes companies on their knees and makes them giants," says John Crouse, a boating historian and public relations man for Aronow. One company that Genth rescued from receivership and built into a world-renowned outfit was Wellcraft. Another was Chris-Craft.

Genth and Aronow had been friends for more than two decades, tracing back to their early racing days. As president of Thunderbird, Genth had bought two of Aronow's first companies, Formula, and later Donzi Marine.

"The last time I saw him in person, in mid-January, we rapped for a little bit," Genth recalls. "He said he had some ideas he wanted to talk about a little later on. Don always had good ideas. This was something we had talked about in general for a few years. Putting Donzi and Aronow and Genth—the legends—together. We figured we could form one hell of a company with his new ideas."

But when Aronow phoned his friend at his office in Sarasota a couple of weeks later, their conversation disturbed Genth. It was strange, Genth remembers, not typical of the man he had known for so many years. "Don said, 'How soon can you come over here?' and I said, 'Shit, Don, I'm right in the middle of a few things here.' "

"I need to go over some things," Aronow urged, "I have a good idea. My noncompete clause is up with Cigarette and I've got a couple of new boat ideas for the two of us. Two names—Genth and Aronow—we could just knock the ass off the thing. How soon can you come to Miami?"

"Don, I can't go over there this week. Why don't we sit down at the Miami Boat Show next week and go over this."

"We gotta do it right now, believe me, I need to get with you right away. I've got to see you right now," Aronow urged.

Time seemed critical to Aronow, Genth recalls. "Don said, 'We have to put this thing together in a hurry. I need to know your thinking.' It was probably the only time in all the years I've known him that he was serious, real serious. He was on a time schedule, no question about it."

Then Aronow changed the subject. He talked about getting older, about how well things were going with his horses. He and his son Michael were partners in a stable in Ocala, Florida, and they had over a hundred horses. He told Genth that Michael was taking over the business and that he was proud of how he was handling it. He talked about his current project, Blue Thunder, the boats he built for George Bush's Drug Interdiction program.

Genth chided him about the boats. Bush's alleged "war" on drugs in south Florida was a local joke. "I said, 'Don, you could sell an ice maker to an Eskimo. Those boats are absolutely horrible for what Customs wants to do with them . . . that offshore work. They can't keep them running. And they're so slow they can't even get out of their own way.' " Genth says that in conversations Don would some-times say "my friend Bush" so he kidded him and said, "Goddamn, you must have a friend to sell those boats."

Aronow took no offense—one of the traits that made him popular was his self-deprecating sense of humor. "Don laughed his ass off," Genth remembers. Then Aronow began to reminisce about some of the powerboat races they had been in. "It was like he was looking back over his life and reliving it," Genth says. "We talked about how damned competitive we had been and a lot of the old 'war' stories. Don enjoyed talking about racing again together. It seemed to put him in better spirits."

Although they teased each other and talked about old times and even made plans for the future, the conversation troubled Genth. "I got a really funny feeling right after I hung up, I don't know, he just —now looking back on it, it was spooky as hell. I know he damn well knew something was up, that he didn't have much time. It was spooky. I even said to my wife, 'Don is really up to something, he was really on a time schedule.' "

Don also called Willie Meyers that same week and said he wanted to talk to him in person. He asked him to stop by his USA Racing Team company, the firm that made the Blue Thunders. Meyers did, and Don told him that he was thinking of taking his family to the Bahamas for a while. He said he wanted "an out-of-the-way place that wouldn't be too boring." A place that would keep Lillian happy and where he could teach his six-year-old son Gavin to water-ski. "Can you recommend a good hideaway?" he asked.

Meyers was intimately familiar with the Bahamas. He had spent almost two years scouting locations while working on the James Bond movie *Thunderball.* He had also performed underwater stunts there for the TV series *Flipper* and *Sea Hunt,* in which he had doubled for Lloyd Bridges.

If anyone knew an out-of-the-way spot it was Meyers. Willie said he would think about it and get back to him. They talked a few days later, on January 30, and Meyers recommended some places on Eleuthera, one of the lesser-known islands. Aronow said he'd let him know when he was ready to go so that Meyers could set things up for him.

In a small apartment in South Beach, thirty-three-year-old Patricia Cordell was leaving for work. As she drove through newly trendy South Beach, dubbed SoBe by people who considered it the tropical twin of New York's SoHo district, the pastel panoply of the art deco landscape on the southern end of Miami Beach did nothing to improve her bad mood. She felt tired and overworked.

South Beach, with its tony restaurants, nightclubs, and art galleries, was the latest weekend hangout for the young and monied Manhattanites and movie stars, but as a newspaper photographer and single mother she had little time to enjoy the lifestyle. Besides, she was more familiar with the less-than-glamorous denizens who also inhabited the area: the crack dealers and their customers who turned to petty crime to support their habits. Her apartment had been robbed several times and her car had been broken into more times than she could remember.

Arriving at the *Miami News,* Cordell was given her first assignment of the day. The paper was doing a story on Miami's world-famous high performance powerboat industry for the Monday business magazine. Naturally, it was highlighting Don Aronow. She put her sunglasses back on and headed up to Aronow's factory on Northeast 188th Street, the street Aronow built, better known by one or more of its many colorful nicknames—Performance Alley, Fleet Street, Boatbuilder's Row, Gasoline Alley, Thunderboat Alley.

The Alley is a short dead-end street in north Miami, easily overlooked. A narrow blacktop bordered on both sides by a series of drab, boxlike buildings, occasional vacant lots, and three- or four-story cement-and-iron dry docks. Two canals run parallel north and south of the street. The area has all the visual appeal of a cluster of nuts-and-bolts manufacturers. And yet those few feet of land are known throughout the world by anyone who loves pushing man-made machines as far and as fast as they can go across the seas.

Onto this strip have come kings and sheiks, millionaires and billionaires, drug lords and diplomats, and men who have broken world records for speed. All in search of what one designer calls "toys," state-of-the-art powerboats, ranging from twenty-seven feet to sixty-three feet and beyond, with price tags from $60,000 to $6 million.

It's a busy street now, but less than thirty years ago it was little more than sun-parched dirt, dried-out weeds, and one man. Don Aronow. With one idea. To go faster than anyone ever had on the ocean. On this street he founded six companies and designed and built boats that have won every major boat race in the world. No story on the high performance powerboat industry was complete unless it included Aronow. To many people, he was the industry.

Cordell entered the unimposing office of USA Racing Team. Patty Lezaca, Aronow's longtime secretary, was seated at a desk in the rear and quickly jumped up, demanding some ID. Jerry Engelman, the sales manager, was at another desk in the front of the room.

The phone rang. Aronow was calling from his car parked at the entrance to the Alley. It was a practice he had started recently. He didn't want to enter the building until visitors had been checked out by his staff. Engelman answered, listened for a few seconds, then said, "It's her." A pause and then, "About five five, red hair, slim, pretty." The conversation lasted another few minutes with Jerry occasionally saying "Yes." Then he looked up at Cordell and said, "That was Don, he'll be right here. He's coming from his other place."

They moved outside to look at the dry-docked Blue Thunder boat that would be used as a photo prop. A moment later Cordell turned and saw a figure striding confidently toward her. "He was completely backlit by the sun," she says. "As he walked closer, I realized he was a really big man. That's when I got the impression that this guy was a warrior king. Maybe I've read too many books but—wham!—that's what came into my mind. This man was big, he was silhouetted against the sun and I'm looking up at him. I couldn't see his face clearly. All I knew was he had a really gentle voice. He was smiling and he shook my hand."

She introduced herself. Aronow looked at her thoughtfully. "You know, you remind me of a Modigliani."

That was the first thing Aronow said to Cordell and it wasn't what she had expected. Almost anything but that. She had a hunch that he didn't even know what a Modigliani was—that it was just some name this jock had heard and was now using to impress her. She didn't know that the rugged powerboat racer loved art—and not only was he familiar with Modigliani's paintings but he owned one.

Cordell was accustomed to her male photo subjects' flirting as she worked and tried simply to get the job done without offending them. But Aronow was different. Soon she was telling him about her eighteen-month-old daughter and how hard it was to work and care for her, and that lately it seemed almost too much to handle.

Standing on the deck of the dry dock with the Blue Thunder, Aronow told her about his six-month-old son, how he was sitting up and learning new words. He was smiling, half-laughing as he talked about being a new father again. The charm that had been captivating women for decades was still palpable, still surfacing naturally. Perched atop a forklift, Cordell was watching it all through her camera lens. A moment later his expression changed. The sexy confidence, the sparkling eyes, and the laugh died.

A small boat was slowly moving along the canal by the factory. It hugged the seawall. Aronow became distracted by it, unaware that she was poised to take another picture. As it came closer, his body stiffened, his mouth grew tight, and his face became impassive. Cordell remembers, "He watched it very carefully, the whole time, for the full range of view."

The boat didn't stop or even slow down. When it was out of sight, Aronow turned back to Cordell. His shoulders relaxed and a slight smile returned. But he continued to look back every few minutes at the canal where he had last seen the boat. She tried a few more pictures but it wasn't as easy getting him to smile anymore. She suggested a different setup, away from the boat.

"Let's take it down," Cordell said, gesturing to Engelman to lower the forklift on which she stood.

Aronow looked at her, then hopped from the bow of the boat over to the forklift, making the five-foot jump easily. He wrapped his right arm around her waist, his left arm around her shoulders, and pulled her up against him. "I was surprised, pleasantly surprised," she comments. "Then he said, 'I'll take a ride down with you.' I thought then that if another man had done that I would've stiffened and pulled away immediately. But I didn't. I don't know if his eyes were blue but I got a true-blue feeling out of him. He was gentle and he seemed genuinely interested in me."

She walked over to the huge Blue Thunder engines, wondering

aloud if they could make a good background. Aronow pointed out some propellers and several huge chrome-plated exhaust pipes and said that he had done other good shots next to engines. One had been for a Dewar's ad profile.

"So I guess you've had a lot of pictures taken?" she chatted as she lined up the picture.

"Well," Aronow said quietly, "that was a long time ago." He motioned to Jerry to go back to the office and get the Dewar's profile for her to see. Engelman returned with it a few minutes later.

"The ad was an older process, I assumed from the late fifties," recalls Cordell. "But you could tell it was the same guy and he just looked like every woman's dream of the adventurous man. The dark hair, and something about the face—the strength of it—it wasn't too round, just strong, adventuresome. He was in some kind of racing uniform with a life preserver on. He just looked rugged. Rugged and exciting."

Aronow looked for more than a minute. "That was twenty years ago," he explained, "twenty years or more." He kept looking at it. His shoulders sagged, the light banter disappeared. Then Cordell told him that it could have been taken yesterday and he smiled.

She wanted a picture of him standing on Thunderboat Alley. Although he wasn't enthusiastic about going out onto the street, he agreed. "This is when he started acting really nervous," she remembers. "He couldn't hold a smile for more than a split second. As soon as he heard the click of the camera, his smile faded at a rapid rate."

Before that they had been in the boatyard, hidden from the street. Cordell says, "But out front, he kept looking up and down the street. I was losing his concentration and the conversation had just stopped. I kept having to ask him to look at me and to smile. Then he started to sweat. It wasn't hot. But he had to keep wiping the sweat from his forehead and still it kept trickling down. He kept looking behind me, and the way he was looking started to make me feel uneasy as to what was behind my back. I got a bad feeling."

As soon as she said she was through, Aronow turned and walked swiftly to the office. Once inside, Cordell says, "he was back to being friendly, completely normal again." He pointed to a photograph on the table, telling her that was his son. Then he asked if she liked old photos and she said she was fascinated with historical pictures. Engelman brought out an old cardboard box filled with photos. He spread them across an empty six-foot-long table.

Aronow scanned the contents and found some pictures of the Beatles with him on his boat, from their 1963 U.S. tour. "Don was standing there laughing with Ringo next to him and a couple of the Beatles were climbing into the boat," Cordell recalls.

Seeing her interest, Aronow started pulling out more photographs. "I have pictures of me with all kinds of people," he said. He flipped one after another in front of her—shots of him with Juan Carlos of Spain, in Aqaba with King Hussein, in Kennebunkport with Bush. There were dignitaries and politicians and movie stars, but he paid little attention to the pictures. All the time he was talking to Cordell, listening to her problems of being a single working parent.

Cordell left exhilarated. "He was such a strong man, a powerful man showing an interest in me. I couldn't believe it. When I walked out of there, I thought, Jesus, that was great. I was thrilled for the first time since I've been in Miami. I had met somebody I could get interested in. I was thrilled."

Cordell had just taken the last photographs of Donald Aronow. The picture that she took of him standing on the Alley, arms crossed, scowling, would be used a few weeks later by *People* magazine in its coverage of his murder. In the photograph, just a few feet to the lower left, is the spot where he would lie dying four days later.

On the day after the photo shoot, January 31, 1987, Aronow met with Benjamin Barry Kramer for more than an hour at Ft. Apache Marina, a company Ben managed with his father, Jack. Aronow and Ben had been in constant contact that week. The sudden closeness puzzled many people on the Alley since the relationship between the two had always had an unexplained edge to it. Neither man liked the other. Aronow considered Ben a spoiled young punk, while Kramer viewed Aronow as his nemesis, the "king" of the street well past his prime who had to be dethroned. Still for some time they had been linked together by an association that remained a mystery.

At thirty-two, Ben was considered the most controversial character on Thunderboat Alley and most of the boatbuilders tried to keep their distance from him. Tall, dark, and tough looking, he was considered arrogant, a hothead. His workers complained that he'd sometimes spit on their money before he paid them. Although he was young he had already established himself as a powerboating champion and boatbuilder with a bright future. At the same time, no one trusted him. As Dick Genth put it, "it's obvious that bully is bad. I don't know why Don would have anything to do with him. It could tarnish Don."

Kramer had diverse and unusual connections. In his late twenties, he had been convicted of smuggling marijuana—although he was not caught in the act—and spent a couple of years in south Florida federal penitentiary. While in prison, he got into more trouble—he was accused of issuing orders to a group of lower-level prisoners to beat up a snitch. He hired a former FBI agent turned lawyer, Pete Clemente, to smooth over the problem with the warden.

After his release, Kramer was stopped on a routine traffic violation. Police found $100,090 in cash in a trash bag in the trunk of his Porsche and confiscated it after a sniffer dog reacted to the presence of drugs on it. At the time, he was registered with the U.S. Probation Office as a $24,000-a-year boat captain for Melvyn Kessler, a prominent attorney in Miami. Kessler argued that probably half the cash in Miami was tainted with the odor of drugs, and that the money was a deposit from a customer for a boat, so the cash was released.

Ben's career took a decided upturn in 1983 when he became a superintendent with Marina Bay Associates, a holding company, owned by a well-known California philanthropist, Sam Gilbert. The firm was developing the Ft. Apache Marina on Thunderboat Alley, a block up the street from Aronow's USA Racing. The "fort" consisted of a huge boat storage and repair facility, and a restaurant/entertainment/office building complex. It brought a touch of class and style that hadn't been seen on the Alley before. The typical boat manufacturing facility consisted of noisy, poorly lit rooms with layers of fiberglass dust over everything.

In 1984, Kramer won the world offshore powerboating championship. The win put him into the big time of offshore racing and opened up new business horizons for him. He and his racing partner, Bobby Saccenti, a protégé of Don Aronow's, began to build high performance powerboats under the Apache name.

The money came rolling in and Ben brought his father, Jack, into the company. Soon after, the Kramers and Saccenti disagreed over the direction of the business. They split the company in two, Saccenti calling his Apache Performance and the Kramer company being renamed Apache Racing. Kramer began his own racing team, calling it Team Apache. Florida governor Bob Graham even officially named a day for Kramer's Apache team. In Europe, where offshore powerboat racing is enormously popular, acquaintances say Ben was treated "like royalty" because of the world title.

By 1986, Ben Kramer was living a flamboyant lifestyle. He threw lavish parties, hung out with Sammy Davis, Jr. and actor James Caan at plush Turnberry Isle, and poured "tons of money" into his racing teams. He had a helicopter and a large corporate jet at his disposal. "It was big, a four-engine jet," says Randy Riggs, who had been

Ben's personal helicopter pilot for a while. "It was so large it would've been too big for most corporations." Later when Riggs quit, Kramer hired Don Johnson's pilot to fly him around.

When Kramer first headed up Ft. Apache, there seemed to be some arm's-length dealings between him and Aronow. Within a few years, the subtle ties, and the animosity, between the men increased. But in the last few weeks of January, the relationship changed dramatically. Aronow called and visited Apache often. Both Kramers called him at his company, sometimes several times a day. There was, according to Jerry Engelman at USA Racing, "a tremendous amount of communication between Ben, his father, Jack, and Don those last days. Something was up for sure."

On February 2, 1987, the last full day of Aronow's life, a black limousine with dark windows parked on the street across from the new home in Miami Beach that Aronow was renovating. Some of the workmen noticed the vehicle. It was out of place on the narrow tree-lined street where all the estates had long driveways and ample parking space on the grounds.

No one was seen getting in or out. The vehicle simply remained on the street for a while, according to one of the workers at Don's house, "like someone was inside watching." At the time, Aronow's contractors assumed the limousine was connected with the musical group the Bee Gees, who lived in the estate next door. Despite later inquiries by detectives—the Bee Gees said it had nothing to do with them—no one would ever discover why the limousine was on the street that day.

On that same afternoon, up in one of the factory sections of north Miami, just a few miles southwest of the Alley, a dark blue Lincoln Town Car pulled up next to a pedestrian. Two men were in the car: one had a swarthy complexion, dark hair, a broad chest and shoulders. The other was muscular with a ruddy complexion and sandy-colored hair. The light-haired occupant called out, "Hey, buddy, where's Gasoline Alley?"

Because it's so removed from the main thoroughfares, the Alley is difficult to find even for people who live in Miami. The pedestrian pointed the driver in the right direction and gave the men a general idea of how to find it, adding, "You're just a few miles away." With that one of the men in the car laughed and said to the other, "How about that, we drove twelve hundred miles and came pretty close."

That night Don and Lillian went to the movies. They ran into Ken Whittaker, the former agent-in-charge of Miami's FBI office, and his wife. It was a fortuitous meeting for Whittaker. He had been planning to get in touch with Aronow. He needed a favor. Whittaker was involved with a law school function and the committee was hoping to get Vice President George Bush to give a speech. As Whittaker comments, "everyone in Miami knew that if you needed a favor from Bush, you spoke to Aronow." Don agreed to talk to the Vice President.

TWO

The Last Day

The early morning of Tuesday, February 3, 1987, began as the quintessential Miami winter day: the sky was an unmarred expanse of blue, the subtle scent of salt water and tropical flowers permeated the air, and the warm ocean breeze rustled through the palm trees. Aronow was at his new estate. Some furniture had already been moved in and the decorating was just about complete. He planned to move Lillian and the children from their nearby Sunset Isle home in the next few days.

The new house was located in one of the most exclusive sections of Miami Beach on North Bay Road. Miami Beach is a long, narrow island that runs parallel to Miami and is connected to the mainland by several causeways. In between is Biscayne Bay. The office complexes, the businesses, and most of the crime and the problems of any large city are generally confined to Miami proper. Much of the "Beach," as it's called, is comparable to the suburbs—although a wealthy one—of a large metropolitan area.

Miami Beach has three main areas. The northern section of the island is mostly country clubs and upper-income homes. The middle section is perhaps the most famous, with its stretch of towering grand old hotels and high-rise condominiums that seem to run the length of the Atlantic side of the island. Further south is the art deco district that flourished in the fifties and sixties, all but died in the seventies, and is once again booming.

North Bay Road is quiet and residential, befitting the wealthy inhabitants. Each house has the de rigueur pool and lanai, many have Jacuzzis and tennis courts, and expensive cars (at least two). The bayside estates are all protected with iron fences or high stucco walls and sophisticated electronic alarms.

Aronow's new home was huge, encompassing 10,000 square feet, and like most of the estates in the area, almost totally hidden from the road. There is a high wall with a wooden gate at the main entrance, and a little farther down the road is the service entrance —one entire wing of the house is set aside for the help.

The new home was a stunning leap from Aronow's previous one in size, location, and appointments. He had paid $1.2 million out-right for it—there was no mortgage—and he was making more than two million dollars' worth of changes. He wanted everything to be perfect. The house was important to him, because it was important to Lillian. It was his ultimate present to his second wife—the woman about whom one friend said, "Don considered Lillian the crowning achievement of his life." It was a somewhat surprising statement in light of Aronow's remarkable past.

Lillian Crawford Aronow seemed to affirm and validate to her husband all that he had accomplished. She was thirty-five, tall, slim, with shoulder-length auburn hair. A former model with the presti-gious Wilhelmina Agency and a WASP from the New York Establish-ment. Before she married Aronow in 1979, she had been a frequent guest on the Palm Beach social circuit, dating Herbert Pulitzer, the newspaper heir, and King Hussein, who frequented the social scene. It was well-known that Hussein was "crazy about Lillian," as one socialite put it, and had reputedly offered Aronow a million dollars not to marry her.

On the last morning of his life, as had become his habit, Don left his Sunset Isle home and made the five-minute drive over to North Bay Road. He wanted to see how the final interior painting was going. At about eleven, "Old Mike" Kandrovicz joined him in the kitchen. He needed some more money to pay the contractors. Aronow opened his briefcase and pulled out a thousand dollars from one of many large bundles. Old Mike had been around Don long enough not to be surprised by the sight of a briefcase filled with cash.

Don was in an expansive mood, laughing, making plans. The phone rang, and he answered. His jovial expression froze, then dissolved. He was silent. His skin blanched as he listened to the caller. He looked agitated. He glanced up, caught Mike's eye, and turned away.

"I can't," Aronow spoke nervously in low tones. "I can't keep doing that. My name is getting known up there."

There was another prolonged silence. Then Aronow said, "You write the letter and send it to me and I'll read it."

The caller spoke again. Aronow responded, "This time I want to know who the guy is. I want his name. I want to think about it."

He jotted a name on the small pad in front of him. Noticing Old Mike peering at the writing, he tore the page off and stuffed it in his pocket.

"I don't know," Aronow spoke into the receiver. "Let me think about it."

No names were mentioned in the brief conversation, but a few things were obvious to Kandrovicz. And surprising. Aronow knew the caller, and it was someone powerful enough to tell him what to do, and to scare him. It was also obvious that Aronow was being pushed to do something against his will.

The conversation ended abruptly. Aronow sat still for a minute, not looking at his friend. Then suddenly he stood up, saying, "Let's get going. I've got to take care of something. I'll meet you back at the office later."

The friendly chat was over.

That same morning across the bay in north Miami, two agents from the Drug Enforcement Administration were on a stakeout. They had been conducting a loose surveillance of Thunderboat Alley for several months. Equipped with long-range telephoto cameras, they would observe the activity from the roof of one of the few high rises in the area. Other times they'd sit for hours at the entrance to NE 188th Street drinking coffee, eating hamburgers and french fries from the nearby Burger King. Watching and waiting.

It was well-known over the years that the Alley was a magnet for smugglers looking for ever faster boats to outrun Customs and the Coast Guard. In the seventies, the dopers made little attempt to hide their vocation. But as government agents surveilled the area ever more intensively, some began to downplay their trade. Now, as DEA agent Dave Borah explains, there are two forms of smugglers.

"You've got the gringos," says Borah. "They're more regular guys. They look a lot like Sunday school teachers and they drive Toyota Corollas. Your Cubans and Colombians are more of the gold flash, they want everyone to know they're in the dope business. They're not worried about the government. They want to show their competitors that they're doing better. We seized a Mercedes and the whole hardtop was removed and everything in there was gold-plated—the steering wheel, the gearshift, the dashboard."

Sometimes the vagaries of the business created an odd couple. One straight looking, the other bedecked and bejeweled. "A lot of times you'll find a Cuban and a gringo together," Borah explains. "Your Cubans like the gringos because they can trust them with the money. In the dope business, a lot of times the gringos got their own organization, mainly marijuana. The Cubans, Colombians, and Latins have their own and you're looking at cocaine. But they mingle a lot."

Even when the flashy dealers try to downplay their money, their attempts to appear unobtrusive fail miserably. Few outside the business carry briefcases stuffed with several hundred thousand dollars in cash, no credit cards, and no form of ID. Nor do many men sport solid-gold Rolexes with diamond bezels and three or four diamond studs in one ear. "This *Miami Vice* stuff isn't just off the wall," Borah notes. "These guys drink Dom Pérignon and flash the cash. We checked out a Julio Iglesias concert and right around me I saw twenty people with portable phones. Why would you take a phone to a concert?"

Eventually all of the dopers make their way to Thunderboat Alley, and because of that, the "go-fast" boat industry as it is called has received increasing government attention. So much so, that one joke among local DEA agents is that half the people at offshore powerboat regattas are undercover feds—FBI, DEA, Customs, IRS—and the other half are dopers and wiseguys.

The feds are kept busy watching and photographing their suspects. The smugglers are there to keep up on the latest advances in their professional appurtenances. And the wiseguys "just wanna have fun." Many of the powerboat racers are considered heroes by the mobsters, who particularly like their "rough around the edges charm."

But when there are no competitions, the agents keep sporadic tabs on the Alley. The street is rife with the potential for all types of criminal activity—from smuggling to money laundering to tax fraud —more than enough to quicken the pulse of any dedicated agent.

On the day of the murder, the two DEA agents on stakeout saw Aronow's familiar white Mercedes 560SL—by now they knew most of the people who worked on the Alley—turn onto the street a little past noon. It pulled into the Ft. Apache lot. Aronow stepped out and entered the building. The agents had seen him visit Apache quite a few times in recent weeks. This time he was there over an hour. Not long after, the surveillance terminated. Nothing much seemed to be happening and the agents had enough for the day. Within a few hours they would deeply regret their early departure.

At about two P.M., Aronow arrived at the USA Racing Team facilities. He was dressed casually. Despite his money, he dressed like most of the men on the street. He had on one of his favorite outfits, a sport shirt with his initials, heavy white cotton jeans, a nautical belt, Top-Siders, and no socks.

The USA Racing Team facilities consisted of two long and narrow factory-style buildings that ran side by side from the street to the bank of a canal. One building served as a warehouse for the completed boats; the other was for manufacturing and offices.

Patty Lezaca and Jerry Engelman were seated at their desks in the main office area. Aronow's office was separated by a glass partition. He had another office upstairs, but he rarely used it anymore, except to make private phone calls. Lately he preferred, even insisted on, meeting with people in the more public first-floor office.

A superficial scan of his office offered few clues to his extraordinary achievements. It was a surprisingly small room, informal, a large utilitarian desk and chair, some cluttered shelves. Powerboating magazines were mixed together with copies of the *Wall Street Journal.* On the walls were several sloppily mounted pictures of Aronow on the Blue Thunder with various politicians. There were some with George Bush and Paula Hawkins, a former U.S. senator from Florida.

Trophies were scattered about, piled carelessly on top of each other. The silver had begun to tarnish on some, others were coated with dust. They were part of the past. A legendary one—the inscriptions testified to that. Still, to Aronow, the past. He was a man who liked to look forward.

This afternoon he was particularly agitated. He had little to say. Lezaca told him that a reporter from the *Miami News,* Jim Steinberg, had called. He went up the stairs that led to the second floor. There, he returned the call. Steinberg, who had interviewed Aronow a number of times, was writing the story that would accompany Pat Cordell's photographs. Steinberg explained that he was looking for some local color for the piece. "So, Don, have any drug smugglers ever tried to buy boats from you?" Steinberg began.

All the boatbuilders had stories, Aronow was no exception. He loved talking to the press, regaling them with anecdotes. He was considered very accessible and always good for a few funny stories— even at his own expense. But not on this day. He tried to dodge Steinberg's questions and seemed a bit short-tempered. Steinberg, who had a good working relationship with him, was surprised.

"Come on, Don," he coaxed. "Have any drug dealers ever tried to buy a boat?" It was meant to be a harmless question—certainly not one that would offend a high-performance-boat builder. In Miami, most boat manufacturers know the integral role that their products play in the drug world. And most adhere to a certain code—it's not their business to judge the background of a customer. If someone wants to buy a boat and he has the money, he can. The only prevailing caveat is if someone comes out and says he's a drug dealer—then you don't sell to him.

Although none admit doing it knowingly, most manufacturers assume that they have sold boats to smugglers. Aronow himself said many times in interviews that he was sure dopers had bought some of his boats—he and everyone else knew that his Cigarette was the most popular drug-running vessel on the Gold Coast waters.

But on this day, the question and the subject seemed to bother Aronow. He weighed his remarks carefully. He was serious, businesslike—clearly not enjoying the typical give-and-take he usually had with reporters. "I suppose they have," he finally responded. "It's hard to tell—you can have your suspicions. My business is with law enforcement."

Steinberg tried to smooth things over by changing the subject and Aronow responded. The conversation lasted a little longer, and Aronow gradually became more like the man whom Steinberg knew. He mentioned plans to build some new types of boats and said he was hoping to "get back into offshore racing."

Then he changed the subject. He boasted that his current company, USA Racing Team, built a high-performance 39-foot catamaran. He mentioned that he had just sold his $150,000 Blue Thunders to Jordan's King Hussein and various law enforcement agencies in several Middle Eastern countries. But, he added, most of the Blue Thunders that he produced went to the U.S. Customs Service.

As soon as he hung up, his black mood returned. Coming downstairs, he saw a memo on his desk. It was a copy of a written confirmation order that Jerry Engelman had sent to MerCruiser, a company that manufactured the Blue Thunder engines. Don had ordered a million dollars' worth of motors by phone, and Jerry had followed up with a letter. When Aronow discovered it, he blasted Engelman.

"What'd you put it in writing for?" he yelled. "Now we're stuck, we'll have to pay for it if we change our minds."

"But Don, we need them." Jerry tried to assuage his boss, but it was futile. There was an edge to Aronow's anger that Jerry hadn't seen before and there was no reasoning with him.

Through the glass partition Jerry noticed a scruffy-looking man wearing a baseball cap, T-shirt, and shorts enter the office. It was a chance to extricate himself from the scene with Aronow. Maybe it was a customer. Anything, he thought, to get Don off his back. He shot out to greet the guy. "Hi, I'm Jerry Engelman, the sales manager."

It was a little before three o'clock, a half hour before the shift ended at most of the Alley's boat factories. A half hour before the narrow, empty road became congested with workers and cars.

The man appeared to be in his late forties, very tall, about six feet four, very well built and muscular, with sandy-colored hair. "He was as big as Don, and that's unusual," Engelman says. Mike Kandrovicz, who had popped into the office at the time, noticed that the man's face and legs were sunburned. It reminded him of the way Northerners look after their first day in the Florida sun.

The man told Engelman that he wanted to speak with Don Aronow personally. Jerry turned to Aronow, who had been observing from his office. He strolled out and the stranger said, "I've been calling all week trying to get in touch with you, Don." Aronow was surprised—no one had given him any messages—and he turned to Patty, eyebrows raised, questioning. She shook her head. No, she didn't take any calls like that.

"I work for a very wealthy man and he wants to make an appointment to buy a boat," the man explained.

"What's his name?" Don asked.

"I'm not supposed to say, but he's very rich."

"I don't make appointments," Aronow said. "Bring your boss in. And I can be here within a few minutes."

Then the stranger started rambling. He looked directly at Aronow and said, "My boss took me from the gutter and gave me a job. Everything I have I owe to him. I'd never turn my back on my boss.

I'd do anything and everything for my boss. I'd even kill for him. Yeah, I'd even kill for him."

Patty couldn't understand what the guy was talking about, why he would tell them that. It was just stupid, she thought to herself. Engelman thought the guy seemed "wired up, though not on drugs."

"What's your name?" Aronow asked.

"Jerry Jacoby."

"You're not Jerry Jacoby," Don said, "I know Jerry." At one time Aronow and Jerry Jacoby had been partners, until Jacoby moved back to the New York City area to open an automobile parts distributorship.

Engelman looked quizzically at Aronow with a look that said this guy is strange. Any minute, he kept thinking, Don is going to make a typical Aronow move, grab this guy by the collar, and tell him to get the fuck out of here. But Aronow didn't move. Finally he forced a hollow laugh. "Let's see some ID."

The stranger grandly slapped his front pockets. Then his back pockets. "What d'ya know?" he snickered. "I forgot my wallet."

Aronow looked at the man but said nothing. Lezaca and Engelman remained silent. Why, they wondered, doesn't Don get rid of this guy? He seemed almost reluctant to touch him.

Finally Aronow told the stranger, "I can't talk to you anymore. Why don't you let Jerry show you the boats." He gestured to Engelman to take the man back into the warehouse and show him the boats. Then Aronow told Patty he had to leave. But the man darted quickly ahead of him to the exit, calling over his shoulder, "No, that's all right, I ain't the guy with the money. Show 'em to the boss." And he dashed out.

Engelman was surprised that the stranger turned down the invitation. In the year that he had worked at USA Racing, only one other person had ever turned down an opportunity to see the Aronow boat factory up close. That time it was a process server who was posing as a potential customer. That man had no interest in boats—he was there on other business.

Aronow made a quick phone call from Engelman's desk phone to his friend Bobby Saccenti at Apache Performance a little way down the same street. Then he left the office, calling out to Patty, "See you tomorrow."

After Aronow had gone, the bizarre conversation kept running through Jerry Engelman's mind. It reminded him of some past incident. Then he remembered. On the previous Thursday, he had taken a phone call at the USA Racing office. It was a woman named Kathleen who said she was calling for her boss. And she had used the same words to describe her employer that the man had just used: "My boss is a very wealthy man. He wants to buy a boat from Mr. Aronow. When will he be in the office?"

Aronow's schedule was erratic at best and Jerry was never really sure when Don would be in the office. In the last few months, he had developed the curious habit of parking down at the end of the street or a few blocks away and calling the office from his car phone, just as he had when Pat Cordell arrived for her appointment. The conversation was always the same: "I'm on my way in," he would say, "anyone there waiting to see me?"

With this in mind, and not wanting to lose a potential customer, Jerry had suggested to the woman that "Don might be in tomorrow morning. I'll give him the message. What's your boss's name?"

"I can't give you his name. I can only tell you that he's very wealthy."

Jerry tried once more. "Why don't you give me your name and phone number and I'll have him call when he comes in. Then you can talk to him yourself."

"I can't give you the number because I'm calling from a pay phone in Palm Beach." Then she hung up. The entire conversation had struck Jerry as odd. The woman had had to keep putting coins in the pay phone to continue talking. It seemed strange that she wouldn't have a calling card or a business number to charge the call—especially when it was regarding buying a boat worth at least $150,000.

She never did call back, Jerry realized. Nor was it the only peculiar phone call that had come into USA Racing. He had taken a number of phone calls in the past few weeks from people wanting to know where Don was and when he would be in the office, but who wouldn't leave their names.

The stranger had disappeared by the time Aronow got into his car. He drove his white Mercedes coupe the few hundred feet down to the Apache complex. He went in to talk to his friend and protégé Bobby Saccenti.

Saccenti headed Apache Performance Boats. He was younger than Aronow, but like his mentor, he had come from Brooklyn to Miami and found success in the boat business. "He was from Coney Island and I was from Sheepshead Bay," says Bobby. "We came from practically the same neighborhood. It was a poor area, and we were poor neighbors. That's probably why he liked me right off."

Saccenti says that Aronow stopped by to check on his recovery. Bobby had suffered a basal skull fracture and extensive nerve damage to his face when he "stuffed" his boat during a race. Mike Brittain, who owns a company that makes boat accessories, was also at the firm.

The three men joined some of the workers and exchanged friendly barbs for a few minutes. Then Aronow interjected the thought that had apparently been uppermost in his mind. He asked Saccenti, "So what do you think—is Ben in?" Saccenti shrugged his shoulders. Aronow started walking toward his car, saying, "Maybe I'll stop by and see him. Well, see you later, kid."

A little farther down the street on the other side, a dark blue Lincoln Town Car with fancy hubcaps was parked. The car had been there all the time that Aronow was in Apache. Waiting. At three-ten P.M. Aronow stepped into his car. As he backed his sports convertible onto the street, the Lincoln pulled out from behind a parked car and approached the Mercedes from the opposite direction. The driver's window was down.

When the Lincoln pulled alongside Aronow's car and stopped, it wasn't unusual. Lots of strangers came to "Don's street" to talk about boats, say hello, take his picture. It was the part of being a legend that Aronow enjoyed.

Suddenly the driver pulled out a .45 semiautomatic pistol and reached almost into Don's car. Aronow instinctively raised his left arm. A bullet smashed the gold, inscribed watch that Rolex had given him to commemorate one of his world championships. There was a split-second pause. Then five more shots cracked the air.

The sound brought people running out from the various boat companies on the street. They saw the window of the Town Car roll up and the driver navigate an expert 180° turn behind Aronow's Mercedes, across the grass, over a wooden railroad tie that lined the edge of the street, and back onto the blacktop. There was no speeding, no frantic squealing of tires. The driver was calm and deliberate.

As the Lincoln headed toward the Alley's exit, a light-colored pickup truck suddenly pulled out behind it and stopped for a moment in the middle of the street. Then it followed. Turning right at the corner, the Town Car picked up speed, almost hitting a young boy crossing the street. Within minutes the dark blue car and the pickup disappeared into the labyrinthine streets of north Miami. Neither would ever be found by the police.

Ben Kramer and his father, Jack, were behind Ft. Apache, putting a boat into the canal. Jack recalls, "A secretary with big tits came running behind the marina and said 'Don's been shot' over and over so fast that we didn't understand what she was saying at first." When they finally did, they dashed to the street and saw Aronow still in the car. "An orthopedic surgeon who had come to check on Bobby was there holding Don's head up," recalls Jack, "and he said to us, 'Don't look at this, you don't want to see it.' So we left." The Kramers were the only ones to leave the scene so quickly.

Bobby Saccenti was in his office when several of his Cuban workers came running in to get him. They didn't speak English so they began calling him, making *pop pop* sounds. Saccenti thought at first they were trying to tell him that the fans in the glass-cutting room had broken down. But they seemed frantic and kept pointing for him to follow. Outside he saw Aronow's car, with the door open and another of the boat workers, Bobby Moore, standing next to Aronow.

Aronow was slumped over the wheel of his car, the engine still running, the air conditioner still humming. Saccenti helped his wounded friend from the vehicle. He had been shot in the wrist, the throat, the chest, the abdomen. His aorta had been hit—blood was spurting out from his body. He was gasping for air. Saccenti clutched at his friend, saying, "Breathe, breathe deeply," trying to will the strength into him.

The surgeon, soon joined by an ambulance crew, attempted to stem the flow of blood. But almost as fast as they applied a bandage to one of the gaping holes, the cloth turned red. The circle of blood in which Aronow lay grew thicker, then wider, until its diameter was almost the length of the man within it.

A crowd of more than a hundred people stood silent in a huge circle, transfixed by the sight. Forced to come to grips with the mortality of the man who had seemed indestructible, larger than life.

"An ambulance arrived and a team of paramedics jumped out," Saccenti recalls. "They came out with pumps, cut his clothes, put a shock suit over his legs, and started putting needles in him. I was in the street smashing a pump down, a foot pump. Everybody was working on him." Aronow was choking and the medics forced him to regurgitate. Then they rolled him on his side to stop and wedged a stick in his mouth to stop him from swallowing his tongue.

One of the paramedics sensing the shock in the huge crowd asked, "Who is this guy?"

A worker replied, "That's the king. He built this street."

Mike Kandrovicz arrived as they were inserting an intravenous needle into Aronow. "He was really shot up," says Kandrovicz. "The first shot hit him in the wrist where he must have put his hand up to ward off the bullet. He had a hole in his shoulder going into his heart. The bullet that went through the right-side car door must've been the one that burned a line across his chest and then went out the other door. The killer must have leaned in through the window because he was shot in the groin. That must've been the one that went through the floor. One bullet missed him."

Old Mike said, "See, Don, I told you it doesn't hurt. You're going just like I did. But you gotta come back, Don." Kandrovicz didn't think that Aronow could hear him, but he hoped. He also hoped that he was right when he had told him that dying didn't hurt. "I guess he felt the first shot, in the wrist. He must've felt that one 'cause you don't die from getting shot in the wrist. But I don't think he felt the ones after that."

The first IV bottle was empty. The medic set up a second one and handed it to Old Mike. "As fast as they put it in him, it was coming out," Kandrovicz says. One of the medics was desperately looking for something to plug the holes, the blood was pouring out so fast from Aronow's back.

The lifeblood of Don Aronow would continue to seep onto the hot, dusty street that he had founded so many years ago for almost thirty minutes.

In an office a few feet away from where Aronow lay, dying, the phone rang. Ted Theodile, the owner of Magnum Marine, another company founded by Aronow, was in his second-floor office reviewing a design. A large bay window on one wall enabled him to overlook the work being done on two 63-foot luxury yachts. The noise from the saws and hammers in the hangarlike building was kept to a minimum in his office by special acoustic insulation.

Theodile's intercom buzzed. His secretary had a wildly agitated client on the phone who wanted to speak to him immediately. He took the call. It was an oil sheik in Bahrain. "He was very excited and he kept saying, 'What has happened? What has happened? I hear they just shot Don,'" Theodile recalls.

Ted hadn't heard anything. He was convinced that his client had somehow misunderstood. He stood up from his desk and moved over to the window. The large two-story-high doors to the facility were open to the street, and as he looked down, he could see that something was happening outside. "The police and fire engines were there," he recalls, "and a crowd of people were standing around. I couldn't believe it. My client was right. I was right there, but I heard about it from halfway around the world."

A medically equipped Bell rescue helicopter arrived at the scene at three-forty P.M., about twenty minutes after it was dispatched and almost thirty minutes from the time the call was placed. A few minutes later the helicopter was in the air—with Aronow aboard and flight medics pumping his chest to keep him alive. He was put on artificial life support, though his wounds by now were dripping clear IV fluid. Four minutes later Air Rescue One landed at Mt. Sinai Medical Center.

Lillian Aronow arrived at the medical center shortly before the helicopter. She was taken into the nurses' office to wait while the emergency room doctors made a desperate effort to save her husband. As a staff psychologist joined her in her vigil, a call was transferred from the hospital switchboard to the office. A nurse answered and then handed the receiver to Lillian. The caller hissed, "Is that son of a bitch Aronow dead yet?"

THREE

Nothing evokes the image of Miami as much as a sleek powerboat shooting across the turquoise waterways leaving a brilliant white wake. No one was more responsible for this sight than Don Aronow. He infused his boats with a style, grace, and sexiness that had never been seen before. And he pushed himself and his creations faster than anyone had ever gone before on the open seas.

In the early sixties when Aronow first came to Miami, the city was a refuge for the aged and sickly; for winter-weary retirees and big-city mobsters; for legal and illegal aliens fleeing one or another oppressive regime; adventurers looking for a new thrill; and misfits, people who for one reason or another were out of step with most of America. It was a city built by the most exquisite dreamers, like Flagler and Plant, and like all dreams it was dying.

By the eighties Miami was a great mystical phoenix rising from the ashes. A new mecca, the city of the future, a hot, vibrant magnet for all who sought a new life, a new chance. A place where fortunes were made, almost overnight, and no one looked too closely at how they were made. A place with so little past that new money became old money within a few years.

In many ways, Aronow both reflected and created the image of modern-day Miami, "America's Casablanca." Colorful, hot, free spirited. A city of mystery, harboring secrets. And an element of toughness and danger lurking just beneath the carefree veneer. Life in Miami is for those who don't mind living on the razor's edge. To many it's the air of combustibility slashing every so often across the deceptive serenity that makes life in Miami so alluring.

It was in the tropical glitz of Miami that Aronow became, as one friend put it, "top gun." In a city that breaks as many rules as it makes, where the entrepreneurial spirit is alive on both sides of the law, and where men take their play seriously, he found the perfect environment.

Don Aronow arrived on the Miami scene in the winter of 1961 with a characteristic swagger, a larger-than-life story, and plenty of money. "This big, dark-haired guy who looks handsome enough to be a movie gangster starts buying from me," Howard Abbey, one of the old-time boatbuilders, remembers.

"You know Miami boat companies—maybe half a dozen or more go in and out of business every year," he explains. "This Aronow drives up in a Jaguar XKE and gives a good order. But I check Dun and Bradstreet on him anyway. You know what? They said he was reported to have several companies in Jersey but refused to give D and B any credit data."

"So I asked him about payment," Abbey recalls, "and he takes a clip of hundred-dollar bills out of his pockets and pays me cash. You don't argue with that. To get paid by a small boatbuilder, you usually have to be the first to catch him if and when he collects on a boat."

Aronow was clearly not the typical transplanted Northerner. Although he was retired, he was young, in his midthirties, and he had plenty of money. He told his new friends in Miami that he had made his fortune in the New Jersey house construction business. But despite his success and the fact that he had just built a new mansion in New Jersey for his family, he quit the business to move to Miami after one harsh winter.

He said one day he was sitting in his new home on the top of a hill in South Orange, New Jersey. A long, steep drive led to the house, and when it snowed, he practically had to climb up to the house on his hands and knees. One week there were two snowstorms. He was fed up with the cold weather, he said. So he turned to his wife, Shirley, and swore that "if it snows for a third time this week, we're leaving New Jersey forever."

Whenever he told that story, he'd pause and grin as he prepared for the punch line: "It did and so did we." He took his three young children out of school, packed their bags, and "retired to Florida." Other times he gave different reasons for leaving: he "just became bored with the construction industry"; he "had made more money than I could ever spend"; or "there was no more challenge in building houses."

Despite his legendary fondness for talking and interviews, and his ability to weave one racing story after another, Aronow spoke little about New Jersey. "That was one thing he was real tight-lipped about," says Norris "Knocky" House, who traveled around the world with Aronow during the racing years. "He just didn't talk about his early years."

He told a few stories, but for the most part he never elaborated on his family life in Brooklyn or how he had made his fortune except to say that it was in the construction business. Most of his friends agreed upon a few facts: that Aronow's childhood was tough. And in the course of only a few years in business, he had become very wealthy.

While he was a lifeguard at Coney Island in the late forties, Aronow met Shirley Goldin, whom he described as "the prettiest girl on the beach." They married, and upon his graduation from Brooklyn College in 1948, he went to work as a physical education teacher at a Brooklyn junior high school. He once said that when he was in college his idea of being really successful was to be a phys ed teacher. "The instructors got good money and wore nice-looking clothes," he explained. "I didn't think there was anything else you could want."

When he was about to become a father for the first time, he discovered that his teaching salary wasn't nearly enough to support a family. He joined his in-laws' small construction company. A couple of years later, he left to start his own company. His first "office" for his new company was in his car. Within a few years, however, he was building shopping malls, housing projects, and office complexes. His business was enormously successful. According to his construction superintendent, Lenny Sendelsky, "he made millions."

In less than seven years, Aronow rose from a construction manager with a small company to owning a multimillion-dollar firm. He had a collection of antique cars and drove a white Rolls-Royce to work. He moved his family to South Orange, where he built a huge mansion. Shortly after the home was completed, Aronow packed up his family, moved to Miami, and never returned.

· · ·

Cruising along the Miami River in his sport fishing boat during his first season in Florida, Aronow began to meet men caught up in offshore powerboat racing. A three-letter man in college for football, wrestling, and track, he was immediately intrigued by the challenge of the rough physical and mental competition required by the sport. "This was where I could use my heart and my head," he said.

"He would drive up to see about his boat in a Rolls-Royce or a Jaguar," says Jim Wynne, a boat designer and champion racer. The rugged racers took one look at Aronow and pegged him as a playboy. They laughed that the first time Aronow raced would be his last.

Offshore powerboat racers pride themselves on their rough-and-tumble sport. To prove just how rugged they are, they relish the story of when fighter Rocky Marciano decided to go along in one Miami-Nassau-Miami race. By the time his boat reached the halfway point at Nassau, Marciano had had enough. Bruised and bleeding, he hopped off the boat and refused to get back in saying it was "too tough, at least in the ring I can hit back." He took a plane back to Florida.

Sportswriters of the day called it the era of "iron men and wooden boats." "Everyone was talking about the Miami-Nassau-Miami race," Aronow later recalled of those early days. "They talked about how tough it was, and how tough the men were who ran in it. Dick Bertram was the current champion." So Aronow set a goal for himself: to beat Dick Bertram in the next Miami-Nassau race in 1962. It was his first contest. He raced a little wooden boat that he called *Claudia* after his daughter. He came in fourth out of fifty-nine. "He damn near killed himself trying to win," recalls Jim Wynne.

Aronow later explained his approach to life: "Doesn't everyone want to win—unless you've got a real mental thing, then why be a loser? It's a matter of how much effort you're willing to put in. Those who put the most in, get the most out. They're the winners."

In the next few years, Aronow raced successfully but not expertly. He pushed his boats so hard that most of them broke before he ever crossed the finish line. He became known as The Animal, a man capable of any human or mechanical excess. Nothing seemed to discourage him from his goal—not exploding engines, broken boats, or crashes. He once declared, "It's not a race unless you get hurt." To that end Aronow on various occasions broke bones, tore muscles, and endured extensive internal and external injuries.

A photographer who often covered Aronow's races speculated, "You wonder why they call it a sport. There are no spectators out there cheering and you take the beating of a boxing match for hours with no time out between rounds. And offshore, if you're hurt, you can't even quit. You have to keep going until you reach land."

It was in this world that Aronow grabbed his share of history. He traveled faster in his powerboats than any other man in the world, breaking all records for speed. "In racing circles, Don was as famous as Mickey Mantle was in baseball," says John Crouse, racing historian and publicist for Aronow. "But Don was bigger and better. Mantle didn't create baseball, but Don created modern offshore powerboat racing. It's no exaggeration to call him the father of powerboat racing."

The day in 1962 that Jim Wynne, a champion powerboat racer, met Don Aronow was a day that changed the course of both of their lives. In his first competitions, Aronow raced boats made by others. But he quickly became frustrated with the designs and decided, as he put it, "to build the finest rough-water boat in the world."

Wynne was meeting with a craftsman at Howard Abbey's boat shop. He noticed a meticulously shined brown Rolls-Royce pull up and a big, athletic-looking man emerge. Wynne and Aronow were the same age and had similar racing interests, but Aronow was a whole new type of character from the typical powerboat racer. For one thing he had money.

Aronow and Wynne were introduced. Both men were having Abbey build a wooden boat. Aronow's was the traditional flat-vee bottom; Wynne's was a new design, a deep-vee, that he had evolved from one that designer Ray Hunt had created. Aronow immediately sensed the potential and asked Wynne to design one for him. Although he was clearly a novice at powerboating, Aronow was so confident, so set on building a revolutionary boat, and so persuasive that Wynne was soon caught up in his vision.

Jim Wynne and Waltman Walters, a naval architect, designed the first three boats Aronow produced. The men began experimenting with designs. Deciding that wood was obsolete, Aronow switched to fiberglass. He continued to narrow the vee of the hull for a finer entry point. The result was the Formula 223.

He established Formula Marine Company, primarily as a racing stable. Wynne raced on Aronow's team then along with Jake Trotter, Alan "Brownie" Brown, Britain's William Shand-Kydd and Lord Lucan. "We didn't win many races but we made the world sit up and take notice—and we knocked them dead with class wins," Aronow recalled.

Against the advice of many of Miami's best boatbuilders at the time, who told him that the average boat buyer didn't want to race and wouldn't pay top dollar for a boat that did, Aronow advertised his designs as if they were Ferraris. He finished them off with all the racing touches: sports-car steering wheels, racing stripes. And he added splashes of luxury—teak interior trim and custom hardware that hadn't come with racing boats before.

In 1964, a little over a year after he started the company, he sold the mold for his 27-foot model to a North Carolina group. He sold the rest—the name, the two remaining boat designs and molds—to Thunderbird Products, then led by Dick Genth. Formula was the first of many companies that he built and sold soon after, again contrary to conventional wisdom that said run with a company while it was hot.

He bought much of the land on a weed-filled dead-end street in north Miami. Each time he sold a company, he moved to another lot —next door or across the street from his former company—and started a new, competitive business. When asked why he would build a company only to sell it soon after it became popular, he gave the typical Aronow answer: "It was like building tract housing. I was more interested in developing new models than in production. After I sold it I'd say, why did I do that? Maybe I should have just taken a vacation instead."

But there was more to his strategy than simply boredom. "He was a genius at what he did," notes Don Soffer, a friend and developer of Turnberry Isle, one of Miami's most famous luxury condominium complexes. What Aronow did was to create and sell a succession of boat companies, all of which have become world-class winners. As he himself said one time, "I'd race the boat, make it famous, and then market it."

Aronow kept the Formula plant. In his sales contract with Thunderbird he agreed not to go back into business making boats similar to the Formula. No sooner had the ink dried on the contract than he called Wynne and Walters back and directed them to develop a new and different line. He removed the Formula name from the building and painted the new name, Donzi Marine. The name was given to Aronow by one of his girlfriends. He thought it sounded sexy and foreign. Soon people all over the world were talking about "Donzi, the new Italian boat."

By this time offshore racers were hitting speeds of 70 mph. In one Miami–Key West race, G-force meters were mounted in several boats. They recorded shocks as high as twenty-five g's. (By comparison, the Apollo astronauts endured about ten g's during lift-off. The shuttle takeoff is even smoother today.)

In 1965, six teams opted to use Donzis, and Aronow soon found himself racing against his own designs. In one competition, Jack Manson, a racer who had won the Key West competition earlier, was running a standard 42-footer. The Donzis, about half the length, were like pesky little mosquitoes zipping around him. He cursed Aronow later, exclaiming, "Those damned Donzis of yours were all around—ahead of me, right behind, pushing all the way." Aronow laughed and said, "We'll put that in print." Sure enough, his ads soon carried the slogan "Another Damned Donzi—that's what racing competitors call them."

Aronow won his first big competition in 1965. He and Bobby Moore raced the *007*, a 28-foot Donzi, in the Miami-Nassau race. He had finally achieved his goal: he beat both Dick Bertram and Jim Wynne. On winning he said, "I've been waiting four years for this moment." He set a world record in that race, averaging 56 mph in the 363-mile race.

Spurred on by his victory, Aronow decided to try to top his own record in the Gateway Marathon—from West Palm Beach to Lucaya, Grand Bahama, and back. The contest became famous throughout the racing world as a testament not only to how much physical punishment the racers endure but to how difficult it was to beat Aronow. Even when he was handicapped by a weak boat.

He and his codriver, Dave Stirrat, showed up in a featherweight 27-foot Donzi named the *008*. Aronow, as always, was experimenting with materials, designs, and engines in his efforts to go ever faster. This new version of his *007* was cut so low that it was difficult to keep it from turning over even when it was tied at the dock. It was built for speed in calm waters. But there were rough seas on the day of the race. Aronow had also been tinkering with the thickness of the hull, making it so thin that when he was inside the hull with a flashlight just before the race, the light was seen shining through. It looked like a jack-o'-lantern.

As they approached Grand Bahama Island, Aronow caught up to Wynne, but a mile from the finish line a prop blade flew off Aronow's propeller. He and Stirrat decided to go for the win anyway, and they left the throttles at full speed. The vibration was almost unbearable. The vee-drive broke, the shaft began to leak, and the boat started to sink. Still they continued. Finally the boat was so waterlogged it could hardly move. Wynne crossed the finish line only twenty-eight seconds ahead of them just as Aronow's boat was almost underwater.

The men climbed onto the dock, badly battered. Stirrat's face was covered with gashes and he could barely walk. Aronow's hands were so riddled with deep bloodied cuts and blisters from the vibrating wheel, he couldn't open them. He taped up his hands, made repairs to his boat, and after the race's one-day layover, cajoled another racer to be his codriver. (Stirrat couldn't make the trip back.) The return brought even worse weather, with swells reaching ten feet high. They slammed the little boat around mercilessly. Still Aronow came in only minutes behind Wynne's much bigger boat.

Later the same year, Aronow broke a world record, averaging 70 mph in the Around Nassau Sweepstakes. Right after the highly publicized record breaker, he sold Donzi. The timing was as usual perfect and brought him the best possible price.

Aronow was by now an intimidating competitor on and off the water. When he sold a company, the new owners were starting to ask him to sign noncompete clauses. He always did. And he always managed to get around them.

He had a number of business interests by then. In one interview he said he had counted up sixteen businesses that he owned in 1966 —everything from an industrial park to a company that prefabricated big tracts for slot-car centers to a shrimp boat.

Despite a noncompete contract with Teleflex, which had just purchased Donzi, Aronow started his third company, Magnum, next door to his original Formula plant. It was with Magnum that Aronow hit his stride. His worldwide sales plan was conducted not through magazine ads but on the water in races.

His Magnum designs reached a peak with the Maltese Magnum. "It was a breakthrough," he later commented, "a great boat, the forerunner of all the deep-vees today." All during these early years, his boats were evolving into the now-famous shapes seen throughout the racing world—sleek lines with hulls that barely touch the water.

In a way, he was the inspiration for the television show *Miami Vice,* which featured Aronow-style designs in the opening credits. Michael Mann, the creator of the show, said that he got the idea for the series when he first came to the tropical city and saw these boats speeding across Biscayne Bay. He said he knew immediately that he could produce a "hot, visually exciting" action show in Miami.

In his Magnum office, Aronow hung a sign on the wall among the boat and horse photographs. The sign more than anything he ever said summed up the philosophy by which he measured out his life: "Nothing in the world can take the place of persistence. . . . Talent will not. . . . Genius will not. . . . Education alone will not. . . . Persistence and determination alone are omnipotent." Beneath it he had written: "Make what you do today important. For you give a day of your life to it."

. . .

The second half of the sixties was when Aronow became the undisputed star of powerboat racing. The sport was conducted on a world circuit by then, and Aronow had both the chutzpah and the money to send himself, his boats, and his throttleman, Knocky House, all over the world.

"Those days were great, absolutely fantastic," says Knocky, chief mechanic, test driver, and racing partner during many of Aronow's victories. House, a former Olympic gold medalist for wrestling and a two-time all-American lacrosse player, is a deeply tanned, barrel-chested man with more than his share of boating scars. Among them: three broken ribs, two lost teeth, a fractured nose, and a hip implant, all the result of a lifetime of racing with Aronow. He explains matter-of-factly, "You figure we ran twelve to fourteen races a year, of a hundred eighty miles or more. You get pretty beaten up."

The Aronow-House team began inauspiciously. In one of the first times they were in a boat together, Aronow was driving. Knocky asked, "Do you know where you're going?" Ever confident, always optimistic, Don replied, "Yeah, sure." A few seconds later they rammed into a sandbar.

House says that Aronow didn't always have the best sense of direction, and he made matters worse by refusing to wear glasses even though he was nearsighted. But the men went on to become perhaps one of the most successful offshore racing teams ever. "We built boats. We raced them. And we beat the world," Knocky states. "Nobody could run with us. If they ran against us and beat us, they were lucky."

The year 1967 was when Aronow became unbeatable throughout the world. He had pulled everything together by then—judgment, aggression, athletic stamina, and superb boating designs. He was still racing the smaller boats against his competitors, whose boats were simply outclassed by his designs.

"In 1967, I won the world championship with two twenty-eight-foot Magnums that cost eight thousand dollars apiece," he noted with great pride. One of the boats was the first outboard-powered boat ever to win an international race; another set a world record of 64.5 mph for diesels. He also changed offshore racing history that year by being the first to win the 190-mile French world championship with a single-engine boat.

"One day we were in Europe, then the West Coast, then Mexico," remembers House. "It was a challenge and we both liked it." Aronow logged a number of racing firsts. At Monte Carlo. At Cannes. He shattered another world record in the Miami–Key West race, averaging 58.7 mph. During that race they kept the throttles wide open, although at times they couldn't even see because of the severe rain squalls.

By the end of that year Aronow had snared virtually every racing title and was the first person to win both the world and U.S. championships. And he won the Sam Griffith Memorial Trophy—considered to be one of the greatest powerboat racing honors.

It was Aronow's style that provided the alchemy that transformed the champion into a legend. Miamians and powerboating enthusiasts everywhere followed "Don's latest escapade." During a California race his boat was going so fast that when it hit a huge wave, it shot off the crest and flew into the pontoon of a low-flying TV helicopter.

"We got back into the race," says Knocky House. "We didn't talk for fifteen minutes. We were trying to figure out how we were going to clean our pants before we got out of the boat. I'm just joking. But we were scared. That was the only time we really thought we were dead."

"Don loved to have this image of man against the sea," recalls *Miami Herald* reporter Edna Buchanan. "And he was always having his press agent, John Crouse, write a release about it." Bobby Moore laughs that "Don would get more publicity in one race than the rest of these people would get in two or three years of racing. He knew how to use the papers and the writers."

One highly publicized picture of Aronow with torn shirtsleeves and a painful grimace has been in magazines from *People* to French *Vogue* with the caption noting the beating he took to win one title. The real story behind the picture is far different. Aronow had heard from someone that John Crouse was a fast runner. According to Crouse, Aronow came to his office one day and said he wanted to race. "We're running as fast as we can and I was beating him," recalls Crouse. "Suddenly he tackles me. We slammed into the ground and he tore his shirt and was bleeding."

Crouse took the picture as a teasing reminder to Aronow how he had to win at everything, even a footrace. Crouse says even Aronow was a little embarrassed at what he did to keep from losing. Then Aronow used the picture to his advantage. He had Crouse circulate the photo to the press saying it was taken after a grueling powerboat race.

Aronow enjoyed the stories. Loved to tell them and loved to read them. He particularly liked those that enhanced his rough-and-tough image. And if a story needed some creative embellishment to gain just the right flavor, he wouldn't hesitate to add it. He was fond of his Around Long Island race. Although he and Knocky had strayed from the course and run aground, they still won. When his competitors began to rib him about going off course, he claimed that they were so far ahead of everyone they decided to stop for fried clams.

His flair for telling stories and his real-life adventures kept reporters happy. In all, he had at least three motorcycle accidents, ten car crashes, and an unrecorded number of boating accidents. With each the legend grew.

He and Alan "Brownie" Brown had several skirmishes. Both men worked on Thunderboat Alley, next door to one another. One day, Aronow sped up the canal behind their companies and purposely created a huge wake that washed Brownie's boat onto the dock. So Brownie got his gun and shot out all the lights at Aronow's boatyard next door.

Always wanting the last word, Aronow waited the next day until he saw Brownie on the dock. He hopped into his boat and sped down the canal at 70 mph grinning demonically. He intended to flood Brownie this time. But his throttle stuck and Brownie watched as Aronow's boat shot out of the canal, hurtled airborne for fifty yards, and slammed into a tree.

Aronow and Brownie teamed together in the Houston Channel Derby—a reputedly calm-weather race. But no one had mentioned to the contestants that if there were any oil tankers or ocean-going tugs in the channel, there would be enormous wakes.

"Going over those wakes was just awful," Brownie recalls. "We were jumping so fantastically high in the air that it seemed we could've flown over the tankers. We were running second when we hit some really incredible waves, and that crazy Aronow never let go of the throttle. Within the space of three or four miles we went from a mile behind to a mile ahead. And that was going out of the channel. Coming back, jumping those wakes from the other direction, was even worse. We were flying a hundred feet off of the water. He just had to win." And they did.

Aronow's humor even in serious situations was a boon to sportswriters, adding color to standard racing stories. In 1968, Aronow was in another record-setting lead in the Miami-Nassau race—he had been clocked at 81 mph—when his Magnum 28 caught fire about thirteen miles from the finish line and burned to the waterline.

"My mechanic Knocky and I dive into the water with our life jackets on, all our clothes, even our shoes on," Aronow told reporters after the rescue. "We manage to get into the raft—we're exhausted

—trying to pull away from the blazing boat, which is about to blow any minute, and the crazy thing keeps coming after us. Finally we realize it's attached with a line. I yell to Knocky, 'Cut the line, goddammit, and get your bleeding legs out of the water—don't ya know there're sharks around here?' "

Dr. Robert Magoon, Aronow's closest friend and a powerboating champion himself, remembers that after a tough race in California that should have completely exhausted him, "Don said, let's have some fun. So we chartered a plane and went to the Riverside Race Track because our friend Mark Donahue was racing that day. We landed the plane and grabbed a taxi. Don liked the cabdriver's hat, so he bought it."

Donahue's car had broken down, so he joined them and Aronow said, " 'Let's take off,' " Magoon recalls. "We went back to the plane, flew to Delmar for four or five horse races, and then flew home. Everything was very spur of the moment. That's the way Don was. Always spontaneous, always up for fun."

Aronow thrived on the macho camaraderie among the men in powerboating. Knocky says that Aronow liked to drop by the shop when "all the guys were there—the workers, the mechanics, the salesmen—and we'd all start wrestling. He'd be rolling around the floor with the rest of us." Crouse describes him this way: "Don had the genteel nature of a head-on train wreck."

Willie Meyers recalls one race in which he and Aronow competed in England. "After the race, Don comes over to me and says that all these people kept sticking their thumb up at him along the course. So, he said, 'I just gave it right back to them.' And Don sticks his middle finger up." Meyers says that Aronow thought that the thumbs-up was the English way of saying "fuck you." He says, laughing, "I had to explain to Don that they were congratulating him, not insulting him. We got a big kick out of that."

Aronow again ended the year victorious, winning the Sam Griffith Memorial Race, the 180-mile Hennessey Cup, and the U.S. championship for the second time. And once again he sold the company. Magnum Marine was purchased by APECO, Inc., a photocopy conglomerate.

In 1969, Aronow transcended the title "world championship racer" and gained his share of immortality. He won eight major victories, setting an all-time record for the punishing sport. One powerboating magazine said: "Aronow's performance in 1969 was so phenomenal it can hardly be described."

After selling Magnum to APECO, Aronow promptly moved across

the street to start another company. Since he had once again signed a noncompete agreement, he went to his friend Elton Cary, who owned Cary Marine. It, too, was on the Alley, just down the street from the Magnum and Donzi plants.

With Cary fronting for him, he put together his newest boat design, a 32-footer that he called the Cigarette. He told the press that he chose the name from stories he'd heard when he was a kid hanging around the docks of Brooklyn. At that time there was a legendary 65-foot pirate boat named *Cigarette.* In the darkness of the night, the boat would overtake rum-running vessels, and under the threat of its Thompson submachine guns, make off with the outlawed booty. It was considered uncatchable by both rumrunners and Prohibition agents.

From his first boat, Aronow's designs had evolved swiftly until they reached a pinnacle with the Cigarette. It became the most famous powerboat in the world—he would later recall that every time he raced the Cigarette 32-footer in 1969 he set a record.

The Cigarette was a creation that went beyond appeal to racing enthusiasts. It came to symbolize the best in powerboats. Many still say it is the most beautiful powerboat in the world—a striking combination of aesthetics, power, and purity of line virtually unrivaled.

It's also sexy. Not surprising from a man who once said, "Actually boats are sex symbols. The Cigarette is a sexy boat, but we don't market it that way. It's a man's boat, a machine."

As soon as the noncompete agreement with Magnum expired, Aronow began racing the Cigarette 32. "It was so advanced," Aronow would say later, "that I didn't go wild with it, pushing it full out all the time like I usually did with boats. We still outran everybody— me and Knocky—but you had to be careful with that boat. It was a dangerous machine."

The original Cigarette—the one that would make Aronow a worldwide star—was later sold to two Australian brothers, Val and Paul Carr. They won three races in a row. Then in another race they were thrown from it at 70 mph in the shark-infested seas off Australia. Both men died. Years later, some people would suggest that Aronow's murder might have been revenge for the Carr brothers' death.

Aronow's stellar year began in March 1969 in the Long Beach–Ensenada, Mexico Race where he snared first place and set another world record for speed. Two months later he was at West Palm Beach in the Gateway Marathon where he captured another victory.

One month after that it was on to the Bahama 500—the so-called "Indy of ocean racing."

But this time he was ill. The night before the race he had a serious attack of diverticulitis and a 101° fever. His wife, Shirley, had seen him race with all sorts of ailments and bruises, but she put her foot down: no Bahama 500. Shirley hustled him off to bed despite his protestations. She was adamant—he wasn't going to kill himself trying to race with a fever. She stood guard outside the bedroom door.

Before dawn, Aronow gulped some medication and climbed out the motel window. He told Knocky and the navigator that he would establish the lead, then go ashore in Nassau, and they could finish the race. It didn't happen. For over nine hours, Aronow stood at the wheel, despite his fever. When he began to fall behind the other boats, he shot off the prescribed path, taking a shortcut through a particularly treacherous coral-strewn cay. He won with an average speed of 64.5 mph for the 540-mile course and broke the former eleven-hour record. Shirley didn't realize he was in the race until she turned on the television.

Two weeks later he was in Italy, nabbing second place in the Naples Trophy Race. Less than a month later, still in Italy, he roared to victory in the 214-mile Via Reggio race. He set a 74.3 mph world record that beat his own Ensenada record and would stand until 1973. In the next month he broke more records in France, then California and England.

"We often spent the entire summer in Europe at races because there were three English races, two French races, a number of Italian races," Willie Meyers explains. "We'd ship our boats over and drive them around the continent on trailers."

By the time Aronow completed the October Miami-Nassau Race —in which he again broke all records—he totally dominated the world racing circuit. No one could beat him. He won an unprecedented eight out of eleven races, an all-time record number of wins for one year. (It was three more than the record five turned in by Miamian Jim Wynne in 1966 and Italian Vincenzo Baliestieiri in 1968.)

He was given every honor that powerboat racing had by the end of the year. Again he won the Sam Griffith Memorial Trophy as well as the French, Swedish, and Bahamian national championships. He won the U.S. offshore championship for the third year in a row— making him the first ever to achieve that distinction.

In 1978, John Crouse did a series of interviews with the world's best offshore racers. One of his questions was "Who was the best you ever faced at sea?" Says Crouse, "The consensus was that Don Aronow was head and shoulders above the rest. Aside from beating you in a boat he either built or designed or both, the guy had an uncanny knack for knowing how badly the other driver was hurting. He often got his jollies by giving them a big bushy-browed smile and wave as he crashed past them in giant seas—many times going through this bit of salt-spray vaudeville hurting like hell himself."

Aronow quit racing after his 1969 championship season. He retired with more victories than any other powerboat racer in the world. Many explanations for his decision to stop were bandied about. In one interview he said he quit because several of his competitors had said if he raced in 1970, they were quitting. Another time he said that after almost a decade of physical punishment, he decided to quit while he was on top. But most friends think it was the accident that paralyzed his son Michael that really marked the end.

"It was devastating to Don," Bob Magoon remembers. "Michael was nineteen at the time. He looked like a younger version of his father. While speeding with a friend on a trip to visit some girls in Georgia, they had a blowout. They were going a hundred miles an hour. Michael was thrown through the air backwards against a tree. His spine snapped."

Bob Magoon was with Aronow when the call came from the Georgia emergency room. Magoon, a physician, spoke with the doctors, who told him to prepare his friend. The driver had just died and Michael, in a coma, was not expected to live. "Don refused to accept it," Magoon recalls. "We chartered a jet and flew there in the middle of the night. He got actively involved in everything, interviewing the doctors, and checking every detail."

The accident was particularly painful to Aronow, who had not wanted to bring Michael on races with him for fear of hurting him. He once said, "I wouldn't take my sons out in a race with me because I wouldn't want to take the same chance with them that I take with myself."

Night after night, Magoon says, the father kept his vigil, whispering to his comatose son, "Fight, Michael. Fight. I know you can do it." Michael regained consciousness, but he was paralyzed. Aronow called in experts from all over the world. He read everything he could about the injury and concentrated all his efforts on willing his son to get better. "His son became his project, his immediate concern," Magoon recalls. "When Michael was injured, Don learned everything he could about it. He became an expert on paraplegia."

Bobby Moore says, "Don lost a lot of interest in the races, then. For a time you'd see his helicopter flying over the races, then you'd see it just once in a while, till he dropped out of the scene completely."

Most people assumed the accident took the life out of Aronow. Close friends disagree. "He stopped racing because he was always getting hurt and he felt he couldn't afford to take that chance while his son needed him," explains Knocky House.

Michael recovered, almost a year later, although he remains paralyzed from the waist down. During his recuperation, he and his father founded Aronow Stables. Finally, satisfied with his son's progress, Aronow channeled his energies again into business.

In 1971, although he was out of racing, Aronow continued to dominate the sport with his successive lines of winning boats. His boats had won the past five world titles. Even rookie racers emerged winners in the Cigarette. Asked by a reporter "Who built the best fast boats in the world?" he answered with unmitigated pride, "Me. For offshore boats the Cigarette 35 is probably the best powerboat in the world."

An Aronow boat had become "the" high performance boat to own. Whatever it was called—Magnum, Cigarette, Squadron XII—no one was immune to their cachet. He sold to kings, sheiks, shahs, and presidents. Customers such as the King of Sweden, the Raja Johor of Malaysia, Prince Omad-Al Fayed of Saudi Arabia, the Prince of Kuwait, Rocky Aoki (founder of Benihana) bought his boats, and many came personally to select them. Evel Knievel had one of his boats and so did Red Adair, the oil fire-fighter.

Fugitive financier Robert Vesco ordered one from exile and went through elaborate means to get the money to Aronow. When Vesco decided that he had to have a Cigarette, he was living in the Bahamas, having fled the U.S. on charges of defrauding American investors of millions of dollars. He sent his son, Tony, with a Bahamian check to pick up the boat. But Aronow would only take cash or a cashier's check.

At seven o'clock the next morning, Aronow got a call at his house. A voice on the other end of the line said, "Hello, Don. This is Bob." Aronow asked, "Bob who?" The caller said, "Come on, Don. You know who I am." Aronow started to laugh, and after a couple of seconds of dead silence, Vesco did, too.

Vesco told Aronow to send his secretary, Patty Lezaca, to Nassau the next day and there would be a cashier's check waiting for her. Lezaca picked up the check and Aronow turned the boat over to

Tony. Eight years later, Vesco's boat was found drifting off the Florida coast. It had been abandoned by a drug smuggler who jumped overboard to escape capture by Customs.

The United States government became one of his biggest customers. Lyndon Johnson's Secret Service guards at the LBJ ranch owned a boat that Aronow built for them so they could guard Johnson when he was whipping around in his own Glastron. Johnson quickly noticed that they had a faster boat and appropriated it. The agents then had to buy another Cigarette so they could keep up with LBJ. The FBI also used Magnums to patrol President Richard Nixon's home in Key Biscayne. The Navy scooped up the boats as soon as Nixon left office.

Aronow sold to other governments as well. In addition to Jordan and Spain, he sold boats to Haiti's "Baby Doc" Duvalier. The Shah of Iran also bought a boat, sending his brother-in-law, a general who headed the Iranian Air Force, to pick out the design. When the boat was ready, the Shah sent his plane and a crew of seven to pick it up.

"The Shah was always calling Aronow personally, always trying to get him to come to Iran," Willie Meyers remembers. The Shah was so pleased with his first boat, he ordered another five for his security forces. When the Shah was forced into exile, Aronow remarked, "I guess Khomeini is using my boats now."

In early 1976, Aronow bought back Magnum Marine from APECO. The company hadn't been able to make a go of it and sold it back, as Aronow put it, "for a few cents on the dollar." He shuttled back and forth across the street from his Magnum office to his Cigarette one. Five months later he sold Magnum again.

The buyer was Ted Theodile, who had been the distributor in Italy for Aronow. Theodile changed the focus of the company from the small 27-foot champion, the Maltese Magnum, to much longer (up to sixty-three feet) and more luxurious models. He had tried to talk Aronow into building larger boats, "but Don was always fascinated with the small boats," recalls Theodile.

While most of the people who bought companies from Aronow were never able to maintain the success Aronow had with them, Theodile says that he made Magnum even more successful than in Aronow's time. "It always got to him," Theodile says, chuckling proudly, "that I was able to do so well. Every time he saw me he'd say, 'You wait, you'll come back and ask me to bail you out.'"

In 1979, Aronow sold Cigarette to Hal Halter, who owned a successful boat-building complex in New Orleans. But in just a few months, Halter approached him to see if he might take back half ownership in Cigarette and manage the business on a daily basis. Aronow agreed.

While running Cigarette for Halter, Aronow began producing another boat design, called Squadron, in a plant on the same street that by now housed the most famous names in powerboating: Formula, Donzi, Magnum, and Cigarette. The industry had come a long way and the once-deserted dead-end street had achieved international fame.

By the eighties, Aronow was renowned for his Midas charm. Besides his powerboat firms, he had branched into other ventures with equal success. He began to put more energy into the horse business. His racing and breeding stable had quickly grown to over a hundred horses on an 85-acre ranch in Ocala in central Florida. And he was still breaking records. He broke one for having a winner in two successive Tropical Park Derbys. He also had a contender in the 1983 Kentucky Derby.

Aronow had all the trappings of success and he enjoyed it. He bought a succession of helicopters and hired a full-time pilot. Randy Riggs was on call at the airport for any spur-of-the-moment flight.

He traveled the world with wealthy and powerful friends. He continued to be friendly with George Bush, who had risen from ambassador to vice president. The change in Bush's political status reflected on Aronow, making him more powerful in Florida, and particularly in Miami. Because he "had the Vice President's ear," a number of area politicians and government officials welcomed Aronow into their domain.

Aronow was also friendly with foreign dignitaries. Jim Kimberly, heir to the Kimberly-Clark fortune, recalls one trip when he and Aronow flew to Spain to visit King Juan Carlos, and then to Amman to meet King Hussein. "His Majesty was very fond of Don and he invited him often," Kimberly recalls. "On this trip we met His Majesty at the capital and then we all flew out to his retreat on the Gulf of Aqaba for a few days. We spent a lot of time on the gulf, did a lot of waterskiing. The King is a good sportsman and he tried to race Don, but Don was just too good for it to be any contest."

Aronow enjoyed his association with royalty. He beamed with delight when he came into his office and his employees announced that "the King called" or "you got another letter from the King today." According to Jerry Engelman, whenever they got a call "and the person said, 'The King is calling,' Don would tell us to ask, 'Which one?' The kings always got a big kick out of that."

It was his second wife, Lillian, however, who made him feel he had really achieved the success he had sought since childhood. To Aronow, she epitomized genuine acceptance into the elite world of the WASP upper class. Aronow and his first wife, Shirley, had lived separate lives for almost ten years and they divorced in 1979. A few weeks later he married Lillian, then twenty-eight, a tall, classic-looking woman in the Ralph Lauren image. King Hussein introduced them. But it wasn't just Lillian's looks that attracted Aronow—he always had his pick of beautiful, sexy women.

Lillian was a socialite. She had made her debut in New York society and had been a member of the Junior League. She brought an exclusive status—one gained at birth. Something that Aronow, no matter how hard he ran, would never have. He placed great significance on the fact that she had married him, often commenting that "I wouldn't have a woman like Lillian if I was hauling garbage for a living."

Meyers says, "Lillian wanted to have eight boys, and Don was all for it." A little over a year after they were married, she and Don had their first child, Gavin. His new son pleased Don, and he ran around to the different companies on the Alley passing out cigars and telling everyone, "I've still got it." When they had their second son, Aronow's pilot, Randy Riggs, says Aronow again ran around, announcing more exuberantly, "I've *still* got it."

Aronow sold Cigarette again in 1982 to Integrated Resources, Inc. for $5.5 million. He continued tinkering with his new company, the Squadron, which he renamed the Squadron XII because his noncompete clause with Integrated allowed him to operate another single-hulled-boat company but limited him to producing only twelve boats. The conglomerate was determined not to meet the same fate that the previous purchasers of Aronow companies had met.

While building Squadron, Aronow got an idea that enabled him to get around the noncompete clause: he would build a catamaran. It wasn't a design that he really wanted. He preferred to continue along the very successful lines of the Magnum and the Cigarette. But the design offered a loophole. Since the noncompete clause wouldn't expire until 1987, it was the only way to stay in business. IRI-Cigarette found out about his plans and tried to stop him legally, but failed. Soon after, he started USA Racing Team to build the catamarans.

At the same time, Aronow's relationship with George Bush was growing stronger. Through that association, Aronow's company, USA Racing Team, won the government contract in 1985 to produce boats for Bush's Vice Presidential South Florida Joint Drug Task Group. His company was awarded the contract again in 1986. The government work made life easy for Aronow—it meant guaranteed sales for his company. Everyone on the street knew that Aronow would have the contract as long as Bush was in power. And most expected that the Vice President would someday be president.

As his relationship with the Vice President solidified, Aronow was as always looking to the future. "One time Don said to me, 'If Reagan got shot again and died, wouldn't it be something to know the President?'" Randy Riggs recalls. "Then Don said, 'Imagine being a diplomat. Wouldn't that be great?' I assumed that he was getting real close to the Vice President [Bush]."

By February 3, 1987, life could not have offered much more to Don Aronow. Except time. He was the undisputed dean of the powerboat industry. He had developed considerable influence in Miami and in Washington. Six months before, Lillian had given birth to their second son. He was working on what he called a revolutionary design for a new boat—eagerly anticipating the expiration of the Cigarette noncompete clause the following month. It was even rumored that he was planning a racing comeback in the 1987 Miami-Nassau race. Those dreams came to an abrupt end on that sunny afternoon when he was gunned down.

FOUR

Don Aronow was pronounced dead at four forty-five P.M. on February 3, 1987, forty-five minutes after the Air Rescue helicopter brought him in. It was less than a month before his sixtieth birthday. Back on Thunderboat Alley there had been hope. "We were all encouraged at first," recalls Bobby Saccenti. "We got reports back that he had made it alive to the hospital. That he made it to the machines. Then as night came, the news filtered out that he had died in the hospital."

When word of the shooting came into the monolithic headquarters of MetroDade Police Department, Detective Mike DeCora was at his desk. The other homicide detectives were out on assignment —murder in Miami is a nonstop business. DeCora had no idea that he was about to handle one of Miami's most famous murders—a not insignificant title in what some considered America's murder capital.

DeCora arrived on the Alley about an hour after the hit. The uniformed police, already there, had tried to protect the area as much as possible. The street was roped off with official yellow tape marked CRIME SCENE—DO NOT CROSS. As DeCora ducked under the tape, one of the patrolmen came over to report. There was no weapon, he said, but they had located some shell casings on the ground near the Mercedes.

A large crowd remained on the small street. In roping off the area, the police had stranded a large number of people who worked on the dead-end side of the crime scene. Most of them, except those who left by boat on the canal, would be stuck there for several hours. But it didn't seem to matter. Everyone was straining to watch as DeCora went about his business.

He picked up the shell casings and bagged them. Then he walked over to the grass and looked at the tire tracks left by the Town Car. The heavy railroad tie lining the edge of the grass was splintered where the car had driven over it. He checked out some nearby bushes for a gun. His concentration was broken when a bystander called out to him. He walked over, and the man, a Cuban fiberglass worker, solemnly handed him a Styrofoam cup and pointed to the spot where Don had died.

DeCora looked inside and shook his head. There on the bottom were what appeared to be some links from a watchband. They were wet from drops of coffee that had remained in the cup. He thanked the guy but thought to himself, haven't people ever heard that you're not supposed to touch evidence? Later, the pieces would be identified as links from Aronow's Rolex that had been scattered about when a bullet hit the watchband.

Then DeCora turned his attention to the Mercedes. The car's left door was open and the window was down. Rather than step in the still-moist pool of blood on the driver's side, DeCora went around to the other side. He squatted down and looked at the hole in the side of the door. A large-caliber bullet had exited there, ripping through the metal.

The window was up on the passenger side, the door was unlocked. Still squatting, he opened it and examined the entry point of the bullet. A briefcase was on the passenger's seat. The keys were still in the ignition. He checked the glove compartment, the door compartments, and looked around for shells that may have landed inside. He didn't find any. When he was finished, DeCora motioned for a uniformed officer to have a wrecker tow the car to a police impound area for further inspection.

Even though there were over a hundred people watching him, it seemed that nobody was talking. Kandrovicz says, "Everybody that worked on the street was just standing around. Nobody was saying anything. I'm sure some people saw the murder. But nobody came forward with any information or anything. You could hear a pin drop.

They all knew that Don had been dying there. They all knew him. Most of them had even worked for Don because at one time or another he owned almost all the companies on the street."

DeCora stayed on the Alley until almost eleven o'clock that night, sifting through debris, looking for clues, getting names of possible witnesses, questioning some people. He was joined by several other detectives, who took some people downtown for more questioning.

Everyone was in a state of shock. In the first hours people were so scared that they didn't even want to give their names. The same thought was on everyone's mind—if they'd gun down Don Aronow, they'd kill anyone.

Within fifteen minutes of the shooting, a call came into USA Racing. Patty Lezaca recognized the voice. It was a customer she and Jerry Engelman knew as Paul Rizzo. They had seen him many times at USA Racing. Rizzo was not the type of person you forget. He weighed over 350 pounds and had a fifty-two-inch waist.

Rizzo was sort of a mystery man to the office employees at USA Racing. For one thing, they couldn't understand how Don could enjoy talking with him. The conversation always sounded boring. Rizzo and his friends seemed uneducated and all they ever did was talk about old friends with strange nicknames from Brooklyn—"Hey, you know so and so. Yeah, yeah, you remember that guy, he was friends with what's his name . . ." It went on and on and on. One name after another, one neighborhood after another.

But the most intriguing aspect of Rizzo was the curious way they had to get in touch with him. He couldn't be contacted directly. When Aronow wanted to speak to Rizzo, he had to call a bakery in Tampa and ask for "Pat." When Pat got on the line, Don would identify himself and say that he wanted to speak to Paul. Then Aronow would hang up and within a few hours Rizzo would call back.

There had been a time when Aronow had been in touch with Rizzo quite frequently, when USA Racing was making a boat for him and a seat had to be specially fitted to accommodate his enormous girth. But there hadn't been any contact between the two men in almost four months.

Patty was surprised to hear from Rizzo so soon after the hit. According to Jerry Engelman, it was a short conversation; Rizzo already knew about the shooting and Patty spoke little. The conversation upset her and she didn't tell anyone what Rizzo had said to her. Later, she would deny to Jerry that Rizzo called.

Not long after, Patty received a call from the hospital with the news that Don had died. Placing the receiver down, she swiveled around in her chair to face Jerry. Emulating Alexander Haig, she announced, "I'm in charge now." She pulled out a special secret list that Aronow had made up the week before—a handwritten list of things that she should do if anything ever happened to him. At the top of the list: #1. CALL GEORGE BUSH.

Patty consulted Don's book of private telephone numbers, found the name, and called Bush's private office in the White House. The Vice President acted quickly. He immediately called MetroDade Homicide for a briefing on the murder. He contacted Lillian that evening at her Sunset Isle home and expressed his and his wife, Barbara's, sympathies. He told Lillian that "Don was a great man . . . a hero . . . and a good friend." He added that he would do all he could for her.

For the next few months, MetroDade Homicide would receive calls from the Bush staff inquiring about the status of the investigation. Bush himself kept in regular touch with Lillian for a while and a month later wrote a letter to Don and Lillian's oldest son, Gavin, emphasizing again that "your Dad was a hero."

Don's close friend, Dr. Robert Magoon, was on a ski holiday in Aspen at the time of the murder. He caught a flight back to Miami. "We were all at Lillian's house, the children, close friends," he says. "Lillian asked me to deliver the eulogy. She said Don didn't want a funeral or a burial. And she asked me to make the speech very brief, to the point, because she said Don didn't even want anything said."

Magoon, a successful Miami Beach ophthalmologist, is in some ways a younger version of Aronow. He met Don at a party in the early sixties when Aronow was fast becoming a name in offshore racing. "He was building boats by then," Magoon says. "He came into this party and he was full of life, telling jokes, funny stories. People just gravitated toward him. He was the center of attention. We found out he lived just a few blocks away from me and we became friends."

Not long after, Aronow offered him the chance to go along on a race in the Bahamas as part of the crew. "We went from Palm Beach to Lucaya," Magoon recalls. "It was a real rough race; I didn't know anything about racing, and I got bounced around so much that I almost got killed. We were supposed to stay overnight at Lucaya and then race back the next day. I was so beaten up that I went out to the boat the next day and told Don I was flying back."

But Aronow's navigator had been hurt, so Don talked Magoon into racing back with him. "When we got back to Palm Beach, I got off and said, 'That's it. I'll never go out again.'" But the next year, everyone was gearing up for the Bahamas 500 race and Magoon asked Aronow to build him a small boat so he could enter as a novice. He came in eleventh out of ninety, and his second career began.

Over the next ten years Magoon became a world offshore champion in Aronow's boats. He established a speed record for Miami to New York, and he attempted to cross the Atlantic in a Cigarette but rough seas drained too much fuel. When his boat had to be towed to the refueling station, that officially terminated the quest. "I still have the picture of me and Don, standing by his helicopter," Magoon says. "We had just christened my boat for the transatlantic crossing and we were drinking champagne."

Allan "Brownie" Brown, a manager at Cigarette Racing Team, drove to work early the day after the murder. His office was next to the scene of the shooting, and he had watched as they put Aronow into the rescue helicopter. Brownie met Aronow shortly after Don moved to Florida in 1961. He had worked for Aronow for a number of years in the sixties.

As he pulled into his parking space at Cigarette, Brownie was surprised to see Willie Meyers nearby, leaning up against a car. He was deep in conversation with a senior Drug Enforcement Administration agent named Jack Hook. "They were huddled together and didn't see me. I don't know what they were talking about," Brownie recalls. "Willie doesn't even work on the street. Maybe he was checking on things for his buddy George Bush. I've always thought that Willie had closer ties to the government than he lets on, he doesn't seem to work or anything. But anyway, here it wasn't even seven A.M. and already things were happening."

A paralyzing combination of shock and fear began to grip the street. People were struggling to comprehend the incomprehensible. Aronow had been idolized by many who worked with and for him, was a hero to those who aspired to racing greatness as well as those who could only dream of it. Aronow was the poor kid who made it big and through whom so many others lived vicariously.

The murder sent a chill through another segment of Miami—the wealthy, well-known, and public figures who had associated with him. Recalls *Miami Herald* boating writer Eric Sharp, "I think that there were a lot of guys in Miami, a lot of highly respected guys, who were shaking in their boots when Aronow was shot. People who had private and public images were all worried that their wild running around and the drugs and the sex was all going to come out."

Some of those people were at the Turnberry Isle resort complex, a five-minute drive from Thunderboat Alley. "The Aronow murder was before the Hart and *Monkey Business* thing brought all the press around and all that negative attention," explains Suzanne Johnson, a former consultant to Turnberry, and founder of Cats and Suzanne's, two trendy Miami nightspots. "In the beginning, the place was wonderful! It was the hottest thing going. I mean, they were very particular about who got in so when you got there it was wonderful. Beautiful people. It was beautiful inside—all money and champagne and yachts. The wealthiest people in the world lived there.

"They had movie stars all over the place," Suzanne recalls. "My God, there were beautiful women and drinking and drugs. It was all there—Roman tubs, orgies. The whole top floor was for parties, there were Jacuzzis on the roof and the whole outdoor thing. You could see all of Miami from up there."

Turnberry is a 234-acre erotic Disneyland for men with money. The source of their wealth is unimportant—whether it's inherited, earned through hard work, gained by membership in an organized crime family, or profits from drug dealings. If they can afford it, they're welcome.

As a result Turnberry has attracted a wildly disparate crowd: from not-so-discreet politicians to Hollywood types like producer Robert Evans and actor Jack Nicholson and America's favorite dad Bill Cosby, to sports figures like Vitas Gerulaitis and Tommy Lasorda to the wealthy denizens of Miami's darker underbelly like Joey Ippolito, a convicted marijuana kingpin. One of the most talked about members is actor James Caan.

"James Caan—he was so good-looking," Suzanne says. "He looks awful now. He's trying to make a comeback." Caan hung around with the powerboat racers and was especially friendly with Ben Kramer, Bobby Saccenti, and Joey Ippolito. "Joey Ip ended up in prison because of Caan," says John Sampson, former intelligence officer with the MetroDade Police Department, and now with Broward County's Organized Crime Division.

It was in the strange entangled world of Miami, where connections go round and round in a dizzying web, that the actor who shot to stardom playing a movie mafioso in *The Godfather* met the luckless real-life wiseguy. "Around '81 or '82, Joey Ip was arrested off of Long Island, with a dozen other people," recalls Sampson. "They had eight tons of marijuana. They were using little Zodiac boats to come in from the mother ship.

"The sheriff in the county up there was convinced that another guy was in charge of the ring. I said, wait a second, you got a ring led by a gringo? You got a Joey Ippolito, Jr., arrested on the beach. And you're trying to tell me that you got a gringo who is going to tell Joey what to do? You got your head up your ass because Joey was the boss."

But Northerners aren't aware of the subtleties of power that hold sway in Miami's multiethnic drug world. As Sampson explains, "I said bullshit. They had a guinea in the woodpile. The Italian would give them Northeast marketing. A rich Colombian doesn't come over and give dope to another rich Colombian. Or a gringo. Or a Dixie Mafia doesn't pick up all this shit and give it to another shirttail. He's going to go for the big dons. Know what I'm saying?"

Sampson says the sheriff was unconvinced. "Anyway Joey Ip did his time," he continues. "I think he was sentenced to eight. Got out. And he and Tony Scotto, the ILA [International Longshoremen's Association] guy, went to visit Jimmy Caan in Cal-i-for-ni-a. And because of that, Joey's parole was revoked and he was sent back in."

Joey Ippolito also shared a mistress with Don Aronow at Turn-berry, recalls Don Soffer. "Donnie," the developer of Turnberry, is perhaps best known now for his yacht *Monkey Business*. He and Aronow were very close. Suzanne recalls, "Don Aronow came over a lot."

Soffer enjoyed the titillating gossip that surrounded his creation and its unrepentantly chauvinistic atmosphere. He himself chris-tened one of his boats *Be Right Back*—his favorite saying to his ex-wife before he'd disappear for several days. He employed small-time models like Donna Rice and Lynn Armandt and beautiful young women, nicknamed "Donnie's girls," as Turnberry hostesses. Ar-mandt was the manager of these "party girls." Their job responsibil-ities were open-ended.

On the day after Aronow's murder, according to Suzanne, Don Soffer received a phone call at his Turnberry Isle office. The voice on the line said only two words: "You're next." Soffer immediately hired five bodyguards. At six the next morning, he boarded the *Mon-key Business* and headed out into the Atlantic. He remained out of sight for a week.

Willie Meyers, Brownie, and Soffer weren't the only ones up early the day after Aronow's murder. In Miami, top MetroDade Homicide brass were having a seven A.M. meeting—prompted in part by the fact that George Bush had personally called the evening before. In attendance were department head Lt. Clint Wonderly, Sgt. Mike

Diaz, who would oversee the investigation, Mike DeCora, who would be team leader, and detectives Steve Parr and Archie Moore.

"Bush's office was calling right from the beginning, wanting updates and so forth," recalls Detective Archie Moore. "They called subsequent days for quite a while. Everyone here figured we better do this right and make sure we cover all the bases 'cause we got the White House looking at us."

DeCora briefed them on what he had observed at the crime scene. Then Wonderly and Diaz decided to assign ten detectives to the case. In a city that often seemed to accept murder as part of the regional fabric, the killing of Aronow attracted significant, immediate attention. The specific manpower assignments and the day-to-day investigation were up to DeCora, although he would report to Diaz.

DeCora told Parr, thirty-three, to "blow smoke" with the family, as Parr described it; other investigators would check the backgrounds and names that popped up in connection with the murder. Archie Moore, nicknamed The Mole by Homicide because of his accounting skills, would review Aronow's financial records.

Shortly before nine, DeCora, Parr, and Moore arrived at USA Racing. Patty Lezaca, Jerry Engelman, Old Mike Kandrovicz, and Aronow's attorney, Murray Weil, were already there. As the employees answered the phones, giving out information on the memorial service, the detectives started their work.

They focused on Patty the first day because she was Don's secretary and had worked for him the longest of anyone on the staff, almost fifteen years. A trim woman in her midforties, Patty was devoted to her boss and listed as an officer in many of Aronow's corporations.

DeCora and Parr started going through the company files with her, looking for deals that were outstanding, boats in progress, anything that might give a clue to the murder. Patty made things difficult. "I could've told them that she wouldn't tell them a thing," Engelman comments. "They were wasting their time with Patty." She wasn't about to talk and she had warned Engelman and Old Mike not to say anything.

At one point she told the police vehemently, "Don was loved by everyone, he had no enemies, because if he did, I'd know about it." Parr and DeCora looked at each other, then Parr issued the classic retort, "Well, he must have had at least one."

The detectives talked briefly with Engelman and Mike. They asked questions about the man who had come into the office just minutes before Aronow was shot. Later both men complained that the police didn't pay much attention to what they said.

Patty wasn't the only witness who was difficult for MetroDade to handle. "Murray Weil seemed very agitated, a constantly nervous fellow," says Parr. He claimed to be ignorant of Aronow's legal work, although he had been Aronow's lawyer for almost twenty years. Weil, Parr says, was unhappy about being dragged into a murder investigation, and the prospect of police scrutinizing his legal work apparently added to his anxiety. Most of his responses to the detectives were variations of "I don't know anything about that."

As the investigators began looking through Don's desk, one of them picked up an address book and flipped the pages casually. Suddenly he stopped. There was King Hussein's private number. On another page was that for Juan Carlos of Spain. "That book really blew their minds," chuckles the *Miami Herald*'s Pulitzer Prize–winning crime reporter, Edna Buchanan. It was one day after the murder, and the enormity of the mystery that ensnared the police was just beginning to hit.

Aronow was a complex man with a complicated life. There was his business empire in which he was a director of five corporations as well as head of three others. The detectives learned that Aronow had been brought to court at least three times in the last year of his life to settle business squabbles. Frances Wolfson, the ex-wife of Elton Cary, one of Aronow's partners, was suing both her ex-husband and Aronow, claiming that the two men had attempted to defraud a company all three of them owned.

There was also the persistent rumor that Aronow had developed a revolutionary new powerboat design that would knock his competitors—even the Cigarette—out of any serious competition. Engelman notes that "Don hadn't been able to build anything other than catamarans for five years because of his Cigarette noncompete clause. But that was about to expire—six weeks after he was killed. I think that's pretty curious."

His customers, as well as his friends, past and present, made an international *Who's Who*. He was friendly with men who had powerful enemies. As one boatseller on the street put it, "he sold patrol boats to the Israeli government—they've sure made their share of enemies. And then he sold to the Arabs."

Another suggested that it had something to do with his racing stables. "Don was really involved with the horses in the last few years. He was always at the Calder track. A lot of real tough-guys hang around there—maybe somebody got burned by one of Don's horses."

Quite a few people on the street thought that Ben Kramer of Apache might have had Aronow killed. A few of the boat workers claimed they saw Ben and Don having a loud, angry fight behind the Apache building just the day before the murder. With Kramer's reputation, particularly his hot temper, there were many ready to believe he could commit murder.

But when MetroDade checked Kramer out, they found he had a good alibi. "After a while doing this you get a feeling for whether someone is telling the truth," says Parr, "and we felt that Kramer didn't have anything to do with the murder. But he was definitely worried about something."

Rumors and facts began to swirl and mix until no one was sure of anything. Billy Yout, a spokesman for the Miami office of the DEA, suggested it could have been a drug hit. A MetroDade detective said the murder resembled a "gangland-style execution." But a day later Bill Johnson, the MetroDade Police Department spokesman, quickly jumped in and called that description "premature." Someone else mentioned a similarity between the execution of Aronow and that of Bobby Seal, a protected government witness and informant against drug smugglers.

Police from nearby Hollywood, Florida, contacted MetroDade Homicide to tell them that Aronow was not the first north Miami boatbuilder to be murdered. There were two others, whose murders remain unsolved. Men who had once had a boat firm on the Alley. The first hit was that on thirty-seven-year-old Thomas Fitzgerald Adams, in 1983. His murder seemed to epitomize the shocking violence that could only be found in Miami.

Adams was shot during an infamous Miami high-speed chase on Interstate 95. In a typical *Miami Vice* story line, Tommy had been doing business with some Colombian smugglers. When he decided to branch out on his own, his former associates were unhappy.

Shortly after he became a free-lancing smuggler, Adams left work as usual and headed out to the interstate. He was followed by four cars filled with "Colombianos." Their cars surrounded his. They whipped out Uzis and blasted hundreds of rounds at Adams as they careened along the highway at 80 mph.

Adams's partner in their defunct boat company, Eugene Otis Hicks, was murdered a few months later, in June. Hicks had been convicted in 1977 of conspiracy to import marijuana into Florida from the Bahamas. He fought the conviction for six years. Just before he was to begin serving a four-year sentence, Hicks, who lived in Hallandale on the same street as Ben Kramer, was stabbed to death in his home.

Although there were some coincidences in the murders, and the three men knew each other, Hollywood and MetroDade detectives concluded that there was no link. As Hollywood detective Jack Hoffman said, "The similarities are that they were in the same business, had businesses near each other, and were killed."

John Crouse was angered by the comparisons. He issued a statement that day saying, "I don't believe there is any link in their deaths. Adams and Hicks were sleazy operators. Don Aronow was a classy man—he was a multimillionaire with a very conservative political point of view and had nothing to do with these people."

Crouse's opinion was backed up by U.S. Customs and the State Attorney's Office. Customs had gone on record a few days earlier stating that Aronow was not under investigation by them for any connection with drug smuggling.

The U.S. Attorney's Office also said Aronow was not under any investigation. According to Ana Bartlett, executive assistant U.S. Attorney, "when Customs undertook the Blue Thunder project there would have been a real reluctance to deal with anyone under any kind of suspicion because it would look bad." She said that Aronow and Customs officials "were very friendly. Of course he made a lot of money from his contract with them."

With all the mystery surrounding the murder, the big question on everyone's mind was who would dare to kill such a good friend of the Vice President of the United States? More importantly, who would think he could get away with it?

During his first interviews, Mike DeCora asked Jerry Engelman and Patty Lezaca to do a composite on the man who came into the office the day of the murder. Patty claimed the man had a mustache, Jerry and Mike Kandrovicz said it was a few days' stubble. In separate questioning, another witness who had driven by the dark Lincoln Town Car as it waited for Aronow gave a different description. He said the guy had dark, receding hair and a dark complexion, broad shoulders.

At a press conference a few days after the murder, the police released a composite. Spokesman Bill Johnson said, "The information we have is that this person was driving the car and would be a suspect. We would like to talk to him. We're looking for this particular person." When Patty and Jerry saw the sketch, they both said, "That's not the guy we saw."

Mike DeCora flew in a police helicopter to check the canals, the parking lots of nearby condominium complexes such as Turnberry Isle, and inland quarry pits, hoping to spot the Town Car. But it had simply disappeared. Many on the Alley still believe that it will be found at the bottom of one of the hundreds of canals that criss-cross Miami. The waterways are infamous for being a quick, easy, and often secure place to dispose of anything—bodies, weapons, drugs.

Police had also been told that seconds after the shooting a light-colored pickup truck followed the Town Car. But no one could identify the man or the vehicle, and no one ever came forward to claim giving chase.

There was confusion about the contents of Aronow's car. Mike Kandrovicz claimed that Aronow had two briefcases—one filled with $180,000 cash—in the front seat of the Mercedes. The detectives said that he was wrong.

Engelman also insisted that Aronow only had one briefcase that day, at least in the office. "We bought him an expensive new one for Christmas," he remembers. "He thanked us and told us how much he liked it, but we never saw him use it. Don always used that old beaten-up one. He called it his lucky bag. That's the only one he had when he left the office."

Kandrovicz stuck to his story. "I said to DeCora, look at the police photos." The detective pulled out a picture of the interior of the car taken right after the murder. Kandrovicz states emphatically, "It showed two briefcases on the seat of Aronow's car. DeCora was surprised. He said he'd look into it. But he never said anything to me about it after."

Typically the Miami winter has clear, balmy, sunny days. On February 5, 1987, the day they held a service for Aronow, it rained heavily. Still friends and acquaintances came from around the world. The wealthy arrived at the chapel's entrance in limousines. Those less fortunate had to try to find parking spaces several blocks away and then walk through the rain.

The service was held at one o'clock in Riverside Memorial Chapel, a small building on the Beach. The service was secular, although Aronow had been Jewish. Almost two hundred people—from multimillionaires to laborers—attended. "That's the kind of guy Don was," says Bobby Moore. "He hung around with kings and princes, but he never turned his back on the little guys. He treated everyone the same. He never forgot his roots."

They crowded the chapel, spilling out of the pews into the aisles.

Pat Cordell was immediately struck by the number of young, attractive women there. "It was like the funeral scene from that movie *The Man Who Loved Women*," she says.

The sense of uneasiness that had hung over Miami since the murder was almost tangible. Many of the mourners had the feeling they were being watched, perhaps sensing the plainclothes police and security people sprinkled throughout the chapel. Everyone who entered the building was noted. As Knocky explains, "I didn't notice any cameras, but I had the feeling they were there. That the police knew everyone who was going in and out the door. I guess they figured these people were going to show up."

Bob Magoon spoke for the family and gave the eulogy. "There wasn't much crying," he remembers. "Just shock and disbelief. How could he be gone? Lillian was in shock all the time. It was very difficult. The doctor gave her some medication. I doubt very much if she realized the whole situation."

It was a short, simple service, lasting less than a half hour. As Lillian had requested, Magoon spoke briefly of his friend:

> As Lyndon Baines Johnson said in his first address to Congress after the assassination of John Fitzgerald Kennedy, "All I have, I would have given gladly, not to be standing here today." There is no point in discussing the material and business accomplishments of Don Aronow. We all know them. He was a fierce competitor. He did not know how to lose. No matter what his endeavor, he always came out on top. . . .
>
> Don Aronow's life can best be described by Auntie Mame's famous quote: "Life is a banquet and some poor sons of bitches are starving to death." Don did not starve to death. He said to me in one of our discussions that he had faced death on numerous occasions and that he lived his life to the fullest and would never have any regrets.
>
> Don would not wish us to mourn for him, but to remember him for the all-male, exciting person that he was. He was a man's man; a woman's man; a man for all seasons. A ten-year-old boy once told me that when he grew up, if he had one wish, it would be to be Don Aronow. I asked him why and he replied, "Because he has everything." And he did.
>
> Don was one of the most charismatic people to be around; always laughing, joking, no time for pettiness or petty people. When Don walked into a room, the room would pulse with his incredible energy. . . . Don died as he would have wished, with his boots on and front-page headlines. . . . Those of us who knew and loved him know that he could never tolerate growing old and being sickly. . . . Don, my dear friend, I will truly miss you.

As the mourners left the chapel, rays of sunlight were shining through wispy gray clouds. Michael Aronow went outside to talk to some of the reporters, telling them that "my dad was a great man. We just don't get it, that's what is so sickening. He dealt with every kind of person in the world. The best and the worst. He came from Brooklyn and he wined and dined with royalty. It was such a god-damn cowardly act. It wasn't played by any of the rules he always played by. He was a sportsman."

The rest of the family spoke with no one, departing quickly through the side door. It was a disappointment to many of the friends who felt close to Lillian and Don. Some had the impression that Lillian was cold and aloof. None realized that she feared she might also be murdered.

One famous person was noticeably absent from the service. George Bush did not appear either in a personal capacity as a good friend of Don Aronow's or in a professional capacity as head of the Vice Presidential South Florida Joint Drug Task Group. The method of the murder and the speculation surrounding it were apparently too much for the man who was looking forward to 1988 and his own bid for the White House. It was the beginning of George Bush's publicly distancing himself from the Aronows.

On Thursday, February 5, 1987, the same day as the service, police spokesperson Bill Johnson announced that "there is nothing at this point that helps us narrow this case down." That evening a group of people dropped by Murray Weil's home, including Bob Magoon, his wife, Nancy, and Rocky Pomerance, the former chief of police of Miami Beach.

Someone asked how the investigation was going. Magoon said that it looked as if it was going to be a very tough case. "Don was probably my best friend and I knew him as well as anybody. And it's impossi-ble for me to think who could've done it. I mean, he had so many different lives. Trying to figure this thing out has to be tough."

The conversation turned to the police sketch that had been issued. Magoon mentioned that Jerry Engelman and Patty Lezaca disagreed with each other's composite and that they both disagreed with the one that ran in the newspaper. No one could understand the discrep-ancy between the eyewitness accounts. "I don't get it," Magoon remarked. "How can the descriptions be so different? Why can't they agree?"

What Magoon and the others present didn't know, and what Ho-micide investigators were only beginning to suspect, was that two men were involved in the incident. The sandy-haired man who came into the office, and a dark-haired man who drove the Lincoln. The confusion would sidetrack the investigation for some time.

"Who's murdering the millionaires of Miami?" had already become a popular question on the well-heeled cocktail circuit by the time Aronow was gunned down. "He wasn't the first millionaire to be killed here in the last couple of years," says the *Herald*'s Edna Buchanan. She sums it up succinctly in her inimitable style, "It's been tough luck for millionaires in the last few years."

There was Stanley Cohen, a wealthy developer found dead in his bedroom eleven months before Aronow's murder. He had been shot four times. There was the murder of the wife of millionaire Anthony Abraham, a former ambassador to Lebanon who owned a number of car dealerships. He posted a big reward, but nothing ever came of it. A millionaire lawyer who owned several HMOs in Miami was shot outside his home in Miami Shores.

Their murders confirmed what most Miamians already knew. Regardless of the location or the price tag on the real estate, there was no place on the Gold Coast where one could feel completely safe. While the drug-dealing shootouts that had forever removed the old image of Miami as a sedentary paradise for sunworshipers peaked in 1981—when Dade County ranked number one in the U.S. with 621 murders—it still remains one of the most violent areas in America.

"Some people compare this situation to the frontier days in Dodge City," quips Buchanan. "That's not accurate. We have more people shot in a bad week in modern Miami than were ever shot down in the entire history of old Dodge City."

Most of the mayhem in Miami has been attributed to Colombian drug dealers and their personnel, many simply hirelings taken out of the mountains of Colombia. "One day they were riding around on horseback barely eking out an existence," says Edna, "the next day they were brought to Miami by drug lords, put into a Mercedes or a Porsche, and armed with high-powered weapons."

Buchanan, who covered many of the murders at that time, recalls, "The Colombians would hit somebody in the middle of a shopping center at high noon just because they were impatient and didn't want to wait until they got him on a lonely street at night."

The 1979 hit at Miami's Dadeland shopping mall came to epitomize just how impatient and unconcerned the Colombian dealers could be. The assassins entered the mall wearing bulletproof vests and carrying more than a dozen guns, including silencer-equipped automatics and submachine guns. They found their quarry, a rival dealer and his bodyguard, who had stopped to buy some liquor, and riddled the fashionable glass-and-chrome mall interior with thousands of bullets. Hundreds of patrons scattered for cover and many were wounded. All to kill one man.

The unparalleled violence of the "cocaine cowboys" was merely the first wave to batter the city. The stage had been set for a new Miami that would splash blood onto its pastel palette. A year after the Dadeland shootout, Castro unleashed a whole new terror on Miami. As part of a deal arranged with President Carter, the Cuban dictator agreed to allow some of his people to migrate to America. He scoured his country for the most ruthless criminals and killers, the mentally deranged and retarded, and packed them into boats with other emigrants in the Cuban harbor of Mariel.

One group after another, the Marielitos, the Haitians, the Jamaicans, would set sail for Florida's tropical shores, eager to outdo their predecessors and hungry for the new American way to wealth— drugs. As Lucy Fitts, spokesperson for the MetroDade Police Department, notes, "We're now most concerned about the Jamaicans. They are really violent."

Heat, guns, passion, and old-world machismo. The combination swept over Miami and changed the landscape forever. Now almost everyone carries a gun, whether it's a small gold-colored revolver perfect for a woman's evening bag, a .45 in the glove compartment, or a legal semiautomatic Uzi that virtually guarantees hitting the target even from a moving car. There's more than a bit of the frontier mentality in Miami, and guns are often the final arbiter in this tropical melting pot.

A few days after the memorial service, police questioning of Lillian Aronow began in depth. She was still in shock and heavily medicated. Much of the initial weeks is a blur to her. She recalls that Steve Parr, the detective assigned to the family, "stayed by my side, walking me around Sunset Isle asking question after question. Mike DeCora was with him a lot, but he just listened. Parr did most of the talking."

Lillian and DeCora seemed to clash from the beginning. It was Palm Beach socialite versus MetroDade cop. Lillian, who describes herself as "the adult child of an alcoholic," is a health fanatic who eschews the cocaine and booze that had been a staple on the Palm Beach circuit. DeCora is far removed from the splashy social milieu of Lillian and Don. He wears cowboy boots with his suit, smokes constantly, and has a snub-nosed .38 strapped around his ankle. He's not facile with "dinner patter." As Parr says, "he doesn't talk much, he's very tight-lipped."

Because he spoke so little, Lillian didn't realize that DeCora was actually in charge of the police efforts. Several days into the investigation he surprised her by saying, "You only talk to the young guys," a reference to Parr's youth. "Parr did all the talking, so I thought he was in charge," explains Lillian. "He's in his thirties and DeCora's in his forties. I know he thought I was spoiled and rich."

DeCora's interactions with Lillian didn't erase that impression. "We were at her place and the black nanny brought this young kid out," he says. "It was Don's youngest son. And I said to Lillian, 'How old is he?' and Lillian looked at the nanny and said, 'How old is he?' The kid was six months old, but she had to ask the nanny. No wonder all these rich people are fucked up; they all think their mommas are black."

Lillian was equally confused by DeCora's outlook on life. "Later when he came to my new home on North Bay, he looked around and said, 'Why did you want to leave your Sunset Isle home? That was a real nice place.' I mean, what kind of a question is that—how can you even compare the two houses?" Lillian felt that DeCora was "totally unconcerned. I know that he hates me. He can't relate to people, all he cares about are his pet birds. I hate that man."

The relationship between the widow and the detectives wasn't helped by the way MetroDade dealt with Aronow's watch. Lillian had been told that the detectives had the specially engraved Rolex. "I kept asking them for it because I wanted to give it to Gavin as a reminder of his father and all that he had done," Lillian explains. "The cops said they would return it. Finally DeCora came over with an envelope. I opened it up and there were a couple of broken links inside. That was it. That's when they told me they didn't have the rest of the watch. All that time they let me think I would have Don's championship watch for Gavin. It was like a real slap in the face."

After three days, the relentless questioning stopped. Parr told Lillian that they had "pretty much" ruled her out as a suspect when they learned how much money her father had left her. "I was flabbergasted," she remarks. "Here they thought I might have done it. They were wasting time on me instead of looking for the killer."

The daughter of New York yachtsman James Crawford III, Lillian had inherited at least a million dollars after her father's death the year before. "I don't know what I would have done in those months if I didn't have my own money because the estate was all tied up," she says. Nor did the motive of money seem that strong when the detectives found out that she had turned down far wealthier suitors, including King Hussein.

But the police were not alone in their initial thoughts about Lillian. The Miami Beach rumor mill was working overtime with stories. It seemed to be the stuff of novels: "Beautiful-young-woman-marries-wealthy-older-man-and-murder-follows." Speculation was further fueled by Lillian's past. Aronow was her third husband. She had divorced her first, and her second husband had died in his thirties.

Donald Aronow's "Last Will and Testament" was made public on February 11, 1987. He had willed the bulk of his estate to Lillian, their two young children, his two sisters, and his three older children from his first marriage. He left nothing to his first wife, Shirley Aronow Parker, although he had given her a generous divorce settlement in 1979 that included $1,000,000 in cash, a $1.2-million waterfront home in Coral Gables, $15,000 a month for two years, and a Rolls-Royce.

He left his two young children, Gavin, six, and Wylie, six months, a larger share of the estate than he did his three grown children by his former wife—Claudia Hay Kimmel of Manhattan, Michael, and David in Brick Town, New Jersey. In his will he wrote that he left them smaller shares "not because of any lesser love and affection. All my children are dear to me, but it is merely recognition that the children born of my first marriage were provided for by me during my lifetime and all have reached majority."

The *Miami Herald* reported that his estate "was worth in excess of $1 million in stocks, bonds, and real estate." It included his Miami Beach home and a New York condominium. It noted that this estimated value was believed to be far below its worth. Later that figure would be revised to $7 million. And as detectives began to untangle his complicated businesses, the estimate would once again be revised upward to at least $21 million.

The family was stunned by the revelation of several secret codicils that Aronow had insisted Murray Weil draw up two years before his death. First, he had removed Bob Magoon as his personal corepresentative. Then, he had placed Michael Aronow's share of the estate in an irrevocable lifelong trust, meaning that his thirty-six-year-old son would never have control over his own money. Most surprising was that he called for the total liquidation of all his businesses—including those he shared with Michael—within one year of his death. The proceeds, he directed, were to be added to his estate and then divided.

Weil had clearly been opposed to the codicil specifying the liquidation of the Aronow business empire. The men met and discussed the matter several times in February 1985. The lawyer warned Aronow that public disclosure after his death would dramatically affect the sales prices of the various companies.

Aronow was insistent. So Weil suggested that he put the codicil in a letter, have it notarized, and refer to the letter in the will. That, he maintained, would at least ensure some privacy regarding the liquidation and prevent a fire sale. This approach, he urged, would enable the family to get the best price for the holdings. But Aronow refused. He wanted it delineated clearly and publicly in the will. At his death, he wanted everyone to know that his interests were to be liquidated within a year.

Bob Magoon maintains it was completely out of character for Aronow to insert such a clause in his will. From his teenage years on, Aronow had tried to extract as much money as he could from every venture. Whether it was the time in college that he purchased a used tank from the U.S. Army surplus and sold it for a handsome profit or the way he always knew the best time to sell his boat companies and get the highest value. This provision was one of the first times Aronow's thinking didn't have profit as a primary goal.

About a week after the will was filed in Dade County Probate Court, Michael Aronow called Randy Riggs, Don's pilot, who had been listed as a witness to the signing of one of the disputed codicils —the one that put Michael's money out of his personal control for life.

Riggs was surprised and pleased to hear from Michael. He wanted to talk about his former boss. "I was upset over the murder," Riggs explains. "I still had some unresolved feelings about Don and I wanted to talk about it with Michael." But Michael only wanted to talk about the circumstances under which the codicil had been signed: "Did my dad have three witnesses present at the moment when he signed it?"

The circumstances under which Aronow signed the codicil were critical. It could mean the difference between a legally enforceable document and one that could easily be broken. Riggs dashed Michael's hope by insisting that "Don came over and asked me to go over to Cigarette with him." There, he said, the three witnesses had signed the document together in the appropriate manner.

Don's will also upset Bob Magoon, but not for financial reasons.

Originally Magoon had been named as Don's personal corepresentative, and at the time of Aronow's death, Magoon believed he still was. When he learned about the revision, he was puzzled and hurt. The two men had been very close. There had been no falling out or even a mild fight, and he could not understand why Aronow had made the change, especially without telling him or offering an explanation. Only one thing was clear. Aronow never did anything without a good reason.

A few weeks after the murder, Alex Rizzo, the cousin of "Paulie," the man with the Tampa bakery connection, dropped by USA Racing unannounced. Patty Lezaca was alone. Jerry Engelman no longer worked there. Alex told Patty that he was there to pick up a $300,000 custom-built boat for his cousin. There was a snag, however. He only wanted to be charged $50,000 for it, claiming that Aronow owed him a $250,000 credit. There was no receipt—he said that Paulie hadn't needed anything in writing.

Lezaca promised to look into the matter and Rizzo accepted that. Then he brought up a new subject. Five months earlier, when Paulie had test-run his previous boat in the canal behind USA Racing, Jerry Engelman had taken some pictures of his cousin and the boat. Alex wanted them.

Patty said that she didn't know anything about them, and that Jerry didn't work there anymore. Alex told her to get Jerry on the phone. "He said he was at the shop," recalls Engelman. "He wanted the pictures that I had taken when he got his boat. And the negatives." When Jerry had developed the film, none of the pictures came out. "I don't understand it," he told Rizzo. "In all the years I've been taking pictures, this is the first roll that didn't come out. I'm sorry, I'm really sorry."

"I apologized profusely to the guy," says Engelman. "It was all I could do, they just didn't come out." Finally, Alex seemed satisfied that Jerry was telling the truth. He hung up and left the office.

The weeks after the memorial service were chaotic at the Aronow home. The new house was ready and Lillian would have to move soon. She was still in a daze. Despite what others may have speculated, she had been in love with Aronow. She had also let him manage their lives. She had wanted a strong man, a protector, someone whom she could count on and who made her feel secure. "Someone who would bring me roses," as she put it.

Aronow had been that type of man. He was in many ways an

anachronism, a product of another age, a time when men sheltered their wives, made all the decisions, and kept problems from them. As Mike Kandrovicz put it, "He kept his wife out of the business. I could never bring up business when his wife was in the room."

That was all over for Lillian now. Her safe, secure world had changed completely and forever. She had to cope not only with her husband's death but with the frightening aspect of how he had died. She wondered whether she, too, would be murdered—even after Aronow's death, the phone calls and hang-ups continued. She had no one to turn to and in desperation she alternately turned to everyone and then to no one.

Jacquie Kimberly stayed with Lillian for a while. Jacquie knew Lillian from her Palm Beach days in the seventies, and they had remained close. Jacquie, the ex-wife of the Kleenex magnate Jim Kimberly, had made headlines in the sensational 1982 Pulitzer divorce trial because of her ménage à trois with Herbert [Peter] Pulitzer and Roxanne in a Howard Johnson's hotel room. Unlike many other well-known people who were starting to pull away from Lillian, Jacquie was undaunted by the gossip. She and her former husband had had their share of publicity—beginning with their marriage. Jim was forty years older than Jacquie; they began dating when Jacquie was seventeen.

"Lillian was around Palm Beach for years," Roxanne Pulitzer recalls. "I first ran across her when she was married to Lee Kinsolving. He died, then she dated Herbert. This was all before I married Herbert. She was one of those girls you see at parties. She was always very well dressed."

The first time Roxanne actually met Lillian was at a party. "Herbert introduced me to her," Pulitzer says. "At that time I used to see her with different men, not just one. I never really connected her with one man until I saw her with Don. And then I saw them quite a bit because they would frequently be at the Kimberlys' and we would be there also. I saw them at parties. That was when we were all happy."

After their marriage, the Aronows often went to the Kimberly home in Palm Beach and the Kimberlys visted them in Miami. Sometimes they attended the boat races together. The newlywed Aronows had also occasionally crossed paths with Herbert and Roxanne, who were married at the time.

Roxanne recalls that when she saw the Aronows at various affairs, "I thought they looked very much in love, they were always laughing and having a great time. I got to know him better than her. At so many of those black-tie affairs you couldn't sit next to your husband, so lots of times I was seated next to Don. He was a great dinner partner, great sense of humor. He had something—a lot of charm, his smile, his sense of humor—he was really fun to sit next to. And he would really focus on you, make you feel special."

While Jacquie was staying with Lillian after Don's death, she called Roxanne. "It was February tenth, my birthday," Roxanne recalls. "Jacquie and I haven't seen each other since '82, but she always calls me on my birthday and at Christmas."

Jacquie told Roxanne that the home was "like a fortress" with people all over. "She said there were secret agents and people with guns all around the place. Jacquie found it nerve-racking. She told me that Lillian was a complete and total wreck," recalls Pulitzer. "I mean, what can you expect—now she's a young woman with two dead husbands."

FIVE

No one—not MetroDade, Lillian or Bob Magoon, who stayed close to Lillian and the children after the murder—can really put their finger on how it happened. All that seems to be known for certain is that Rocky Pomerance, the former police chief of Miami Beach, appeared on the scene. They aren't sure how he became part of the activities or even when. Magoon thinks it might have started when Pomerance dropped by the Weil home the night of Aronow's memorial service.

Lillian thinks that she might have asked Pomerance after the service to check over the house and grounds for her. She says that "there were very strange things going on at my house. Lots of security problems and people being seen on the grounds at night. I had Rocky over there in the middle of the night a couple of times because of these very weird things that were happening."

After the memorial service, Steve Parr was at Homicide Division when his phone rang. "I got a call one night. I was working the case," he recalls. "It was Pomerance. He said, 'I'm here at Mrs. Aronow's, is there anything you can tell us? Was it a robbery?'"

Parr ducked his questions and Pomerance became annoyed that

he wasn't getting any information. The conversation didn't last long. Later Parr heard that Pomerance "called the brass upstairs, and I'm fairly sure that he got anything he wanted. He talked to a particular chief. I'm sure whatever he got it wasn't much, because we didn't have a motive. It was obvious it wasn't a robber. We all knew it was bullshit that it was robbery."

Almost immediately, Pomerance took control of the disorganized situation at the Aronow house. After he spoke to the police, he turned to Lillian and said, "Those guys at MetroDade are good, but they're just overworked. Lillian, what you need is an attorney. And maybe a private investigator of your own. You want to get the guy who killed your husband, don't you?"

With that, Richard Gerstein, a cohort of Pomerance's, appeared on the scene. Lillian thinks that Pomerance had told her that she needed a lawyer and suggested "how about Dick Gerstein or James Jay Hogan?"

Lillian called Bob Magoon and said that she was thinking of hiring an attorney to oversee the investigation. She wondered what he thought of Dick Gerstein. She also mentioned Hogan, a defense lawyer. Magoon opted for Gerstein because he was a former prosecutor.

Gerstein is a well-known figure in Miami. He was one of the state's biggest vote-getters, elected state attorney for Dade County an unprecedented five times in the sixties and seventies, and he held the position longer than anyone else. A World War II bomber pilot, a war hero who lost an eye in combat, he looks like a mean Yul Brynner. During his public-service years, he was skillful at public relations and headline-making cases.

He was included as a minor character in the book *All the President's Men* by Woodward and Bernstein. Bernstein had sought Gerstein's help in following up on the Watergate burglars who came from Miami. He was impressed with Gerstein's public record. But when he mentioned to a federal agent that Gerstein might be helpful in the investigation, he wrote in the book that the agent said, "It pisses me off that Gerstein is a member of the bar."

The remark was no doubt a reference to the belief held by many federal authorities that "Bad Eye," Gerstein's moniker in some circles, was less a defender of the law than supposed. Rumors of organized crime "affiliations" dogged Gerstein during his years of public service and private practice.

In 1974, while still state attorney, he was subpoenaed before a federal grand jury that was looking into links between public officials and organized crime figures. Meyer Lansky was a target of the investigation. Called along with Lansky and Gerstein was one of Gerstein's longtime aides, David Goodhart.

According to the *Miami Herald*, after Lansky was called, Goodhart and Gerstein were questioned before the grand jury about "meetings on three separate Saturdays on Lincoln Road [Miami Beach] with Hymie Lazar, a gambling-junket operator whom police sources describe as a close associate of the underworld figure Meyer Lansky." The state produced pictures of Goodhart giving Gerstein cash. Both men claimed it was ten or twenty dollars because Gerstein had forgotten his wallet and needed money to get home.

In 1982 the U.S. Attorney's Office investigated charges by an informant that Gerstein allegedly was taking drug money to be laundered in Panama. Despite on-again, off-again probes into his activities by federal authorities, he has never been indicted or convicted of any crime. To many people in Dade County, not privy to the sordid allegations, he remains a highly regarded member of the community. Both Bob Magoon and Lillian knew him only casually before Don's death, and because of his public service, they respected him.

Magoon was optimistic when Gerstein and Pomerance became involved. As Don's best friend, he felt a deep commitment to Lillian, and to himself, to see that whoever killed Aronow was brought to justice. But he was beginning to feel that he was in over his depth. "I was stunned when the people started asking me about different parts of Don's life," he recalls. "There were things that even I didn't know about, and the investigation was complicated with hundreds of possibilities."

The first thing that Gerstein did was hire the private investigation firm of Riley, Black. While MetroDade Homicide didn't try to squelch Lillian's efforts to solve the murder, they resented the clear implication that they weren't up to the job. "Her reasoning for hiring a P.I. was that she was dissatisfied with our investigation," Parr explains. "We said that she could hire anyone she wanted to, but they weren't going to find out a great deal."

MetroDade Homicide also felt it was out of place to give Lillian their private feelings that the Riley, Black firm was, according to Parr, "a real sleazy group of people," and that "there have been rumors about Gerstein for years."

Living at the mansion didn't ease the pain for Lillian. In fact, it sharpened it. The new house had been her idea, her dream. Aronow had gone along with it to make her happy. "You know, a house is really more for the woman," Magoon explains. "He wanted Lillian to be happy." Now the house had a morbid atmosphere. Don had died just a few days before they were to move in, and everything around her reminded her of the ten months they had spent renovating it. Mementos, such as the large set of ivory tusks in the den that Don had picked up on one of his many overseas adventures, were everywhere.

Despite the presence of Lillian's mother, Michael and his family, and Lillian's two children, the house retained an "unlived-in look." It was stately, not comfortable. And Lillian felt completely alone in it. She spent much of her time in bed locked in her room. She slept often, rarely able to do anything else.

Near the end of February, Rocky Pomerance brought William Riley over to meet Lillian. His immediate focus was on Don Aronow's financial papers. "The first thing Bill Riley told me," Lillian recalls, "was that someone could easily break into the house and take Don's records. That I should move them someplace safe."

Then he told her she and her children could be in danger. "He said she could be attacked in broad daylight in her car just as her husband had been," says Magoon. "He decided to teach Lillian how to drive in an antiterrorist fashion. Driving in the left-hand lane in multiple-lane roads so that no one could drive alongside and shoot her. And getting a car with tinted windows. Things like that."

After Pomerance and Riley left, the idea that somebody might be skulking outside waiting to get into her house terrified Lillian. She started thinking about the confidential things she had there. "I thought, what if they get in here? What could they find?" she recalls. "I had all these letters that Hussein had sent me. They were old love letters. I decided to burn them. If anyone broke in and found them, people wouldn't understand."

Soon rumors were whipping around the Beach that Lillian was "deep-sixing" documents. "It was one of the help who talked, and I think I know who it was," says Lillian. "She hates me and told her friends, who told everybody they work for." The story that Lillian was destroying incriminating documents wasn't the only one that was making the rounds. "They were saying that I was seeing Hussein again. That we were having an affair," she says angrily. "It was all bullshit."

After this incident, Lillian had Murray Weil draw up a confidentiality agreement and made all her employees at the house and at USA Racing sign it as a condition of continued employment.

With the private investigation under way, Gerstein turned his attention to Michael Aronow. After his father's murder, Michael had talked to the media. He was also conducting his own investigation of sorts. Gerstein and Pomerance told Michael that he had "to stop acting like Sherlock Holmes, trying to find Don's murderer. Let the P.I. do his job."

During these early months, Lillian was still receiving many hang-up phone calls, even though she changed the number several times. Pomerance added more security. He arranged for a protection service run by a former Israeli agent to take care of her. The agent stayed in the house for weeks, sleeping downstairs on the couch.

While she was nervous in her home, Lillian was also uneasy whenever she ventured off the estate grounds. One day as she pulled out of her driveway, she noticed a van with heavily tinted mirrored windows parked not far from the gate. It caught her attention. Then she noticed it in other places around Miami Beach when she was running errands. She had the distinct feeling that the occupants had photographic equipment inside and were taking pictures of her.

She also believed that her phone was being tapped. "I could tell, it was the clicks and other sounds. I finally had it. I screamed into the phone, 'You fuckers have had it, I'm going to get George Bush after you.' She hung up and called Bush. He calmed her down and promised to look into it. "After that it stopped," she says, "there was no more tapping on my lines."

As the investigation proceeded, Bill Riley personally kept Lillian updated on developments. One of the first things he reported on was Jerry Engelman. Riley told Lillian that they had determined that Engelman could not possibly have been where he said he was at the time of the murder.

Engelman told the private investigators that after the big sandy-haired guy left, he had walked the few hundred feet out to the canal and was looking at the water when Don was shot. Riley said his men had paced out the route that Jerry said he took and that he had to be lying. Lillian started to become suspicious of everybody.

Riley also told her that there was a possibility that Don had been murdered by the CIA or some "feds gone in too deep." He suggested that Don might have been killed because he had helped spearhead the government's antismuggling efforts. That some agents had eliminated Don as a favor to the drug kingpins who were assisting the CIA-backed "freedom fighters" in Nicaragua.

Lillian knew that Don had worked with various federal agencies as well as foreign governments, including Israel's and some Arab countries. He had been friendly with the Shah of Iran and had done business with him. "Baby Doc" Duvalier was having him build a

USA catamaran but fled Haiti before it could be delivered. Panama's strongman Manuel Noriega had also contacted USA Racing about purchasing some boats. An international conspiracy seemed quite possible, especially after an old racing friend of Aronow's stopped by to see Lillian one night.

Roger Hanks was a friend of Don's and a former CIA agent. "He came by to see me a month or so after Don died," Lillian recalls. "He scared the shit out of me one night. He told me that I had to leave town, take the kids, da da da, all this stuff, because of the information he had from CIA people. Otherwise me and the kids would be killed. He said he had heard about this because he had 'prominent sources.' "

Lillian turned to George Bush, knowing that with his connections as former head of the CIA he could check on the story. She told him Hanks's story. Bush later called her back. "He said to me, 'Lillian, you're fine.' He said that 'ex-CIA people are really off.' That's the truth."

Bush told Lillian to "stay away from Hanks and all spooks," she says. "He said he knew a lot of them, they're just off, they've got problems, lots of problems, he said." She adds, "They're just crazy, the ones that I've met, every single one of them are crazy. They like to play games, cloak-and-dagger bullshit. They're all caught up in their little world."

After the Hanks incident, Lillian snapped out of her haze. She was determined to take charge of her life and become more actively involved in the investigation. She decided to offer a $1,000,000 reward to catch Aronow's murderer. She was convinced that the longer the investigation went on, the less chance that it would ever be solved.

Riley reluctantly agreed with the idea of a reward, but thought it was too much money. "Lillian, a million bucks will bring every kook in south Florida out of the woodwork. How about fifty thousand dollars?" Lillian was not swayed. She called Murray Weil and MetroDade's Mike DeCora to tell them her idea. They both said that a million was too much.

On March 22, 1987, a $100,000 reward was announced for "anyone producing information leading to an arrest and indictment of Don Aronow's murderer." All tips were to be phoned into Riley, Black. The *Miami Herald* carried the story, and Lillian placed several ads in south Florida newspapers. Then she waited.

Bill Riley arranged for a small van to cruise Thunderboat Alley and north Miami. For a while it drove up and down the short street on which Aronow had reigned for so many years. A sign hung down each side of the van—one in English and one in Spanish—asking for information about the murder and announcing the reward. "It was disappointing," says Magoon. "The investigators told Lillian that they had gotten only a couple of calls."

While the private investigation firm hadn't come up with anything except the analysis of how long it took Jerry Engelman to walk the hundred feet from his office to the canal, their fees were mounting. "They were doing very well," says Steve Parr. "They probably made well into the five figures off of Lillian. Could be as much as fifty thousand dollars."

Evidently, for this kind of money Bill Riley felt the young, beautiful, wealthy, and recently widowed client deserved his personal attention. According to Lillian, one day at her house he said, " 'Lillian, after this is all over, you and I should get together and have dinner.' I just stared at him and said, 'You've *got* to be kidding.' "

While Don Aronow was not a household name, he was well-known in world sporting circles. His death, and especially the circumstances surrounding it, attracted local, national, and international attention. His murder was reported on network evening news, and a number of national publications decided to send correspondents to Miami. Journalists came from *Esquire, People, Playboy, Sports Illustrated,* and the *Washington Post.* The murder also caught the attention of the Washington office of *60 Minutes* and the producers of *20/20.*

Since the Aronow family was declining interviews, journalists coming to town gravitated to John Crouse, Aronow's publicist for twenty years and now the self-proclaimed spokesman on Aronow's life. Crouse, fifty-seven, who looks like an aging blond surfer, always speaks as if he's addressing a large audience without benefit of a microphone. He's been writing about offshore powerboat racing from the early days of the sport in the sixties. He is a client's dream publicist—he has a talent for creating high-drama, colorful adventures and mythic traits—and he remains consistently unhampered by the facts.

After working in the shadow of Aronow for two decades, Crouse enjoyed the spotlight. "He was fielding calls from all over the country," says a close friend. "He sees himself as the historian of powerboat racing and the keeper of the flame for Don's memory."

Some of the journalists evidently didn't appreciate Crouse's value. "He was really pissed at this producer from *20/20,*" says his friend.

"The guy came down from New York and they went to lunch. Then the guy made him split the bill. John was furious. He wouldn't talk to him after that."

Producers of *60 Minutes* had better luck. "Chuck Lewis is the advance man for Mike Wallace," Crouse explains. "He was especially interested in solving the murder and I spent a lot of time with him. He wanted to use the show's clout to help in tracking down suspects. Lewis told me that he liked doing that—solving unsolved mysteries —and that he intended to break the Aronow case. I think he spent a lot of time in Miami investigating. He thought it was amazing that someone could kill a friend of the Vice President and get away with it."

Jerry Engelman also heard from Lewis. "This guy calls me up. He says, 'I'm Chuck Lewis from *60 Minutes*. So who killed Don Aronow?' I thought, what an asshole. If I had anything to say, I certainly wouldn't have said it to him. I told him that I really only worked for the guy for a short time and that I didn't know anything."

Evidently Lewis's style of interrogation didn't work with Mike DeCora, either. He remembers, "This guy from *60 Minutes* calls me up and wants me to drop everything and go running out to the crime scene to show him what happened. I told him to take a hike."

MetroDade wasn't in the market for publicity on the Aronow case or anything else for that matter. It had had more than its share of media attention in recent years and was still recovering from its role in the Miami race riots, as well as from fallout from the notorious "Miami River murders" in which Miami city cops were convicted of drug dealing and murder. "The cops are paranoid," observes *Herald* reporter Edna Buchanan. "That has been the trend down here because so many of them are corrupt, so many have been indicted."

Once Lillian had been eliminated as a suspect in the murder of her husband, the detectives began pursuing other leads. The most persistent rumor—what else does anyone think of in Miami?—was the drug connection. The scenarios were endless. "Don could've been hit because he always wrote the names of people who bought his boats in his books," suggested Don Soffer. "Maybe the smugglers thought he was informing on them."

Some people had heard a rumor that even before he began making boats for the government, he was secretly putting transponders into his boats so Customs could easily nab smugglers hiding in the waters off the Keys. After all, people noted, Aronow had been friendly with Bush even before Blue Thunder. If he had been helping the government and the smugglers found out, then the dopers might have decided to make a lesson of him.

In Miami the drug world is never far away. The signs of a darker life are everywhere, intruding into the bright pastels. The aura of drugs has hung heavily especially over Thunderboat Alley since "go-fast" boat makers first moved to the street. For a time, drugs and boats zipped up and down the canals, unhampered.

The style of powerboat that Aronow created played an essential role in the drug smuggling industry. His boats were so fast that they became the main means of drug transport into the country. Federal agents couldn't even begin to match the speeds of his go-fast machines. While Customs and DEA agents became frustrated and powerless against Aronow-style boats, the smugglers were gaining a stronghold and their numbers were increasing rapidly.

In the late seventies, the role of go-fast boats changed, but still remained integral. Instead of being the primary means of transport, they became the final link in a sophisticated smuggling operation. They provided the last mad dash toward the mainland, with the contraband cargo brought into the Gold Coast waters by freighters and planes.

"The druggies bring between three hundred and a thousand pounds of cocaine in a day," says DEA agent Jack Hook. "They fly it by light aircraft from South America to the Bahamas. They have four, maybe five, speedboats at particular coordinates on the ocean and the aircraft flies by and drops the duffel bags of cocaine. The smugglers divide the bags among the five boats—they know Customs can only stop one boat at a time. If they stop one or even two, the other boats get through." The loss of one boat and its cocaine cargo are considered an insignificant operating expense.

"We have a lot of powerboats for sale down here at government auctions," Hook explains. "The Cigarette is still the most popular, then there's the Midnight Express brand. There are a lot of brands down here with those big performance hulls. They have different engines, but they're all high-powered, very expensive, fast racing boats that the dopers use."

Aronow had been very public about his disdain for drugs. "Don didn't like dope dealers in general," says Knocky House. "He thought they were a disgrace to the country and they were helping to ruin it. People who were running drugs or fooling with them, he called them dirty. He had deep feelings." Bobby Moore says, "I know in my heart that Don wasn't mixed up with drug people."

Eventually the drug connection was discarded by MetroDade Homicide. "We heard all those theories," says DeCora. "We checked out the transponder idea, but found that the batteries just wouldn't last that long for them to be useful to anyone. And we talked to the DEA and the U.S. Attorney's Office. All the feds said they had nothing on Aronow."

Then the police began pursuing a new angle—a vengeful husband. The idea that it was a crime of passion was spurred on when the story spread that Aronow had been shot in the groin. Some people thought that it was more than a coincidence, especially in light of Aronow's legendary reputation with women. His onshore exploits were almost as well publicized as his offshore ones.

Jack Kramer offers one example of Aronow's reputation: "I was in England, in some little town where there was a boat race. I was with one of the racers and we drove by this building and the guy says, 'That used to be a hotel. When Don was here for a race, he stayed there and fucked a lot of the town women there.'" Kramer, half laughing, half admiring, adds a historical perspective: "It was incredible, even in another country, there was a place where Aronow had screwed some women. It was like 'fucking George Washington slept here.'"

Perhaps, the detectives thought, Aronow had slept with the wrong woman. A twist on the French aphorism *cherchez la femme*. Only this time they were looking for the man behind the woman. While the idea of "macho" is passé in most of this country, it's still strong in south Florida where many men retain the Latin-influenced concept of machismo. "There's more macho here in Miami, in Dade County, per square inch than any other place in the world," as Edna Buchanan asserts.

"We learned that there was a real bad fight at the Calder Race Track not too long before the murder," says Steve Parr. Police discovered that Aronow often went there with Eileen Taylor, wife of Skip Taylor, a Miami defense attorney. "The argument was between Don and Skip," Parr says. "Skip was warning Aronow to stop seeing his wife."

Eileen was well-known to the staff at USA Racing but not well liked. "She's rich and snotty," says Jerry. "She's used to hanging around with millionaires." He describes Eileen as "in her midthirties. Sometimes she didn't look too good." Then he elaborates in an unfortunate choice of words, "But other times she looked like a killer. Well . . . I don't mean a killer."

When the detectives questioned Eileen about her relationship with Aronow, Eileen told them that "she and Don were casual acquaintances who just happened to bump into each other at the track," Parr relates. "But her statements contradicted what others had said about the relationship." MetroDade eventually concluded that neither Skip Taylor nor Eileen had been involved in Aronow's murder.

Jack Kramer—still burned by the persistent innuendo that his son Ben was involved in the murder—thought the police should have investigated Taylor further. "Here he was seeing the guy's wife," he says. "And he was shot in the balls, I hear. You know those defense attorneys, they deal with bad dudes all the time. All Skip would have to do is make a phone call. Know what I mean?"

While MetroDade was running into dead ends, Lillian's private investigators weren't getting anywhere, either, even though by this time she had four men managing the investigation: Gerstein, Pomerance, Riley, and Warren Emerson, a detective who worked for Riley and was brought in to do the footwork.

Emerson's methods puzzled a number of people. Many witnesses recall Emerson's showing up on their doorstep within a few days of MetroDade's questioning them. Emerson always asked the same questions of the witnesses: "What did MetroDade ask you?" and "What did you tell them?" The interviews with Emerson rarely went any further; he seemed satisfied by just knowing what information MetroDade had acquired. None of those questioned by Emerson ever felt that he was interested in learning anything else or in discovering new information. It would be a while, but finally Lillian, too, would conclude that none of "her people," as she called them, ever turned up information that led anywhere.

Richard Gerstein had dropped out of the investigation. He was apparently occupied with "home improvements" not long after Aronow's murder, according to William Cagney, a former member of the South Florida Federal Organized Crime Strike Force. The Strike Force, composed of FBI agents, U.S. Attorneys, and state and local law enforcement authorities, targets people who they believe may have some connection with the mob. Gerstein had often been the subject of conversations on the force, says Cagney. Recently, the fed grapevine had been enjoying a new tidbit.

"I hear Dick undertook some major house renovations. He had the fence around his home fortified and a wall built between his house and the street," says Cagney, now a prominent attorney in private practice in Miami. Apparently Gerstein was no longer interested in the waterfront view that the front of his Miami Beach home offered, either. "They say he had several bayfront windows that overlooked Miami Bay removed, and the space filled in with concrete."

Cagney, who has followed Gerstein's activities for years, chuckles as he muses, "I wonder what he's worried about?"

On May 12, 1987, Miami's legal community was stunned by a court decision made concerning Don Aronow's will. Lillian's lawyers, the high-powered local firm Mershon, Sawyer & Johnson, convinced the Dade County Probate Court to break one of the irrevocable codicils that Aronow had insisted on inserting into his will.

The provision that Aronow's business holdings be liquidated within one year of his death was revoked. One of the lawyers from the firm stated, "We argued that it was not in the best interest of the estate and those interested in the estate."

Aronow had obviously been completely aware of the codicil's implications. And the provision was clearly important to him. But his wishes were not to be followed. The law firm's argument apparently convinced the court to make what many estate lawyers consider an extraordinary decision. As Raphael Steinhart, a Miami attorney who dealt with Aronow in some real estate transactions put it, "I've never heard of anyone breaking such a provision. It's very unusual."

The decision gave the family power to dispose of the businesses when, and if, they wanted. On May 12, Circuit Judge Moie Tendrich signed an order nullifying the one-year limit. While Tendrich signed the document, it was Judge Featherstone who actually made the decision, according to Tony Fernandez, chief bailiff in the probate court. Coincidentally, Judge Featherstone is a Gerstein appointee as well as a protégé, according to Steve Bertucelli, director of the Organized Crime Division.

By the end of May, virtually everyone involved had to admit that the investigation seemed cold. There were no new leads. Nothing had come out of the reward. No one had any better idea why Aronow had been killed. MetroDade stopped returning Lillian's calls—they had nothing new to tell her—and they were mired in more murders, among other things.

As Edna Buchanan once wrote about the lot of the Miami policeman, "Miami cops are subjected to everything that is ugly or evil: drug smuggling, money laundering, mass murder, the Mafia, deposed dictators, foreign fugitives, illegal aliens, serial killers, street people, spies, terrorists, international intrigue, bombings, grave robbing, exotic diseases, bizarre sects, bizarre sex, animal sacrifice, voodoo, gunrunning, vast wealth, utter poverty, crazy politics, racial tension, refugees, and riots."

And as more bodies piled up, detectives found less and less time to concentrate on a three-month-old murder. The *Miami Herald* had stopped its almost daily coverage of the story. Most journalists from various magazines and news shows had left—with no story other than "everyone loved Don."

With her husband's will broken, Lillian decided to continue the operation of USA Racing at least for a while. In her first appearance at the company as the new owner, she dressed in what one employee described as "one of those tough masculine type of outfits that some of the businesswomen wear." And she announced to all, including Michael, that "I'm the boss now. That's boss with a capital *B*."

Immersing herself in the business, Lillian learned that Panama's strongman, General Manuel Noriega, was interested in buying some Blue Thunder patrol boats for his agents. She decided that she would handle the deal herself, so she arranged to go to Panama to meet with Noriega personally.

She mentioned to George Bush that she was going to Panama. He strongly advised her against it. "He told me that there were a lot of bad things going on with that guy and that I shouldn't have anything to do with him," she recalls. "So I canceled my plans. Then later, it came out that he was a drug dealer."

After the February 1988 indictment of Noriega by federal grand juries in Miami and Tampa on charges that he was a drug trafficker, Bush went on record insisting that he hadn't known about Noriega's drug activities before the indictments were announced.

As Lillian became more involved in the day-to-day running of USA Racing, the reality of her husband's death was finally settling in, as it was with his friends and associates on and off Thunderboat Alley. It had taken a while—somehow Aronow had always seemed indestructible. But the arrogance of the killers continued to haunt everyone.

Bush told friends he was still shocked by the fact that the murderers of a man so close to him had simply driven away from the scene and within minutes become part of the faceless American fabric. He continued to visit Miami, overseeing his Vice Presidential South Florida Joint Drug Task Group from his office adjacent to the state-of-the-art Blue Lightning command center in a downtown federal building. On many of the trips he went fishing with Willie Meyers. The two men had become close since Aronow's death and they spoke of Don often.

On one of their fishing outings, Bush told Meyers that although his staff continued to monitor the investigation, MetroDade Homicide had little to report. He said he was pessimistic about the murder ever being resolved, so much time had passed. He thought they would have a chance if the federal government became involved. "I just wish," he told Meyers, "that there was some federal aspect to the murder. If the killers crossed state lines. Then I could get the FBI involved."

Bush's pessimism was shared by many in Miami as one theory after another had been brought to light, explored, and reluctantly dismissed. But speculation on why the larger-than-life sports hero had been gunned down continued to dominate talk on the Alley. And some thought that his murder suggested another side of the legend that only a few people knew.

BOOK TWO

SIX

By June 1987 when I arrived in Miami on assignment for *Playboy* magazine, Thunderboat Alley was quiet. Four months had passed since Aronow had been killed, and the off-season lull was in effect. Many workers on the street were laid off, and those who remained were seeking refuge from the relentless Miami summer sun. Everything was hot to the touch: the parked cars, the blacktop, the handles on the doors of the boat companies. Heat waves emanated from the ground. Occasionally a truck or car roared down the Alley, whipping up the arid dirt that bordered the narrow road.

The Aronow murder remained unsolved. Most of the detectives on the case had been reassigned, the killing swiftly slipping into the dusty backlog of unsolved murders in Dade County. Little new had come to light. The tributes and remembrances no longer ran in the papers. USA Racing had really ceased to exist on the day that Aronow died, although many of the employees and family members continued to show up at the office. The goal was simply to maintain the illusion of an operating company until it could be sold. King Hussein eventually would intercede for Lillian's sake and coax some of his business associates to buy the company.

Still there was an unsettled air that hung over the city. A feeling that there was far more to the murder than seemed apparent; that something was going on in the darker world of Miami. There was a growing sense of distrust even among some of the people who had worked on the Alley and had known each other for years. Many cast reappraising eyes at each other—wondering if the other knew something about the murder, or worse, had somehow been involved in it.

Even Lillian began to feel it. One of her first social outings after her husband's death was a dinner in Miami. Vice President George Bush was there. He had taken phone calls from her in the last few months as she sought his advice on various matters. But his manner changed when they were in public. At the dinner, she says, "he waved and smiled that smile of his, but he wouldn't come over. He sent a Secret Service agent over to sit with me and keep me company for a while." She had the distinct impression that he did not want to be seen with her.

The *Miami Herald* society editor also noted the exchange and agreed with Lillian's feelings. George Bush was avoiding her. It seemed curious that a man who had been personally and professionally close to Lillian's husband would essentially snub the widow the first time he came across her in public. Lillian wondered what made Bush have this reaction. "I said to my mother the next day that this man is definitely guilty about something," Lillian recalls.

When Aronow was gunned down, Jerry Engelman and the staff at USA Racing had been completing the final specs for the renewal of the coming year's Blue Thunder government contract. It was, as far as everyone on the Alley was concerned, a "sure thing" that Aronow's contract would be renewed. With his death, however, Customs lost no time in handing the contract over to Cigarette—the company it had always wanted, and no doubt would have hired if George Bush had not been friendly with Aronow. But Lillian thought there was more behind Bush's change in attitude toward her than simply embarrassment about the transfer of a boat contract.

In life, as in death, it was difficult to know with Aronow what was myth, what was reality. Since his move to Miami in 1961 mystery surrounded him, especially his early background. There were lots of stories, and Aronow and his publicist, John Crouse, encouraged them. Magazine articles and interviews contradicted one another. Even years later, some of his closest friends would disagree on almost everything about him, especially his pre-Miami years.

He was from Brooklyn; he was from New Jersey. His father ran a candy store; he was a taxicab owner; the manager of a gas station. The family was "dirt poor"; the family had lost a fortune in the Depression; they were typically middle class. Aronow was a war hero serving on ships that made the treacherous Murmansk run against German wolfpacks in World War II; he never saw active duty. Shirley's family was wealthy; the family was just getting by. His in-laws loved him and set him up in the construction business; he "had something" on Shirley's family and the family hated him.

The same uncertainty and ambiguity that characterized his life would become even more pronounced when those around him struggled to comprehend the reasons for his murder.

The door to USA Racing is open. Inside is a preppy-looking man slouched against a desk. A blond woman is reading at another desk in the corner, and at the largest desk in what was once Don Aronow's office is a man in a wheelchair. It's Michael, Aronow's oldest son—there is a definite resemblance. The office is quiet. When Aronow was around, it bristled with activity—he was like a walking charge of electricity. Those days are clearly gone.

Everyone in the room greets me expectantly, assuming I'm a customer. I introduce myself, explaining that I'm doing a story on Aronow. The blonde jumps up and starts waving her arms. "We can't talk to you," she cries in alarm. "We can't talk to nobody. Lillian says we're not supposed to talk to anybody. Get out of here!" She is Patty Lezaca, Don's longtime secretary and an officer in several of his corporations and holding companies.

Michael pushes himself toward me in his wheelchair. Out of Patty's line of sight, he catches my eye and mouths the word *later*, gesturing with his hands not to push the subject. Patty is standing a few inches in front of me, repeating that I must leave.

I drive a little down the street, watch the activity for a while, then drive back, where I can see the door to USA Racing. After about twenty minutes, Michael wheels himself out into the middle of the street, looks up and down, then spots me and waves. His wheelchair is on the same spot where his father had posed for his last picture, the one in *People* magazine.

We return to the office. The preppy is gone; Patty remains. Michael apologizes about the earlier episode. "What can I do for you?" he asks. I wonder what progress the police have made. "They're working their hardest," he says. "I don't know, we don't know, we're hoping they'll come up with something, they're trying their best."

The family still has no idea about the motive for the murder. "It's unbelievable," Michael explains. "That's all, it's a real mess. There's no rhyme or reason to it." Patty comments that USA Racing had been getting peculiar phone calls for about three weeks before Don was killed. She says they had checked with Jerry Jacoby (the name given on several of the phone messages and the name given by the big sandy-haired man), and he had denied calling the office.

We talk about Don and boat racing. Michael says his father never encouraged him to race, that he had actually tried to discourage him. "My father kept raising the age limit," he explains. "And then I had my accident. So I never did get to race with my father." Michael and his father did go into business together with Aronow Stables. "My father didn't know the details of horse breeding," Michael says. "He just liked the racing, the sport." As we talk, Patty sits at her desk, staring despondently at the papers on it.

Michael says he'd be willing to cooperate on a story about his father. "Sure, if it's done nicely," he emphasizes. "That's all that counts." Why wouldn't it be? I wondered at the time. So far every story, every article about Aronow, has created a larger-than-life champion. "I idolized him until the day he died," Michael offers. "I got to know my father on a European trip one summer and during the year after my accident. I knew him as well as anyone."

But he can't explain why his father changed his will and inserted the peculiar provisions that denied Michael from ever having direct access to his inheritance. He shrugs his shoulders, saying, "Who knows why he put that in his will—and about selling the company— that was a while ago. My father was unpredictable. We never knew what he was up to. He kept me off guard." Michael suggests I call him in a few days so we can talk more about his father.

Aronow and success seemed to be intertwined. Everyone remarks on the success that Don achieved at every stage of his life. He never failed. When other boat makers were losing money, Aronow was making more than ever. No one else in powerboating could even begin to match his wealth—as one boat designer noted, "most guys in this business don't have two nickels to rub together. But Don, he always had plenty of cash."

While most of the powerboat builders barely survived, Aronow was singularly successful. Even those who bought his thriving firms were unable to match the success he had with them, and often the new owner soon went under.

Art Grace, the horse-racing reporter from the *Miami Herald*, knew Aronow through his breeding and racing activities. "He was a very interesting person," Grace comments. "Liked by some, hated by others." He says that Aronow was "the kind of person who seems to me, anything he touched he was awfully lucky with. The building business initially. The boat business. The horses. The success he had is fascinating. It happened a number of times. It wasn't lightning striking once—it hit him a lot."

Aronow's publicist and longtime friend, John Crouse, is expansive on the subject of his hero. "He had a lot of different sides to him, very aggressive, big, strong, athletic," Crouse says. "Rather independent. He didn't seem to have too much fear of anything."

Crouse comes close to suggesting that Aronow almost single-handedly saved the Free World during World War II—or at least the Russkies' posteriors. "He made the deadly Murmansk runs in the Merchant Marines," Crouse explains excitedly, expanding on the story that has been in various sports magazines since the sixties. "Made several of them," he emphasizes. "That was the notorious run where we went up to Murmansk to save the goddamn Russians' lives and they were shootin' at our guys when we got off the boats with their stuff. Murmansk, Russia. Up in the North Sea. And the Germans probably sank most of the ships that tried to make the run. That was literally what saved the Russians in the early part of the war. That was what Don did."

He does not explain how Aronow, who was born in 1927, served in the Murmansk convoys (or even the war for that matter), which took place in the early forties. Don would have been only fifteen years old.

Crouse goes on to say that while Don didn't bear any physical scars from his war exploits, he did carry psychological ones. Not long after Aronow arrived in Miami, he was at a football game sitting in the stands with Crouse. As the audience cheered, suddenly there was a loud cracking sound, like a gunshot. Aronow ducked under the bleachers covering his head with his arms. Crouse explains, "It was a firecracker, but Don was still reliving those war days."

Jerry Engelman is at the Apache Bar, part of Ben Kramer's Ft. Apache Marina complex. It's a hangout for workers in the Thunderboat Alley companies. It also attracts customers who come searching for powerboats, as well as people from the surrounding area who simply want to soak up the atmosphere. I had expected a dingy, sawdust-on-the-floor hole-in-the-wall. Instead the bar is pristine, with highly polished wood walls, shiny patio furniture, and docking facilities. A window catches the intense sunlight and offers an unobstructed view of the waterway. The wood and brass glisten.

The customers, mostly men, are low-key, dressed in casual hot-weather attire. The waitresses are exactly what one would expect in this male bastion, friendly, built, and spilling out of tight black short-shorts and white halter tops. The sexual roles in this industry are clearly delineated. We order beers.

"Everybody liked Don," Jerry states matter-of-factly. We talk for a while about Aronow's success in business, how he dominated the street, and his racing exploits. "You really don't know what it takes to race powerboats," Engelman says. "I rarely go over seventy, but recently I went out in a boat that goes ninety. I had a helmet on. The wind grabs the visor and it feels like it's going to rip your head off. You've got to be in real good physical shape. The abuse these guys take. The pounding. It's just—whatever macho is—that's it."

Engelman, a transplanted New Englander, had practiced both criminal and divorce law in Connecticut before he and his wife moved to Miami. Engelman got a job selling boats. He was reading a story on the Blue Thunder operation in the *Miami Herald* and noticed that it contained a mistake. He called USA Racing to tell them that they should have the paper print a correction.

"A man answered and I told him about the error," says Engelman. "We started talking about powerboats in general, and then the Blue Thunders. Then this guy says, 'Listen, why don't you drop by the office sometime. If you're looking for a job, we'll talk.' So I told him that I might just consider that, and I asked him for his name. He says, 'I'm Don Aronow.' Shit, I thought, all this time I've been talking to Don Aronow. I was blown away."

Jerry jumped at the chance to meet Aronow, job or not, and stopped by the office the next week. "We talked for a while and Don asked me what kind of salary I wanted. I don't know why, but I just had the feeling that with him, I'd get only one chance," Engelman says. "If it was too high, he'd just say something like 'We'll get back to you' and I'd never hear from him again. There'd be no bargaining. No give-and-take. So I lowballed it and got the job."

Engelman finishes his beer and leaves the Apache. A few people who have overheard the conversation and Aronow's name stop by the table to talk. They all have the same story. Death has elevated Don Aronow to almost mythic proportions.

By six P.M., most of the people in the bar have left. A man sitting quietly at a table a few feet away has been listening to the conversations with a hint of amusement. He's noticeably different from the others. More formally dressed, prosperous looking, and authoritative in an understated way. He's wearing an impeccably tailored suit, a silk shirt, and a solid-gold Rolex. There's something more. He's obviously a man with knowledge and many contacts—the type of man that when you ask how he knows something you brace yourself for the answer.

I ask if he knew Don Aronow. He did, he replies, they had business dealings in real estate. I expect to hear the usual litany. Instead he pauses, his face expressionless, and he says nonchalantly, "He was a prick." It's the first negative comment I've heard. We talk for a while about some of his ventures with Aronow. He says that Aronow's business strategy was always "to squeeze you for a penny, and then another nickel."

So you think he burned somebody in business? Maybe that's why he was killed? The man looks directly at me, shakes his head, and states, "It was a message from a long time ago."

"Don was like a rock star, he was always surrounded by women," says Alan "Brownie" Brown of Cigarette. "They just gravitated to him. He was the greatest cocksman I've ever known. If there was ever a man who could lay women end to end around the world, it was Don. He must've fucked six or eight hundred wives in the last twenty-five years. He was a real charismatic guy and the women loved him."

Brownie is reminiscing in his office at the Cigarette Racing Team, which Aronow sold for the second and last time in 1982. It's a few hundred yards away from the Apache Bar. The room looks like someone's basement workshop. Papers and sketches are strewn haphazardly on the desks and on the floor. The smell of the chemicals from the fiberglass material used in the boats permeates the room. There are two other desks for the staff members who share the office. People keep walking in and out as we talk about Aronow.

Brownie is not at all what one expects. But then again as I've started to learn, nothing on the Alley is what it seems. For one thing, the men are much smarter, savvier, and more ambitious than I had imagined. Perhaps it's the powerboating sport—the attention it focuses on brute force and strength—that makes one wrongly assume that the participants are all muscle and little brain.

With his full head of white hair and matching goatee, Brownie resembles a college English professor more than a renowned developer for go-fast boats. He speaks in a careful and precise manner, punctuated by thoughtful pauses. He dresses like most men on the street, casual pants and shirt. He's observant and has a remarkable memory. He met Aronow more than twenty-five years ago, right after Don moved from New Jersey. As we talk, the conversation drifts to Aronow's women. Brownie chuckles, points up to the ceiling, and jumps up from his chair. "Follow me."

We cross the room. Around the corner is a hidden hallway, and a small spiral staircase. As we climb the iron stairs to a private room, Brownie says that when Aronow owned the company, it was a well-known secret that he took one of his secretaries here at lunchtime. "He made this his bedroom apartment, and every day they'd come here for a quickie," he explains. The room is worn, windowless, and unused now. There's a large shower with Italian tile (Brownie points out that it is big enough to have a party in) and a bidet. Vestiges from the Aronow days.

The conversation turns to the boat business and Aronow's high performance machines. "The people who buy these boats are rich and these are their toys," Brownie comments. "It's turned into a hell of an industry and Don really started the whole fucking thing."

I ask how Don made his money, but Brownie shakes his head and replies, "Not any way that I want to discuss. I've always said that he'd rather make a dollar through subterfuge than make five dollars straight up. It was a game with him."

Brownie won't talk about Don's experiences in New Jersey, either. "There's nothing that I want to repeat," he emphasizes. When pressed, he offers only that "Don did what he had to do to make a lot of money. Other than that I really wouldn't want to discuss it. But he certainly was a guy who did whatever needed to be done. A go-getter."

"What else did Aronow like to do?" I ask. "He liked women. He liked fast boats."

"No," he contradicts, "he hated boats."

That surprises me. So what was it all about? Just making money?

"Yeah, mostly," he agrees. "I don't think he ever made too much operating the company. He made it when he sold the company. He did like building boats, but he had no interest in going out boating."

"So why did he race?"

"To prove a point," he explains. "He started out poor and Don always wanted to be the best at everything. He put a great deal of himself into everything and he was an incredibly bright man. He learned very quickly."

We talk about the reaction on the street to the murder. "I think it must have been some kind of organized deal or they would have found something out by now," Brownie speculates. "It's been a long time and they haven't turned up anything. I've heard every fucking theory. I never thought Don ever had anything to do with drugs, except selling lots of boats to them."

Selling boats to dopers is a profitable business. Back in the old days—the seventies—drug smugglers used to haunt the Alley in search of fast boats. Because the boats were always being lost to Customs or abandoned, the smugglers gave a lot of repeat business. In recent years, small planes have begun to replace some of the boats.

Brownie mentions one company that was probably the last to specialize in the drug trade. It was started by Bying Goode, who once worked as Aronow's manager at Cigarette. Goode ran Cigarette when Aronow was racing. Then Goode started his own company, a venture that quickly landed him in prison.

Goode built 37-foot boats and equipped them with five outboard engines. It wasn't difficult for anyone in Miami to figure out the purpose of the boats. If you still didn't get the point, there was always the name, Midnight Express. But despite the obvious, the feds were unable to nail Goode for his boats. He was nabbed for laundering drug money and disguising cash payments.

Brownie hasn't heard any rumors about Aronow's being involved with drugs. He comments that the DEA and the police in Miami publicly stated that they didn't think Aronow had anything to do with drugs as far as importing them.

He says that some people have speculated that the murder might have had something to do with Don's business style. "He was a very, very friendly guy with a terrific sense of humor," he explains. "But he was a ruthless son of a bitch despite all the eulogies. He fucked everybody financially. He always did it with a smile. It wasn't like he would steal money out of your pocket. But like, you're dead."

Despite his merciless business dealings, Aronow was still popular. Brownie repeats what I've heard from so many people. "He had one of the most unbelievable personalities I ever saw. He was great fun and he always enjoyed life."

Like everyone else on the street Brownie has thought a lot about the murder. "I'll tell you the parts that don't make sense," he says. "Unless it was somebody trying to prove a point to somebody else. If I gave you the job of shooting Aronow—you know the geography here—you could lay across the canal in the woods over there with a deer rifle and a scope, and when Aronow went out to his car, which he did several times a day, you just blast him one time in the ear and nobody would ever know. You could just walk away. Why they did it the way they did, doesn't make any sense at all."

I comment that the broad-daylight hit sounds like a message.

"It sure sounds like one," he agrees.

As friends and acquaintances begin to talk about the real Aronow, the conversation quickly turns to sex. The same demons that drove Aronow to best others in races and in business seemed to drive his sex life as well.

When the police were looking into the possibility of the murders being committed by a jealous husband or lover, they asked Shirley Aronow Parker if she thought he was cheating on his current wife. She rolled her eyes, observing wryly, "It would really be unlike him if he wasn't, because he always was, all his life." On the night of their honeymoon while Shirley was in the shower, Aronow told friends that he "screwed the chambermaid in the other room of the suite."

After their divorce, Shirley married a well-known New York architect, Alfred Browning Parker, but it didn't last long. Friends say she was still really in love with Don. Shirley obviously shared the sentiments of many of Aronow's associates. As Randy Riggs put it, "The guy was a heartless son of a bitch sometimes, but he was a great guy."

Edna Buchanan calls Aronow a flagrant womanizer. "Always was," she emphasizes. "Everyone knew it. He never tried to hide it. There was a woman he put up in this high-rise condo on the bay. The current wife—when the police asked her about him seeing other women—said, no, no, of course not. So she either hadn't caught on or didn't want to admit it."

John Crouse agrees, "As most everybody who knew him thought, his major foible was women. He did love women. He came alive around women. He sparkled and was never at a loss for things to say."

Yet still for all his braggadocio and his undeniable attractiveness to women, Aronow's affairs sometimes took a farcical turn. He was always worried about his wife—first Shirley, then Lillian—or a mistress dropping by the office unexpectedly and catching him with another woman. More than once a girlfriend charged into his office to chastise him for not calling. Although he discouraged Lillian from visiting the office, he devised various strategies for the rare occasion when she did. Then he rehearsed his employees in handling any of a half dozen situations involving women.

If he was upstairs in his private office with a woman and his wife dropped by, the office employees were supposed to tell her that he had taken one of the boats out for a test drive. He said this would explain why his car was at the company but he was unavailable. If he was out with another of his girlfriends, they were to say that a business meeting came up unexpectedly.

Never one to leave anything to chance, Aronow would periodically quiz his staff: "I'm upstairs with someone. Lillian comes by. What do you say?" The employees would repeat the proper answer. Then he'd propose another scenario. What if he's at home and Eileen Taylor, for instance, wants to get in touch with him? Then they were to call him at home and say, "Mr. Taylor just called for you, and it's important." The "mister" was an added precaution in case Lillian picked up the extension. (To avoid such problems in the future, Don was having a sophisticated phone system installed in his new mansion that would have precluded Lillian from listening on an extension.)

Jerry laughs when I tell him that Eileen Taylor denied to MetroDade Homicide that she was having an affair with Don. "Bullshit," he says, laughing. "How about when she'd go upstairs looking like she had just stepped out of a beauty salon and come downstairs an hour and a half later with her hair pulled back into a ponytail like she had just stepped out of the shower?"

Eileen was one of a number of women whom Don was seeing at the time of his death. Once when he developed a rash and the doctor advised him not to have sex for a few days, Don told him earnestly he couldn't go that long without it. Randy Riggs says, "I don't know the term for it, but it's like a sickness. All the man wanted was sex and money. And sex more than money. He said to me a number of times, 'Boy, I'll tell you, when I die, and they cut my brain open, all these cunts, millions of cunts are going to fly out.' And he was very proud of that."

Aronow was part of a notorious crowd that frequented Miami's Turnberry Isle. The group was considered so debauched that Miami's old-time mafiosi who frequented the condominium were shocked right down to their pinky rings. John Crouse mentions, "I have a friend who is a mafioso type—one tough son of a bitch. And he said, 'John, I wouldn't want to tell you what happened.' It must have been mixing ménage à trois, ménage à God-knows-what, and Aronow and they were all smoking pot. I don't know what-all they did."

Aronow kept a mistress, Missy Allen, at Turnberry. In the late seventies—just before Don met and married Lillian—he was in love with Missy. "He used to see her all the time," Riggs recalls. "She wanted to get married. And I think he did, too. But he told her no.

He told me that she wasn't the kind of woman he needed for a wife. I remember we were flying somewhere in the helicopter right after he had told her no, and he was really broken up about it."

Aronow continued to see Missy after his second marriage, always at lunchtime when he wouldn't have to explain his absence. When Missy realized that Aronow would never marry her, she became the mistress of two other men in addition to Aronow: Bobby Rautbord and Joey Ippolito. Rautbord, also a former world-champion powerboat racer, once owned Miami's Carriage House Restaurant, while Joey "Ip" is the former powerboat racer who was busted off Long Island for smuggling eight tons of marijuana.

Aronow was a fierce businessman. Some say that he was toughest on those he thought could afford to be cheated. "If the right guy came in here, he'd shear him like you'd shear a sheep," says Bobby Moore, his former racing partner, who now has his own company, a custom-rigging shop. "A high roller—if he could afford it—Don would take him. The little guy he'd give a break before he would a guy with a lot of money." Moore is familiar with some of the stories about Don's business dealings: "I hear he screwed some people around here, but I have never known it."

Randy Riggs, who started a silk-flower wholesaling business with his wife, also says Aronow pulled some fast deals. But like Moore, he says they involved people who had money. One was a business agreement that Aronow made with Hal Halter, a New Orleans boatbuilder. The first time Aronow sold Cigarette it was to Halter. "Don's style was to get as much money as possible for his company," Riggs explains. "He'd overvalue things and then he'd start taking things back.

"I remember he took a whole forklift back. A six-thousand-dollar forklift. He sold it with Cigarette to Halter and then got a truck and took the whole garl darn thing back because it wasn't on the list. He said, 'Hey, it wasn't a part of the deal.' Don had purposely omitted it from the contract hoping Halter wouldn't notice. Hal thought he was getting the whole thing. In Don's mind, he wasn't. So he took it back."

Making money was central to Aronow's makeup, but there was something even more important than money. He needed to best others. Whether it was a matter of a few hundred dollars or a few million, he was exhilarated by outwitting other people. It made him feel proud—and more than equal to those who never had to scrape for survival.

The young Don Aronow had been an ambitious hustler, too. Even as a Brooklyn teenager, he was fixing up abandoned machines in junkyards and selling them for a tidy profit, outwitting older men who tried to take advantage of his youth, and always looking for ways to make money.

Michael Aronow says that when his father was in his early twenties, he and a friend had the idea that they could buy a surplus World War II tank cheap, fix it up, and sell it for a profit. The tank was in the middle of Manhattan and they had to bring it back to Brooklyn. There was a problem. Civilians couldn't put a tank on the road.

So Don went to an army surplus store and bought a uniform. Michael says, "My father drove the tank through the heart of Manhattan. The police thought he was with the military so they gave him an escort. That was my dad."

Near the entrance to Thunderboat Alley is Magnum Marine, another company started by Aronow, now owned by Ted Theodile. The two-story building has several rooms running along one side on both floors. The rest of the hangarlike area is open, and two large boats are receiving finishing touches. There is a 43-foot powerboat and a 63-footer. Both are luxury items, aesthetically impressive, all the more so for their combination of speed and size.

Theodile, a northern Italian, moves with a characteristic European grace. He proudly takes me on a tour of the factory. As we cross the work area, the fiberglass dust that covers the floor collects on our shoes. The noise of sanders and saws rises and falls. We have to climb small ladders to get up onto the boats. A dozen workers are scurrying over each one. Although the hulls are made by a type of mass production, each boat is individually completed by master craftsmen.

The interior of the large boat is all leather and suede, in shades of pewter. The master bedroom has a huge bed and is surrounded by high-tech video and stereo appurtenances. The boat has two engines, each one approximately the size of a small car, each with 2,000 horsepower. It's being made for a Japanese customer—many of Theodile's clients are from the Orient in recent years. This boat will sell for about $6 million.

Theodile, too, has thought about the murder and has a sense of something larger, evil, behind it. "The very fact that this guy used a dark Lincoln Town Car, four-door sedan, which in Florida is very rare," he muses, "it's not that you see a lot of dark Lincolns here."

They had a description of the car, he emphasizes, but the police

couldn't find it. "Just that makes me think there is something organized about this," he says. "Florida's a peninsula. In a way it's a
simple state to control because after the guy did the murder, an hour
later, the police were informed all the way to Jacksonville and the
state police were informed on the road. There are very few roads,
you know, that get you out of Florida."

In the very early stages of the investigation, the police went to
Magnum often and talked to the workers, but nobody knew anything
about the murder, or so they claimed: why it happened or who did
it. "I don't think it has anything to do with this area," Theodile says
pensively. "I think this comes from far away. That's my feeling at
least. My gut feeling, my epidermal feeling, is that it isn't something
that originated here."

Theodile saw the Mercedes in which Aronow was shot before the
police took it away. "I'll tell you one thing," he intones. "Only one
bullet didn't hit him. It exited through the right-side door. The hole
was as big as an inch with all the metal sticking out. Just looking at
that really made me cringe. A gun that does that—it's not a jealous-
husband weapon. I never realized it, but talking about it now, I think
this is a professional thing. Somebody wanted to make absolutely
sure he wouldn't survive."

Theodile is one of the few who will go on record as saying he
didn't like Aronow. "Stories about Aronow I have plenty of," he
comments. "But I don't know if I'd be happy to divulge them, if you
know what I mean." He does mention the time that Don cheated
him out of a boat mold.

When Aronow sold Magnum he agreed that the price included
everything. Then as he often did, Don tried to take back some inven-
tory, in this case, one of the molds. Knowing that Aronow would just
make a few minor changes and start building other boats, Theodile
refused even to sell it back to him. Aronow stormed out in anger,
and Theodile thought he had outmaneuvered Aronow.

A few days later, a man stopped by Magnum. He said he represented a Canadian company and he wanted to buy a Magnum mold.
Since he was from another country, and therefore represented no
serious threat to Magnum's business, Theodile agreed. They set a
price of $15,000. The man told Theodile, "Look, I've got some cash.
Why don't I give you a thousand dollars now and you can give me a
receipt saying 'paid in full,' and when I pick it up, I'll give you
another fourteen thousand dollars in cash." Theodile agreed. The
next morning, Aronow showed up at Magnum with the receipt and a
sheriff with a court order directing Theodile to hand over the mold.

Theodile allowed them to load the mold onto a truck and leave, but he was furious at being conned out of $14,000. After the truck left, he grabbed a publicity picture of Aronow from the office wall, threw it on the floor, and stomped it to pieces. "Don't ask me where he got a judge to sign a court order in the middle of the night," he says with pointedly raised eyebrows.

Still, Theodile comments that Aronow was too much of a presence in the industry and on the street for anyone to murder him for his shady business practices. "Everybody on the street knew Don," he explains. "And whether you liked him or you didn't, he was Don Aronow. He invented all of this and people had a certain pride in him, in what he accomplished. The fact that this business existed was because of him. I just don't think anybody in this business would have done that to him."

While a uniform picture of Aronow was emerging from talks with his friends and associates, there seems to be little agreement on the details of his murder. Some people say the killer had sandy-colored hair, others say it was dark hair. The question of whether he was an amateur or professional, Latino or Anglo, brings heated debate.

Jerry Engelman recalls the strange visit by the big, sandy-haired man to the USA Racing office minutes before Don was shot. The man was definitely not a Latino, and he spoke without an accent.

Mike Harrison, who works at Cigarette in the parts department, saw the murder from a perfect vantage point thirty yards up the street. He says there was only one man in the Town Car. He was dark, but not Latino, broad-shouldered, and he drove in a calm, certain manner. He didn't panic or try to drive off quickly. Even the actual firing of the gun was deliberate, with a brief pause between shots to take aim. Harrison, a gun enthusiast, says the weapon was a .45, and that the man was alone in the car.

Despite what the newspapers had originally printed, it seemed that there were two people involved in the hit, not one. One man flushed Aronow out of his office, then the other, the shooter in the Town Car, took over. He waited patiently until Aronow's car was in the right position, then slowly pulled alongside and fired. Another bit of overlooked information was the pickup truck that had followed the Town Car immediately after the shooting.

A professional hit was the only reasonable conclusion. Former Florida chief homicide investigator Harold Young, who solved the famous 1985 Benson "pipe bomb" murders, comments, "The dark Lincoln Town Car is sort of a trademark of a status mob hit man. It's a symbol that he's a heavy hitter. The .45 he used is a goddamned cannon—you don't find druggies or amateurs using that. That's not exactly the kind of gun that you just happen to carry around. It's real powerful and you have to know how to use it. It's got a hell of a kick to it." Since neither of the men was Latino, a drug motive seemed less likely.

A few people at the scene also said that Aronow was shot in the groin—a characteristic touch of some mob hits, intended to show great antipathy for the victim as opposed to the more commonplace "nothing personal, just business" motive. "Shooting in the balls is the Mafia's way of emasculating a guy—they like to do that," Young says.

The two-car scenario is another tactic that professionals use. The second car is a "crash car." Driven by the killer's partner, the crash car blocks others from following the shooter. If necessary, it will ram any car that tries. The object is to ensure that the trigger man gets away from the scene. Even if the crash car is wrecked at the scene, there's no way the cops can hold the driver. He's completely in the clear.

"Everything about it says Mafia," Young concludes. "They like to leave telltale signs so that the right people get the right message." The sign is the way in which the hit is done. In this case it was bold, out in the open, on a public street.

Young isn't surprised that MetroDade Homicide has made no progress on the case. "They've probably concluded the same thing —that it was a mob hit," he says. "And they know there's nothing that they'll really be able to do about it. They'll never catch the guys. Even if they did, they'll never convict them. The witnesses would either change their testimony or disappear."

A confident, daring, well-coordinated Anglo team. A "kiss of death" message. A smoothly orchestrated hit and getaway. Instead of solving the mystery of the murder, these insights only raise more questions.

Why would the Mafia put out a contract on Don Aronow?

SEVEN

The brief conversation I had in the Apache Bar with the well-dressed stranger keeps surfacing: "It was a message from a long time ago." It seemed melodramatic, theatrical, the type of thing a character might say in a film noir murder mystery. In 1987, in the sun-brilliant world of Miami, it seemed incongruous.

Still there were many things about Don Aronow that didn't seem to fit. The way he died. Some of the friends he had. The fact that he was one of the few men on the street to make money. Even the intrigue surrounding his early days: his astonishing rise to fortune and his abrupt departure from New Jersey in 1961.

John Crouse, like Don's other Miami friends, knew little about Aronow's early New Jersey days except the few bits of information Don had given him. He had told Crouse that Shirley's family was very wealthy and owned a huge construction company in New Jersey. Then again, he had told Crouse he had been in the Murmansk runs. But other than that, Aronow seemed to have placed a heavy veil over his early life.

"I'd like to know about it," Crouse tells me in response to questions about Aronow's early life. "It's just natural. Hell, I made a hero, a legend out of this fucking guy for twenty years. I'd like to know if I made a legend out of a guy too much so. I think the clues are going to come out of up North, and not here. When you start finding how, you know—what he says he did up there just doesn't jive."

Shirley Parker Aronow's voice sounds warm and adoring as she talks about the young Don Aronow she fell in love with four decades before. "He was a five-letter man at Brooklyn College," she says. "He never did any of these things as a hobby. He wanted his letter. He was out to *win,* and he did."

She says the first year they were married, Don was offered the role of Tarzan. A man came to the Coney Island beach where he worked as a lifeguard and wanted to sign him up for a screen test. Shirley was thrilled. But Don turned it down. He thought it would be better to finish college. He said they couldn't guarantee anything other than to sign him to a contract for a year. "I thought, well, what could be better, you know," she recalls. "The best thing in the world, and he said no, no, he had another year of school and he wasn't going to stop. He had plans for himself even then."

Shirley and Don married in 1948. He had just joined the service. "That was most peculiar," she remarks thoughtfully. "He joined the Marines and got out and went into the Merchant Marines." Suddenly she changes the subject. "Look, I can't talk anymore, I've got to be at Sotheby's at three. I'll tell you what, I'm going away next week and when I come back, I'd be happy to get into it."

Lenny Sendelsky's first job out of high school in 1951 was as a laborer for Shirley's father, Max Goldin, who owned a small construction company. Goldin had begun his career as a house painter in Brooklyn. Later Shirley's two brothers joined their father in a house construction business in New Jersey. Not long after Aronow married Shirley, he left his job as a physical education teacher and joined his in-laws as a project manager. Within a few years, he decided to branch out on his own.

"The way Don got started in the business—I don't think, I don't think it would be appropriate to tell you how he got started, and how he got his money from the father-in-law," says Sendelsky. Then he relents, explaining that in 1954 Aronow coerced Shirley's father into "giving him some up-front money and promising to give Don X number of dollars for five years." According to Lenny, Aronow threatened to turn Max into the IRS unless he underwrote Don's independent construction venture.

After Don left Goldin Construction, taking Lenny with him, Max Goldin "pretty much didn't last very long," Sendelsky says, laughing. "They tried to hang in there for maybe another three years and they faded away." While Goldin's luck plummeted, Aronow's fortunes soared.

Sendelsky says he never met a shrewder businessman than Aronow. "He was a dynamite guy, a dynamo; Don was a pusher and a driver and a hustler," he explains. In seven years, from 1954 to 1961, Lenny says Aronow built and developed several thousand houses, a shopping center, a nine-story apartment building; developed a hundred acres of commercial properties and office complexes, a million and a half square feet of industrial buildings, and more than thirty factories. Other developers called Aronow and Sendelsky the Gold Dust Twins because "everything we did, we did it well and made money at it," Lenny explains.

After Aronow "retired" to Miami in 1961, he urged the twenty-eight-year-old Sendelsky to relocate there so they could start a new construction business in Miami. Lenny didn't want to move, so Aronow proposed another idea. They could be partners with Sendelsky in New Jersey and Aronow in Miami. It was the only time Aronow offered an employee a partnership. Still, despite their amazing track record of success, one business relationship with Aronow in a lifetime was enough for Sendelsky.

Lenny comments cryptically, "I didn't think it would be in my best interests for us to be partners." Then he adds, "But Don and I was friends right up until the end."

Eddie Cohen is a retired New Jersey attorney who also worked for Aronow in the early days. He recalls Aronow with a mix of fondness, amusement, and awe.

"He was only twenty-eight when I met him," Cohen, seventy-five, says. "If he had stayed here instead of running down to Florida—he left at an early age—he would've been a billionaire. You wouldn't believe it. It's unbelievable what he did. There are billionaires who weren't as good as he was building hotels in Tel Aviv."

Cohen doesn't know anything about Aronow's background or his childhood. "Don never spoke about that," Eddie says, "though I do know that Don was born in not a fancy family."

He tells me that Aronow "liked girls." In what can only be called an understatement, Eddie observes, "He liked it, I guess. He was big and strong and very handsome. There were hundreds of women. Shirley was an attractive, decent woman. She believed in him. Never dreamed anything could go wrong with their marriage. He used to do things in the daytime. He said, 'If you're going to do things, you do things in the daytime.' But he didn't have any regular hours, you know. She thought he was a saint."

Cohen says that Aronow was too aggressive for Shirley's father, that he was always pushing to build more. This made Max Goldin nervous and eventually Don left. Cohen confirms Sendelsky's story about Aronow's blackmailing Shirley's father with the threat of the IRS, but then adds that he doesn't want it to get around. "It's a tough story," he notes. "Don got his money. He was rough. Everyone admired him. You had to admire him."

As in his later years, Aronow took care to separate his business life from his personal one. Despite the close association he and Cohen had in business, Cohen knew little about Aronow except that he used to go into New York a lot. He and Eddie never socialized. "I didn't know who his friends were when he was in New Jersey," he comments. "Don kept his private life private. Oh, here's one funny story. He had a date in New York with a recommended girl, you know?"

"No," I reply. "A 'recommended girl'? I don't understand."

"Recommended," Eddie repeats in a louder tone. "She was recommended."

"Oh, you mean like a . . ."

"Yes, yes. So he, he was very unusual," Cohen continues. "Anyway, he had this date in New York, so he tells his wife he had to go to New York on business. And she said, 'Gee, I have to go, too,' you know. So what's he gonna tell her? No? So he puts her in the car and they go to Manhattan and his mind is working furiously—how the hell is he going to get rid of her? So he rolls up on the other side of the Holland Tunnel and suddenly pulls into a parking place, and jumps out, saying, 'I'm late, you take the car and meet me later.' He grabs a cab and does what he has to do." Cohen starts chuckling again. "He was an amazing guy."

We talk about Aronow's stellar rise in business. "He was aggressive, positive, an unusual man," Eddie recalls. "He did what he wanted. He was determined. I have never met anybody like him in my life." Cohen, an expert in real estate, met Aronow in December of '54 just after he left Goldin's company. Eddie still remembers their first conversation.

They were driving to Rahway to look at a piece of land for development. "On the way Don told me that 'anybody who does business with me winds up with money,' " Cohen recalls. "And you know? He was real young but he was right. It's hard to explain to you, he was ahead of us all. He changed my life. I guess he changed a lot of people's lives. Just about everybody's."

Aronow started out on his own with a project in Cranford, New Jersey, a twenty-house job. "Then he began building in Woodbridge and Edison," Eddie says. "Nobody told Don what to do, he did it all himself. He didn't take any recommendation or anything. He didn't need it. He really built property wherever he went. Lenny [Sendelsky] told me the other day that Don figured a job for $12,999. Figured it to within twenty-five dollars of what it actually cost, and that's the way it actually worked out. Incredible, you know?"

Cohen says with obvious admiration in his voice that Aronow "made $4,500 on a $13,000 house. A hundred-odd houses. And he closed them all in six weeks. From the time he bought the land till he sold the [completed] houses on it. He did about seven or eight of these major housing projects."

Despite the extensive construction, Aronow never encountered problems with unions or laborers. "He never had any problems getting along with people except politicians," Cohen says. "But in New Jersey you don't bother with politicians."

Cohen suggests that I contact a woman from his office, Barbara Chase. "She knew Don very well," he explains. "Tell her I said to call, she can tell you lots of stories about Don."

Before we conclude, we talk briefly about Aronow's murder. Does he have any idea why Aronow was killed?

He responds, "Maybe Don was making love to a gangster's wife. Who knows?"

Barbara Chase doesn't want to reminisce about Aronow. She cuts me off as soon as I say I'm writing about him. She says she doesn't have anything to say. When I tell her that Eddie Cohen suggested she might have some stories for me, she states icily, "Eddie's an old man who talks too much." The phone disconnects.

David is Aronow's youngest son from his first marriage. He, like Michael, seems open and willing to talk about his father. But neither seems to know much about Don's pre-Miami days.

David is in the construction business and builds in the same areas of New Jersey that his father did. But the two rarely spoke about the construction business. "Dad kind of played that stuff down," David explains. He recalls just one time being on a boat with his father "and he pointed over to the shore and said, 'I built all over there.'"

Don's accountant, Sid Kravitz, never spoke to David about the

construction business while Don was alive. After he died, Sid told
David stories about Don's construction days. "Things like closing a
lot of houses from the time that he went under contract until the
time he closed the last house was six weeks—unbelievable stories
like that," David recalls.

No one has been able to explain why Aronow left his multimillion-
dollar construction business so abruptly. David can't shed much light
on it either. He says one day his father just said that they were
moving south. They flew to St. Thomas in the Virgin Islands where
Aronow intended to live. After a few days they suddenly moved to
Miami Beach, where they stayed for some time at the Americana
Hotel. It was all spur of the moment, but David doesn't know any
more. He suggests I ask Sid Kravitz—"he knows all about the construction days."

Sid Kravitz is in his office in Union, New Jersey, the same city where
Aronow Construction had its office. Sid was Don's accountant for all
of his business life, including Don's twenty-five years in Florida.
Although several members of Aronow's family have told me to contact Sid for stories, when I do get in touch, he doesn't want to talk.

As soon as I explain that I'm writing about Aronow's early construction days, he quickly cuts me off. "I don't want to talk about it."
Another disconnect.

Lillian Lust is Don's sister. David Aronow called her "the family
historian." She lives in Forest Hills, New York. She says she isn't
sure that she wants to talk to me. I tell her I'd like to know about
Don's military service. "Don was an able-bodied seaman," she says
stiffly, "in the Merchant Marines." I ask if he had to lie about his age
to get into the service early.

"No, he was in legitimately," she explains. "You had to be eighteen, and he was older than that."

"Did he ever go to Russia—to Murmansk—in the service?" I ask.
"No."

I point out that if he was older than eighteen, then he must have
missed World War II entirely. She agrees, then says it's a waste of
time for us to continue talking. She also advises me not to bother
calling people in Brooklyn and New Jersey about Don's past.

A few days later Michael Aronow calls to say that he won't be meeting me for lunch as we had agreed the previous week. In fact, he
won't be saying anything more about his father. "I just can't talk

about it," he comments. "I would, I just don't want to, I've talked about it too much, for too long now." He adds that his mother, Shirley, has also changed her mind about cooperating and won't be talking anymore either.

Why are they so negative all of a sudden? "I just don't want to see my father's name tied into this and that; probably half of it's bull anyway," Michael responds. "It makes great reading, but it's non-sense, it'll just end up becoming such nonsense, that's all. What's the goddamned point?"

I also hear from the Aronow family attorney, Murray Weil, who wants me to stop working on the Don Aronow story completely. "I know the legal position," he says, "as far as enjoining someone from publishing, the First Amendment prevents that from happening. As to the ramifications after that, that's another story."

I ask Weil how he is dealing with other media people. His voice trembles with emotion as he answers. "Do you know what I do with them?" he asks rhetorically. "I don't even speak to them, and any-body who asks me, I tell them not to speak to them, too."

Suddenly, no one wants to talk about Don Aronow's New Jersey days. When I broach the subject, the family and associates become nervous, agitated, and even hostile. Why does Don's construction career seem to touch a raw nerve?

"I heard that Aronow had been run out of New Jersey," says Eric Sharp, the *Miami Herald* boating reporter, who has spent some of his free time investigating Aronow's murder. "I heard that from somebody who knows a lot. We heard that he was hiding out in a hotel down here. I got that from a guy who is connected to bad people. The guy who told me about New Jersey is the brother of a very, very bad guy from that area."

When Michael Aronow was still talking to me, he had once elab-orated on his father's "retirement." He recalled that his father came home from work one day and announced that they were leaving New Jersey immediately. Don told the family that they could take only what they could pack into a suitcase and carry onto the plane. The rest of their belongings, including the furniture and Don's valu-able antique-car collection, were left behind. Although it was prime boating season in Miami, he also left his boat up north. The sale of his newly built estate and his immensely lucrative business were arranged after he left. All the paperwork was handled long distance.

"It was in February or March of 1961," Michael said. "He took us all and we left for the airport, parked the car, and went to St. Thomas. I was eleven and Claudia was eight, and David was whatever, four. [My parents] were kicking the idea around, the Virgin Islands, but we ended up in Miami. We lived at the Americana Hotel for a while. [My Dad] he wanted to, you know, retire."

Sharp has more details about that stay at the Americana. "They kept their bags packed for quite a while in case they had to run for it again. They lived like fugitives, day to day, ready to get the hell out of there if they had to." Sharp's source also told him that Don kept $20,000 in cash on hand with him in the room to fund another escape if necessary. "I was told that he thought they might have to pick up and leave in the middle of the night, but they didn't. They stayed at the hotel for ages, months and months."

In 1959 a young Don Aronow made another spur of the moment trip to the Caribbean. He had come home to Shirley and said that a friend of his had teased him about his beard, saying it made him look "swishy." "He came right home and told me to get a nurse for the weekend for Michael, who was eight then, Claudia, six, and David, the baby," Shirley told a reporter years later. "Then we took the next plane to Puerto Rico and checked into the best hotel so we could get a suite with a big terrace."

Despite the hot tropical weather, Aronow had worn an overcoat. Shirley had recalled that "Don had his coat up around his beard when we registered, and people in the lobby must have thought we were bank robbers on the run. As soon as we got to our room, Don shaved off his beard and then went out on the balcony to tan the white patch around his chin. All his meals were sent in, and he wouldn't leave the suite to go nightclubbing or shopping with me." A week later, they returned to New Jersey.

Shirley apparently never questioned the circumstances of the fifties Puerto Rico trip, nor did she question the family's abrupt departure from New Jersey in 1961. The unusual circumstances of the hasty trips suggest that Aronow had twice felt he needed to get out of New Jersey quickly. Once for a week, the second time permanently. If Eric Sharp's story about Don fleeing New Jersey was true, who were the "bad guys"?

Don Aronow made his first fortune building thousands of Levittown-like houses in northern New Jersey—in then undeveloped rural towns such as Union, Middletown, East Orange, Perth Amboy, Cranford, and Kenilworth. The construction industry in the area was under strong mob control during those years.

"The northern New Jersey housing construction business in the fifties was a hotbed for organized crime," says John Davies, executive assistant to the New Jersey State Commission on Investigation, which tracks the mob. "Especially in the building of thousands of suburbia tract houses." Davies also authored an SCI study on Mafia infiltration of the 1950s housing industry in north Jersey. "In the fifties, New Jersey was a highly corrupt state," he asserts.

Several Mafia families vied for control of the burgeoning New Jersey construction business in those days. "The Gambinos were big in the whole metropolitan New York area—Carlo Gambino and 'Harry the Horse' Saltstein even had their fingers into Levittown," Davies notes. "The Vito Genovese family had Jerry Catena in place in north Jersey, in the town of Union. Catena was very close to Meyer Lansky." Lansky, the "chairman of the board of organized crime," was a cofounder of the Genovese crime family with Vito's predecessor, Charles "Lucky" Luciano.

Davies listens intently to the Aronow construction legend, and then laughs. He says that someone who was able to put up large numbers of tract houses and apartment buildings in the fifties in north Jersey "would have had to have some 'cooperation'—to put it mildly." The fact that it was accomplished in seven years by a young man in his late twenties? "No one," Davies explains, "could have done that alone during that time, especially a man without money behind him."

For a contractor merely to survive in this environment he would have had to play ball with the mob to a certain extent, Davies believes. To flourish and expand, he would have to be "in bed with them, unless he had an independent financial base."

Aronow had no such financial reserves. His salary when he worked for Shirley's family was the same pay he received as a physical education teacher at a Brooklyn junior high school. A few years later, when he started Aronow Construction, he was the father of two young children. Shirley's father was barely surviving in the industry and went out of business just a few years after Aronow left. Don's own parents, according to Michael Aronow, ran a gas station. Yet Don Aronow's successes were, by any standard, astounding.

Eric Sharp's investigative efforts provide more details. He hears from his "connected" source that Aronow was a Mafia-controlled contractor while in New Jersey. He also learns that Don fled to Puerto Rico in 1959 because "he had taken large amounts of money from the mob. Money that was going through his companies, a lot of it was sticking to his fingers. Phenomenal amounts of mob money. They found out about it, and they were very unhappy about it. It got very unhealthy for him to stay around." The Aronows fled to San

Juan. Some power behind the scenes reconciled Aronow with the mob, and he returned to New Jersey and resumed his construction activities.

Interestingly, Aronow's permanent "retirement" from the construction business a year-and-a-half later coincided with a bloody Mafia turf war going on in the northern New Jersey construction industry. Winter 1961 saw the skirmishes escalate to such violence that many mobsters and their affiliates fled the area. It was a state of siege. James Truly, the Chief of Police of Union, recalls how the docile, mob-controlled area suddenly turned into a brutal battleground. "It's ironic," he says. "I happen to have a brother-in-law who was slightly involved with them years ago, he handled the book for the area. He went on to own the Halfway House restaurant in Mountainside. He testified in the Kefauver hearings in Congress on the mob. Testified under the name Carmine Brooks. He knew the whole crew, but he's dead now. But a lot of the tidbits I know was because of him."

The chief doesn't remember Aronow, but he does recall that in early 1961 the town of Union, where Aronow's office was located, was the focal point of a statewide mob battle for control of the New Jersey construction industry. The area had been controlled by Gerardo "Jerry" Catena, the number two man in the Brooklyn Genovese crime family. Suddenly, a Mafia upstart, Simone "Sam the Plumber" DeCalvacante invaded the territory.

Those on the losing end of such a struggle would clearly have an incentive to get out of the area quickly. Especially someone like Aronow who already had one strike against him and probably couldn't count on the support of his own crime family. "So who won the war for the construction business—Sam the Plumber or Jerry Catena?" I ask.

"Sam the Plumber," Truly says. "You know he still runs this whole area."

Being on the wrong side in a turf war was bad enough for wiseguys, but at least they knew violence was part of their "job" when they signed on. For mob business associates and front people, who felt they were insulated from the darker side of their crime family's business, it could be a nightmare.

When things got too hot, many fled south. According to former Miami FBI head Ken Whittaker, the word was out in New York and New Jersey that Miami Beach offered much-needed refuge. In addition to the northern New Jersey construction war, there were also two brutal mob battles going on in Brooklyn during the same period.

Mob business associates and wiseguys fleeing for their lives went to Miami Beach's Americana Hotel to seek the protection of the most powerful man in all of organized crime: Meyer Lansky.

Next to the Americana was the Singapore Hotel. There Lansky conducted his business. "Lansky had his office at the Singapore," says Whittaker. "And he used to walk over to the Americana and sit in the lobby all the time. He saved a lot of wiseguys. If Meyer granted you sanctuary, nobody would dare touch you. Nobody."

After their departure from New Jersey for the Virgin Islands in the winter of 1961, the Aronows soon wound up at the Americana.

The hotel was more than just a safe haven. It was the "in" place for wiseguys. "The Fountainebleau [Hotel] had fallen on really bad days and the smart money guys used to stay at the Americana," comments Whittaker. Hardly the place one would expect to find a multimillionaire with a wife and three small children who were used to living in a luxurious, custom-built home.

The suggestion that Aronow had finally been forced out of New Jersey during a bloody Mafia turf war answered many questions. It explains why a man with his drive for money would—at the age of thirty-three—abruptly walk away from a business "that made millions" and move to a hotel room in what was then a sleepy retirement town. It also explains why Aronow contacted Lenny Sendelsky so soon after he left and suggested that they start up again, but with Aronow in Florida. And why Sendelsky, a twenty-eight-year-old construction superintendent would be reluctant to resume a relationship with his "gold dust twin"—even with the lure of a partnership.

After more than half a year of calling the Americana home, Aronow finally left. He bought a house but didn't have to move far. It was four blocks away, still close enough for Lansky's protection.

On a hunch that Aronow's mob connections didn't end when he moved to Miami, I call Brownie at his office at Cigarette. "How well known was it that Don had connections with wiseguys?" I ask.

"Oh, I don't know," he says slowly. There's silence, and then, "I don't think it was any great big secret. Don knew lots of those guys."

Brownie first met some of Aronow's mob friends in the early sixties. "The first year Don and I showed at the New York boat show, in 1965, we had a really big-time guy," he recalls. "Dominic Ciaffone. His gang name was Swats Mulligan. He used to come up and sit in the booth. I didn't know exactly who he was, but he had something to do with organized labor and stuff from New Jersey."

Swats came often to visit Aronow when he owned his boat company Donzi and then Magnum. "I met that one guy on countless occasions," Brownie says. "He spent a lot of time with Don at the office. He'd hang around sometimes for six hours at a time."

One time, Brownie and Aronow were in a restaurant with Swats in Fort Lauderdale. Swats kept staring at one of the customers at the next table. "He said, 'I know that fuckin' guy.' He promptly gets up and goes over and says to the guy, 'Didn't I put five bullets into you in an elevator?' And the guy said, 'Yeah, Swats, how ya doin'?' Swats said, 'I thought you were dead,' and he says, 'No, I lived, I'm fine.' And they both laughed."

Dominic "Swats Mulligan" Ciaffone was "a sinister-looking motherfucker," Brownie recalls. "He had those eyes. He used to tell all kinds of stories about making strikes and breaking strikes. He talked about—whatever you call that kind of ice pick with a crossways handle. They used to cut those things off, shorten them up so that two or three inches stuck out. He said you could tell you got a good hit if you could hear the air coming out of the lungs. When everybody else was fistfighting, they were fighting with those things."

Swats was a mob enforcer and hit man according to Bob Magoon. Aronow once told Magoon a story of how Swats broke into a union in Brooklyn. "They sent Dominic and this other guy to this hall," Bob Magoon recounts, "and there's this big guy at the front door who won't let them in. And another guy next to him. The big guy says, 'No way you're going to get in there.'

"Dominic was not a big guy, but he turns around on the guy, walks up to him with an ice pick in his hand, and whoosh! Gets him right in the lung, you know. Gets the other, whoosh! The two of them drop like flies and Dominic looks at his friend and says, 'See, I told you there'd be no problem,' and they walked right in. When Don told me that story, he said, 'I want to be on that guy's good side.'"

Pete Clemente, a former FBI agent and now a lawyer in Miami, is familiar with Swats Mulligan. Clemente worked Organized Crime in New York and Florida and speaks fluent Sicilian. "Swats Mulligan used to come down to Florida quite often," he says. "If there's anything I'm sure of, it's that Swats Mulligan is a member of the LCN [La Cosa Nostra]. He was a 'made' member of the outfit, no question about that."

Being a "made" man is a great honor in the underworld. While many men may be associated with a crime family or involved in some way with its activities, only a select few are officially brought in as members. They must be of Italian extraction to be "made." The initiation ceremony varies, but it's said to involve pricking the candidate's finger with a pin or sword to draw blood and having him swear an oath of secrecy. Membership is for life. As Jimmy "the Weasel" Fratianno once put it, "you go in alive and go out dead."

Once a man is officially made, his status is greatly elevated. He receives a share of the family's take on its illegal activities. He has the protection of his family behind him and is extended "respect" by the organization wherever he goes. No other crime family can touch him or encroach on his territory. If anyone does, the full wrath and power of the organization will come down on him.

Clemente expresses regret that he didn't keep his LCN cards from his FBI days. He explains that the LCN card "could contain the name and address of the individual, date and place of birth, various associates. His position in the organization—whether he was a *capodecina*, soldier, or a *soldo capo*, or underboss or what. It would have a history of his criminal activities, if he had a record, and the area that he would usually frequent."

Fortunately, New Jersey SCI's Justin Dentino still has old LCN records. He says Swats was definitely a high-level member of the Mafia. "Subject deceased," he reads from the file. "Green eyes, looked Irish. Five-seven, two hundred ten pounds. Had a winter place on one hundred twenty-third Street in North Miami. FBI number 208775, date of birth 3/24/1903. It says here his main area of expertise was in labor-racketeering and he had a hidden interest in a record company."

"Labor-racketeering" is a catchall phrase for the ways the mob can control an industry by influencing labor practices. In the construction business, it can involve offering liberal financing to contractors. Building requires a strong cash base. Rapid expansion of a construction company, the type of growth Aronow achieved, requires almost an unlimited supply of capital.

Labor-racketeers often take over unions by force and intimidation to gain access to pension funds. But the most common ploy involves using the union as a weapon against contractors and other employers. Once their people are in control, the mob can then extort immense sums from builders by simply threatening strikes or sabotage. Naturally, mob-affiliated builders didn't have such problems. Aronow, according to those who worked with him in New Jersey, never experienced union difficulties or sabotage.

Swats's involvement in the record business may also explain the mystery surrounding the death of famous singer Jackie Wilson. According to Brownie, "Swats Mulligan owned Jackie Wilson." In 1975,

Wilson collapsed on stage during a performance and spent nine years in a permanent vegetative state until his death. Doctors were never able to determine the precise nature of Wilson's condition—they thought he might have had a heart attack—and he never recovered. But just prior to his "attack," Brunswick executives Nat Turnapol and Carmine De Noia had been indicted by a federal grand jury investigating the company for allegedly failing to issue royalties to its artists. Because of his sudden comatose condition, Wilson was unable to testify at the 1976 trial, which found Turnapol guilty. The conviction was later reversed on appeal.

Despite many successful albums, neither Wilson nor his family have ever received a single penny from the record company, according to a 1988 investigative report on *Entertainment Tonight.* The producers of the Eddie Murphy movie *Coming to America* told *Entertainment Tonight* that they sent royalty payments for use of a Wilson song to CBS Records, which now owns the label, though it pays a licensing fee to Brunswick. Wilson's family says they never received those payments either, according to the report.

When asked in 1988 about the Wilson situation by *20/20,* a spokesman for Brunswick said that records pertaining to Wilson's twenty-year recording career had been destroyed at the time of the 1974 federal investigation. They were also at a loss to explain how Nat Turnapol's son got writing credits on some of Wilson's records, even though he was only four years old at the time. Jackie Wilson died in 1984 having never regained consciousness.

"I always thought that [situation with Wilson's illness] was real suspicious," muses Brownie. "I always likened it to the Sonny Liston thing, where the mob bought him and he didn't take a dive when he was supposed to and he OD'd although he didn't use drugs." Brownie suggests that Swats may have thought Wilson was going to talk to the grand jury and arranged to have him kept permanently quiet.

Don Aronow had a very unusual friend in Swats Mulligan. Not many people can count Mafia assassins among their circle of acquaintances. The relationship evidently afforded certain privileges. In 1967, Don was made privy to confidential Mafia plans involving a murder.

One morning Aronow received a phone call at his Donzi Marine office. When he hung up, he started laughing and told Brownie that the call was about a mutual friend of theirs, John "Johnny Futto" Biello. The caller told Aronow that if Johnny Futto owed him any money, he'd better collect it that day. "It really cracked Don up," Brownie recalls. "It seemed pretty bizarre to me. The next day Futto was shot dead, and all of a sudden it made sense."

John Biello's body was found on March 18, 1967, in a Miami Beach parking lot. There were four bullets in it. The hit was described by Vincent "the Fat Man" Teresa, who was the number three man in the New England mob at the time, in his autobiography *My Life in the Mafia*.

Biello had been a captain in the Vito Genovese family and a friend of Joe "Bananas" Bonanno, the Brooklyn don and Mafia "Commission" member. In 1964, Bonanno told Biello that he was going to consolidate all the New York families under his control by "whacking out" some bosses.

"Biello was a treacherous bastard," Vincent Teresa wrote. "He was one of those who tipped off the bosses about what Bonanno was planning to do. Then, when the mob kidnapped Bonanno and held him while the old dons decided what to do with him, Biello was one of those who voted to have Bonanno whacked out. Bonanno never forgave Biello for his treachery."

Joe Bonanno's philosophy, according to Teresa, was "to put people who rubbed him wrong, to sleep. . . . Make the guy think you're his friend until the right time comes, the right setup, and then you make your move like a tiger. That was what Bonanno did with Biello. He never let him know there were any hard feelings. Then it happened."

Vincent Teresa met Bonanno at the airport in Miami and drove him to the Dream Bar Restaurant. There a Genovese wiseguy talked with Bonanno privately, and Bonanno then left immediately for the airport for a late-night flight back to Arizona. "It was either the next day or two days later," Teresa wrote, "when I read in the paper that they had found Biello's body. . . . Now Biello was a big man. He had interests in a record company, and he was the hidden owner of the old Peppermint Lounge in New York and another in Miami that made a bundle out of the twist craze. He was a millionaire with a lot of influence, but he was still a walking dead man as far as Bonanno was concerned."

Knowing that someone had been targeted for murder on the orders of a Mafia chieftain is not information that the typical person has. Yet, Don Aronow knew about the planned hit on Johnny Futto just hours after Joe Bonanno left Florida on an eleven P.M. red-eye flight to Arizona.

· · ·

Aronow was close to other high-ranking Genovese members besides Swats. In the sixties, he used to go deer hunting in upstate New York with Joey Pagano, a convicted heroin trafficker. Pagano is no ordinary "made" guy. According to the *Valachi Papers*, Joey Pagano made his Mafia career by executing a man in 1952 for the notorious Charles "Lucky" Luciano.

Luciano, with his childhood friend Meyer Lansky, seized virtual control of the Mafia in the U.S. in 1931 with a carefully executed "mass extermination" of forty Cosa Nostra leaders. After he snared the highest position in the Mafia for himself, Luciano chose Vito Genovese as his underboss.

Luciano fell victim to Thomas Dewey's crusade against racketeering, and in 1946 he was deported to Italy, though he continued to influence mob activities in the U.S. While in Italy, Luciano expressed the wish that Eugene Giannini, a narcotics trafficker, be killed because Luciano considered him an informer. (Lansky actually made the suggestion to Luciano). Vito Genovese then told Joseph Valachi to hit Giannini. Vito had an ulterior motive. It was a favor for Luciano, but it also helped Vito consolidate his growing power within the family.

Valachi got three East Harlem kids—rising hoodlums in line for membership in the family—for the actual execution. Two were brothers: Pasquale "Pat" and Joey Pagano. The third was Valachi's own nephew. The hit went down. On September 20, 1952, the body of Eugenio Giannini was found in a New York City gutter. He had been shot in the head.

According to Valachi's memoirs, "the Cosa Nostra membership books, we call them books but there ain't no real books, it's just the expression we use," had been closed since the early 1930s. After World War II there were a number of "proposed members," but the books weren't officially opened until 1954. Among those brought in by Valachi were Pat and Joe Pagano.

The Pagano brothers also played a role in what may have been the Mafia's initial contact with the infamous "French Connection." In 1952, Valachi sent Pat Pagano to Marseilles to make contact with Dominique Reissent, a Corsican who imported morphine base into France for conversion into heroin. A deal was made to purchase fifteen kilos of heroin, worth about $165,000. When the shipment arrived in the U.S., Valachi paid off the participants. They were given a choice of money or drugs as payment. Joey and his brother opted for the "junk," according to Valachi, and he gave them two kilos of pure heroin.

It was only the start of an ambitious career for Pagano. As a member of the Genovese crime family, Joey has had a diversified career "in labor-racketeering, entertainment, shylocking, gambling, and extortion," says NYPD Intelligence's Lt. Jack Clark. "He was a money-maker, he brought big money into the family. He was one of the biggest money-makers ever in the Genovese family."

Joey's bailiwick was northern New Jersey, the Bronx, parts of Westchester and Rockland counties. He had a place in upstate New York, in the Catskills, where he took his friends hunting, says Clark. There are suggestions that Pagano is still active. According to Clark, his name was mentioned in several newspaper articles regarding a 1987 mob hit in New York.

Another man who often went hunting with Aronow and Pagano was Moishe Levy. While Levy is not a member of a crime family, Clark comments, "they say he's affiliated with the Genovese family on the fringes." The alleged association is due in part to Levy's apparent friendship with mafiosi and particularly the fact that he had been partners in a record company with "Tommy Ryan" Eboli, the number two man in the Genovese crime family. Eboli murdered "Tony Bender" Strollo in 1962 to assume his position as underboss to Vito Genovese. Ten years later, Eboli himself was murdered.

Apparently Don Aronow's mob connections weren't a well-guarded secret. A number of his friends and associates were aware that he was close to wiseguys.

Aronow's pilot, Randy Riggs, says that Don once told him that he did something for the mob back in New Jersey and that they had given him a nickname that meant "balls of steel" in Italian. "So I'm sure that there was a depth to him," Riggs says. "It wasn't out in the open, and I think that whatever happened before Florida with the Mafia, with the Ciaffone guy that came and visited him at Donzi— whatever relationship he had with those kind of people grew out of the early days."

Riggs explains that over the years "Don was very good. If he was involved in what some people speculate he was involved in—with the Mafia and all that—he kept it out of the office. He was very good. He didn't involve anybody in it directly or indirectly."

Jerry Engelman says one person in particular was concerned about stories of Aronow's mob ties getting around: Willie Meyers. After the murder, Meyers expressed alarm that such relationships might reflect poorly on Vice President George Bush and Secretary of State George Shultz, both of whom he became close to after the Aronow shooting.

"He was real sensitive about anything [about Aronow] that could be construed as negative against Bush," Engelman recalls. "Early on, I had gone up to talk to Willie and asked him about a Mafia connection [with the murder], and as soon as I said it, Willie said, 'Well, Don wasn't Mr. Nice Guy, he hung around with a lot of those guys.' And he rattled off shit like names, dates, places, Mafia stuff." In particular, Meyers specifically mentioned Don's friendship with Swats Mulligan.

Engelman asked Meyers if the Vice President was aware of Aronow's close relationship with a Mafia hit man, but Willie declined to answer, suggesting instead that Jerry should put the Aronow murder out of his thoughts.

EIGHT

Long before Don Johnson and *Miami Vice*, there was Meyer Lansky. And before Miami was the home for dopers and their drugs, there were wiseguys and their money. Although the flamboyant escapades of the druggies have riveted the crime spotlight, the Mafia still retains its insidious presence. As always the mob works in a covert way, leaving the high-flying smugglers to capture the covers of *Time* magazine, the attention of law enforcement, and the outrage of the public.

"Don't get lost with all this narcotics stuff," Arthur Nehrbass, former head of MetroDade's Organized Crime Bureau, advises me. "There still are a lot of organized crime cases that are nonnarcotics that are being made here all the time. Virtually every major American Mafia family is here in south Florida in some form or another."

The Mafia influence in Miami goes back to the forties. It came to fruition when Meyer Lansky and Tampa boss Santo Trafficante, Jr., made their pact with Batista to open more casinos in Havana. By the fifties, the mob was a dominant force in Miami.

Lansky was the architect for the deal that created a financial bridge between Miami and Havana. In 1952, Lansky agreed to restore Batista, the ousted ruler of Cuba, to power. In return the dictator would allow him to set up his casinos. Batista agreed wholeheartedly. The sum of $3 million that Lansky deposited in Batista's Swiss bank account and the promise of 50 percent of the take was an offer he couldn't refuse. Working behind the scenes in Cuban politics, Lansky assured Batista's recapture of the presidency despite strong opposition.

From then on Batista would deal only with Lansky, who in turn represented the interests of all the American Mafia families in the casinos. Chartered flights brought high-stakes gamblers to Havana from all over the United States. The profits poured out of Havana and into Miami. The operation was so successful and there was so much money around that Lansky left New York and moved to south Florida.

Then Castro came along in 1959 and shut it all down. But by that time, Miami was mobbed-up and Meyer Lansky was the biggest man in town. Or more precisely, in the underworld. He had shown the mob that they could, in a sense, buy entire nations. Later, it was said that Lansky did in the Bahamas with Prime Minister Pindling what he had done in Cuba with Batista.

There were other reasons why south Florida was quickly becoming a mob magnet. "It was an emerging state," Nehrbass says. "There was lots of money coming here, and whenever there's a lot of money coming in, the mob is going to be around." Making it all the more attractive was the fact that law enforcement was lax. "Miami was a vacuum that anybody could move into," Nehrbass explains. "Anyone looking for investment could come here without any problem because the state wasn't controlled by any family. It was and still is an 'open area.'" Most other mobbed-up cities are considered "closed."

Since the city was officially "open," many wiseguys came to vacation in Miami, striking up relationships and deals with members from other families, and even retiring along the Gold Coast. As one agent says, "As far as the mob is concerned, Miami is the sixth borough of New York City."

Edna Buchanan has followed the Aronow case with passing interest. She was on leave when the murder happened and so she didn't cover it. She mentions that a friend was in Geneva at the time of the murder and that Swiss TV broke into the regular programming with the news of Aronow's death.

Edna—as she is called by everyone in south Florida—is slim, blond, and could easily look at home in a *Town & Country* profile of south Floridian society. Her looks are at odds with her work. After years of being on the scene of some of Miami's most grisly murders, she has become a celebrity—Disney is doing a movie about her life. She is warm, friendly, and unaffected by her elevated status.

She agrees to see me and we meet on the fifth floor of the *Herald* building. It looks like every other newspaper office: an enormous room extending almost the length of the building, overcrowded with many drab functional-looking desks. Papers, computer printouts, and photographs are piled high on each desk.

Edna says that MetroDade Homicide hasn't made any progress on the case. "Nothing is happening at this point, they just don't know what to pursue," she comments. When I mention that I've come across information that connects Aronow with the mob, she tells me a story she heard.

Shirley Parker Aronow told some friends that after the 1961 move from New Jersey, Aronow had been making payments to a "big-time mobster." The mobster died in the early 1980s, and not long after Aronow stopped the payments. This went against the code of the underworld. Because the mobster's wife was still living, Don was supposed to keep making payments to the widow. Some representatives for the widow told him he had to keep paying. He refused. The men told Aronow that it would not be forgotten, and that he would be sorry he dishonored the man's memory.

Edna hasn't heard anything else to support the theory that Aronow had Organized Crime (OC) links, but she suggests several contacts. She wishes me good luck, although she says she thinks it's going to be tough getting anything on Aronow. "This guy's been in the public eye for twenty-five years," she points out. "Something would've come out." Then she adds, "You would think."

On the morning of his murder, Aronow received a call and spoke about his reluctance to continuing "writing letters."

I contact Ken Whittaker, one of the men whom Edna had suggested, hoping he can shed some light on the role Aronow may have held in the mob. Whittaker, an FBI agent for twenty-seven years, started his career in the New York area and has more than a passing familiarity with La Cosa Nostra. An attorney, he now runs Whittaker Investigations with his son, Ken, Jr., a former Miami-area police officer.

Reluctant to mention Aronow's name, I recap that a well-known owner of a company may owe his success to a connection with organized crime. He receives a telephone call and his response is that he "can't keep writing letters," that his name "is getting known up there."

"In other words, he doesn't want to do any more endorsements for them," Whittaker says. "You say he's a pretty prominent figure in the state. Political?" he asks. He explains that there's a significant difference depending upon whether the political party the man is associated with is in power or not. I tell him the man is a business-man connected with an incumbent national figure.

He says it sounds like the man is getting concerned about blowing his clean cover. "His name is surfacing too much," he explains. "And he's getting worried that he might be publicly associated with the wrong people."

He suggests that the businessman would be "a shill, a beard, perfect to call on someone in the administration because he is so clean looking." He pauses, then asks again, "He's got a pretty good image? He's up there?"

I say the man had clout in the highest levels of the U.S. govern-ment.

"Well, now you're making me more impressed," he comments. "You can use it in several ways. One of the most popular I know would have been to really twist him. That's what they do. Take years to twist 'em. They keep him in a position where he would never endorse anything bad. And so the guy is swayed to go along. If he does that too often, which is what it sounds like this guy is telling these people—things that have been blown up or things that have become questionable have surfaced—then he's telling them, listen, I'm getting too well-known. I'm losing all my effectiveness."

Ultimately, he explains, the real problem is that "the beard is always concerned about himself. These guys, you know, they like to play with fire, get all the good, but all of a sudden they see the walls potentially come tumbling down." The description seems to fit Aronow's telephone conversation on the morning of his murder.

Whittaker gives me a rundown of the ways in which the mob uses "legitimate" businessmen or clean fronts. He explains that each member of the crime families has a personal preference for one type of scam or racket, and then he rattles off the most popular methods, including taking over a legitimate company with good credit, running up big debts, then declaring bankruptcy; forcing a company to buy supplies only from other mob-controlled companies; running hi-jacked goods through otherwise legitimate firms; insuring a company to the hilt, then torching it.

Then there's one of the cornerstones of mob financial activities:

money laundering. Certain companies are highly suitable for laundering large amounts of illegally generated cash: fast-food restaurants, vending machines, auto dealerships. Big-ticket businesses that often deal in cash are good for laundering.

When I ask about the high-performance boat business, Whittaker laughs and comments, "Boat business. Huh. That's the things people do. You're right. I would say you would not be wrong on speculation since you tell me a boat business. You could coast on a hull number because one of the worst things in the world, the toughest things for law enforcement [to unravel], are those boats with the hull numbers."

The luxury powerboat business, with its machines easily costing several hundred thousand dollars, lends itself ideally to laundering cash. One of the easiest ways is for a builder to "sell" nonexistent boats. A bagman hands over a couple of hundred thousand dollars in cash, supposedly for the purchase of an expensive boat. The boat maker writes up a bill of sale with an imaginary hull number. The builder deposits the cash, pays taxes on the money, and voilà! Dirty cash becomes clean bank deposits, and the money is free to be used as the mob wishes. Later, it's almost impossible to prove whether the boat actually existed.

Since Brownie had been a manager for Cigarette after Aronow sold the company, I ask him if he had ever noticed anything strange about the company's records. He had. "There were lots of missing hull records—who bought what boat," he recalls.

"Did you ever think that with Don hanging around with all these mobster types, they were into his companies?" I ask.

Brownie says he never thought about that since Don didn't have any need of financing. He was a pretty wealthy guy, he points out.

Maybe that was why he was wealthy, I suggest.

He hesitates, considers the suggestion, then says, "Well, that's logical, isn't it?"

Don Aronow had a proclivity for cash from his construction days on. "He usually had ten grand in his pockets at any one time," says Jerry Engelman. Lillian Aronow agrees, commenting, "He was very lucky at the track." Old Mike Kandrovicz insists that Aronow had two briefcases, at least one with $180,000 in cash in his car with him the day he died. That wasn't the only time.

Kandrovicz says Aronow asked him on a number of occasions to take briefcases of cash home with him overnight or for a weekend.

"Don always carried his money in a briefcase," he comments. "I took it to the bank and stuff like that." There were times when Old Mike took home briefcases with almost a quarter of a million dollars in cash. "That was only when somebody would buy a boat or two at Cigarette and they'd buy it at night," he says. "Those boats run into large amounts of money. And I would take it home. Don didn't want to put the money in the night box, the safe deposit box."

John Crouse, who is close to Kandrovicz, says this happened quite often. "But why would Don have some poor guy take home this ton of risk, with this kind of money?" he asks. "Old Mike could've gotten murdered for that. In fact if the people that gave Don the money cottoned on to it, they could've killed this guy in a heartbeat and gotten the money back. Now why would a guy take home or have somebody go home and stash cash, big cash amounts? Then have him bring it back the next day. When I think about it, laundering makes a lot of sense."

The *Miami Herald*'s Eric Sharp tells me that "there are people who believe Aronow was a continuing front for all sorts of illegal money activities going on down there." He adds that he heard through his "connected" source on the Alley—the same one who told him that Aronow fled New Jersey for his life—that "an old Mustache Pete" who had moved to Miami had been using Aronow's boat companies for laundering money and apparently had been doing so for years. Cigarette and other firms. But especially Cigarette."

According to Sharp's source, the Mustache Pete—a Mafia term for an old and honored member of La Cosa Nostra—owned a share of Aronow's boat businesses and Aronow had been paying him off for years. Then around 1983, the mobster died. Aronow cut off the payments. The man's family went to Aronow. Sharp relates what his source told him: "The family went to Aronow and they said, 'The family gets paid as long as you live' since the old mobster was the one that got Aronow started." Sharp's story also backs up the one that Edna Buchanan had told me about the old-time mobster who controlled Aronow. And it takes on even more significance when I discover that his source ("the brother of a very, very bad guy" from New Jersey) was Aronow protégé Bobby Saccenti.

It was Cigarette that was far and away Don's most successful company. The first time he sold the company—at its peak in 1978—the new owner, an experienced and successful boatbuilder, was unable to make the company work. So Don bought it back, cheap. If a mobster was behind any of Don's companies, Cigarette would be the one. But the question remained: who was behind it all?

. . .

Trying to find the real Don Aronow is like chasing shadows in the noonday sun. Every so often you catch a glimpse, but it quickly disappears. Aronow was so dominant a figure for so many people— over the course of several months I've had dozens of people tell me that he literally changed their lives—that everything else is obscured by the intense glare of his light. But there are shadows, and I'm convinced that they lead into a much darker world.

There had been numerous *Miami Herald* stories recounting Don Aronow's racing and business exploits over the years. There had also been a tiny item that ran in the paper in 1974. The article was about a federal grand jury investigation into mob-supported gambling. David Gerstein, the former state's attorney who came to Lillian's assistance after her husband's murder, and his protégé Richard Goodhart, had been called to testify. So had Don Aronow and his son Michael. The target of the investigation: Meyer Lansky.

Both Aronows invoked their Fifth Amendment rights and later testified only after being granted immunity. Was it simply coincidence that Aronow was subpoenaed in connection with a Lansky operation? This was the third time I had run across Lansky's name while delving into Aronow's background. Lansky had been aligned with Jerry Catena, the Genovese underboss who controlled the northern New Jersey construction industry until Sam the Plumber took over. Lansky was also the protector of the wiseguys who fled to the Americana Hotel from the New Jersey and New York mob wars in the sixties.

While not Italian, Lansky was by any account one of the most respected and feared crime bosses—the "chairman of the board of the national crime syndicate." He died in January 1983 at the age of eighty.

"Lansky was a patron for many Jewish people in the mob," says former FBI agent John Yablonsky, who was assigned to Lansky in the seventies. "He was well-known to be almost fanatical about business. He always looked for ways to make money. It was the only thing he was interested in. When he died, he was worth over four hundred million dollars—although officially his estate was valued at a hundred twenty thousand dollars. Everything else was hidden, in Switzerland or in trust with front people. He was a very complex man."

Until his death, Lansky was closely aligned with Brooklyn's Genovese crime family, the same family with which Aronow's wiseguy friends were connected. Once he left New York and moved to Florida in the fifties, Meyer established many businessmen for use as clean "front people." Many of Lansky's financial operations, in fact, relied heavily upon so-called clean businesses for mob purposes. One of his particular talents involved running skimmed Las Vegas casino profits through legitimate businesses.

"Skim" is cash illegally removed from the tables in the casinos before it gets to the counting rooms where it is offically recorded. In the sixties, Las Vegas gaming authorities estimated that Lansky skimmed $3 million cash a week. His operation was simple yet effective. A runner would pick up a briefcase in Nevada with about $200,000—the most you can usually get into a briefcase in smaller bills—and fly it to wherever it was being laundered. Yablonsky says they followed many couriers to Miami.

From Miami, the bagmen simply hired a plane, helicopter, or boat. Within hours at most, they arrived on one of the islands off the Gold Coast: the Caymans, Bahamas, British Virgin Islands, or the Netherlands Antilles. The money was deposited in secret accounts and the first leg of the operation—money movement—was complete.

Once the cash was in the bank, Lansky was free to wire the money anywhere in the world. Often the next stop was Switzerland, a frequently used ultimate repository, or Liechtenstein, a tiny principality a few hours drive from Zurich on the Austrian and Swiss borders that is gaining in popularity among drug smugglers. Often there would be a second challenge: getting the money back into the U.S. so it could be used "legitimately."

One popular method especially favored by Lansky was to arrange a "loan" from these offshore banks to a front person back in the U.S. Since tax-haven countries have strict secrecy laws, no one would know the original source of the money, and it could be used to set up a new company, buy real estate and businesses, or purchase major durable assets such as planes, helicopters, automobiles, and boats.

Although the front would sign for the asset and use it as if it were his own, it was always very clear that the property belonged to Lansky or another high-ranking mobster. It never became the property of the front person. Basically, the mob was parking its assets with people they trusted. Crime families would use the property as they saw fit. Only a front-man with a death wish would think otherwise.

Lansky's financial methods were so discreet and clever that most of his activities are still the subject of great speculation. Despite the intense interest of law enforcement over half a century, Lansky and his empire remained an enigma to the day he died.

Near the end of his life, Meyer granted a rare, brief interview. He was outside a Miami courtroom for his appearance before a grand jury. Reporters had shown up hoping to learn something about the world's most mysterious and powerful crime figure. One journalist asked if he would at least "acknowledge his financial wizardry—underworld or not."

He laughed. "No, I wouldn't. Ha ha. I'm going to the poorhouse."

Which poorhouse? the reporter asked.

Lansky smiled. "You'll spend your whole life guessing, won't you?"

Since Lansky was considered such a major OC target, there have been many agents assigned to him over fifty years, some spending just a year or two on him. Locating those who tracked him more than ten years ago proves difficult. A man in Virginia who keeps lists of former FBI agents provides some names. Many have retired or moved on to other parts of the country; some are dead. The ones I do find can't connect Aronow and Lansky.

There is no luck at the court records either. Five years after his death, Lansky's records at the Dade County Probate Court are "unavailable"—though normally they would be considered public record. When a clerk punches Lansky's name into the court's computer for me, it prints out nothing but the name. "Wow!" the clerk exclaims. "I've never seen anything like this. Somebody cleansed the whole file, every single entry. It's like the man never even existed."

Tony Fernandez, head bailiff of the probate court, says that Judge Featherstone, a Gerstein protégé, ordered the Lansky records sealed. Even after his death, Lansky's influence still extends into the heart of the judicial system.

The name Lansky reminds Fernandez of an incident involving Mrs. Lansky. "Judge Featherstone was telling her that she would get such and such an amount a month from the old man's estate," he recalls. "She was upset, she wanted it all at once and she said, 'Hey, Judge, why can't I have the whole fucking amount now?' "

Fernandez says he jumped up and said, "Ma'am, you can't talk like that in here." But the judge said, 'No, that's okay, leave her alone, this is a free country.' " Judge Featherstone also handled the Aronow will and the unusual breaking of its key provisions.

Aronow's friends have never mentioned Lansky. John Crouse laughs when I ask him if Aronow knew Lansky. I get the same reaction from many of Don's closest friends. But Knocky House, who raced with Aronow in the glory days of the late sixties, says, "Sure. Don knew Meyer Lansky from the old days." The "old days," he says, were Aronow's construction days in northern New Jersey.

Randy Riggs never saw Don with Lansky: "I just heard him talk about him. A lot of these conversations weren't directed to me. I'd just be there." Bob Magoon knew that Aronow was friendly with Lansky, but he says, "So what, I knew him, too."

Magoon was Meyer's ophthalmologist for a time. Although he can't recall who first referred Lansky to his practice, he says he enjoyed talking to him when he was in for his eye exams and that he found him to be "a quiet, simple Jewish man, very intelligent and very well read." As surprising as it sounds—before his financial genius surfaced, Lansky began his career as the founder of Murder, Inc.—many federal agents share similar impressions.

John Crouse is stunned when Magoon confirms the acquaintance. He becomes angry, saying that some of Aronow's friends have accused him of tearing apart Aronow's reputation. "Magoon said, 'Why don't you leave Don's memory alone?'" Crouse relates. "So I said, 'You reap what you sow, Magoon. If Don was friends with Meyer Lansky and all these other guys, then he was into something.'"

Crouse says he had a fight with Magoon about Lansky. "I told him, 'So you think that Meyer Lansky was this nice little old Jewish man? So much for you as a character reference, Magoon.' You know, these people think you have to make heroes out of these people even if you find they have clay feet. I like Don. Don was a colorful, dynamic guy and I miss him still. But that doesn't mean that this stuff isn't starting to unravel.

"I'm not going to make it out like it didn't happen," Crouse continues. "Don was still an animal out there. A phenomenon at sea. And building those boats. He did some incredible things in his life. Al Capone loved kids, I hear. Well, that's the way it is."

Meyer Lansky shunned the spotlight as avidly as many far less powerful people sought it. A physically small, wiry man, he always worked behind the scenes, choreographing and managing the mob's activities. His secretive ways often deluded even those who specialized in observing the Mafia's activities.

When the "Boss of Bosses," Vito Genovese, died in prison in 1969, there was a great deal of public speculation about who would become the new head of the Mafia in the U.S. But as one federal agent recalls, "the real boss of bosses was still the same—Meyer Lansky. He anointed and then removed the Italians at his will."

To many federal agents, particularly those who worked Miami, Lansky is the "one that got away." Although he was engaged in criminal activities from his teenage years, he spent only three months of his life in jail. For more than fifty years despite the best efforts of various government agencies, he held the reins of power in the organized crime underworld, nurturing it from a small group of criminals to a multibillion-dollar-a-year global empire.

Part of Lansky's success at eluding conviction was his arm's-length attitude toward his business. He usually dealt with his front people through intermediaries to shield them so that their identities are virtually impossible to determine, even now.

Pete Clemente, who during his FBI days was also assigned to Lansky, once tried unsuccessfully to bug Meyer's home to find out some of his business associates. For some reason, the bug never worked. Clemente adds, "Meyer was extremely reclusive and mild mannered. Very discreet. He used public telephones for the most part, he changed the telephones that he used. You'll never be able to figure out who he was in business with in a million years."

Feds were never even able to figure out if Lansky was a "made" man. Clemente comments, "There is a divided opinion on Meyer as to whether the Mafia made an exception and made him. Or whether he was never able to become a member because he wasn't Italian. The better opinion is that he never became a member. But nobody except Meyer and one or two people who are dead know."

Clemente adds, "He was always a gentleman. I remember one time this guy and I were doing surveillance on him and [Lansky's second wife] Teddy asked my partner, 'What's a nice young man like you doing in the FBI?' And Meyer told him he would be a lot better off working for IBM."

When Lansky died, many law enforcement OC experts believe that his empire was taken over by an alleged lieutenant, Miami attorney Alvin Malnik. "There are a lot of opinions about this, but that is just what they are—opinions," says Art Nehrbass. "And to give you any concrete facts I would be hard pressed to do it. They are just theories, [but] the smart money says that Malnik took over for Lansky, but nobody could prove that."

John Sampson, who met Meyer on one of his OC watches, says, "Intelligence on Meyer was very, very sketchy. And I don't know if there is anybody who can give you a good definition of his empire." Sampson says he thinks it would be impossible to determine the identity of front people involved with Meyer. He points out that while his group at MetroDade thought Al Malnik was tied into Lansky, "we had a running joke that the prize would go to anyone who ever could get a picture of Lansky and Malnik together." No one ever claimed the prize.

. . .

While the police may never have ascertained a definite connection between Lansky and Malnik, Don Aronow believed there was one. "Yeah, Don was friendly with Al Malnik," says Randy Riggs, oblivious to Malnik's reputation with law enforcement. "He would talk about Al Malnik and Meyer Lansky. They had a kind of relationship according to Don."

Riggs doesn't know whether Malnik and Aronow had a business association. "They just spent time together doing favors for each other," he explains. "Back in the late seventies Malnik had a helicopter and sometimes he would use Don's helicopter or Don would use his. Don didn't talk to Al Malnik every day but . . ." His voice trails off.

Aronow frequently asked Riggs to fly Malnik to various places using Don's helicopter. "He [Malnik] built a ranch up in Boca Raton, a really elaborate, huge farm with all kinds of stuff on it. So I'd fly him up there," Riggs says. Although he never flew Malnik to the Caribbean, Riggs says he's sure Don went there with Malnik's helicopter.

Riggs often flew Aronow to the Caribbean. Sometimes it was a quick trip at lunchtime. One of the first trips he took with Don and his mistress was right after he began working for him in 1975. "I flew Missy and him over. I had my camera and I was taking pictures of him and Missy. Toward the end of the three-day trip my camera disappeared. It was locked up in the damned helicopter and I always suspected that Don took it because at the end of the trip he handed me two hundred dollars as a tip."

Riggs believes that for some reason Don didn't want anybody having the photographs. "And he didn't know who I was at the time because I had just started working for him," he explains. "Don controlled everything about him. If he wasn't happy with something, he controlled it. He could've taken the camera and not paid me a nickel, but I believe the two hundred dollars was for the camera, no doubt in my mind."

Alvin I. Malnik, Miami restaurateur, multimillionaire, lawyer, jet-setter, claims to be a misunderstood guy. A man too friendly for his own good. That's how he explains the enormous OC cloud that has hung over him since he made his first million two years after graduating from the University of Miami Law School.

The owner of Miami's famous The Forge Restaurant, Malnik has many well-known friends and acquaintances including the royal family of Saudi Arabia; Italian actor Giancarlo Giannini; Meshulam Riklis, the superwealthy head of Rapid-American Corporation and perhaps more notably the husband of Pia Zadora; the ubiquitous Brooke Shields. His client roster has included people such as Sammy Davis, Jr. and Jimmy Hoffa.

But investigators say he also has links with members of organized crime, specifically Meyer Lansky, Vincent "Jimmy Blue Eyes" Alo, and Sam "Mr. Miami Beach" Cohen, who was indicted for skimming millions from the Flamingo Casino with Lanksy in the early seventies. (Cohen went to prison; Meyer, of course, didn't.)

Of these unfortunate associations, Malnik told the *Miami Herald* in 1982 that "the friendships I chose to make were perhaps not provident or in my best interests. If I like somebody, I like somebody. I don't go around examining if this relationship is good for me or bad for me. . . . Maybe it's naive. I've always been that way." He called the alleged Malnik-Lansky alliance "an incredible, inescapable myth, an albatross around my neck."

Despite their suspicions, the feds were never able to put Lansky and Malnik together. Most of the government's witnesses to the relationship were convicts and payrolled informants. But at least one time the feds came close to getting the hard evidence with a credible witness. A man giving a deposition remarked offhandedly that Al Malnik had brought him to a restaurant to meet with Meyer Lansky. The man said he left as soon as he realized it was the godfather of organized crime.

The feds were thrilled. Pinning anything on Lansky and an associate was almost impossible, and now they had an executive linking the two. A few days later the witness suddenly recanted his story. He said he couldn't swear that it was Lansky whom he met with Malnik.

According to the former *Miami Herald* "Mafia hunter" and investigative reporter Hank Messick, Malnik was instrumental in helping to manage Lansky's vast empire and was "involved in complicated syndicate deals ranging around the world." Malnik's alleged involvement with Lansky first came to the attention of the FBI through an illegal wiretap of Malnik's office in 1963. They reportedly heard wide-ranging discussions on such topics as plans to "buy" the Bahamian government, details of stolen FBI reports, and a conversation regarding Jimmy Hoffa.

On October 27, 1979, Malnik was secretly recorded by the FBI as part of the Abscam investigation. The discussion was the purchase of the Aladdin Hotel in Las Vegas, which gambling officials had ordered sold because of suspected organized crime infiltration. The prospective buyer was an Arab sheik, in reality undercover FBI agent Tony Amoroso.

In the FBI tapes, according to the *Miami Herald,* Malnik said the hotel would cost $105 million, plus $10 million extra in cash "to swing the deal." When asked who would get the bonus, Malnik responded, "Nobody's gonna volunteer that they're receiving it, because the people who are going to receive it, uh, will never under any circumstances be identified or acknowledged as having received it." FBI agents say the money was a secret payoff, most probably to Lansky, though Malnik denied it and was not charged with any crime.

Shortly before Lansky died, Malnik missed being the victim of an apparent mob hit. The *Chicago Sun-Times* reported on March 7, 1982, that "a bomb that wrecked a yellow Rolls-Royce at Miami's posh Cricket Club has investigators eyeing the possibility that Chicago mobsters had a hand in the caper.

"The bomb, obviously meant for the car's owner, Miami mob figure Alvin Malnik, went off Wednesday as a parking valet started the engine. The car jockey was blown from the auto but survived. . . . Since Malnik is a protégé of longtime Miami crime chief Meyer Lansky, the best guess is that young-Turk Miami mobsters were sending a message to the aging Lansky: 'We're taking over.'" Not long after the bombing, Malnik left the country for several years and lived in the Middle East.

When Don Aronow heard about the car bombing, "he shook his head and laughed," Randy Riggs remembers, "and said, 'Al's gonna get it yet.'"

Ken Whittaker invited me to drop by his office at the Whittaker Building in Miami. He's surprised to learn that the man I've been investigating is Don Aronow. "My grandson went to preschool with his son," Whittaker says. "My wife and I saw Don and Lillian the day before he was killed. We were in line at the movies. I wanted him to talk to George Bush for me."

Whittaker's even more surprised when I tell him that it had come to my attention that Aronow not only hung around with wiseguys but possibly did business with them. His eyebrows shoot up at the suggestion that a man so close to Vice President George Bush might have mob ties. He grabs the phone and calls another former agent and they talk about Aronow. Had the other man ever heard of any connection between Aronow and the mob?

The agent says that he had questioned Aronow in 1976 after John "Don Giovanni" Roselli was murdered. Roselli was a capo mafioso in the Los Angeles family who at one time had been assigned to smooth things in Hollywood for Chicago crime boss Sam Giancana. With Giancana, Roselli was also involved in the so-called CIA-Mafia plot to assassinate Fidel Castro.

Roselli had evidently fallen out of favor after he testified before Congress on the matter. He was found in a 55-gallon drum floating in Miami's Biscayne Bay. His legs had been cut off and stuffed in beside his body. Just before he was set to be questioned, Sam Giancana was shot to death in his home in Chicago, presumably over the same matter.

Some people believe that Roselli and Giancana were murdered not because of the feeble 1963 plot to murder Castro, but to cover up a deeper, far more explosive secret: that Meyer Lansky and Santo Trafficante had ordered the murder of John Kennedy because of his administration's vigorous (and effective) pursuit of organized crime. Consistent with this idea is the fact that Jack Ruby knew both Lansky and Trafficante. The mob was particularly incensed that after their helping John Kennedy with the presidency, he allowed his younger brother to repay them by attempting to break up organized crime.

Whittaker asks the agent why he had interviewed Aronow about the Roselli murder. The agent says he couldn't remember, that it might simply have been because Roselli had been found floating near Aronow's company. Meyer Lansky was also interviewed about the Roselli hit, the agent adds.

When he finishes his conversation, Whittaker says he's going to check some of his sources to see if anything pops up about Aronow. He doubts that anything will come of it. "Meyer was very careful," he says. "That's why he never got caught."

Later I ask around the Alley if the FBI ever talked with anyone else about Roselli. Aronow appears to have been the only one questioned.

A few days pass and Whittaker apologizes that he hasn't come up with anything. He explains, "I spoke to one of my sources and he says no connection to his knowledge [between Aronow and Lansky]. The other guy that has knowledge about the Florida connection— you know, whether the DEA would have anything on our boy over on the Beach who's been dead now for five years—you know what I mean? He hasn't gotten back to me." Whittaker talks in code: the "Beach" is Miami Beach, the "boy" is Lansky.

"So we don't have anything there yet," he concludes. "The other guy is out of pocket. I've reached out to someone in New York, New Jersey, and they haven't come back to me yet. Let me keep pushing out the word." Meanwhile, he gives me another contact to try: Jarvis "Jerry" Armstrong, another former FBI agent. "Try Jerry, but he hasn't been in Miami for almost twenty years."

• • •

Jarvis Armstrong was assigned to surveil Lansky from 1968 to 1970. Then he left Miami. He's retired now and lives in Kentucky. He says that the Bureau started tracking Lansky back in the 1920s, remarking that they had several rooms filled floor to ceiling with files on his activities. I ask if he ever made a connection between Lansky and Don Aronow.

"Did I ever hear of Lansky with Don Aronow?" Armstrong repeats my question thoughtfully. "Yeah, I ran across that name, spelled A-r-o-n-o-w. I came across that file. I recall that one. He was, saw him with him [Lansky] in south Miami when he [Lansky] lived in south Miami. Saw him with him, you know? Took the tag number. [Ran] the tag number. Informants, we had where he [Lansky] went, places he frequented."

"You saw him with Aronow on a number of occasions?" I ask.

"Right."

"Do you have any idea what Aronow was doing with Lansky—you saw them at business meetings?"

"Any time he [Lansky] was talking to somebody, it was business, I can assure you of that," Armstrong states positively. He says Meyer "seemed to be very friendly, a relative or something. He was awfully friendly with him [Aronow]." He adds that the two men shook hands and were very cordial with each other.

Armstrong says he has no idea what kind of business the two men might have had. "He was *with* Aronow," he emphasizes. "That's the thing. He [Lansky] talked to a lot of people, and sometimes you wouldn't find out till years later what was going on."

Armstrong explains that Lansky would have good use for a clean businessman, especially in financing. "They put him in business, get him to money-launder, filter it through there," he says. "Maybe a guy wanted this done, wanted that done. You know he had—Lansky had—all kind of contacts."

Since Armstrong left Florida in 1970, he is unaware that Aronow had become an important figure in Miami and a government contractor for the Vice Presidential South Florida Joint Drug Task Group. Nor had he heard about the murder. After a brief rundown of Aronow's life up to Blue Thunder, I relate the events of his last day, including the message that the killer gave to Aronow in the office.

"Hmmm. Sounds like they were telling him 'you forgot your friends,'" Armstrong says. "Whatever they told him in there was a message that meant something to him. Those guys play rough. There's no way out, they use you up."

"Do you think they were exploiting his connection with George Bush?" I ask. "Is that something the mob does?"

"Yeah," Armstrong states.

"Does it surprise you that a Lansky associate was friendly with Bush?"

"Well"—Armstrong pauses—"Lansky had a lot of friends in high places that I don't have."

"To say that Meyer had influence is the understatement of the century," says John Sampson. Over the years allegations have been made linking Lansky to the CIA, Naval Intelligence, Papa Doc Duvalier, Senator Barry Goldwater, LBJ aide Bobby Baker, and innumerable prominent businessmen including Huntington Hartford and the elusive billionaire D. K. Ludwig, once considered the richest man in the world.

Lansky may have even had power over J. Edgar Hoover. According to journalist Pete Hamill, some wiseguys claimed that Lansky got photographs of Hoover, a closet homosexual, which insured Meyer immunity for the rest of his life. "During the thirties, when Lansky was reorganizing the Prohibition mobs into a multinational corporation, Hoover never bothered them," Hamill wrote.

In later years as the mob diversified, Hoover refused even to acknowledge its existence—preferring instead to look for "Reds" under every bed. His steadfast refusal to deal with the mob for over thirty years has never been explained. It was only after his death in 1972 that the Justice Department made any headway at all in its efforts to indict Meyer Lansky.

Throughout the years Lansky's name has surfaced in the most surprising circumstances. He may have had a longtime connection with former president Richard Nixon. Nixon lived in Lansky-Batista–controlled Havana for a time in 1940 and once considered opening a law office there. Instead, he moved to Washington and asked for a $61-a-week job in the government division that supervised retread tires. Coincidentally, the lucrative East Coast retread-tire racket was controlled by Lansky.

In 1946, Nixon announced his candidacy for Congress, and Beverly Hills attorney Murray Chotiner showed up as a consultant on his campaign staff. Chotiner counted Lansky's childhood friend and Las Vegas partner "Bugsy" Siegel among his numerous mob-connected clients. During the period 1949–52, Chotiner defended clients in 221 organized crime cases. He was killed by a hit-and-run driver in Washington, D.C., during the Watergate scandal. His death remains unsolved.

In later years, another thread may have appeared. During an OC watch on "Jimmy Blue Eyes," Lansky's liaison, John Sampson says he "came across a guy, Victor Piansadosi. He was supposedly the bagman for Tricky Dicky. He brought money to Nixon, one of the stories I heard. This is stuff that nobody else knows, I mean nobody. We discovered Victor in '77 and nobody had ever heard of him. But if you look at the Meyer Lansky file, page one from a long time ago, you see under 'associates' Victor Allen. But it turns out to be [Victor] Piansadosi. Interesting, huh?"

During the last month of the Nixon administration, a $36-million skimming charge against Lansky was dropped "because he was too old."

Ken Whittaker is delighted that Jerry Armstrong could help me. "How about that," he says. "That's great. We have two retired FBI types here, and we have my son, and we have retired Bureau guys on an ad hoc basis. Like I said, if you ever need information any- where in the world, we have guys, former agents who are natives of those areas. Why don't you come by for a cup of coffee, say about three o'clock and tell me all about it?"

At his office his pride turns to astonishment when I tell him Armstrong spotted Meyer Lansky meeting with Don Aronow. "He actually saw them meeting together?" he asks incredulously. "Don and Meyer? Where was this? What were they doing?"

I explain that Armstrong says they were meeting for business purposes on more than one occasion. Whittaker still can't believe it. "How did he know it was Don?" he asks. When I tell him that Armstrong ran his license plate, he looks at me in stunned silence.

We review the situation: Aronow's meetings with Lansky and Mal- nik, his relationships with Genovese wiseguys and murderers, brief- cases filled with cash delivered at night, an apparent Mafia hit. Could there possibly be any innocent explanation for all this?

Whittaker stares up at the FBI emblem on his wall. "You know, we have an old saying in the Bureau," he says slowly. "If it walks like a duck and it quacks like a duck—it's a duck."

Art Nehrbass, who served as head of the FBI office in Miami in the late seventies before taking over MetroDade's Organized Crime Bu- reau, had heard about a possible connection between Aronow and the mob. "There were rumors and stuff like that, but nothing con- crete," he comments.

Nehrbass is intrigued by the stories of Aronow's having briefcases filled with money. He explains, "If he's getting briefcases filled with cash, one or two hundred thousand at a time, there are cases that go back to the year one in which this was the accepted way of getting Mafia profits out of their casinos." He asks where Don traveled and whether he cleared Customs all the time.

Aronow went frequently, sometimes once a week, to Bimini, Cat Cay, for lunch. His pilot, Riggs says that Aronow used both his own and Malnik's helicopters for trips to other parts of the Bahamas, especially the downtown casino at Freeport. Quite often they were able to enter the islands without clearing Customs.

The downtown casino in Freeport is in the Lucayan Beach Hotel, owned by Resorts International. Although the company has repeatedly denied allegations that organized crime elements are, or ever have been, involved in its operations, *Life* magazine in the sixties alleged that Lansky and the Mafia had penetrated the Lucayan Beach and other casinos in Freeport. In 1967, the *Wall Street Journal* reported that the Lucayan Beach casino was staffed by American veterans of Lansky's Havana and London casinos, in violation of Bahamian law.

Clarence Jones of the *Miami Herald* wrote in 1967 that so much money was being raked in by the casinos in Freeport that "it had to be mailed, parcel post, to New York banks in cardboard beer cartons." Jones noted that the cartons full of money "hinted at wholesale skimming from the casinos."

Art Nehrbass speculates that besides skimming the Nevada casinos, Lansky would want to skim his Bahamas casinos as well, "so he wouldn't have to make the split with the Bahamian government. And if a guy is doing a lot of travel over there in a private aircraft, it's possible there's movement both ways—so it could be taking money into this country as well as taking it out."

Aronow bought his first helicopter about 1969, at the same time he founded Cigarette. Riggs isn't sure how many helicopters Don had before he started working for him in 1975, but he says there were six or seven long-range jet helicopters from 1975 to 1982. "Some of them could carry seven people, though we usually just had two," he recalls. "Without refueling, you could go three hundred miles."

Changing helicopters every year could serve a useful money-movement purpose, Nehrbass says. "A new one with a new number every year would make a lot of sense if you didn't want to excite a lot of attention to a helicopter that has been making weekly or monthly trips," he points out. "If they're really Lansky's helicopters, then he [Aronow] might be the only one who uses it, if he's the only one running errands for Meyer. Or it's for whoever wants it, [such as] Al Malnik as another guy in the Lansky group."

An IRS agent who investigates Caribbean money-laundering operations says that no one has ever been able to locate any of Lansky's half-billion-dollar personal empire since he died. "If Lansky was behind Aronow's companies, then see if anything unusual happened to them when Meyer died," he suggests. "Sooner or later whoever took over for Meyer would get around to asking Don for those things back that really belonged to the mob."

He adds one other bit of advice when looking for front people: "My motto is follow them assets," he says, laughing.

Dade County records show that on the day Lansky died from lung cancer, Aronow scooped up promissory notes worth almost $4 million from his boat company and transferred them into his own name. The notes were related to nine valuable parcels of commercial property on Thunderboat Alley. According to the IRS agent, such a transaction is consistent with Aronow's rifling the company to prevent whoever else was involved from "getting at the goodies first."

Aronow's helicopter buying spree also came to an end at the same time. FAA records show the one he ordered several months before Lansky died was the last one he ever had. The helicopter, a Bell Jet Ranger, was the one Aronow took to Islamorada for his boat ride with George Bush. In 1985, Aronow, who was notorious for always extracting as much money as possible from any deal, simply gave the half-million-dollar aircraft away.

I would soon discover that the recipient had organized crime associations. And it would turn out that the man was the key to the murder.

The irresistible Donald Aronow. (John Crouse Associates, Inc.)

Don with his first wife, Shirley, in May of 1971. Through two decades of marriage, Shirley consistently refused to believe rumors of her husband's philandering and his mob connections. (*Miami Herald* photo)

Don and Lillian in 1983. Marriage to the blue-blooded Lillian, who was formerly girlfriend to King Hussein, validated Don's success in a way that his business achievements never could. (*Miami Herald* photo)

Don's most magnificent creation ever, the "Cigarette," nicknamed the Ferrari of the open seas. (John Crouse Associates, Inc.)

After Don fell and lost an impromptu foot race with John Crouse, he ripped his shirt and had Crouse take this photo as an example of the rigors of boat racing. (John Crouse Associates, Inc.)

Aronow posing with a model of his "Aronow Unlimited," the fastest catamaran in the world. Ben Kramer would keep the mold for his own and build the world champion Apache 41-foot catamaran. (John Crouse Associates, Inc.)

Vice President George Bush, Donald Aronow, Treasury Secretary Nicholas Brady, and Willie Myers set out for the high seas on "Blue Thunder," the 30-foot catamaran the government purchased for its drug-interdiction force. (White House photo)

When Pat Cordell took this last photograph of the champion sweating nervously on Thunderboat Alley, it was bullets, not government questions, that Aronow feared. (Photo by Pat Cordell)

MetroDade Homicide investigator Mike DeCora inspects a gaping hole made by the only one of six shots that missed Aronow's body. (Photo by Guy Montanari)

Federal probation agent Rory McMahon's relentless pursuit of Ben Kramer ultimately brought down Lansky, Inc.'s billion-dollar operation. (Photo courtesy Rory McMahon)

Meyer Lansky, for fifty years—until 1983—the real godfather of organized crime in America. (*Miami Herald* photo)

Ben Kramer with close friend, Turnberry patron, and fast-boat groupie James Caan. (John Crouse Associates, Inc.)

Left: Richard Gerstein, Dade County's most popular district attorney ever. His career was dogged by rumors of ties to the mob and to Meyer Lansky. Center: Rocky Pomerance, former chief of police of Miami, who came to Lillian Aronow's assistance.
Right: Former Lansky attorney Melvyn Kessler, later convicted along with drug kingpin Ben Kramer in a massive drug-money-laundering case. (*Miami Herald* photos)

Aronow's Purple Gang associates, Frankie Viserto, Jr., and Paul "Rizzo" Caiano, were suspected of running the Genovese family's heroin importation operations. (Left: FCI photo. Right: NYPD photo)

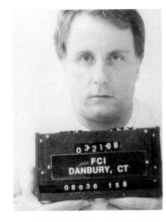

Jack and Ben Kramer, father and son drug kingpins. Jack liked the good life, and Ben treasured his macho image in and out of jail. (Left: *Miami Herald* photo. Right: AP Wide World photo)

Left: Italian actor Giancarlo Giannini, at left with Al Malnik—Miami restaurateur, multimillionaire, lawyer, jet-setter—who claims to be a misunderstood guy. He calls rumors of his association with Meyer Lansky "an incredible, inescapable myth—an albatross around my neck." Right: Gerstein protégé, former judge David Goodhart, who was subpoenaed to a 1974 federal grand jury along with Meyer Lansky, Richard Gerstein, and Donald Aronow. (*Miami Herald* photos)

Robert Young (alias Taylor), the convict indicted in March 1990 for the murder of Donald Aronow, despite the fact that none of the witnesses could identify him. (*Miami Herald* photo)

Chicago hitman Wayne Bock, whose list of suspected murders spans twenty-five years, fits the description of the tall, sandy-haired stranger who flushed Aronow from his office into the hands of the assassin. (Left: Tom Burdick photo. Right: police photo)

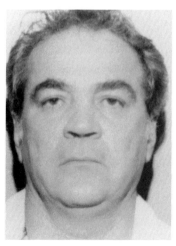

Witness composite of Aronow's murderer (left) is a match with mug photo of Chicago hit man Frankie Schweihs, according to a homicide investigator. (Chicago PD photo)

NINE

It is late August 1987. The beginning of what some call Florida's "mean season," when hurricanes and thunderstorms sweep over the tropics. A time when anyone who can leave, does. The days are unrelentingly hot and humid. Even the palm trees are scorched by the merciless sun.

The nights are better. After sunset, the city takes on the steamy splendor of an equatorial capital. The breeze is strong and warm. The scent of summer flowers becomes more intense from the heat. Brightly colored lights are reflected from the houses and the buildings onto the waterways.

On the Alley there's a strange air. A few times recently fully armed DEA agents in gunboats have cruised down the canal that runs behind the street. Docking at the Apache Bar, the agents hop onto the deck, strut around the complex, and brandish fierce-looking weapons. They never speak to anyone. A few minutes later they jump back into their boats and head out the canal to the bay.

There are other disconcerting signs as well. During one of our conversations Brownie comments that "there are all kinds of strange people going up and down the street. A lot of black-tired cars lately.

Some type of Fed cars." A flustered Jerry Engelman says that he was accosted on the Apache docks by a man who asked him if he knew Don Aronow. "He looked like a lot of Don's wiseguy friends who used to show up from time to time," Jerry says nervously.

Engelman, who had come to Miami to enjoy the relaxing lifestyle, didn't want to be involved in the Aronow case any more than he already was. He shrugged his shoulders and said no and tried to walk on. The man stopped him again and said, "sure you did, you knew Aronow." Jerry reluctantly confirmed that, yes, he did know him. The wiseguy pressed, "You used to work for him, didn't you?"

When Jerry again nodded the man said, "Aronow was a fucking snake in the grass. You oughta forget you ever knew him."

One hint of what's up comes from an unexpected source, a man familiar with some of the illegal activities going on behind the scenes. We meet when the shift is over, at the dead end part of the Alley, near an abandoned concrete plant. He had promised to check out Bobby Saccenti "in a peripheral sort of way," as he described it, because Bobby had been the last man to talk to Aronow before the shooting. It was Saccenti that Aronow went to immediately after the strange visitor left his office.

"Ben is a very likable guy if you know him," he says. "He's like a big kid. I don't think that the Kramers had anything do with Aronow's death. If you're working on the homicide angle and the possible implication of Ben Kramer and Jack Kramer, I'd be inclined to have nothing to do with you."

The man says he doesn't know of any ties between Ben and Don other than boat racing. "Ben's a very knowledgeable person about boats, things nautical," he comments. "He's a very intelligent young man. I have no knowledge of Ben doing anything wrong—direct knowledge—of anything illegal."

He also has praise for Ben's father, Jack, calling him a very likable gentleman and charming. Despite his closeness to the Kramers, my contact is hard-pressed to describe Jack's business. "Well," he explains, "you know, he's been into different businesses. This business and that business."

He stops talking as a boat powers by on the canal. A lot of people on the street commute by boat and he's concerned that somebody might see him talking to me. He turns away. Once the boat passes, he starts to talk again and a strange look comes over his face.

He blurts out, "They're currently, you know, I think Apache, the Kramers, are currently under federal investigation. I don't know, maybe tax. And possibly, ah, possibly maybe Jack. From the standpoint of, you know, overseas funds, that kind of thing."

"Money laundering?"

"Well, ya."

"How do you know?"

"Don't ask me. And don't mention my name. You'll get me killed."
He repeats, "You'll get me killed."

He pauses. I don't know how to respond to what he has just said.
My silence encourages him to continue. He asks, "Does the name
Shaun Murphy mean anything to you? Shaun Murphy was the officer
of some off-island corporation. Banking, investment. Some people
were sending money to these offshore companies. This guy Shaun
Murphy was arrested and is cooperating with law enforcement. I
guess these federal grand juries are looking into this kind of stuff."

It's a last gasp of information. He is clearly agitated now. "That's
all I'm going to say," he concludes. "But under no conditions use my
name, because I want to reveal something to you. I've had contact
with Ben Kramer. I'll help you all I can with the Aronow story. I'll
try to do some digging, but lay off the Kramers, you know?"

No one seems to know Shaun Murphy or how he is connected to
Thunderboat Alley. At least nobody admits it. Finally, I call a senior
Justice Department official who has talked to me previously. He says
Murphy is part of Operation Isle of Man, a massive federal-level
multiagency investigation.

The name was selected because that was the location of an offshore bank that was discovered to be part of the "looping" of laundered money. The investigation began at New Scotland Yard and led
ultimately to an accountant in the British Virgin Islands: Shaun Murphy. Deciding the best thing for him to do was cooperate, Murphy
came into the interrogation with his arms full of client records. Included in his roster were drug smugglers and mobsters who were
laundering huge quantities of money.

Vast amounts of cash—possibly as much as a billion dollars—
moved through Murphy to banks throughout the world, including
locations in London, Switzerland, Liechtenstein, South America, and
the Far East. Murphy played a pivotal role in the cycle. He was
frequently the first drop-off point for cash as it left the U.S. on its
way to being "looped" and "cleansed" through Liechtenstein or
Switzerland. Then he often wired money back into the States, usually
in the form of "loans."

Typically, the cash was routed to Murphy via the U.S. Virgin
Islands. Because it's American territory, there are no forms that have
to be filed to transport currency there, and it's a short flight from
Miami to St. Thomas. Anyone can simply carry a suitcase full of

money onto the island. It's all purely legal because it's still the U.S. Then one steps onto any of the hundreds of small boats in the bay, crosses over to Tortola, which is part of the British Virgin Islands, and walks straight into a bank. In a matter of minutes the money is out of the U.S. and out of the reach of the IRS and law enforcement officials. For those who prefer a bit more discretion, there are the services of "facilitators."

Murphy was such a facilitator of offshore money movement, the money being furnished to him through middlemen, mainly lawyers. The lawyers were used so they could claim client-attorney confiden-tiality and protect the sources of the money. British and U.S. inves-tigators tracked back through the lawyers to the sources of the money, and then forward through Shaun Murphy to see where the money was going. According to the Justice official, they tried to prove the likely source of the cash, which they assumed was narcotics in origin.

"Does Operation Man involve Ben Kramer?" I ask.

"I can't tell you," he says. "You'll just have to wait and see."

It wasn't a long wait.

Throughout the day, Friday, August 28, 1987, there were more black-tired cars than usual on the Alley. This time there were also some more expensive-looking management-type "fed cars." They flitted back and forth for hours. Then, a few minutes before three-thirty P.M. when the workers were scheduled to finish their shift, the area around the Ft. Apache Marina erupted into action.

Dozens of patrol boats entered the waterway that ran alongside the Alley. On the street, cars and trucks from various government agencies descended on Apache. Federal agents in blue pullover jack-ets with POLICE on the front and the name of their agency on the back—FBI, DEA, IRS, Florida Marine Patrol, MetroDade Police—hopped out of their cars, yelling, "This place is seized by the federal government!" and flashing warrants. They were armed with all types of weapons from M16s to shotguns to pistols.

They rushed into the Ft. Apache Bar, shouting at the customers who were trying to scurry out of the building. Brownie had just sat down a moment before so he decided to finish his beer and watch the action. "When I walked out into the marina, they had everyone out against the wall," he recalls. "And on the canal it looked like a fucking armada."

The agents held everyone while they checked their IDs. They ran the information through a portable computer terminal at the pay phone that linked to the National Crime Investigation Computer (NCIC) in Washington. Brownie recalls, "This guy that took mine was the head guy, he was really well dressed, had a gold badge and a fancy thing over his pocket. And while we're waiting for my ID check, he's talking to me, and Saccenti from next door came right up to the gate. This guy says, 'Is that Bob Saccenti?' and I said yes, and he went sprinting over there and walked Bobby back to his place."

Jerry Engelman, who has the uncanny knack of being in the center of action on Thunderboat Alley, was also caught in the Ft. Apache raid. He was sitting in his office on the third floor. When he glanced out the window, he saw a patrol boat pulling up to the marina. "It was moving far too fast for normal docking," he recalls, "and then they threw these big fenders over the side and slammed up against the dock."

He watched as agents jumped off the boat. A few seconds later, he heard footsteps in the hall and suddenly five DEA men charged into his office. Engelman had a yellow legal pad on his desk with several days of notes on it, including customers' names for orders. An agent grabbed it and began perusing it. Another agent demanded Jerry's driver's license and wrote down his address and social security number.

"When we got outside, there were TV crews, satellite trucks, and there were TV helicopters overhead," Engelman recalls. "And all these guys who worked for Apache Marina had yellow T-shirts on that said 'Apache.' They had all of them quarantined over by the service shop."

It took more than four hours before everyone was processed and freed from Ft. Apache. The marina part of the complex, with over two hundred boats in storage, was sealed for a week while federal agents searched each vessel. Most were released to their owners. But a few, those containing even small quantities of dope, were confiscated. The agents also seized the multimillion-dollar Ft. Apache complex under a U.S. Justice Department action that charged that it was built entirely with narcotics money.

A little farther north, DEA and IRS agents were securing Kramer's enormous boatbuilding facility in Hollywood, Florida, where he manufactured his highly regarded Apache speedboats. It, too, was appropriated along with his $2-million yacht, *Sea Witch*.

In all, the government ultimately seized almost $200,000,000 worth of Kramer's property in locations throughout Florida, Michigan, and California, including a number of prime commercial locations in Los Angeles County. Their most valuable seizure was Kramer's California card-playing casino which generated $2 million a week in profits. It is the world's largest legalized card-playing casino, dwarfing even Donald Trump's Taj Mahal gambling operation.

In the early evening the day before the Ft. Apache raid, on a posh island just off the coast of Miami Beach, Ben Kramer and his girlfriend emerged from a $300,000 penthouse in Biscayne Cove on Williams Island. The private, security-conscious island was developed for the wealthy Miamians seeking security and freedom from the crime that plagues other parts of the area. Williams Island is also famous for the fact that part-time resident Sophia Loren is one of the developers and has appeared in advertising endorsing the complex.

Ben and his girlfriend were on their way to the airport. She was taking a flight to visit her mother in Brooklyn, New York. He was on his way to a powerboat race in Bay City, Michigan—he had already shipped his $400,000 Team Apache race boat—and his girlfriend planned to join him there later. As they headed for his new black Porsche 928, a group of federal agents jumped from the shadows.

William Grieves, an FBI agent on the scene, says they "lucked out" at Williams Island. "They came out," he recalls, "and we got them both out on the front driveway. Ben looked surprised, but he's been through the mill before, so it wasn't like too big a shock. But his little girlfriend was so scared she was shitting like a dog, like a dog trying to shit a peach pit or something. We had a hell of a time getting her calmed down."

A DEA agent on the scene says Kramer's girlfriend had good reason to be scared. "She had marijuana in her purse, a couple of bags. And the biggest frigging dildo you've ever seen in your life." He laughs, adding that one of her suitcases was filled with "sex toys."

Ben was arrested. The indictment that resulted in Kramer's arrest in Miami came out of the Southern Illinois Federal District. He was charged with importing at least a half a million pounds of marijuana into the U.S. with a street value close to a billion dollars. The government also charged him with the more serious crime of operating a "continuing criminal enterprise." Another sports celebrity, Randy Lanier, the Indianapolis 500 rookie of the year in 1986, was indicted along with him.

· · ·

After Kramer was taken away, the agents entered his penthouse condo. Inside they found a photo album with pictures he had taken of himself with his Colombian drug connections. They also found an extensive library of porno videotapes and some homemade videos. On one, Ben had recorded his tour of the Colombian ranch where he bought his highly prized Santa Marta Gold marijuana.

In the video, Ben and several Colombian "cowboys" drive around the ranch in a four-wheel-drive Blazer, covered with Apache Race Team stickers. The "travelogue" includes a stop at the beach while they shot at the sand and the ocean with a large arsenal of silencer-equipped automatic weapons. One agent in the raid laughs, "Benny was Pancho Villa with this fucking bullet thing across his chest, acting crazy, shooting the guns off."

But perhaps the most surprising find among Kramer's possessions were originals of Gary Hart's early primary stump speeches. They were locked in Ben's safe at the Ft. Apache complex. This was not the first time there was a subtle link between the former senator's downfall and the narcotics kingpin.

Both Ben and Gary Hart hung out at Turnberry Isle, the resort built by Don Aronow's longtime friend Donny Soffer. A key female employee at the resort was Lynn Armandt, the woman whose phone calls to the *Miami Herald* terminated Hart's political career. Armandt had at one time been married to a Miami drug dealer thought to be associated with Kramer. Armandt's husband vanished one night and has never been found.

"When he disappeared, Armandt put in a missing person's report," says one DEA agent on the Kramer case. "Then his car was found, with machine gun holes and there was blood in it. And then they found Ben Kramer's phone number in the glove box."

Until his arrest, Ben Kramer lived a lavish lifestyle and brazenly went about his business of building the largest marijuana smuggling empire in history. Incredibly, during all but eight months of this time he was on parole from a 1978 smuggling conviction and was under the close supervision of a federal probation officer.

The August 1987 bust and indictment of Kramer was by no means the first effort to get him as a drug kingpin. In early 1983, his probation officer, Jo Ann Pepper (the late Congressman Claude Pepper's niece), had asked the Hollywood, Florida, PD to investigate her suspicions that Ben had resumed his smuggling activities, or more likely, that he had never stopped. Two Vice detectives, Ronald Raccioppi and Joseph Nickmeyer, joined Pepper in tracking Kramer's activities and found what they called "red flags" all around.

By the middle of 1983, they convinced a judge to order a "pen register" on Kramer's phone. A pen register records the telephone numbers of outgoing calls but not the actual conversation. It's often the first step in getting the court to agree to a complete, or "Title 3," wiretap.

In a report prepared for the court by Detective Nickmeyer on the results of five months of pen register recordings, he noted that "an unusually high number of calls were made." Daily telephone logs attached to the report show that for the months June–October 1983, a total of 6,615 calls were made from Kramer's phone.

The phone logs also indicated that hundreds of calls were made from Kramer's number to the office and home of prominent Miami attorney Melvyn Kessler during the period. The logs also showed frequent calls to Barranquilla, Colombia, a town with one main industry: drugs.

During this period, Kramer was also busy traveling extensively and requested numerous "travel permits" from Pepper. He told her he was employed as a part-time consultant for Los Angeles real estate developer and philanthropist Samuel Gilbert and as a lighting consultant in Jack Kramer's company. The demands of his work supposedly required travel throughout the U.S. as well as Europe and the Caribbean.

As part of their investigation, Raccioppi and Nickmeyer surreptitiously picked up Kramer's trash in December 1983. They found residues of cocaine and marijuana and receipts from a November trip to the Pierre Hotel in Manhattan. The receipts show that on November 27 to 29, 1983, Ben stayed at the hotel, one of the city's most expensive. He was listed as a frequent and valued guest there. Under "special request" on the reservation slip was handwritten "Best Suite available, Daniel knows him."

Ben paid the full rate for the suite, $1,750 a night. His total bill for three days was $10,097.02. He paid in cash. (Ben also liked to stay at the Plaza. In the same trash container, the detectives found another receipt for the same period, which showed that on one day at the hotel he spent $2,852.34.) His hotel records showed numerous phone calls to locations throughout the country. Several intriguing calls: those made to a prestigious Washington, D.C. law firm with government connections.

Ben's high living was not restricted to out-of-town trips. In various surveillance records he was seen in Mercedes sports coupes, Porsches, private planes, and a $2-million yacht. When questioned, his explanation to the probation officer was always the same: these "belonged to friends." He also spent lavishly around Miami. More receipts found in his trash indicated he spent a lot of time at Joe Sonken's Gold Coast Restaurant, in Hollywood, Florida. A June 1983 bill showed Kramer had run up a tab at the restaurant of $5,293.25.

On December 21, 1983, Pepper made an unannounced visit to Apache Boats where Ben had secured his third part-time job, this time working for Bobby Saccenti. Pepper was suspicious of the alleged boss-employee relationship and noted in her log: "Employer Saccenti in office with Subject [Kramer], but Subject appeared to be in control."

Kramer had requested of Pepper permission to travel to South America "on business" for Gilbert's international division, but Pepper balked. "Advised S [Subject] he would not be allowed to travel to Venezuela or Colombia, as he is on probation for narcotics trafficking and he does not need to be exposed to that situation again. S became upset, indicated he would be contacting his attorney." (In the meantime, while waiting for official clearance, Kramer continued clandestine trips to South America via the Caribbean in his private jet.)

By the end of 1983, Pepper, Nickmeyer, and Raccioppi concluded that Ben had returned to drug smuggling on a grand scale and had personally made $3 million that year. They had surveilled him in New York, Florida, and the Bahamas and had amassed a considerable body of incriminating evidence against him. All three were confident that they could soon get his parole revoked and that additional smuggling charges would be brought against him.

They were wrong.

Pepper's recommendation to the Washington, D.C., office of the U.S. Parole Commission that Ben's parole be revoked was denied. Kramer's attorneys then filed a suit in federal court against Pepper alleging "conflict of interest" and forcing her removal as his probation officer. The two Hollywood detectives were not only unable to get a Title 3 wiretap, they couldn't even get an extension on their pen register. Despite their best efforts, they were unable to find a single prosecutor on a local, state, or federal level who was interested in pursuing charges against Ben. Both detectives subsequently resigned from the department.

The 1983 efforts by Pepper, Raccioppi, and Nickmeyer to prosecute Ben Kramer, like those of many others during the seven years he was building his empire, had inexplicably fallen into a legal black hole.

· · ·

On August 31, 1987, the Monday after the Ft. Apache raid, Kramer was taken before a U.S. magistrate in federal court in Miami on the federal warrant from the Southern District of Illinois. Bail was denied.

For Kramer this was just the beginning of his legal problems. Three months later he was indicted by a Southern Florida District federal grand jury, partly on the basis of testimony from Shaun Murphy. These charges—unlike those in the Illinois case—included Ben's father, Jack; Miami attorney Melvyn Kessler; Los Angeles businessman and philanthropist Samuel Gilbert; and Gilbert's son, Michael. In a massive 70-page, 44-count racketeering indictment unsealed on November 25, 1987, the men were charged with running a Colombian-sourced drug importation operation and an international money-laundering scheme.

The focus of the Florida case was on the movement and laundering of narcotics proceeds. The indictment charged that the group controlled an elaborate network of bank accounts, companies, and active businesses that stretched from the Caribbean to London to Liechtenstein to Los Angeles. Their operation processed the enormous amounts of cash that came in ever faster as Ben's drug operation grew, converting it into clean funds. The linchpin in the scheme was Cortrust, a company formed in Liechtenstein to take advantage of that country's strict bank secrecy laws. It served as the ultimate looping point of most of the funds.

From Liechtenstein, money was transferred through a host of other companies in the Caribbean. The money then came back to the United States in the form of "loans" to front corporations. According to the indictment, the defendants then used the laundered money to develop private and commercial real estate, to buy companies, and to purchase luxury items such as boats, jet planes, and cars.

The laundered drug money was also used to build the grandiose Ft. Apache Marina and to cultivate Kramer's growing reputation as a boatbuilder and racer. To mount campaigns for a powerboating racing championship can easily run into millions of dollars a year. Kramer also used the money to fund Randy Lanier's Indianapolis 500 racing team.

The government claimed that Jack Kramer directed the funds through a portion of the laundering network and invested the profits in the U.S. by acquiring and maintaining assets through foreign and domestic corporations. Sam Gilbert was accused of assisting in the laundering of the profits, and of providing a fake job for the ex-convict Ben Kramer to use as a cover for illegal activities.

Mel Kessler was charged with making the wire transfers that laundered the money, as well as providing the legal expertise to set up the companies in Europe, the Caribbean, and the United States. As U.S. Attorney Leon Kellner explained in a press conference, "no narcotics organization is made up solely of smugglers. It also involves the professionals. They are the people who hide the assets."

At a December 2, 1987, bond hearing for the Florida defendants, the government requested that Kessler be kept in custody. They claimed that he traveled throughout the world, had access to a fortune in drug money, and was a danger to the community. But twenty-four well-known defense lawyers came to Kessler's aid in the courtroom. Five testified that Kessler was nonviolent, a man of his word, and a lawyer who had known about the impending—though supposedly secret—indictment for at least a year. The court ran out of time before all the plaudits from the lawyers could be heard.

The judge assigned Kessler a $1-million bond and he was released after he posted 10 percent. The government agreed to a $250,000 bond for Jack Kramer. Sam Gilbert died of cancer the day the indictment was announced, and his son Michael Gilbert was a fugitive for a time before he turned himself in.

Although the Florida federal case was massive and impressive, the Illinois federal charges were far more serious for Ben Kramer. Conviction under the new stringent "B" version of the Continuing Criminal Enterprise 648 statute brings mandatory life imprisonment without chance of parole. As FBI agent Robert Duker, who headed the Illinois investigation, bluntly put it, "It's a casket case. You go in, you come out in a casket."

Ben Kramer's national distribution operation was first tripped up by just twenty bales, about a thousand pounds of marijuana. This insignificant amount within the total operation was all the Illinois feds needed. "The guy [with the twenty bales] was four steps removed from Kramer," says Duker. "It was a slow process of hammering and squeezing, which led us first to four people who were leaders in [Randy] Lanier's distribution network. Lanier had the most exposure as far as being the guy who you traced the marijuana to."

From Lanier, Duker discovered six channels of distribution or major customers. "Our investigation came up through three of them," Duker notes. "And once we got to the level below Lanier— those people that had contact with Lanier and the other two principals—then we used them. Basically we worked our way up to Lanier. We didn't start out with him. Three major people rolled over at once. When they rolled over, all their numerous workers rolled over and substantiated what they said."

Illinois authorities constructed a three-part scenario to Ben Kramer's importation-distribution operation. Ben arranged for the purchase of marijuana in Colombia. A second partner managed the transportation from Colombia to the States—usually by sea barge. Lanier worked with the distributors once the cargo reached the U.S. He coordinated the drug-dealing network through a toll-free beeper system.

While others beneath him have "flipped," Lanier has been of no help in getting to Ben. "He'll never roll over," Duker predicts. "But we don't need Lanier. When you get as big as Kramer, you leave a lot of tracks. And you depend on people keeping their mouths shut. And when they stop keeping their mouths shut, you've got problems."

Duker notes that Florida has had years to do something about Kramer but never made a move on him until Illinois stepped in. His impression is that there are some Florida officials ready to go lightly with Kramer. "Florida indicted him on very similar charges down there," he says. "And then they tried to get him down there where he could cut a deal, turn over some money to them. We fought them on that."

Duker says that Kramer was trying to pit the Florida feds against them. "We said to Ben, you're just the same as anyone else," he relates. "You're gonna end up cooperating and get a deal. Plead straight up or go to trial. The deal was he didn't want to cooperate with us. The deal was he doesn't get a deal unless he does. That's our policy up here. We're not going to change things for him just because he wants to give back fifty or a hundred million dollars."

Duker says he doesn't care whether Kramer ends up making a deal or not. "We have Ben cooked in this case, we're going for the jugular. He's going bye-bye forever."

TEN

In the months following the government seizure of the Ft. Apache Marina complex, business dropped off "to almost zero," a barmaid comments angrily one afternoon. "Look at this," she says as she pulls a folded check out of her tight short-shorts. "United States Marshals Service. My paycheck is from the goddamned U.S. government. They're running the whole marina. Look around here, there's nobody here. How am I going to make a living with this shit?"

The bar is deserted. Later a man and a woman come in, wander around, check out the ceiling, and make notations on a clipboard. When the barmaid asks what they're doing, they explain that they're insurance agents. "We're revising the policy on the marina," the female agent says. Now that the government owned the marina, the Marshals Service was increasing the insurance coverage.

The Ft. Apache bar had been a good source of leads in the past. Now it seems no one is eager to drink or hang out at a bar run by the feds. Gone are the bejeweled Rolexes, cellular hand-held phones, and diamond pinky rings. Absent are the deeply tanned men in open silk shirts. No longer do sleek black Midnight Expresses (the boat designed to carry dope far and fast in the waters off the Gold Coast) tie up at the Apache docks.

The Rumrunner on 179th Street and Biscayne, about nine blocks south of the Alley, has become the new hangout. Brownie's white mane appears in the middle of the biggest and loudest group of people. He has his arm around a woman thirty years his junior and he's telling jokes. Everyone is laughing. "Hey, buddy, let me buy you a drink," he yells at me. "Let me introduce my friends. They write for *Powerboating* magazine. They're doing research." It's just past noon on a Wednesday and everyone is already glassy-eyed.

After a while, the crowd drifts away and Brownie starts talking about Swats Mulligan. "You know Don was a great admirer of Swats. The name Cigarette comes from Swats's rumrunner boat. That's how Swats started in the Mafia, as a rumrunner during Prohibition."

"Swats ran the famous *Cigarette* rumrunner?" I ask in astonishment.

"He had two boats. One was called the *Cigarette,* and the other was the *Hijacker.* Swats used them to rob other rumrunning boats. They were armed with machine guns and had triple engines; they were very fast for their day." Brownie is surprised that I didn't know that Don named the Cigarette boat after a rum-running vessel. "Hell, I thought everyone knew that," he comments.

"Sure, everyone knows that," I agree. "But they don't know that he named it that because his friend was the rumrunner." Aronow had told the press that he had heard stories about the rumrunner *Cigarette* when he was a kid hanging around the Brooklyn docks.

Looking at Aronow's life was like peering through a kaleidoscope. Just when you think you have it in focus, it twists a little to reveal a totally new perspective.

We're interrupted by a deeply bronzed, well-dressed man who pats Brownie on the back as he walks by. "Yo, To-ny," Brownie yells. "How the fuck ya doing?" Tony grins as he recognizes Brownie and joins two people at a table outside near the water.

"That's Tony Roma, he's one of the boys," Brownie says. "He started the restaurant chain Tony Roma's. The first one was a few blocks from here. A lot of small-time guys hung out there. I wouldn't know the big ones, so I don't know if they hung in there or not."

Brownie says that Tony is a legitimate businessman. "He made all his money by opening all the Playboy Clubs for Hefner," he explains. "And when he retired or got fired or whatever from that, he bought [the first] Tony Roma's here."

"He's a great host, a great restaurateur," Brownie comments expansively, adding that Tony takes care of his friends. "You know, one of the former managers here at Rumrunners, he used to be a driver for one of the big guys. I don't know which one, but he went away to 'school' for about forty years. And the guy took his driver down to Tony and said, 'This is my boy, take care of him [while I'm gone].' And Tony put him to work."

Our conversation twists and turns and eventually makes its way to Ben Kramer. Brownie's heard that the government eventually plans to sell Ft. Apache Marina, with a minimum bid of $4 million. "Speaking of property on the Alley," he continues, "you know when Don died, Cigarette Racing Team looked into buying USA Racing's land and buildings. We needed more space at the time, and it would've been handy to have those two buildings. We were very surprised to find out that Aronow didn't own the buildings or the land."

"So who owned it?"

"Some company called Super Chief South."

Dade County land records is on the ninth floor of a state building in downtown Miami. The room is filled with thirty or forty microfilm reading machines. The window shades are drawn tightly all day so people can read the screens. The projectors put out a lot of heat and their fans are noisy. The room is packed with people waiting to use them, and when someone gets up, there's always someone ready to pounce on their spot. Everyone is testy, and the place smells like a locker room.

Finally it's my turn. I insert an index tape and look up "Aronow." Page after page of Aronow's activities flash by. Wading through the listings is a tedious process. Every time I decide to look at a document, I have to relinquish my microfilm machine and wait in line at a teller-like window for a different roll containing the detailed documents. There are a large number of listings under "Aronow." Most of them turn out to be associated with Thunderboat Alley. The stories I had heard were right. At one time or another Don owned virtually all the land on the street.

Then I find what I've been looking for: a listing for "Aronow" and "Super Chief South." Book 12,628, page 2,022. It's a promissory note and deed made on August 29, 1985, between "Donald Aronow, individually and as Trustee," and "Super Chief South, Inc., a Florida corporation whose post office is 3030 N.E. 188th Street, North Miami Beach." The document is for the sale of a parcel of land somewhere in Dade County. To a nonsurveyor the location is not clear. The land transferred is:

A portion of the SE1/4 of Fractional Section 3, Township 52, Range 42 East, Dade County, Florida, being particularly described as follows: Commencing at the SW corner of the SE1/4 of the NE1/4 of the SW1/4 of said Fractional Section 3, Township 52 South, Range 42 East, thence run S89 56'45" along the south line of said SE1/4 of the NE1/4 of the SW1/4 of Fractional Section 3 for a distance of 450 feet; thence run N00 39'25"W for a distance of 185.83 feet; thence run N89 20'35"E for a distance of 842 feet to the Point of Beginning of the property herein described, said point lying on the East boundary line of that certain property deeded by Naule Industries, Inc. to Rick and Mitchell, and described in Deed Book 630, at Page 58, of the Public Records of Dade Country, Florida . . .

The description goes on and on with technical data. The terms of the sale: Aronow received a small down payment, $100,000, and a note for $600,000.

The document doesn't list any address for Don Aronow. But the address of Super Chief South—3030 N.E. 188th Street—is the same as that of Aronow's company, USA Racing. It appears to be simply a transfer of land from one of Aronow's companies to another of his many corporate shells. A "paper" transfer for tax purposes would explain the small down payment.

There is something visibly different about this document when I compare it to other Aronow transactions. Most deeds and notes connected with Aronow are two pages. This one is ten pages of print so small that even with the microfilm reader it's almost impossible to read. All the other land transactions list the location by street address in addition to the customary surveyor specs.

This deed contains no street address. The only way to determine the location of the land is by comparing the specifications to other plots of land in Miami. I figure the Alley is the best place to start. Further research indicates that the land described on the deed is identical to that of USA Racing.

The document also contains one small paragraph buried in the end of the contract. "Item 27" catches my eye:

This mortgage shall also be security for the payment of the indebtedness owned by USA Racing, Inc., a Florida corporation to the Mortgagee, Donald Aronow, in the amount of $473,600, to idemnify Donald Aronow from any personal liability under the Retained Title Agreement between Bell Helicopter Textron, Inc. and presently USA Racing, Inc., which contract had been personally guaranteed by Donald Aronow. A default in the payment of said contract shall constitute a default under this purchase money note and mortgage as well.

According to the clause, Don bought a helicopter "on time" for USA Racing and personally guaranteed the payments. (It appears to be the helicopter he used when he went to meet George Bush at Islamorada.) As of the date of the deed in 1985, Aronow was still in debt to Bell Helicopter for it.

Item 27 was apparently designed to insure that USA Racing would continue to make the payments. It also strongly implied that Super Chief South was buying the company USA Racing, Inc. with its helicopter in addition to the parcel of land, although there was no specific mention of this in the document.

If Don owned Super Chief South—if it was just another of his corporate entities—why have Murray Weil write in protection to ensure that payments continue to be made to Bell Helicopter? There was only one inescapable and surprising conclusion: Don Aronow and Super Chief South were completely separate.

It was a company sale disguised in the form of a land deal. And only one clause at the very end of the note—an obscure item buried in a convoluted document—revealed the true nature of the transaction.

On the following page was the notary seal of Murray Weil next to the corporate seal of Super Chief South. And the signature of its secretary and president: Jack J. Kramer.

The Kramers owned USA Racing.

Just seven months after he had been awarded the government contract to build drug interdiction boats, Aronow secretly sold the company to a drug kingpin. In 1985, Don Aronow wasn't building the famed Blue Thunder boats for America's War on Drugs.

The nation's largest marijuana smuggler was.

ELEVEN

"Watch Out Dopers! A crack of 'Blue Thunder,' faster than a shiver, stable as a platform, is about to become the state of the salt-watery art on the side of the law," the *Miami Herald* reported February 5, 1985. The occasion was the announcement of the awarding of the Blue Thunder contract to Donald Aronow by U.S. Customs Commissioner William von Raab.

"The man who designed the roaring Cigarette speedboats, favorite vehicle of ocean-going drug smugglers, has built a better boat, one that will snuff out the Cigarettes," continued the article.

A week after the announcement, on Valentine's Day, a laughing U.S. Senator Paula Hawkins and smiling von Raab posed with Aronow for a group photograph at a ceremony commemorating the historic contract. It marked the first time that the Vice Presidential South Florida Joint Drug Task Group would get its own specially designed interceptor boats, rather than having to rely upon seized vessels. It was a symbol of the Reagan/Bush administration's new commitment in the war on drugs.

But within seven months Don Aronow's role would become merely a facade. Ben Kramer was actually the man with the contract.

The same Ben Kramer who was regularly smuggling barges in from Colombia crammed with so much marijuana that it usually took his crews three full nights of work to unload them.

How did Ben Kramer pay Aronow for the company and the contract? With freshly laundered "narco-dollars" that had gone through a six-stage international cleaning process. The Blue Thunder company had been purchased with drug cash "looped" first through Shaun Murphy in the British Virgin Islands, then Liechtenstein, back to Murphy, and through two companies in Los Angeles before finally arriving cleansed in Miami ready for the purchase.

In the months following the clandestine takeover, USA Racing completed critical development stages on the boat, then began building and delivering them to Customs.

Only a short time after the Blue Thunders were in service they became the butt of jokes. One of the first times I spoke to Edna Buchanan about Aronow's murder, she quipped, "Maybe the government did it. They're upset because the Blue Thunders don't work. They're lemons and they're always being repaired."

When George Bush came to Miami three months after the clandestine Super Chief South deal, *Herald* columnist Carl Hiaasen wrote:

> George Bush is back in town this week, spreading his mirth and irrepressible optimism about the war on drugs. I would never suggest that the man is making a pest of himself, but every time I turn around he's down here, giving the exact same speech to the same bunch of people . . .
>
> During the most recent trip, I considered inviting George to stop over for some Triscuits and Cheeze Whiz, but it turns out he was too busy with matters vice presidential. No wonder. Look what fell out of his pocket as he boarded Air Force Two for the flight home:

memo to: THE VICE PRESIDENT OF THE UNITED STATES
    from: STAFF
      re: MIAMI SCHEDULE

9:50 Arrive at Miami International

9:51 Denounce Communism

10:07 Get in limousine. Wave in a friendly manner, even if no one recognizes you.

10:35 Climb out of limousine. Keep waving.

10:36 Climb aboard US Customs sleek anti-drug speedboat known as Blue Thunder. Try not to mention the fact that Blue Thunder costs $150,000 and hasn't caught a single smuggler—it's still a very nice boat and Customs went to a lot of trouble waxing it up for you. Also: Be sure to wear black safety goggles that make you look like a panelist on the old What's My Line.

10:45 PHOTO OPPORTUNITY. Drive the Blue Thunder in circles around Biscayne Bay. Please be careful with the throttle and try to remember that boats don't have brakes. And if you should see a real smuggler, for God's sake, turn around and go the other way as fast as you can.

11:15 Drop in on Vice President's drug task force. Make sure nobody's been using your office. Check to see if there's a large pile of confiscated drugs for convenient PHOTO OPPORTUNITY.

11:30 Press Conference to announce that the U.S. is "making progress" in the war on drugs. Ignore reams of evidence to the contrary. If pressed by rude local reporters about how we could possibly be doing so great when the entire state of Florida is knee-deep in cocaine, prepare to give STANDARD OBLIQUE VICE PRESIDENTIAL REPLY #226 . . .

Throughout 1986 the *Herald* and the *Miami News* carried a number of more serious stories about inexplicable problems with the Blue Thunder boats. The *Miami News*'s Scott Spreier wrote: "You remember Blue Thunder. That's the buzzword for U.S. Customs' high-powered, $150,000 offshore speedboats touted as the latest weapon in the war on drugs.

"Turns out the two 39-foot vessels assigned to the Treasure Coast [north of Fort Lauderdale] have been landlocked as of late with engine trouble. The folks at Customs weren't too excited about talking with the press, afraid, I guess, that news of the breakdowns would send a Colombian armada heading this way."

Spreier goes on to ask, "Just how effective are these vessels, designed by Don Aronow?

"Well, according to . . . tight-lipped federal lawmen, the pair in use on Treasure Coast have yet to make a drug arrest. Six months ago I wrote a column about the economy and efficiency of using such high-priced, high-powered toys to battle drug smugglers. My concerns have not been allayed."

The *Herald* reported about the same time: "Blue Thunder, the U.S. Customs' fleet of high performance boats, has lost some of its roar. . . . A 440-horsepower engine in one of the $150,000 boats had to be overhauled twice since it arrived in the area last January [six months before]." When queried by the *Herald,* Customs official Gregory Jansen declined to comment on how many other Blue Thunder boats were broken down in south Florida.

"We don't want to give that information to the drug smugglers," he told the paper.

At the end of yet another of his Blue Thunder boat rides around Biscayne Bay, Bush told the press in response to questions about the program, "It's really too soon [to tell about Blue Thunder]. We're in this as a marathon, not as a sprint."

But the Blue Thunders weren't even limping along.

Don Aronow had continued to keep in regular touch with the Vice President despite the mounting and publicized difficulties surrounding the Blue Thunder program. Aronow spent much of his time trying to conjure up good press for Blue Thunder—a goal that was becoming increasingly difficult. Unable to stem the mounting negative press in Miami about the boats, he turned to high-powered friends overseas to improve his image. One was King Hussein.

During one of Hussein's visits to the States in spring 1986, Aronow, ever the salesman, enticed Hussein into buying a boat. He evidently hoped that Bush would be suitably impressed by the international appeal of the Blue Thunder. After Hussein left the country, Nicolas Iliopoulos, the royal boat captain, wrote to Don from the Royal Palace at Aqaba.

THE ROYAL PALACE

P.O. Box 99 Aqaba, Jordan

May 18, 1986

Dear Don & Lillian

Once more thank you for your great hospitality during our visit to Florida.

"Haya" (the new Bertram 54') arrived safely in Aqaba on May 14 and after days of cleaning she has now proudly taken her permanent position among the other royal yachts.

His majesty enjoys your catamaran "Hashim" immensely.

The last few days we had King Juan Carlos and Queen Sofia as guests. We only used "Hashim" running up and down Aqaba Bay.

King Juan Carlos was very interested in the boat and inspected it very closely. Why don't you send him a leaflet with the particulars. Your boat was also very much appreciated by President Hosni Mubarak of Egypt and he was very thrilled to drive her.

Well, I am catch up with paperwork now. I did enjoy America a lot this time. I am serious thinking of immigrating to your part of the world and I feel I am wasted here (except for H.M.).

    Yours sincerely, Nicolas

It was a terrific PR coup for Aronow—two kings and one president praising his boat. When Aronow received the letter, he immediately forwarded a copy to George Bush. Within a week he received a reply:

June 6, 1986

Dear Don:

Thanks for sharing with me that fascinating letter from Nicolas Iliopoulos. Incidentally, King Hussein is going to be our guest here for dinner in the not too distant future. It sounds like their boat "Hashim" is running well. I can repeat that my old Cigarette, the "Fidelity" is running well too. I've had her out a couple of weekends and the engines have been humming.

    I hope our paths cross soon, my friend.

                        Warm Regards, /s/ George Bush

Customs was also working hard to restore Blue Thunder's reputation as well. Numerous "photo ops" on the boat were held, the stunning visuals of the Blue Thunder streaking across the glittering Miami seafront swaying those impressed by the facade rather than the reality.

Customs also made a Blue Thunder boat ride a must for visiting VIPs. One article in the *Miami Herald* had reported, "The original Blue Thunder was so busy . . . showing off for politicians and reporters that it didn't catch a single smuggler for 17 months." Another reported that "since the boat's unveiling . . . it has become a tourist attraction for visiting government dignitaries" and "diplomats from Italy and England and television crews from as far away as Pittsburgh and Buffalo."

On June 28, 1986, a *Miami Herald* story ran:

MISS LIBERTY TO SMILE ON BLUE THUNDER

If you tune into the Fourth of July celebrations in New York Harbor next week, take a close look at the first boat in the International Naval Review.

Not the battleship *Iowa,* which will carry President Reagan down the Hudson.

Take a look at the little blue-and-white boat right in front of the president's. . . . If all goes as planned, that boat will be the Blue Thunder, pride and joy of the U.S. Customs' fleet.

The 39-foot catamaran, prized for its speed and maneuverability, was hauled to New York this week, Customs spokesman Malcolm Ferguson said Friday.

When the battleship *Iowa* came into view carrying President Reagan to the Liberty Island festivities, Miamians searched their TV screens for Blue Thunder. But the boat wasn't there.

Blue Thunder headquarters is located in the Miami Customs building, in the heart of the city that many believe was revitalized by drug money, in a state whose number one industry is narcotics. The building, surrounded by spectacular high-rise offices, is a modest, nondescript edifice. Blue-jacketed agents scurry in and out. I tell the guard at the front desk that I'm looking for the Blue Thunder tour.

Without looking up, he points down the hall. Following his directions, I proceed through a long corridor. It ends in the back of the building on a waterway. A Blue Thunder boat is docked on the canal. Nearby, a camera crew is waiting. I ask a man holding a Minicam if this is the boat tour of Blue Thunder. He shrugs his shoulders saying, "*Je ne parle pas d'Anglais,*" and points to the boat where two Customs agents, a large black man and a petite woman, are huddled over the engine compartment.

The man, the driver, is adjusting something on one of the Blue Thunder's enormous engines. "Okay, try it now," he says to his partner. She hits the starter and the dual engines turn over, but they don't start.

"Excuse me," I interject. "Is this the Blue Thunder tour? I think I've missed my group."

"Well, sir, they were here yesterday. You can come with these gentlemen and the lady. But you'll have to wait, we're having some problems."

I join the camera crew. One of them speaks English. She says they are from Paris, and they're doing a TV special on drug smuggling in America. They had wanted to go out on Blue Thunder at night and film a drug bust, but they were settling for a ride around Biscayne Bay at noon.

While the man continues tinkering with the engines, I climb onto the boat and sit in the passenger's seat. The boat has a plush interior and the seat is comfortable. To a landlubber, it's an impressive-looking boat. Curiously it's painted black. A black Blue Thunder.

"Maybe we can have them all come back later," the woman whispers to the man. He grunts. Finally, the engines start. It's been ten minutes. I don't know how long the French crew has been waiting, but they look very bored.

Everyone piles on. Our driver puts on his mirrored aviator sunglasses, nudges the dual chrome throttles, and we start down the canal and out into the bay. It's a smooth-riding boat and seems to have power. The driver begins to relax, and he starts talking.

"This is the Blue Thunder boat, the centerpiece of the National Drug Interdiction effort headed by the Vice President of the United States." Then he adds as an afterthought, "Mr. George Bush," presumably for the benefit of the Parisians.

"Is this the boat that Don Aronow built?" I ask.

"Yes, sir, it is," he replies. "You know, I knew the man. I went up to the factory and saw them building these boats. Damn shame what happened to him."

It's a clear, beautiful day. We turn south, picking up considerable speed on the calm, tropical waters of Biscayne Bay. The boat leaves a long, white, curving wake that is directed back toward the downtown Miami skyline. In the noonday sun the glass and mirrored buildings sparkle. The water is a Caribbean turquoise. The French anchorwoman suddenly points and exclaims with delight, "Mee-am-mi Veece! Mee-am-mi Veece!" as her cameraman pans the Minicam across the spectacular scene.

The Customs agents look pleased.

Suddenly the driver puts on the overhead flashing lights and sounds the sirens. We pull alongside a pleasure fishing boat; the small craft, weighed down by the weight of seven Hispanic passengers, is lumbering along. The cameraman hurries over to the side of our boat and focuses on the fishing boat, hoping no doubt that someone on it will pull out an Uzi or start dumping pouches of cocaine overboard.

"Hello there, sir, U.S. Customs," our driver yells. "Sir, how are you today?"

"Okay," says one of the seven. All the men on the boat look up at us, their faces conveying a look of quiet exasperation.

"We're just checking," our driver explains. "Where are you going?"

"We're just fishing."

The agent peers closely at the boat and then asks, "Sir, didn't I stop you last week?"

"Yeah," the man says, nodding patiently. "You did."

"Well, okay, sir, have a nice day."

After we start up again, the driver announces, "They were riding low in the water. That's why I pulled them over. A boat that rides low in the water is one of the things we look for. They could be carrying contraband." In a sheepish aside to his partner he says, "I thought I recognized them, we stopped them a few days ago." Then he shoves the throttles hard, and we start moving at a fast clip.

The wind blows everyone's hair straight back, and the roar of the engines makes it impossible to talk. I check out the woman Customs agent. She looks to be in her early twenties. She's pretty, blond, about five three. She's got a pistol on her hip, but in another outfit she could pass as a cosmetics model at Bloomingdale's. No wonder she has Blue Thunder VIP tour-guide duty.

We cruise around a little longer before returning. On the dock I ask the female agent, "So how many drug smugglers have you caught?"

"None, I've just been doing this for a few months." She used to be an IRS agent. Her job was to freeze the assets of people who owed money to the government, but she became bored and quit after a year.

"I wanted to get some excitement so I transferred to Customs," she says. "But it's been pretty slow. I want to go up to Fort Lauderdale. There they actually hunt for smugglers. Here we just take people out for rides, mostly."

"How are these boats?" I ask.

She explains that they are having a lot of problems with them.

"We have to treat them real gingerly, and we can't really open up with them."

"Why? What happens?"

She pauses. "The engines, they . . . blow up a lot."

Deciding to get an expert opinion on the antidrug boats, I look for Brownie during his "regular office hours" at the Rumrunner. Despite his cavalier and extroverted personality, Brownie has a reputation as one of the best high performance boat product designers in the business, and he holds a number of patents on his work.

"Blue Thunder?" he roars. "You mean Blue Blunder, don't you? The fucking thing is so undependable. It's a dog. If he [Aronow] sold six or seven of them to the public, that was a lot. I doubt he sold that many of them."

Brownie elucidates the problems with the boat. He says that the Blue Thunder is a 38-foot Cigarette cut into two, with a wing that is too narrow for its length to be aerodynamic to any extent. He notes that the "wing" connecting the two halves of the catamaran hull where air rushes through is too small. Because of that, the boat reaps none of the positive benefits usually expected of a "cat" design—especially lift and speed.

Despite Aronow's pronouncements about the catamaran design, Brownie says that Blue Thunder really isn't a catamaran at all. "It's just a wet, slow deep-vee," he notes with disdain. On the Alley, calling a boat wet is about as bad as it gets.

After Aronow produced one of the first Blue Thunders, he took Brownie for a test ride in it to get his opinion. "He brought it down without a deck on it to take a ride," he recalls. "It only went fifty-six miles per hour with a pair of four forties [440 horsepower engines] in it. And that was without the added weight of a deck!"

Aronow had asked him to look at the boat from his perspective as a catamaran designer. Brownie recalls, "I said, 'Don, this is going to be the first boat in history that's going to combine all of the bad habits of both a deep-vee boat and a catamaran.'" Brownie laughs again, adding, "Well, Aronow was a master of selling anything."

The problems of the Blue Thunder went far beyond simply making the boat too narrow, according to Brownie. He says everything is wrong with it and proceeds to rattle off a litany of flaws. In addition to being poorly designed and losing essential aerodynamic lift, it's too heavy by two thousand pounds, made of the wrong materials, has gasoline rather than the more dependable diesel engines, and has feeble stern drives. Because the boat is too heavy and lacks lift, it requires massive engines that even then are required to work far too hard. Consequently, as the Customs woman had said, they blow up.

If the boat had a fatal flaw, Brownie says, it's the mismatch of the stern drives and the powerful engines. "Blue Thunder's TRS drives are weaklings," he says. "Those drives wouldn't take any gaff." The drives—like a transmission on a car—transmit the power from the engines to the propellers, and when the drives go, the engines start spinning freely without the resistance of the props in the water, over-revving almost instantaneously. It's like driving on the highway at 75 mph in a car, pressing the gas pedal to the floor, and then shifting into neutral. With one big difference.

With engines the size of Blue Thunder's, the result is serious. The engines "redline" and often literally tear themselves apart. A 1,000-pound engine breaking apart at tens of thousands of revolutions per minute is a sound that's as close as you can get to that of an explosion on a boat without throwing a match into the gas tank. Sometimes as it disintegrates, the engine parts become red-hot, high-speed steel projectiles that smash their way through the walls of the engine and fly off into space.

"It's called grenading," says Brownie. "You know, like a grenade. So now you know why Don always had Willie [Meyers] along to handle the throttles and Bush just steered the Blue Thunder on his boat rides." He winks: George Bush was kept far away from the engines.

The *Miami Herald* had reported in 1986 that one Blue Thunder blew two engines in just six months. The replacement cost with labor for blowing an engine: about $50,000 for the engine and another $10,000 for the drive, almost half of the original cost of the boat. Brownie points out that it's not surprising the boat had such an abysmal interception record. "At sixty grand a pop per engine/drive, what thirty-five-thousand-dollar-a-year Customs stiff—who wants to keep his job—is really going to open up with it?"

Is Blue Thunder good for anything?

"Well, it's more stable than a deep-vee if your primary job is sitting out there, fucking around waiting for something to happen," Brownie says.

"You mean cruising around the ocean at a slow speed?" I ask.

"No, I mean sitting still and waiting for someone to go by. They're good for sitting still out there."

The problem didn't result from Ben Kramer's lack of design skills, either. Brownie says that Kramer knew how to make a good boat. "He knew what he was doing," Brownie comments. "I was always impressed with the Apache product. Ben built world-class boats. Take his forty-one-foot catamaran. It won the world championship in 1986."

How could two of the best powerboat builders in the world produce the Blue Blunder?

Blue Thunder wasn't just a poorly designed boat. Brownie had pointed out that it had a critical design flaw that undermined its entire mission. When a Customs agent on patrol spotted a smuggler, his overriding thought wouldn't be catching the suspect, but nursing his engines so they wouldn't "grenade."

Brownie's analysis reminded me of Dick Genth's last conversation with Aronow, a week before the murder. Genth, a highly regarded boatbuilder who heads Donzi Marine, had told Aronow that "those boats are absolutely horrible for what Customs wants to do with them . . . that offshore work. They can't keep them running. And they're so slow they can't even get out of their own way." Genth, like Brownie, knew Aronow's sales ability and added, "Don, you could sell an ice maker to an Eskimo."

Aronow had "laughed his ass off," Genth recalled. "He said the boats weren't worth shit, that . . . you can't put enough horsepower in them for what they needed to do with them."

Aronow's joking about the Blue Thunders with his friend was probably his way of trying to explain the unexplainable—why suddenly the master builder couldn't put out a good powerboat. At the height of his career, he was failing on a grand and public scale. His high-profile antidrug crafts were being ridiculed in the press and even by his close associates.

In private, Aronow was very concerned about how he was being perceived. He talked to Jerry Engelman several times about the effects the problems with the Blue Thunders would have on his reputation. "Aronow at this point had a lot riding on his ego and the publicity," recalls Jerry, "and no way was he going to see it go down the drain." In a surprising move, Don covered out of his own pocket the cost of replacing the TRS drives with sturdier ones—at $20,000 per boat on a number of the government's boats. It was an uncharacteristic action and highlighted just how worried he was.

Aronow took great pride in his reputation as a boatbuilder. His world-class boat designs and his racing championships were his real accomplishments. They didn't result from LCN associations, as his construction success most likely had. Now he was hamstrung, everything coming undone because of a secret deal that he had made with Ben Kramer. A man he detested.

Unlike every other time in his long career that he sold a company, Aronow went to great lengths to conceal the transfer of USA Racing and its Blue Thunder contract to Kramer. When Aronow sold it, he told his employees not to tell anyone. "He tells me to keep it a secret," recounts Old Mike. "He said to keep it on the Q.T., 'cause he figured that, you know, it wasn't gonna, maybe it wasn't going to go over [with Customs].

"Then Ben came in and said nothin' was going to change, you know," Old Mike continues. "We didn't know whether we were going to have a job or not, you know, when you sell a company. Ben said, naw, nothin's changing. I knew Ben before he bought the company. I mean, I like Ben."

Old Mike says after the sale Jack and Ben would come over to USA Racing. He recalls, "The both of them would come over, but they didn't take over or nothin'. Don said he would maintain the office upstairs, and they would be downstairs. That was it, that's all they said. And then, everything, the company ran like nothin' happened, running the same way [as before]."

Jerry Engelman joined USA five months after the sale to Kramer. "Don made a point of telling me, you know, he didn't want the connection with the Kramers known." Jerry says that Aronow tested his employees on this issue as he did on how to fend off calls from Lillian on his whereabouts.

"The subject would come up," Engelman recalls, "particularly because there had been the sale, it would come up. 'What's the connection between Apache and USA Racing?' and the proper answer: There wasn't any. It was an instruction on how to answer, on how to handle a certain type of question. He never specifically mentioned that deal to me, ever, it never crossed his lips in my presence. All I know, I know from Ralph [another Aronow employee] and [Old] Mike and fill in the blanks."

Aronow was particularly upset about Kramer's decision to transfer USA Racing's Mark McManus to the Apache facility in Hollywood. McManus was considered one of the best plant supervisors in the high performance boatbuilding business. To cover up the transfer, when a call came in to USA Racing for McManus, the staff was to say that Mark was in the bathroom. Then they had to quickly call Apache in Hollywood and give him the message. Engelman explains, "Mark was a big man [to Aronow] and he didn't want anyone to know he no longer worked for him anymore. Don was real touchy about that."

Jerry didn't consider the subterfuge peculiar for Aronow. "Not in the context for him," he says. "It was just another one of those hush-

hush things for Don that we weren't ever supposed to talk about, like these enormous chunks of hashish he used to keep in his desk upstairs to smoke when his girlfriends came over. Or that often he had Patty [Lezaca] sign his signature on documents and then notarize them because she was a notary. She did a pretty good imitation of his signature, too, but I could tell the difference."

He chuckles as he recalls some of the irony of the Aronow days. "You know what I mean?" he explains. "A notary notarizing a fake signature that she herself forged. That was just Don. But to tell you the truth, I never really did understand the thing with the Kramers."

I drop in to see Steve Bertucelli, director of Broward County Sheriff's Organized Crime Division in his Fort Lauderdale office.

"Did you know that in 1985, Ben and Jack Kramer secretly bought the U.S. government's Blue Thunder boatbuilding company, and they did it with laundered narcotics money?" I ask.

Bertucelli looks apoplectic. "What??? Jesus fucking Christ! Those fucking Blue Thunders. I knew it, I knew it. I always knew there was something fishy about those goddamned boats."

TWELVE

Three weeks before Ben Kramer bought the Blue Thunder company, on August 9, 1985, he was at a mandatory meeting with his probation officer. He was in his fifth year of parole from his 1978 drug-smuggling conviction, and he still had to report regularly. His probation officer, Rory McMahon, surprised him with a request for a urine sample to test for drug usage.

"Here we are standing in the fucking men's room and I'm standing there watching Benny pee into a fucking bottle," recalls McMahon. It's standard practice to accompany parolees into the bathroom to insure that they don't substitute someone else's urine. "So we're there and he's telling me that he's going to be meeting with the top man from the Florida branch of the National Drug Task Force and some bigwigs from Customs."

McMahon found the notion so absurd that he didn't pay any attention. "I said, 'Sure, Benny, right,' and he said they all wanted his opinion on building drug interceptor boats and that he was going to be taking over the contract to make boats for them. And then he hands me the bottle and says that he might be meeting George Bush, too, if he's in town. And if I didn't harass him and I minded my p's and q's, he might even invite me to go to the meeting."

Ben also brought up another of his favorite topics in the men's room that day: Donald Aronow. "He said that Aronow was an overrated piece of shit, and he was going to blow him right out of the water," says Rory. "Aronow was the old dog and his days were come and gone. Benny was the new kid on the street with all the hot ideas. Typical Benny. He's got his fucking head in the urinal but his mind's in the clouds, thinking, 'I'm the greatest, I'm going to be meeting the Vice President discussing business,'" says Rory, chuckling.

The drug test results came back a few days later. Kramer tested positive for cocaine. He contested the results and had his lawyer offer voluminous "scientific" documentation to support his contention that taking vitamins had thrown off the test.

The following week, on August 16, there was activity in a Liechtenstein bank under Kramer's account for Cortrust. Some of his drug profits were moved out of Cortrust into another Kramer corporate shell, Troon Mortgage Investments in the British Virgin Islands. Then Kramer's facilitator, Shaun Murphy, wired $508,180 from Troon to the United States into the account of C.G.L. Investments in Los Angeles. It was recorded as a "loan." From C.G.L. Investments, the newly cleaned money was transfered to the account of a rare-coin company also in Los Angeles.

Four days after the money had arrived in Los Angeles, Super Chief South was incorporated in Florida. The money was transferred to the company's new bank account in Miami.

On August 29, 1985, in Murray Weil's Miami Beach law office, Jack Kramer presented a $100,000 check to Don Aronow. It was a down payment for the purchase of USA Racing, Inc.; its $10,000,000 Blue Thunder contract; the land and factory building; a $500,000 Bell Jet Ranger helicopter; nine high performance boats worth $1,200,000 in various stages of production; and all the manufacturing equipment, molds, furniture, and fixtures at the location. The remainder of the agreed purchase price—a paltry $600,000—was to be paid off over twenty years.

For a $100,000 down payment, Kramer was getting assets worth at least $5 million in addition to the prestigious and lucrative government contract that could be worth tens of millions over the life of the project. Also as part of the agreement, two valued employees—Randy Riggs and Mark McManus—were permanently transferred from USA Racing to Apache. It was the first time in his business career that Aronow sold so much for so little.

"Follow them assets," the IRS agent had advised me months before when I was trying to determine the mob figure who "controlled"

Aronow. But Aronow's helicopter, his assets, and his company had made their way into the most unexpected hands: a thirty-year-old drug-smuggling boat racer and his father, the owner of a commercial lighting company.

Aronow was at the zenith of his life in 1985. He was friends with royalty and high government officials. He was "top gun" on Thunderboat Alley. His racing achievements assured him of lasting fame, and his legendary Cigarette set the standard for beauty, speed, and popularity by which all other powerboats were measured. Yet, he was becoming enmeshed in secrets with a man thirty years his junior who was viewed suspiciously by almost everyone who knew him. As Dick Genth had bluntly put it about Don and Ben, "it's obvious that bully is bad. I don't know why Don would have anything to do with him. It could tarnish Don."

Even Bobby Saccenti, despite a long-term relationship with Kramer, was wary of Ben. "Whenever he [Saccenti] had to make a deal with Kramer, he used to call his brother [in New Jersey] to come down and go in with him," says Bob Magoon. "Bobby's got a family history of mob. He's the young kid in the family, and they all protect him. His brothers, one of them is real Mafia, a hit man. You don't mess around with Bobby because he calls his brother in." Federal agents and MetroDade Homicide allege Lou Saccenti is a hit man and a made member of the Genovese crime family.

What power did Ben Kramer have that caused Aronow to give him USA Racing and its government contract for essentially nothing, and made Saccenti seek the protection of a reputed Mafia killer whenever he had to talk business?

Bell Helicopter, a division of Textron, Inc., has its office in Ft. Worth, Texas. Aronow had purchased at least ten helicopters; someone there should remember him. Ed Lette does, and has surprising information about the helicopter Aronow purchased four years before his murder. Lette says the note on the helicopter was paid off in October 1985. The total price of the chopper was $465,970. The full payment of the outstanding loan—approximately $325,000—was made soon after the Super Chief deal. Ben Kramer already owned the helicopter at this point. Yet the payment was made directly to Textron from Aronow Stables.

In the Super Chief promissory note Murray Weil had inserted "Item 27." It insured that the payments (which were a whopping $5,500 per month) would continue on the Jet Ranger's loan after Don sold USA Racing. However, just a month after Kramer got the helicopter, someone was paying off all the money owed on it. Was it Don's money? Or was Ben using Aronow again, this time to front the buyout through Aronow Stables, a company that Don still owned?

There were only two possible explanations—neither legal. Either Aronow was acting as a conduit for what was surely $325,000 of Kramer's drug money and running it through a legitimate company, Aronow Stables, to avoid government detection. Or he was shelling out his own money for a helicopter he no longer owned—and it was being used by a man who was telling his probation officer he was making only $25,000 a year. From either perspective, Aronow was helping a drug smuggler, at considerable risk to himself.

In response to my question of whether there was anything else unusual about the helicopter's records, Lette flips through the rest of his file. He mentions that Aronow had been planning to transfer the chopper to another of his companies on June 28, 1985, according to a letter Textron received. Not long after, however, Randy Riggs, as Aronow's vice president, sent a letter cancelling the transaction.

It was the mention of the helicopter payments in the August 29, 1985, promissory note that provided the first solid hint that something unusual was going on between Kramer and Aronow. Now, the June 28, 1985, letter from Randy Riggs to Bell Helicopter was another interesting clue. It suggested that within four months, at most, of the February Blue Thunder contract announcement, Kramer was making his move to grab USA Racing and the helicopter from Aronow.

I call Riggs. When I mention the helicopter and the Super Chief deal, he becomes agitated. "This is a very real situation for me right now," he says. "I know that Ben's in prison, but Jack Kramer's out [on bail]. I'll try to be helpful, and as a book goes, I have no problems there. But when it comes to trying to solve a murder, and I say, yeah, this guy came in or Ben threatened this guy or I saw this amount of cash or Don did this, well, I don't want to get involved in that. You see things, but then, you don't see things. Don's dead, and I want to stay around."

As soon as I mention Jack Kramer, he terminates the conversation. "Here I am," he says nervously. "Jack's gonna be riding in the damn helicopter with me Saturday [at the boat races], which I'm not happy about, but the guy that's paying me to do it says do it, so I have no choice. Don always told me something, and I haven't really lived by it because it's not my personality, but he said, 'You talk, you lose.' And he always said that. He said that weekly.

" 'You talk, you lose,' " Riggs repeats. "I can hear him saying that. I can see his face telling me that right now. And here I am talking to you."

I drop by to see a DEA agent who had participated in the seizure of some of Kramer's assets hoping he might have more information about the Jet Ranger. After being cleared through security by intercom, I'm buzzed through a door that looks as if it could withstand a direct hit from a bazooka. We settle in an empty conference room. There's a mostly eaten birthday cake on the conference room table, Styrofoam cups and paper plates are strewn about. "It was one of the secretaries' birthday today," the agent says. "Want some?"

As we split the remnants of the cake, I ask about Don's helicopter. "Aronow's chopper?" he says. "Hmmm. I don't know if that's the same one that Ben was using in his offshore powerboat racing or not. I know Ben had a big Lockheed Jetstar, four engines. It's really not that good for a corporate jet because it's so big, it uses so much fuel." The agent says when Ben realized that his days were numbered, he unloaded the plane. "Hold on, I'll see where the jet was taken to."

He leaves the room and returns with some files. "It was traded. Right outside of Chicago. A place called Trademaster's International. When the [DEA] agent went by using the address they gave [for the aircraft's transfer], there were three names on the door. But not that one. That name wasn't even there."

The agent says he can't help me track the helicopter. He doesn't have time. He says he's "got bigger fish to fry than a $500,000 aircraft that may or may not have been paid off with Ben's narco-dollars." Ben is already incarcerated, held without bail pending the trial, but there are still problems with the case. Kramer's activities stretched around the globe, and tracking down the details of the operation is painfully difficult. There are brains behind Kramer's organization and someone is keeping one step ahead of the feds.

The smuggling organization has continued to move the cash, despite Kramer's imprisonment. The feds thought they had cornered $14 million in Liechtenstein and Switzerland. Then they found it had disappeared. At first they thought it had been wired to Hong Kong because there were some transactions there, but they were unable to locate it. "We're not really sure where it's at now, and we're losing fourteen million," he says disgustedly.

Despite the problems, the DEA agent says that one of Kramer's pilots is giving them a better picture of how Kramer operated: "He would fly Kramer to the Caribbean first and then to South America. On some flights the guy said there were duffel bags and duffel bags stuffed with cash."

"How much?"

The DEA agent looks at me. "We just really don't know," he says, shaking his head. "Millions. Sometimes they would carry the cash stacked in big igloo coolers, those hundred-quart coolers, like the ones you see on fishing boats. Depending on the denominations, in the smaller denominations they were used to, each one could hold a couple of million dollars."

Our conversation turns to a high performance offshore boat race coming up that week in Sarasota, often of interest to the feds. He suggests that I go. "Maybe Jack [Kramer] will introduce you to his friend Sammy," he says. "You know, on one of Sammy's appearances on the Johnny Carson show, at the end he looks at the camera and says, 'Hey, Ben, man! I luv ya!' "

Sammy Davis, Jr., was close to the Kramers. Sammy's wife acted as a celebrity announcer at Ben's 1985 Apache Offshore Challenge Race. (The same race for which the governor of Florida issued an official proclamation declaring it "Apache Offshore Challenge" day in Florida.)

Since Ben's up in Marion prison with convicted Colombian king-pin Carlos Lehder in a 23-hour-a-day lockup and Jack's been in-dicted, the agent says he's lost interest in attending the races. "But I can guarantee you, at any given offshore powerboat race there's going to be federal agents all over the place. The only thing is, if you see any of us there you recognize . . ." He pauses, waiting for me to fill in the blanks.

"Yeah?" I'm not getting his message.

"Don't say hello." He laughs.

The Sarasota offshore regatta is one of the big events of the circuit. The day before the actual race, tens of thousands of spectators invade Long Boat Key to get a look at some of the sleekest and fastest powerboats in the world.

The area is filled with large tractor trailers carrying the boats and equipment. The crews are busy working up to the last minute making final adjustments. Spectators stand around gawking at the powerful machines, their engines belching out clouds of smoke when they start. For the duration of the event, the crews and especially the drivers are celebrities, attracting throngs of bikini-clad groupies.

A local TV station provides live coverage, and the regatta has the atmosphere of one giant Fourth of July picnic.

The race headquarters is at the Long Boat Key Club, but everyone from the Alley is at the Sheraton bar. Brownie is there, and as usual he's got a good-looking woman by his side. Also as usual he buys me a drink. I ask him about Don's last helicopter. He remembers that Don used to land it on the roof of USA Racing, but other than that he doesn't know what happened to it. He seems a little disappointed that he can't help.

"Did we ever talk about Aronow's Air Force?" he says, perking up. "He owned an aircraft company back in the midsixties, I can't think of the name of it. It was up at Lauderdale Exec, or Lauderdale International or someplace. A shitload of planes. It had a lot of planes and it burned down mysteriously. They had a big arson investigation and all kinds of shit."

"Aronow owned the company?"

"I think he had a junior partner, but it was Aronow's company. It burned fucking flat. I think they found a Zippo lighter outside the place right at the edge [of the burn marks]. They never arrested anybody to the best of my knowledge, but I remember it was push and shove whether they were going to get paid by the insurance company."

I ask if Jack Kramer is around. Brownie says he hasn't seen him, but if I'm lucky, Joey Ippolito might show up.

"I thought Joey Ip was still in prison for breaking parole when he went out to see Jimmy Caan," I say.

"He's out again, I saw him a few months ago," Brownie replies. "Joey's got a really fancy restaurant in Point Pleasant, New Jersey. I always enjoy seeing Joey. He's a fucking ton of fun. He was a good racer. Had big balls. Now, his brother is crazier than a fucking bedbug. Louie Ip. Nobody likes to see him. He's rough. I think he's in jail for forty, fifty years, for everything. Drugs, extortion, you name it."

John Crouse, Aronow's publicist, wanders by. When I ask if he's seen Jack Kramer, he launches a nonstop monologue. "Not since Key West [Powerboating World Championship]," he says. "Jack walks up to me and says, 'Here's the *big mouth*,' and shook my hand at the same time. And I said, 'Jack, what do you mean by that?' He says, 'I don't like what you're writing in your column in *Powerboating* magazine about Ben. My Ben-zee wouldn't hurt a flea.' I didn't get hot until I walked away. I wasn't thinking about it, I wasn't planning to beat him up."

Crouse says Ben called him collect from federal prison. Ben wanted to get a copy of *Ocean Race: A History of Offshore Power-boat Racing*, a comprehensive book that Crouse has been working on for the past seven years. But Crouse couldn't decide whether to give Ben a copy.

"I said, 'Ben, there may be stuff in the book that you don't like. I call a spade a spade. You were arrested for a major crime and people don't like that,' and Ben went off on his tirade. He said, 'Hey, I'm not lily-white,' but that he wasn't involved in the stuff that the government says he was. Ben says that he just put people in touch with other people, and they became major criminals. People met in his boat shop then went out doing major conspiracies, but he wasn't the guy.

"I said, 'Ben, some of us are pissed off about drug smugglers, and we're going to do whatever it takes to do something about it. Get rid of some of you bastards. If it takes some of us getting shot or killed, we're going to do it.'"

Brownie looks at me and rolls his eyes. Crouse is the only person on Thunderboat Alley who would talk to Ben Kramer that way.

Crouse says that Kramer understood his position and it made him consider sending his book to Ben. "Kramer and his father have always been good to me," Crouse says. "They like me. I said, 'Ben, you got one complimentary. I owe you that much.' And then he said to come to the prison and he would tell me the real story."

"The real story about what?" I ask.

"The arrest," Crouse replies. "He said that people want him to write books. People want to do a movie. He won't talk to anybody. There'll be a lot of people who'll get hurt if he talks. I don't doubt that that's plenty true. I'm certain he could tell awesome stories."

Then without a pause for air, Crouse launches into his favorite subject: the memorial dinner that he put on for Don Aronow in 1987. Lillian Aronow had boycotted it and had her friends avoid it as well. As a result, almost no one showed up to Crouse's great and ongoing embarrassment. "I did nothing to deserve it, and I don't appreciate somebody chopping on me like that," he says. "It was going to be a toast for Don originally. Well, actually it was going to be a roast but Don didn't want to be roasted. When he was murdered, it just slid off into a memorial. But she and her clique didn't approve and they went behind my back."

His diatribe continues. "You know, in the first place, half that clique that I know have been heavy drug users. They fuck around in orgies, you know, stuff like that. So it kind of pisses me off to be put

down by somebody like that. What a world. Ha! Whatever happened
to a handshake and sit down and talk about things? That whole level
of society is going to be our downfall.

"I think [Don's secretary] Patty Lezaca did a number on her
[Lillian Aronow], too. Believe you me, I'll untangle it. Patty will be
sitting in a pile of shit when I'm done with it. I think that if Lillian
ever found out what she said about Don when the murder was still
hot, she would gag. Those two will cut each other's throats eventually. I don't really care if I don't see or hear from Lillian Aronow
again." Crouse suddenly sees someone he knows at the other end of
the room, waves, and shoots off. Within seconds he's talking nonstop
to his new audience.

Brownie notices Randy Riggs standing at the entrance to the bar.
He suggests that Riggs might know where Jack Kramer is. We've
never met in person, and when I introduce myself, Randy looks
uncomfortable. "No one on the street knows about it," he says,
referring to the Super Chief South deal. "That's where I need to be
quiet." He's also worried that Jack Kramer might see us talking so
he suggests that we get together later. We meet that evening.

I ask him about the June 28, 1985, letter he sent to Bell Helicopter
canceling a transfer of Aronow's helicopter from USA Racing to
another holding company.

Riggs says that immediately after he wrote the letter Ben Kramer
took possession of the helicopter. Murray Weil structured the deal.
There was a big discussion about sending the paperwork into the
FAA. Aronow told Riggs not to file it. Riggs recalls, "I said, 'Don, we
can't sell the helicopter without sending the paperwork into the
FAA,' And he said, 'Yes, I can.' I said fine."

After that, Riggs says he flew for the Apache Race Team exclusively, but he remained on Don's payroll and to outsiders he appeared to work for Don. But Aronow never again flew in the
helicopter after that meeting in Weil's office. Eventually Jack Kramer formally "transferred" Riggs to Ft. Apache Marina and made
him marina manager.

The helicopter transfer in June and the secret sale of USA Racing
a few months later deeply disturbed Randy, and he still doesn't
understand what was happening. "There is a lot of stuff that went on
there, I'm not really sure about it. I wasn't happy with Don." Randy
talked to Aronow about being forced to work for Ben. "Don said,
'You may be working for Apache,'" Riggs recalls, "'but you're still
with me.' In my mind it's difficult to live like that and be loyal to one
or the other."

Randy comments sadly, "He had bought and sold companies all along, but he had never sold me. I always stayed with him. But when he sold USA Racing, I felt like I had been sold."

Randy doesn't like Ben, commenting that Kramer has an inflated ego and he expects to get whatever he wants. After working for Ben for a while Randy quit. "It was best to leave," he says cryptically. "Whether I was scared, I don't want to say."

Randy had nagging doubts and suspicions about Ben Kramer. Just as perplexing as the sale of USA Racing for him was the long-term relationship between Kramer and Aronow. It puzzled him for the ten years that he worked for Aronow and he could never understand what tied the two men together. The more he saw, the stranger the relationship seemed.

Beginning in the mid-1970s, Riggs says Ben used to drop by to see Aronow at Cigarette Racing Team. For a high-school dropout with a part-time job, Ben's lifestyle clearly didn't add up even then. Nor did he bother to try to hide the extravagances. With his hair pulled back in a long ponytail—the trademark style of Miami dope dealers—he was usually driving one of three or four late-model Mercedes he owned. He also flaunted his two new Cigarette boats, a Bertram, and four yachts.

Riggs could never understand why Don would tread lightly around the annoying teenager. Ben didn't seem like the type with whom Aronow would have much in common—he wasn't considered particularly bright, he was disliked by most of the people who knew him, and he exhibited an arrogance that irritated the veterans on the street. Yet, Don let Ben spend hours hanging around the office and his factories.

When Ben got out of prison in 1980 after his first conviction for smuggling, Don had simply given him the 41-foot championship catamaran mold that Ben then used to start Apache Race Team. This really puzzled Riggs who had seen firsthand how tight Aronow was with everything he owned. Aronow always commanded a high price for his prized molds, usually in excess of $100,000. He never gave them away—in several instances he connived to get them back. This one was considered a superior design—one that Aronow could have used to make the catamarans for Blue Thunder.

Aronow also provided the land that Kramer used for his Ft. Apache complex, according to Riggs. The three parcels that housed Ft. Apache went through a holding company, and a fourth piece went directly to Ben and Bobby Saccenti for Apache's racing team.

Ben even tried to cash in on the valuable Aronow name by using

it in early Apache advertising without clearing it with Don. It triggered a lawsuit against Aronow from the new owners of Cigarette,
who claimed violation of their noncompete clause. Aronow settled
with Cigarette out of court for an undisclosed sum.

Ben wasn't content to take just from Aronow. Riggs says that later
Ben tried to extend his relationship with Aronow to Don's friends.
He tried to capitalize on Bob Magoon's championship racing repu-
tation by naming one of the first Apache raceboats *The Dr. Bob
Magoon.* Magoon "went crazy," says Randy, and made Kramer re-
move his name from the stern of the boat.

But it was the Super Chief South deal, Riggs says, that stunned
him the most. He says, "Don specifically kept everyone out of it,
including Patty and myself. He kept everybody out of it, whereas
with all the other contracts, all the other deals, we all were involved.
Prior to Super Chief I had worked with Murray. Me and Patty always
worked with him on contracts."

When Don came back from Murray Weil's office on August 29,
1985, he called all of his employees together, Riggs explains. "He
announced that Ben had purchased the company. But that we were
never, ever, to talk about it with anyone. No one on the street was
ever to know."

After weeks of trying to run into accused drug lord Jack Kramer
"accidentally" at some public event where we could talk surrounded
by the relative safety of others, I decide to stop by his office. He's
out on $250,000 bail on the Florida federal money laundering indict-
ment, and a fed tells me that he is spending a lot of time at the
government-seized Apache plant in Hollywood, Florida. The fed
comments angrily that they can keep him out of Ft. Apache Marina
complex in Miami, but not out of the Hollywood factory.

When the Florida feds were forced to move prematurely on the
Kramers' assets in August 1987, someone made a clerical error in
the seizure application. The federal government had seized all of Ft.
Apache Marina on the Alley and all of the Apache business operations. They had not, however, seized the actual building that housed
the boat-manufacturing facilities. As a result of this technicality, Jack
was free to spend as much time there as he wished—he just couldn't
get involved in the business. Instead, the U.S. Marshals Service
appointed Mark McManus to run the Apache boat-building operations pending the outcome of the trials.

The manufacturing facilities are housed in a block-long building
on a side street in an industrial section of town. I park several blocks

away so no one will see my car and walk the rest of the way to the plant gate. A worker says the offices are on the second floor. At the top of the stairs there is a long, winding corridor decorated with photos of winning Apache racing boats. Walking along, I step across an electronic beam that apparently notifies the office when someone is coming. I look over my shoulder, half expecting to see some muscular bodyguards armed with semi-automatic weapons, but the area is deserted.

No one is at the reception desk at the end of the hall, but loud laughter is coming from the corner office, the general manager's office. I stick my head in, expecting to find Mark McManus. Instead, it's an older man whom I recognize from photographs as Jack Kramer.

He's on the phone. He points me to a couch and continues talking. The office is large, wood paneled, and tastefully furnished. Jack has a large mahogany executive's desk, and it's piled high with paperwork. He's laughing and in a good mood. The call is evidently from a customer and Jack is confirming that Apache will meet their promised delivery date on a boat. So much for the feds keeping Jack out of Apache business.

For a man charged with operating the money-laundering portion of one of the largest drug-smuggling operations in the world, Jack Kramer is not at all what I had expected. He looks to be in his late-fifties, wears glasses a bit too large for his face, and is casually dressed in golfer's type clothes. He's a little overweight with soft, tanned facial features and grayish-black hair that falls on his forehead. His pleasant, even jovial, demeanor reminds me of my uncle—the one who always gave me a dollar bill when I came to visit as a kid.

When he gets off the phone, I tell him I'm writing about Don Aronow. Jack smiles, "Oh, Don, yes, what a great guy. I really loved him. He was really something." He goes on to say that he first met Aronow in the early seventies when he moved from Philadelphia to Florida and that they were close "right up to the end."

Jack is a schmoozer. He's using the same chummy tone on me that he did with the customer on the phone. He continues, "We all used to hang out a lot. We always had a great time with Don." He proceeds to tell me about the time he, his son Benny and Sammy Davis, Jr., had a surprise birthday party for Don. He promises to get me a copy of the videotape they made with all of them singing "Happy Birthday, Don." He says Sammy was a riot and I'll love it.

Don's murder shocked Jack but really didn't surprise him. Jack says Don "screwed too many women for his own good." His theory is that Don was killed by a jealous husband or boyfriend in a fit of rage. He mentions the angry confrontation between Miami attorney Skip Taylor and Aronow at Calder Race Track. "Taylor was really furious, he told him to stay away from his wife. He threatened him, really threatened him, but Don didn't listen and continued seeing her. And then he's killed. And he was shot in the balls, I hear. You know those defense attorneys, they deal with bad dudes all the time. All Skip would have to do is make a phone call. Know what I mean?"

The problem with Taylor reminds Jack of Aronow's fight with another man over a woman. He recounts that King Hussein was deeply in love with Lillian in the late seventies when she was still single and living in Palm Beach. He pleaded with Aronow not to marry her, even offering him a million dollars to leave her alone. "Don went ahead anyway," laughs Jack. "What a guy."

To my amazement, Jack keeps talking nonstop, soon bringing up the subject of drug smuggling. "I don't know what all this fuss is about marijuana," he declares. "It's simply ridiculous. You know even federal judges—Supreme Court nominees—have admitted using it. What's the big deal?" Jack says making grass illegal doesn't stop its use. According to him, it breeds crime. "By making stuff illegal, people just want it all the more. All you do is allow these drug kingpins and crime bosses a way to make lots of money," he says, shaking his head. I don't know what banana boat Jack thinks I've just fallen off, but I'm beginning to get the impression I'm talking to John Crouse's twin.

Jack asserts that marijuana will eventually be completely legalized. "It didn't work with Prohibition, and it won't work with marijuana," he declares. Suddenly, Jack jumps up and suggests that we go look around the plant. He pats me on the back as we walk downstairs.

The Apache factory looks like the boat-building facilities on the Alley, but it's a lot bigger. The Kramers never did anything on a small scale. A sleek, black, 41-foot Apache cat stands majestically on mounts in one of the bays. Jack suggests I climb up and take a look inside. Even though he's old enough to be my father, he helps boost me up the ladder. He climbs up beside me and, as he talks expansively about the superior quality of Apache boats, he jokingly pokes me in the ribs several times. When we climb back down, Jack again insists on helping me down. It finally sinks in—he's been checking to see if I'm wearing a wire.

As Jack walks me outside toward his new Mercedes sedan, he tells me how much he misses Don and how hurt he is that Lillian Aronow has been suggesting Ben was behind the murder. "I just don't know why she says all these nasty things. Ben loved Don. He was our friend." He gives me a warm smile and firm handshake and suggests that I call him the following week about the Aronow birthday video. With that he starts the car, waves, and speeds away. By the time I get to my car, he's vanished into traffic and I lose the opportunity to follow him.

I call several times in the following months hoping to get some answers to questions about the real relationship betwen Aronow and the Kramers, but he's never there. When I ask about the video, the secretary says that Jack wanted me to know that he tried, but he could never find it.

THIRTEEN

When Ben Kramer bought USA Racing and its Blue Thunder contract, he already had three drug-related arrests dating back to 1971, when he was charged with possession of LSD and marijuana. He had been placed on juvenile probation for one year.

In 1974, he was arrested on a state charge of selling marijuana and carrying a concealed weapon during the commission of a felony. Adjudication was withheld, and there was no disposition of the charges.

A year later he was charged in connection with the importation of a ton of Colombian marijuana. When the twenty-year-old Kramer was arrested by two DEA agents, he told them he had been contacted at a marina "by two older, Italian-looking individuals," the agents' report details. According to Kramer, the men asked if he wanted to make a lot of money for one day's work, and Kramer told them "he would like to, but didn't want to kill anyone."

While the DEA agents were detaining Ben and one of his "off-loaders," they overheard Ben telling the off-loader that one of their partners had evidently "talked his guts out and opened his mouth like a sewer and the cops knew everything." A few minutes later,

Kramer told the agents that he would like to "help them get the Italians."

The DEA agents didn't believe that Kramer was simply a young guy trying to make some quick money. Their arrest report concludes, "It is felt that Kramer's statement is totally untrue in regards as to how he got involved in this offense," and that "Benjamin Kramer is the number one defendant in this case as far as culpability."

After his arrest, Kramer was released pending his trial and he fled the area. For two years he was a fugitive living on a farm near Tampa, although he continued to slip back into Miami to visit his family and friends. During one trip home he was arrested by the Broward County Sheriff's Office for the reckless operation of a vessel and charged with resisting arrest and obstruction by a disguised person. Once again, all state charges against him were dismissed.

It took the federal government to nab Kramer. Since there was still the 1975 fugitive warrant on him stemming from the smuggling charges, the police had to turn him over to the federal government. For those charges he was tried and convicted in December 1977. Even then, Kramer almost wriggled free.

"While awaiting sentencing the U.S. Probation Department was directed by the court to prepare a sentencing report," a Justice Department official familiar with the case recalls. The department's recommendations, while not binding, were an important factor in the judge's decision whether to give prison time or probation. Some surprising figures stepped forward to plead for probation for the young, seemingly recidivous, smuggler.

"In an effort to convince the department to recommend probation, a number of influential people interceded on Ben's behalf," the official explains. He suggests that we meet for lunch. When I arrive at the restaurant at the agreed-upon time, he has already finished eating. The waitress is handing him the check.

"It was a good meal," he says cheerily as I sit down. "Thanks." He stands, plunks the check down in front of me, and says, "Have a nice lunch, and hey, don't forget your package there when you leave." He walks off.

Beside me on the chair is a large envelope. Inside are a number of confidential files about Ben Kramer. They are stamped with the markings of a federal agency and they pertain to a variety of Ben's problems with the law.

First in the packet is a card. It is a note from NCIC that Ben Kramer often used the alias Darth Vader Kramer. Also included in my envelope are copies of Ben's high school transcripts from South

Broward H.S., indicating that he had flunked out in the eleventh grade with a 0.6 (out of 4.0) grade point average. His highest grade was a "C" in civics, while most of the rest were "Fs" or Incompletes.

Next was a copy of a telegram sent from a man in a powerful political position:

WESTERN UNION

December 14, 1977

U.S. Probation Department
Ft. Lauderdale, Florida

It has been brought to my attention that you are considering the parole of Benjamin B. Kramer. Mr. Sam Gilbert of Encino, California, who has been deeply involved in helping young people in California, has indicated to the U.S. Probation Department that if the above mentioned individual is granted parole, he will assume the responsibilities for his employment, as well as undertake rehabilitative efforts.

Mr. Gilbert has a community-wide reputation for integrity. I believe he would carry out his duties toward Mr. Kramer in a highly responsible manner.

Senator Alan Cranston

The "Mr. Sam Gilbert" mentioned in the telegram was the same man indicted in November 1987 along with Jack and Ben Kramer in the Southern Florida District drug-money-laundering case.

Senator Cranston wasn't the only member of Congress to take an active interest in the young felon. Senator Stone of Florida had also interceded for Ben with the commission and then became concerned that his recommendation of leniency for a drug smuggler might be misinterpreted by the judge.

A handwritten "Report of Contact," dated December 14, 1977, re: Benjamin Kramer, read, "Laura Hall of U.S. Senator Stone's office got a call from Mr. Gilbert in Calif. ref D. [the defendant] and are concerned about this Federal parolee. I advised her of D's status before the Court and she didn't want to have Mr. Stone's name mentioned to the Judge. Would not want it misconstrued he was interfering w/the Judicial process. I agreed."

Ben's plight was also taken up by a state supreme court justice, who extolled the virtues of Sam Gilbert. A December 7, 1977, letter, from the "Chambers of the Superior Court, Los Angeles, California" was almost identical to the Cranston one, except it added, "In summary, I would only repeat that Mr. Gilbert would be an excellent choice to help Mr. Kramer in his effort to reestablish his life. And I have no doubt both Mr. Gilbert and Mr. Kramer will be successful. Thank you for your courtesy and cooperation."

The letter was signed, "Loren Miller, Jr. Judge, Superior Court of Los Angeles."

Six days later, Judge Miller apparently still had young Ben on his mind. When Miller learned that his December 7 letter didn't reach the parole board, he took no more chances and dashed off a telegram. The December 13, 1977, telegram from Judge Miller explained that "the following was sent to you on Dec. 7. Regret that it did not arrive," and the entire text of his first letter was included.

Kramer was just twenty-two years old in 1977, yet somehow he had mobilized two U.S. senators and a state superior court judge in an effort to keep out of jail.

It's easy to become jaded in Miami.

"Woolworth's sells out of Uzis," read the headline in a local south Florida magazine. The article went on to report that the "five-and-dime" store chain had decided to offer semiautomatic Uzis at one of its Miami outlets. The price $595. The weapons sold out in one day.

There is no other city in America like Miami. It's always slightly out of kilter, as if the residents have played just a bit too long in the sun. But even for Miami the tale of Don Aronow, Ben Kramer, and Thunderboat Alley was beginning to resemble one of *Miami Vice*'s more farfetched story lines.

Here is the Vice President of the United States in his first major role as leader of the War on Drugs overseeing the decision to give a government contract to Don Aronow, a man who has been associated with the Mafia for decades. Then the Vice President writes a letter to the man emphasizing, "Again Don this day [with you] was one of the greatest of my life."

While Customs thinks Aronow is building its drug interceptor boats, he's smoking hashish in his office. All the while ducking calls from his wife, a woman King Hussein supposedly offered him a million bucks not to marry. As Aronow daydreams about a future ambassadorship when his friend the Vice President becomes president, the man who really holds the government contract is a thirty-year-old drug kingpin who calls himself Darth Vader and makes home videos of his dope-buying trips to Colombia.

A U.S. senator, who would become a presidential contender, is urging that this third-time drug offender caught with a ton of dope be granted leniency. And Sammy Davis, Jr., is waving and shouting to a drug dealer on national television, "Hey, Ben, man! I luv ya!"

Finally, two of the best powerboat builders in the world are building the U.S. government's drug interdiction boats—and the Customs Service can't understand why the boats keep blowing up.

Come to think of it, this story was too far out even for *Miami Vice*.

Despite the bizarre twists in the tale, however, nothing that I've found has brought me any closer to the motive for Aronow's murder. I call the man who originally tipped me off to the connection between the Kramers, Shaun Murphy, and the Isle of Man investigation. He agrees to meet me at the "usual spot" near the abandoned concrete plant at the end of the Alley. Going back to basics, the mob connection, I ask him if he ever saw Meyer Lansky with anyone from the Alley.

"Well, no, I never did," he replies thoughtfully, "but I—you know who was a great admirer of Meyer? Ben. Ben was a great admirer of the wiseguys. He was one of these great admirers of Meyer Lansky and other guys. He used to say Lansky was a real neat guy."

"Kramer knew Meyer?"

"Oh." The contact acts surprised. "I guess I didn't tell you. Now this is strictly confidential, you can't ever say I told you. Meyer Lansky was Ben's great-uncle."

Suddenly the Aronow-Kramer relationship came into sharp focus.

Arthur Nehrbass, the former head of MetroDade's organized crime unit and retired agent-in-charge of the Miami FBI office, had once told me that if a man isn't a made member of La Cosa Nostra, he's considered "property," the term the mob would use. That property would be available to other organized crime figures to use, and they would probably have to kick back to the owner of that property.

"Donald Aronow could've been a piece of owned property," Nehrbass had explained, "and they might use him for many things. He would be owned—and could be leased out." Nehrbass had also said that according to the code of the underworld, Don's companies would really belong to the mob to do with as it pleased.

If the Kramer-Lansky relationship was true, it explained many things, particularly how Kramer, just twenty-five years old when he got out of prison in 1980, was able to run over Aronow like a steamroller for seven years, appropriating everything he had.

Bob Duker, the FBI agent who supervised the Southern Illinois Federal District investigation of Ben, has heard about a familial relationship. "I've heard that there is, and I've heard that there isn't," he says. "I mean, we didn't give a shit as far as we were concerned. As far as us, who gives a shit that he's related to Meyer Lansky? We're not worried about who he's related to. You hear a lot of things, that's the rumor going around."

"What about all these people who came to his assistance like Senator Alan Cranston?"

"Well, [Ben Kramer] has a lot of pop," Duker agrees.

A Florida DEA agent familiar with Ben Kramer says there is a family connection. "The word we had was nephew," he explains. "That the mother—or was it the father? One of them was—so Ben was—what does that make him?"

MetroDade Homicide had also heard about the family ties. Detective Steve Parr says, "You know, that sounds familiar. Someone had told us that. I've seen that in my notes when I was going through them not too long ago."

An IRS agent familiar with the case says he wouldn't be surprised. He comments that Mel Kessler used to be one of Lansky's attorneys and that L.A. businessman Sam Gilbert was associated with Meyer as well. "I think Sam Gilbert was more than a front for Lansky. I think he occupied a position of fairly high stature in the Lansky organization. He wasn't a worker, he was a boss." Gilbert, a friend of Senator Cranston's, was known among federal investigators as "the Meyer Lansky of the West Coast."

The agent says that a family relationship would certainly explain how a young punk drug smuggler would be tapped into such powerful figures as Kessler and Gilbert and how he repeatedly wriggled out of his difficulties with the law over the years. "In the past," he says, "Ben's connections have gotten him out of trouble again and again, that's clear."

I stop by the Federal Building to see Kramer's former probation officer Rory McMahon. He confirms a connection. "Yeah, it's through Jack's wife," he says. "She's Meyer's niece. That makes Ben Meyer's great-nephew."

McMahon also comments that all the people surrounding Ben are connected with Lansky. He thinks Sam Gilbert may even be related because Ben called him his uncle. "Then there's Mel Kessler, the attorney who was indicted along with Jack and Ben," McMahon notes. "He used to represent Lansky at one time and was Ben's attorney on his second drug bust in '74. A lot of Ben's attorneys over the years were Meyer's attorneys from long ago. Like Joseph Varon and E. David Rosen. And you know who the registered agent is for Apache Boats? Emerson Allsworth. He was Meyer Lansky's Broward County attorney." He adds that he's heard Rosen will be Jack's defense lawyer in the upcoming Florida money laundering case. Everywhere I look the Kramers are surrounded by the aura of Meyer Lansky.

McMahon stands up, and suggests we leave the building. "I'll show you something. We'll take my car."

He opens a file cabinet and removes a shoulder harness and a large pistol. Seeing my reaction as he straps on the gun, he laughs and says, "The .357 magnum: Don't leave home without it."

We leave Ft. Lauderdale, taking his red sports car south on I-95 until he suddenly veers off across two lanes of traffic to take the Hallandale exit in Broward County. He drives as if he's practicing for the Miami Grand Prix.

We cruise around a quiet residential neighborhood and pull up to a guardhouse marking the entrance of one of Florida's upper-class "secured communities." Rory flashes his badge, and we drive through, finally stopping in front of a large house that borders on two spectacular waterways. A black rottweiler sticks its enormous head over the fence and starts barking.

"Number six sixty Hibiscus Lane, Hallandale, Florida," Rory declares. "This is Benny's half-a-million-dollar house. His wife and kids are here now. The government's in the process of seizing it, though they're letting them stay there for a while."

He puts the car in gear and starts slowly down the street counting houses. "Eighth house," he declares. "Here it is. Number six twelve Hibiscus Lane. This is Meyer Lansky's old house."

"That house over there"—he points across the street—"'Alley Boy' Persico, the brother to Carmine 'the Snake' Persico from the New York Columbo Mafia family. 'Little Ray' Thompson used to live down the street before he got indicted as a major marijuana smuggler. Up on the corner was Eugene Hicks, remember him? His boatbuilding partner on the Alley was Tommy Adams, the guy who was blasted full of holes on I-95 by the Colombians a few years back. Eugene is dead, too. Stabbed to death right in that house.

"On the cross street up there"—he gestures a little farther down the road—"Phil 'Brother' Moscato. He's got pending indictments with the Miami Strike Force. He's New York Luchese family. And Vito DiVanzo's house. He's Luchese, too, tied in with Anthony 'Tumac' Acceturo out of New Jersey."

The mention of Acceturo's name reminds me that Swats Mulligan, the Genovese hit man who was friendly with Aronow, was surveilled meeting a number of times with him in Miami. McMahon isn't surprised. He says they're all connected in Miami and adds that Benny's house used to belong to a relative of Albert Anastasia.

"So what d'ya think?" he says with a big grin on his face. "Nice neighborhood, eh?"

Benjamin Kramer a crown prince in the Lansky empire.

No wonder he acted like a spoiled and ill-mannered scion who expected to inherit his family's fortunes. In his world, filled with second- and third-generation LCN members, young Ben was royalty, mob style, and as such he was accorded "respect" at the world's finest casinos and fawned upon by Mafia groupies such as Sammy Davis, Jr.

Accustomed to rubbing shoulders with mob potentates from an early age, Ben would have no fear of anyone. When he had trouble with the law—as he often did—a vast network of influence and the best attorneys money could buy would always be there for him. Growing up under the watchful eye of Meyer, Ben would learn the significance of U.S. senators, state superior court judges, and high-powered Washington law firms in a way that his high school civics teacher never dreamed possible.

From the time Ben made his first appearance on the Alley as a teenager, there was clearly something special about him. The tough men of powerboating treated him with kid gloves. Some feared him, everyone acceded to his whims.

Mob associate Don Aronow—the man Lansky "took from the gutter" and made into everything he was—would be subject to the caprices of Kramer. Even more so, once the even-tempered and fair-minded Lansky had passed from the scene in early 1983. And what better plaything for the "nautically inclined young man," as one of my contacts had called him, than the great Don Aronow's boat companies?

January 1983 and the death of Meyer Lansky coincides with a pivotal chronological point in the Aronow-Kramer relationship. Beginning in 1983, Ben acquired from Aronow a championship catamaran mold, equipment, land to start his own race team, a championship deep-vee mold, use of the Don Aronow name, two boat companies plus their manufacturing facilities, the best plant superintendent in the business to run them, land for a grandiose marina and bar entertainment complex, and a helicopter along with Don's experienced pilot.

The windfall finally culminated in August 1985 with the best "toy" an up-and-coming drug kingpin could want.

His very own Blue Thunder contract.

So many things, important and trivial, that had been puzzling about the story suddenly fall into place. Such as how Ben was able to build an enormous international drug empire virtually overnight. Or why friend and former partner Bobby Saccenti insisted on bringing his Mafia brother along whenever he had to discuss business with Kramer.

It explained Aronow's meeting with Murray Weil three weeks after he was awarded the Blue Thunder contract to include the unusual additions to his will. The codicils were Aronow's vain attempts to do something in death he knew he couldn't do in life— resist the insatiable young Kramer.

But the "iron-clad" will had easily been broken just three months after the murder by a judge who was a friend of Richard Gerstein, a man with rumored ties to Meyer Lansky himself.

Finally, it answered the most bizarre and troubling aspect of the entire story: why seven months after he got the government contract, Aronow gave it to a thirty-year-old, coked-up ex-con who was the target of a massive international drug investigation. Then desperately tried to keep it a secret, knowing that if it leaked out, it could destroy his relationship with the man who would probably be the next president of the United States.

It didn't explain, however, the peculiar last three weeks of Aronow's life. The frequent meetings and calls between Ben, Jack, and Don where "something was up for sure," as Jerry Engelman had put it. Nor did it solve Don's murder.

One thing was certain. While the "chairman of the board of organized crime" may have died in 1983, "Lansky, Inc." was still open for business.

FOURTEEN

While no one has ever called it Lansky, Inc., the empire that the "chairman of the board" oversaw was bigger and more powerful than any company in the Fortune 500. In the unhallowed halls of the "corporate" underworld, a vast array of "employees" pursued the various interests of Lansky and the mob. Like many major corporations, the "organization" continually diversified its business pursuits, making sure it was never dependent on only one source of income.

Over the years, Lansky, ever aware of societal trends, had guided the Mafia from booze to prostitution to gambling, building an organization that experts could only begin to estimate in the billions. Lansky himself was rumored to be worth $400 million conservatively and more likely a half billion at the time of his death in 1983. Since then one of the most intriguing underworld mysteries for OC watchers has been, what happened to that empire and where did the money go?

The topic has been discussed and analyzed endlessly. There are only two reasonable assumptions. The money didn't just disappear. Neither did the organization. The legacy continues, lived out by players such as the Kramers, Mel Kessler, the Gilberts, Al Malnik,

Vincent "Jimmy Blue Eyes" Alo, Richard Gerstein. And Don Aronow. The more I learned about him, the more entrenched he seemed in that organization. Somewhere in that mercurial world there existed the key to the murder of Don Aronow.

Piecing together the mystery is difficult. As with so much of the underworld, everything is shadowy, insubstantial, and elusive. Facade often obscures reality, fiction appears more real than fact. With a different perspective, a whole new image appears.

On one of my regular trips to the Federal Building, a DEA agent who has given me background material on Florida's drug smuggling hints at yet another facet to Aronow.

"How much do you know about Don Aronow—how he made his money?" the DEA agent asks.

"I think he made a lot of it, first in construction with the mob's help back in New Jersey," I answer.

"I understand all that," he says, smiling. "What ways can you make money in Florida?"

"Real estate, money laundering . . . smuggling."

"How about Aronow from that last standpoint?"

"I never heard he was directly involved in smuggling. I find that hard to believe, though it seems he'd do anything for a buck. Why? Did you ever have any indication he was involved in smuggling?"

"Let me discuss this with somebody, and if there's something, maybe we can dig it out."

That was the end of our conversation that day.

MetroDade has heard rumors about Aronow and the possibility that he was involved in drug smuggling. But they were never able to confirm them. Steve Parr says that Aronow's financial situation has caused them to wonder just how he made his money, particularly in the five years before his death. He points out that those years show a surprising jump in Aronow's net worth—and they haven't been able to account for it.

"You'd need a Harvard MBA to figure Aronow's finances out," Parr says. "We're dealing with a man who had a net worth of seventeen million in 1982 then up to twenty-two million plus at the time of his death. Close to six million bucks—and he didn't do anything. I'm sure if we got a team of CPAs in here we could find out."

For Aronow to have a $6-million jump in his net worth, he would have had to make far more money. As Parr says, "A hell of a lot more." He reflects then adds, "We really can't figure out how he did it."

Parr is referring to some basic accounting principles. For Aronow to have increased his net worth by $6 million, he would have had to earn about $12 million before taxes, under the tax laws that were in effect at the time. According to Jerry Engelman, Aronow's boat business had a pretax margin of 10 percent—which means Don would have had to gross $120 million in sales in order to earn that $12 million legitimately through his boat company.

Yet those years in which Aronow's net worth increased so dramatically were actually years in which he did little business. A noncompetitive contract that he had signed with the new owners of Cigarette kept him virtually out of the boatbuilding business after 1982.

There were no world-famous designs like the Cigarette or the Magnum or the Donzi. Except for some small ventures such as the Squadron XII—so named because all he could build was twelve boats worth at most a couple of million in sales—Aronow was out of business completely. Then George Bush came along and Aronow got the Blue Thunder contract in 1985. But even that generated less than $10 million in sales for the two years prior to Aronow's death.

Don's horse breeding activities weren't doing well either. In the years after the sale of Cigarette, Aronow Stables was hemorrhaging at the rate of fifty grand a month, $600,000 a year. Also, Randy Riggs says that from 1982 until he left in 1985, Aronow never made a profit from USA Racing. Despite this bleak analysis from Riggs—who served as vice president for both Aronow Stables and USA Racing—Aronow somehow added considerably to his fortune.

The numbers just don't add up, notes an IRS agent familiar with the case.

Business realities suggest that he made so much money those last years in other, more lucrative ways. Involvement in Florida's most lucrative industry, drug smuggling, would easily account for his financial success. Although everyone has been vocal about Aronow's hard stand against drug dealing, he was secretly and intimately connected with one of the nation's top smugglers. Aronow crossed between two worlds. It was the darker one that held the key to his murder.

Aronow's friend Paulie Rizzo, the man who dropped out of sight in the months before the murder and then called USA Racing minutes after the shooting, was part of Aronow's other world. Rizzo seemed to be the classic wiseguy, from his penchant to settle debts with paper bags full of cash (always just short of the IRS-alarm-ringing $10,000 mark) to his contact at the bakery in Tampa.

"I had to ask for a guy named Pat and then he would contact Rizzo," Jerry Engelman recalls. "And sometime later Paulie would call back." Engelman couldn't remember the number, and it wasn't in his personal telephone directory from USA Racing.

The Tampa office of the Florida Department of Law Enforcement is surprised when I call to ask if there are any mob message centers in the area that service Miami. Ken Sanz, a special agent, says he knows only one in Tampa. It's for "the Trafficante's [crime family] at the Alessi Bakery." He gives me the number and I call it. A woman answers, "Alessi Bakery on Cypress." I ask for Pat. Another voice comes on the line. I ask if he's Pat.

"Yeah," a male voice answers.

"Can I get a message to Paulie Rizzo?"

"Yeah," he says expectantly.

I hang up and call Sanz, asking him to check on the name Paul Rizzo in connection with Trafficante. Nothing pops up. I suggest that "Rizzo" might be an alias and repeat Engelman's description of the wiseguy: fat, a fifty-two-inch waist, dark hair, and in his forties. Does Sanz know him?

He says it sounds familiar but he wants to know if there is anything special about Rizzo's face.

The only response Engelman has is that Rizzo had a "baby face" and was "well dressed for a fat guy." When I call Sanz with that bit of information, he replies, "Well, your Rizzo sure sounds like Santo Trafficante the Third. The unusual thing about him is he's three-hundred-plus pounds and he's got a baby face."

Sanz says it wouldn't surprise him about Santo and Aronow especially because of Aronow's high-priced powerboats. "Santo Three, he's third-generation LCN, you know," Sanz says. "So he really doesn't like to work as hard as his uncle Santo, Jr., did." Santo III, according to Sanz, is a yuppie wiseguy who likes spending money, living lavishly, hanging around with race car drivers, and frequenting casinos, where he is always warmly welcomed.

The Tampa FDLE office has intelligence that Santo III is bringing cocaine into Tampa and Jacksonville hidden in "gray market" Mercedes-Benz automobiles, though no criminal charges have ever been filed in the matter. "They put it into the battery," Sanz explains. "You can get two keys of coke into a battery. Or heroin. We suspect he's bringing in heroin, too."

Later I show Engelman a full-color blowup of "Santo Three's" Florida driver's license. But he says it isn't the man he knows as Paul Rizzo. Nor does he recognize photographs of other portly guys from the Tampa area such as Santo III's gumba "Little Augie" Panella or Phil Alessi, the owner of the bakery.

Was Paul Rizzo even from Tampa?

"Well, when I called Pat at the bakery and left a message, Rizzo would get back to me, sometimes in an hour, sometimes in a week," says Jerry. "Well, actually there were two guys. There was Paulie, about forty. And there was another one that called himself Alex. Much younger, thirty maybe, also heavyset, shorter. They always came in together. One time I said, 'What's with you guys, you guys related?' They looked at each other and laughed, and they said, 'Oh, we're cousins,' but I didn't believe them."

Engelman found the whole situation with the Rizzos strange. "It was pretty weird," he remembers. "Whenever Don would talk about any of these guys, like half the time he would say, did you ever hear from that guy, or those boys—like he couldn't remember their names. He'd never use the names that I knew. It was like he was fishing, as if the names we knew were aliases, and he knew them by their real names. I always noticed that. He couldn't remember their names.

"Now, the guy called Alex, he would say 'Hey, Paulie' and 'Look at this, Paulie,' so probably his name is Paul. But 'Rizzo'? I doubt it. Paul told me, he sort of confided to me once, that he was from New York State, Brewster. Something like that. And I think I believed him about that. Yet, sometimes they would call to say they were coming by, and they were there in an hour, an hour and a half."

Engelman first met the Rizzos right after he started working at USA Racing in early 1986. They wanted Aronow to build them a USA boat. Later, in June of that year, Alex came in with a check for $75,600 he had received from a Pompano Beach, Florida, boat broker for the sale of another boat. He endorsed it over to Don as a down payment. Jerry suspected that because the name was an alias, the only way "Alex" could unload it was to give it to someone he knew would accept it without identification.

After they gave Aronow the check, the Rizzos would stop by USA Racing with $8,000 cash in a paper bag every week or so. The total cost of the boat was $203,900, all of it paid off in cash except for the initial check down payment. Paulie Rizzo was eager to get his new boat and was always prodding Aronow and Engelman to finish it quickly.

Finally the boat was ready. "When he comes to pick it up, I went out on sea trials with him on it," Engelman relates. "He was crazy. There were like seven boats in all of Biscayne Bay on a Tuesday morning, and he nearly hits all of them. Unbelievable! And I came back to the office thinking this man's a crazy driver. And sure enough, ten days later, he rams the boat head-on into a seawall and he opens up six or seven feet of the bow of the boat. He hit the seawall at like fifty miles an hour. The guy was a madman."

Aronow told Rizzo he could repair the boat so that it wouldn't look like it had ever been in an accident. But Paulie didn't want that. He complained that he could never be happy with a repaired boat, saying that every time he stood up on the deck he would be able to see where it was repaired. When Aronow hesitated, Rizzo flicked his hand as if he were swatting at a fly and in a firm, condescending voice said, "Build me another one."

There was no more discussion. Aronow quickly agreed. The second boat was built with no money down, a rare practice for Aronow. This one was plusher than the first.

"Different engines, more goodies, controls, more customized stuff," Jerry recalls. "Cost a hundred grand more than the first one. Now we got two of his boats sitting there. Presumably he's going to sell the first one. That's when the guy disappeared. So now he owes us for the second boat and he owes us for the repair of the first boat. I remember Don said to me, 'the number is eighteen thousand. If he calls—if anything happens—the repair is eighteen thousand dollars.'"

Although Rizzo had been insistent that Aronow build him a new boat immediately, he suddenly seemed to lose interest. There were no calls and no visits to USA Racing. Every few weeks Don would check with Engelman to see if he had heard from Paulie. "Once or twice I called over to the bakery," Engelman recalls, "but he never got back to me. It was just like he was MIA for months. And the two boats just sat there."

Then Aronow was shot. Fifteen minutes later, Paul Rizzo called and spoke to Patty. Later, she would deny receiving the call. A few weeks after that, the long-absent Alex Rizzo was also back on the scene. He wanted USA Racing to keep the first boat and give Paulie credit toward the new one. And he wanted the pictures of Paulie and his boat that Engelman had taken on the sea trials. "I was scared, kind of, when he called me at home and insisted that I bring him the pictures and the negatives," Jerry recalls. "I said believe me, if I had them, I would give them to you. It was just a dead roll." Engelman's camera had malfunctioned.

USA Racing took Paulie's old boat in trade. Alex took the new boat. For a while, the rebuilt boat sat in the dry dock, then the company sold it to Customs as a Blue Thunder boat.

"It was real nice," Engelman emphasizes. "Plush seats, black bottom, black sides, white deck, black trim. I spent a lot of time on that boat."

The boat description sounded familiar. It wasn't until a few days later that I realized where I had seen the plush black USA Racing boat that wasn't good enough for wiseguy Paulie Rizzo. U.S. Customs had given me a ride in it around Biscayne Bay. It was their black Blue Thunder. Their VIP tour boat, the pride of the fleet, used for all the antidrug photo ops of smiling politicians and foreign state visitors.

The vanguard of Customs' war against drugs was a fat wiseguy's hand-me-down.

In the parallel universe of organized crime, Paulie Rizzo had ties with another wiseguy friend of Aronow's. All the time that Engelman was at USA Racing, he accepted frequent collect calls for Don from a man in Leavenworth Prison named "Frankie." Often, when Aronow was out of the office, Jerry would talk to Frankie. During one conversation, Frankie mentioned Paulie Rizzo and commented on his dropping by USA Racing on the previous day. Jerry wondered how a guy in a Kansas prison could keep such close track of Aronow and Paulie.

Frankie's relationship with Aronow extended beyond phone conversations. Six months before the murder, Frankie's wife called USA Racing. She told Don that she was coming to the office for money. Ten minutes later, she appeared in overdone makeup and an outfit that looked as if it came straight from Frederick's of Hollywood. Don turned to Patty and told her to write a check for $50,000 for the woman. Patty was stunned. She had never seen the woman before and she had no idea why Aronow was giving her such a large sum of money.

Intrigued by the fact that Aronow was giving money to a convict, I stop by MetroDade Homicide to ask about the check. They, too, were curious about it—the canceled check had popped up when they were reviewing Aronow's records. Mike DeCora says they interviewed one of Don's old friends, Joel "Joey" Weichselbaum, currently in prison for tax evasion. They asked if he knew Frankie. Joey did. He also knew about Aronow giving Frankie's wife the money.

Joey and Aronow had been friends for at least ten years. Joey had helped Aronow scam Ted Theodile when he purchased Magnum Marine from Don. It was Joey Weichselbaum who had posed as a Canadian businessman to trick Theodile out of the $15,000 boat mold in the sale of Magnum.

As an afterthought, DeCora mentions that Aronow went to Leavenworth twice in 1986 to visit Frankie.

"What's Frankie's last name?"

"Versato, something like that," he replies.

"What was he in for?"

"I don't know."

DeCora knows. He also knows Frankie's exact name. But it signals that we've come to the end of our quid pro quo conversation. I have nothing else to offer.

Leavenworth Prison has no records for a "Versato." Nor does the National Federal Prisoner Locator service.

A fed agrees to run him through a small portable hookup he's got to the National Crime Information Computer for me. "I got a hit," he says. "But you were off on the spelling. Frank John Viserto, Jr., d.o.b. 1/28/1947. It's V-i-s-e-r-t-o." He says that's all his portable will tell him, but he'll see what else he can get for me.

"Let's see—Joey Weichselbaum," says John Sampson from Broward OCD, who seems to know everyone with any connection to organized crime in the Miami area. He pauses. He likes to make me work for the information. "I don't know. I think I've been getting a touch of Alzheimer's lately." Another pause. "The last I heard of Joey Weichselbaum he was trying to take over ownership of the Jockey Club."

Sampson says at one time a federal organized crime strike force was looking into him, but he doesn't know what happened. He does recall one incident involving Joey's brother, Frank. A man was unloading a cargo container from Eastern Airlines in New Jersey. He had a heart attack. When the police went through his pockets, Frank Weichselbaum's name was there, and two hundred pounds of marijuana was in the cargo crate.

"How about Frankie Viserto? Ever hear of him?"

"I remember the name." Sampson says he's a member of La Cosa Nostra but he can't recall in what connection.

"Weichselbaum seems to know Viserto's business. Joey's no slouch then?"

"No," Sampson says. "I was convinced Joey was pretty big."

Sampson tells me that Weichselbaum was also friendly with another friend of Aronow's. "He was real tight with Joey Ippolito," he explains. "When they were racing off New Orleans and one of the crew got killed in a boat crash, Joey Weichselbaum sent a plane to pick up Joey Ip and the rest of the crew. That's how tight they were."

Joey Ip is second-generation La Cosa Nostra, one of nine children.

His father was an associate of mob chieftain Simone "Sam the Plumber" DeCalvacante of New Jersey, the man who won the bitter Mafia struggle for control of the northern New Jersey construction industry begun in the fifties. Now the Plumber, who hates his nickname, is retired and like many other old mafiosi, lives in Miami Beach. He's famous for his passion for chocolates, insisting that his wiseguy visitors bring him a box.

Joey Ippolito's older brother, Louie Ip, is also mob. John Sampson investigated him at one time. "We did a wire [wiretap] on Louie when I was at Dade, working with Hollywood," he remembers. "Louie was in for a scheme out of JFK where they were bringing in some shit, marijuana and hash."

I ask if Joey Ip had any other connections. "I was talking to a source one time that had information on a steel-hulled, eighty-five-foot shrimper that they picked up with a load of dope on it," Sampson recalls. "A load of grass. Now the guy—the source—had done some good things for the feds. And he was saying that the boat was Meyer Lansky's because the people there were talking about it. And the people who were talking about the boat being Lansky's were guys that I know to be very Italian and very much involved with some offshore powerboat racers. One, to wit, one Joey Ippolito, Jr."

Sampson comments that he's always suspected that the Mafia was involved in Florida's drug business but that he couldn't get anyone to listen. He was also convinced that there was a connection between the drug activities of Florida OC and the New York families. "Anyway," he continues, "the source information [on Lansky] may be kind of accurate. I really don't know. I never really evaluated it because shortly thereafter I worked for an asshole lieutenant and we weren't about to do any more intelligence. But up to that point that's what we were coming up with."

The investigation had ground to a halt when Lansky's name surfaced.

Until his arrest in the early eighties, Joey Ippolito was living in Lansky's old Florida neighborhood in Hallandale. "Around '81 or '82, Joey Ip was arrested off of Long Island, with a dozen other people," Sampson recalls. "They had eight tons of marijuana. They were using little Zodiac boats to come in from the mother ship. He went away for eight [years]."

I tell Sampson that Aronow had a connection with each of the three men. He shared a mistress with Joey Ip, he pulled at least one scam with Weichselbaum, and he gave money to Frankie Viserto.

"Un-u-sual acquaintances," he says.

"Did you ever think that Aronow was dirty?"

"I always had the feeling of it," Sampson says. "But what are you going to do? Just another pretty face. I knew the name. But so few of us, so many of them. Unless you're out there watching these guys all the time, quietly, you're not going to learn anything. You've got to have devotion."

For a man who claimed to have no knowledge of drug smugglers, Aronow was surrounded by them. Each smuggler in turn seemed to know the others and to have both a business association as well as a personal one. They were clearly not small-time dopers, and they all had Mafia connections as well. The journey into Aronow's darker world had just begun.

Frankie Viserto seemed to have surprising clout for a man doing a long stretch in the joint. Paulie Rizzo kept in close contact with him, and Don Aronow not only dashed off a check for fifty grand, he also flew up to Leavenworth to see him. But none of my Florida contacts can place Viserto other than to verify that he's LCN. I decide to branch out—go back to Aronow's roots. A south Florida fed gives me the name of a man in New York who is famous for his knowledge of New York wiseguys.

"Frankie Viserto, original member of the Purple Gang," says Lt. Jack Clark of NYPD intelligence.

"How about the son?" I ask, since the historical Purple Gang was a Prohibition-era gang in Detroit that hijacked liquor from other hoodlums.

"The Purple Gang," Clark repeats with emphasis. "A notorious group of young guys up in the Bronx, East Harlem. They got started in the seventies. All young protégés of Pleasant Avenue. And they became involved in extortion, labor-racketeering, narcotics." Clark explains they took their name from the old gang, but other than that, there's no connection.

"What crime family is that?"

"They're shoots of the Genovese. It was all like eighty guys, maybe more. Paulie Caiano, 'Ray-ray' Recildo—I'm trying to run down the main guys—Frankie Meldish, his brother Joe Meldish, Patty Prisco, Angelo Prisco. There's a whole shitload."

"Was Viserto running marijuana?"

"I would say other stuff."

"Heroin?"

"Heroin, coke—hold on, I'll see if I have anything on him." He comes back on the line. "Lives in upstate New York, Dogwood Drive in Yorktown Heights. Got an FBI, Frankie John Viserto, Jr., also known as Frankie Celese, Frankie Price, and Franz Goodz. And the senior had an address in Fort Lauderdale. That was the father, d.o.b. 1/17/1927."

Clark says that most of the Purple Gang members are second-generation La Cosa Nostra.

"What mob was he with—the father?"

"Genovese," he confirms. "They're all Genovese Purple Gang. They're all basically narcotics. In all, there were a hundred twenty-seven members that we identified as being part of this street gang, or whatever you want to call it."

"Anything on what Frankie went away for?"

"Nope," he says, checking the information in front of him. "And that's all I have on him here in this squirrel file."

"They are liable to kill at any time, at any place. . . . They are young, up-and-coming mafiosi. Much like the old Murder, Inc., they are the hired guns, either used by old-timers (Mafia chiefs) for hits, or working on their own." So concluded a 1979 confidential assessment of the Purple Gang by the Florida Department of Law Enforcement.

As for Aronow's friend Frankie Viserto, he is described by authorities "as a key member and organizer of the Purple Gang. He is a resident of New York who travels frequently to Florida."

In their report, the FDLE also suggested that the Purple Gang was operating with the protection of Bonanno crime family boss Carmine Galente, as well as that of "captains in the Vito Genovese crime family. The young gang is rapidly becoming a major factor in underworld narcotics traffic and violent activities."

While the Purple Gang was based in New York, the FDLE believed they worked out of Florida as well. Their "Intelligence Assessment" dated 2/8/79 concluded that:

1. The PURPLE GANG does exist in Florida and may be using this state as a base of operations as indicated by the presence of several members or associates, and by documented weapons purchases.

2. Intelligence at this time does not indicate that the PURPLE GANG is committing gangland murders in Florida.

3. It is highly likely that narcotics, particularly heroin, smuggling is being engaged in by the PURPLE GANG.

4. Core member FRANK JOHN VISERTO, JR., may continue to direct activities from his Homestead, Fl., jail cell, depending on who visits.

In 1977, Judy Doyle wrote in the *Orlando Sentinel* about Viserto's gang. "It's vicious, arrogant, brutal—and totally dependent on Florida for its supply of guns for crime. Descriptions of New York's newest terrorist group, the Purple Gang, range from its being a renegade faction of the mob to being New York's sixth crime family."

Her story quoted one mob investigator as saying, "They're going back to the old methods like were used in the 1920s such as mowing people down on the street." The article also reported that "the Purple Gang in one year has been linked to at least 17 murders of former gang members, rivals, and suspected informants. . . . Gang members are hired for contract murders by a few of New York's most powerful mobsters to eliminate any forces vying with them for the boss's seat."

According to the article, the Purple Gang pioneered the .22-caliber pistol as a standard murder weapon for Mafia hits. "Mobsters have traditionally preferred heavier guns than the .22 with its bullets that weigh slightly less than an ounce," Doyle wrote. "CIA agents have long preferred .22-caliber pistols, and [for the same reason] the Purple Gang also prefers them because they are easier to silence."

"The Purple Gang remains busy at work muscling in on the underworld action of narcotics, prostitution, gambling, and guns," Doyle concluded. "The feature most observers agree on is the gang's penchant for brutal murders."

Could the Purple Gang be involved in Aronow's murder?

Frankie Viserto spent much of his ten-year confinement in the Leavenworth Federal Penitentiary in Kansas. As the undisputed leader of the Purple Gang, he is a man of considerable influence in the underworld. In prison he was visited by fellow inmate Anthony "Tony Pro" Provenzano, a man close to both Meyer Lansky and Genovese capo Gerardo "Jerry" Catena, the man who oversaw housing construction in Northern New Jersey when Aronow built there.

OC experts say Tony Pro was also part of the Genovese crime family. Tony Pro is most well-known as the man who supposedly ordered Jimmy Hoffa's death. In 1975, Hoffa and Provenzano were supposed to meet in a Detroit suburb for lunch, a "sit-down" peace parlay to settle their long-standing feud. As Hoffa waited in front of the Machus Red Fox Restaurant, a car pulled up with several men inside. Hoffa got in and was never seen again.

Even Tony Pro, as influential as he was with the mob, was impressed by Viserto and cultivated his friendship. During each visit, Tony brought gifts for Viserto of candy and cigars.

In his spare time, Rory McMahon has been checking into Frankie Viserto for me. When we get together again, he says that Viserto was sentenced to fifteen years imprisonment followed by a fifteen-year special parole term in the Eastern District of New York. The sentence was for heroin conspiracy, possession of heroin with intent to distribute, in 1978. He had been indicted with fourteen codefendants on conspiracy to distribute 330 pounds of "white" heroin. Official records show that Viserto, along with two other defendants, Joseph "Little Joe" Solce and Richard "Fats" Rocco, were the leaders of the Purple Gang. All three were convicted. Their files stated that the Purple Gang was the largest heroin smuggling and distribution operation in the United States.

He was also sentenced concurrently to three years in the Southern District of Florida on a weapons charge. Viserto was scheduled to be released December 31, 1988, to his wife's residence in Ft. Lee, New Jersey. His new job, according to the files, would be manager of a pizza parlor in New York City.

"Get this," McMahon says, snickering. "The name of the place is Pizza-Furter, as in frank-furter. On Second Avenue, in Manhattan. So, I guess we know where Aronow's fifty thousand dollars went." Rory explains that the money helped Viserto pull off a scam that wiseguys often use to get out of prison on parole.

Through a front, the wiseguy sets up what appears to be a legitimate business. Then the front offers the wiseguy a job in that business. The prospect of solid employment often convinces the parole commission that the repentant mobster is ready to become a "productive member of society." Once out, he's free to pursue whatever endeavors he wishes, while pretending to his probation officer that he's gainfully employed.

Despite the sleazy, corrupt world that McMahon often traverses, he's been able to maintain his sense of humor—tinged with just the right amount of cynicism. He comments that Frankie will be "working" for Pizza-Furter the same way Ben Kramer "worked" for Apache Boats. While supposedly a consultant for Apache, Ben was actually traveling to New York, the Caribbean, and South America coordinating his international drug empire.

I ask McMahon if he can get the dates of Aronow's trips to Viserto at Leavenworth in 1986. To visit someone is prison, a person has to be approved by the prison officials, then on arrival, the visitor's name and details of the visit, including date, time, and length of stay, are all recorded.

McMahon tries, but he learns that Viserto's visitor list has disappeared. In March 1988, Frankie had been moved to FCI-Danbury in Connecticut. All of his records were transferred there at that time —except evidently the Leavenworth visitor list. In his years working with convicts, McMahon has never heard of a visitor list disappearing. He assumes there is some simple clerical mix-up. But Leavenworth doesn't have them either.

The Leavenworth officials at the prison can't explain why the visitor list was not included in his file. "They should be there," McMahon states, "and they should include all the people who ever visited him. Even the guy at Danbury said that [the missing list] was real unusual. I've never heard of this happening."

McMahon follows up again with calls to both prisons, but they still fail to turn up the missing list. "Real convenient that the list with Don's name on it is missing," he comments.

The list of visitors in Viserto's file had apparently been purged. Presumably it held information that someone did not want available. There were quite a few people—from high-level mobsters to well-known elected government officials—who would not want to see Don Aronow's name on the visitor list for a heroin-trafficking mafioso.

I call the DEA agent who had hinted that he was considering "dishing out" some information on Aronow. I suggest that he was going to tell me that Don was somehow involved in the Purple Gang with Viserto.

"No," he denies. "I've heard of them, of course, but not in Florida. Our information was about Joseph Ippolito, Jr., and Donald Aronow." He says they have a confidential informant who worked for Ippolito before he was imprisoned in 1982.

Aronow and Joey Ip were very close, even jointly supporting a mistress, Missy Allen, before Joey was incarcerated. "They were like brothers," Randy Riggs once remarked. "[Don] he'd visit people in prison. I flew him to Otisville, New York, a couple of years and he'd visit up there. I never went in, but he'd go in to visit people. He told me he saw Joey Ippolito up there. Joey was in for smuggling marijuana." Riggs had added in awe, "Don lived a hell of a life. Whatever life he lived, he lived a hell of a life."

I was about to find out more about the double life of Don Aronow.

"Aronow was working with Ippolito," the DEA agent says. "Our information was that he was building specially designed boats—stripped down with large cargo compartments. The boats would zip out to the mother ship and pick up marijuana. But more important to us, in the late seventies and early eighties Aronow was involved in drug deliveries to his factory. They used his plants for drops at night."

Before the advent of sophisticated interception techniques in the mid-1980s, marinas and out-of-the-way commercial buildings on south Florida canals were favorite off-loading spots. In the brazen, high-flying smuggling days, go-fast boats would whip right up to the docks, unload their cargo, and zip back out to the mother ship for another delivery. The Thunderboat Alley canal was ideal for such purposes, the DEA agent notes, with factory buildings on one side, a heavily wooded area on the other, and workers who minded their own business.

"Aronow would close up the Cigarette buildings, and then Joey's Cigarette boats would come in at night up the canal from the bay and off-load there," he says. Ippolito's criminal organization, he explains, relied exclusively on Cigarettes in the go-fast phase of his smuggling operations. Then he laughs about the use of Aronow's buildings, commenting, "It was an all-Cigarette operation."

The DEA agent takes me by surprise. Despite Aronow's other activities, I thought he would steer clear of direct involvement in smuggling. Basically, it seemed dumb. And Aronow was by no means a stupid man. The slippery money routines, the fast financial maneuvers, weren't surprising. Few people go from rags to riches—despite the notion being deeply embedded in American folklore—without crossing the line somewhere. But drug smuggling?

"So Aronow was actively involved in drug smuggling!" I blurt out in amazement.

"Marijuana and cocaine," the DEA agent notes matter-of-factly.

All during the time that Aronow and Bush were solidifying their friendship, Aronow was already involved in drug smuggling. By the time he was awarded the government contract, the DEA had solid leads that Aronow had indeed been in the War on Drugs—except he was on the other side.

With the Blue Thunder contract, he was working both sides.

The DEA wasn't the only agency aware of Aronow's involvement in drug smuggling. At the time of the murder, the Isle of Man drug task force was also peripherally looking into Joey Ippolito's early-eighties smuggling operations. A fed involved in the Man federal grand jury proceedings says they were aware that Aronow played an active role in Ippolito's operations.

"Don's smuggling activities weren't just a one shot deal, then? It was ongoing?" I ask.

"It was sporadic," the fed says. Ippolito would take over the facility at night, off-load a couple of tons of marijuana, and disappear by morning.

"How could this guy have gone on and done all the things he did with the government's antidrug program?"

"That's easy enough to see," he says. "The government's a big organization, and one hand doesn't know what the other hand is doing."

Even though Ippolito had been busted in '82 in New York, the fed says that a drug case could still have been put together against Aronow for his part in Ippolito's Florida smuggling operation.

"It could all be historical, we don't have to catch them in the act," he explains. He says it was possible his federal grand jury might eventually have indicted Aronow had he lived. He suggests that they might have employed RICO, the federal racketeering statute often used against organized crime bosses and major drug figures.

"It [the charge against Aronow] would've been conspiracy to import and distribute," he explains. "[If we could prove it happened] a number of times, it could've become a RICO." He dismisses the idea that his agency would be dissuaded from a drug-smuggling indictment against Aronow in light of his role with Blue Thunder.

The thought that George Bush was a lucky man passes through my mind. How would the Vice President have explained that the man he appointed to build boats for the War on Drugs was being indicted for drug smuggling? Aronow's murder had ended that potential problem.

Bill Norris is the head of the Major Narcotics Unit at the Miami U.S. Attorney's Office and the top federal drug-prosecution official in south Florida. It was his office that headed the U.S. prosecution efforts in the Isle of Man investigation.

"Was Aronow actually part of a marijuana-smuggling ring?" I ask, seeking an on-the-record confirmation.

"That's correct," he confirms. "We've always harbored suspicions about Aronow because he was a key player in the whole go-fast boat industry."

The go-fast boats were greatly responsible for the growth of what many consider to be Florida's top industry, drug smuggling. The boats were so stunningly fast that in their initial appearance in the coastal waters they left federal agents in their wake, both figuratively and literally. Now, high-performance boats play such an essential role in Florida smuggling operations that many boatbuilders are automatically suspected of modifying boats and knowingly selling them to dopers. And of course, no one was more responsible for the revolutionary development of high-performance boats than Don Aronow.

"We had reliable information that he was involved in off-loading of marijuana at his facilities," Norris continues. "Aronow would leave the lights off and the place unlocked, and then they would deliver the marijuana at night and hide the bales in his buildings."

"And this guy was close friends with the Vice President?"

"Pretty crazy, I agree," replies Norris.

FIFTEEN

When I arrive at Rory McMahon's office in the Federal Building for our meeting, he jumps out of his chair to greet me. His face becomes animated as he removes a file from his cabinet. He had asked a friend to send down some files from the Southern District of New York.

"You won't fucking believe it, I almost shit when I saw it," he exclaims. "I found a 1983 entry on Donald Aronow, and it noted that Don was 'suspected of involvement with the Purple Gang, and that he had offered employment to a Purple Gang member.'"

McMahon says he continued to look through the court files, and he waves some papers triumphantly in front of me. "I found it. A fucking letter of recommendation from Don for none other than the head of the Purple Gang. Frankie 'Pizza-Furter' Viserto. Un-fucking-believable." After supervising wiseguys for years, Rory talks like one.

The records show Aronow sent the letter to attorney James Jay Hogan, who in turn forwarded it to the Federal Probation Department the following week. Taking no chances, Don also sent a copy to Viserto at the penitentiary. It read:

CIGARETTE RACING TEAM, INC.

June 20, 1981

Mr. James J. Hogan
950 S. Miami Avenue
Miami, Florida 33130

Dear Mr. Hogan:

I received a call from Mr. Frank Viserto, Jr. who is in the Miami Federal Correctional Institution. He asked me if I would consider him for a position with our company when he is released; which I had agreed to do in 1980.

I first met Frank and his wife, Rosalind, several years ago at the time his wife was pregnant with their first child. He was with a friend or acquaintance who was purchasing a boat from our company.

He is a real boating and fishing enthusiast.

I have seen him many times, in fact, I met him by accident when he was vacationing in the Bahamas. I was invited to go fishing with him on a friends [*sic*] boat. I was impressed with his boat handling capabilities, fishing prowess and his knowledge of marine electronics.

Although I am not familiar with his background except the fact that he was sentenced to jail, I am willing to accept him as I know him.

We are prepared to offer him a position in our Electrical Department or Boat Demonstrator at the prevailing wages at the time of his release or any prior time or for any rehabilitation or work program that the penal system recommends.

Our company, Cigarette Racing Team, Inc. builds a line of fishing and sports boats and approximately 50 employees are employed in our company. I have owned three marine companies of which we have sold over the past 15 years (Formula Marine, Donzi Marine, Magnum Marine.)

We are the leaders in the world in building high performance, pleasure, and racing boats and we have been World Champions 9 times.

You may use this letter for presentation to the proper authorities for the benefit of Frank Viserto, Jr. or for the Rehabilitation Division of the penal system.

Very truly yours,

CIGARETTE RACING TEAM, INC.
Don Aronow,
President
DA/pl

cc: Frank Viserto Jr.
#08036-158
15801 S.W. 137th Avenue
Miami, Florida 33177

Don's letter of recommendation for the notorious heroin-trafficking mafioso illustrates one way in which the mob uses its "clean" front people. A man with an outstanding public reputation, enhanced by his association with high government officials, lends his support to a convict. He describes the prisoner in innocuous phrases, offers respectable employment, and encourages the government to release the "rehabilitated" man. And another wiseguy is sprung early from prison to get back into his real business.

The letter suggests that Aronow knew Frankie casually, meeting him and his wife, Rosalind (daughter of a Genovese soldier nicknamed "Johnny Lamps"), around 1979. But other people say that the association began long before that. Randy Riggs is certain that Don knew Viserto prior to 1975, and that Frankie and Don met often at Cigarette Racing Team before Frankie's heroin conviction. Viserto would usually spend the entire day with Don, hanging around the office, the way many wiseguys such as Swats Mulligan did. When Viserto was in prison, he spoke to Don often, at times twice a week, according to Jerry Engelman.

While Frankie may have been the "boating and fishing enthusiast" described by Aronow in the letter, most of his time was spent in other, less innocent pursuits. Besides heading the Purple Gang, a group so vicious that it even intimidated "mainstream" Mafia families, Viserto is suspected of being a terrorist and a large-scale gunrunner.

He is close friends with Jorge Antonio Zimeri-Safie, an international terrorist and professional assassin. In 1975, Zimeri-Safie and Viserto were observed at the E. W. Revere Indoor Gunnery Range in Pompano Beach, Florida, where they were firing a variety of high-powered weapons. The operator of the range overheard them discussing their joint travels to Guatemala around the time that a Guatemalan official was murdered. A weapon found at the site of the assassination was traced to Viserto.

A 1979 U.S. Justice Department Organized Crime Strike Force "Intelligence Brief" notes that "Zimeri-Safie heads a paramilitary group in Guatemala which seeks to overthrow the present regime. He is currently being sought by Guatemalan authorities for murder and weapons offenses as the result of a 1975 shootout in which a Guatemalan G-2 officer was killed. The prosecution of Zimeri-Safie [on U.S. gun charges] was the first part of a multi-faceted prosecutive effort by federal Organized Crime Strike Force members directed at hired killers utilized by La Cosa Nostra throughout the United States."

Aronow's friendship with both the Purple Gang leader and the Vice President extended over a decade. While Viserto was gaining control of the largest heroin-smuggling ring in the country, Bush was climbing the Washington political ladder. As Aronow became more deeply enmeshed in Mafia-sponsored drug activities, he clinched a multi-million-dollar government contract. Ultimately by awarding Aronow the Blue Thunder contract, Bush allowed not one but two drug-smuggling arms of the mob to penetrate the government's antidrug program: Kramer and marijuana; the Purple Gang and heroin.

Was the Secret Service asleep at the switch? Why didn't someone pull George Bush aside and warn him?

A Justice Department official who has worked on a number of south Florida's biggest drug-smuggling cases had promised to ask one of Bush's Secret Service agents about the Vice President's relationship with Aronow. Over lunch in a small Miami Beach bistro, he recounts their conversation.

"I talked to my Secret Service buddy [on Vice President Bush's detail]," he reports. "He remembers the name Aronow. He said, 'Didn't he get snuffed?' I said yes. I asked, 'Was there any hubbub about it?' He said there was something, but he couldn't recall." The Secret Service agent wasn't actually assigned to protect Bush until after Don's murder.

The Justice official continues his story. "Then the agent said to me, 'Was there something about this guy being tied into drugs?' I said, 'Yeah, I think it's getting even worse than that. There may even be some indications that he had mob ties.' The agent said, 'Ho-ly shit!'"

The official says he then asked the agent how a mob associate could get so close to the Vice President. "I said, 'Let me ask you something. Do you check out anybody the Vice President is going to be socializing with?' 'Of course!' he said. 'We do record checks. Then we would usually talk to the police in the area, because we don't have an intelligence network sophisticated enough to plug into somebody who's on the fringes. So normally, if it's somebody he [Bush] is going to have more than just casual contact with, we'll run it by the local PD people.' "

The official pauses in his story to explain that the Secret Service uses national computer banks to check for criminal records first. Then they go to the local police, who punch the person's name into their intelligence computers to see if there is any incriminating information on a state level. He says that it's often the local cops who can give them the information that doesn't always show up on the computer. "They may then say, for example, that the guy has never been arrested—but here's the real story on him."

The official takes a few more bites of his sandwich, then resumes his recounting of the conversation with Bush's Secret Service agent. "I said, 'So I would assume that they would get the straight scoop from MetroDade that this guy was in and around all of this drug shit at all times and his possible mob connections. What would you guys do with that? Is that too questionable to bring to Bush's attention?' "

The agent was stunned at the suggestion that the Secret Service would refrain from telling the Vice President that his friend was possibly involved in a drug operation. "He said, 'Too questionable my fucking ass! We would be in there in a minute and we would present it like this: This is what we found. You do with it what you want, but we're telling you, it makes us very, very nervous.' "

As for Bush, the Secret Service agent told the official, "A guy like George, it's one way or the other, right then and there. He would take the advice and not have any further contact, or he'll listen and say, 'Fuck off, I'm gonna do what I want.' " The agent had no idea why Bush, if warned, continued his association with Aronow.

The Justice Department official says that his contact made one other comment about the Aronow and Bush relationship. "My friend said, 'I guarantee you I know what the connection was between him and Bush. It's the boats. The guy loves fucking fast boats.' " The Secret Service agent had called Bush a "boat groupie."

We both laugh, thinking of all the photo ops Bush had given in his Don Aronow–built Cigarette *Fidelity* in Kennebunkport, and Blue Thunder in Biscayne Bay. How different the message is when the story behind the boats is revealed.

The Justice Department official concludes his summary of his conversation with the Secret Service agent by noting, "I got the impression that if the Secret Service boys came in and ran down the scenario about Don's mob and drug connections, George is going back to rule number one: 'I love boats. This guy is the king of the fast boats. And I'm not fluffing him off because you guys think he's too close with this guy or that guy.' "

Rory McMahon is caught up in the connection between Aronow and the leader of the Purple Gang. In his off times he has been pursuing Viserto's background with the same relentless intensity as the detective in Victor Hugo's novel *Les Misérables*. He has scored another hit and sounds excited when I call.

"Hey, you know you were interested in anything else I heard about Big Don's buddy Frankie?" he greets my voice. "Well, you have to see this stuff. I mean this Viserto is one sick fuck." I don't need any more incentive.

McMahon has obtained a 1979 report that offers a broader view of Viserto's criminal activities. Frankie is apparently a twisted version of the Mafia "Renaissance man," with pursuits that go beyond his position as heroin kingpin, terrorist, and pizza-maker.

At the time the document was prepared, Frankie was defined as a "significant criminal" under the Federal Bureau of Alcohol, Tobacco, and Firearms (ATF) enforcement program. ATF agent Robert Harris wrote about Viserto in detail. In 1974, Harris received information that Frankie was looking for thirty automatic handguns with silencers for which he was prepared to pay $1,000 each.

A few years later, in 1977, Viserto was arrested by New York ATF agents on a Florida warrant. According to Harris, Viserto had a sales receipt listing various sophisticated weapons and scopes. Included on the list were two Taser weapons priced at $400, an infrared night scope, and an electronic stun gun that utilized a 50,000-volt charge to incapacitate a target.

Included in Harris's report was a "Memorandum of Interview" with one of Viserto's cellmates, Angelo Kenneth Wedra. According to the report, Wedra met Viserto at the Metropolitan Correctional Center, New York, in 1978. Viserto was there for heroin conspiracy in Brooklyn. Wedra was very friendly with Carmine "Johnny Lamps" Saglimbene, who was a Genovese soldier. When he learned that Viserto was the son-in-law of Johnny Lamps, he struck up a friendship. Soon Wedra and Viserto were having daily conversations at the MCC.

Wedra said that Viserto was fascinated with guns and he had bragged that he had enough guns "to start a war." He told Wedra he was collecting munitions for a potential gang war between the Bonanno and the Genovese crime families. Viserto's allegiance was with the Genovese, his initial connection to La Cosa Nostra.

The interview with Wedra revealed to the feds the murderous aspect of Viserto's personality, particularly his predilection for torture. Frankie told Wedra about the torture murder in the early 1970s of a father and son. Viserto killed them in retaliation for their murder of Johnny Lamps's uncle. Frankie described to Wedra how the victims were choked, tortured, and finally shot.

There were many more murders. Viserto told Wedra that he killed notorious New York loanshark Eli "Joe the Baker" Zeccardi, who disappeared in 1977. His body has never been found. Viserto said that Joe the Baker had often interfered in his arguments with prominent New York mob attorney Gino Gallina, always settling in Gallina's favor. Viserto wanted to kill Gallina, but first, he felt he had to eliminate Joe the Baker. Later in the year that the Baker disappeared, Gallina was murdered gangland style on the streets of Manhattan.

In his conversations with Wedra, Viserto mentioned killing at least fifteen people. As for his long-range plans, he swore that all the witnesses who testified against him in the 1978 heroin trial in Brooklyn would be killed, and that "anyone who testifies against me will be killed."

A particular target of Viserto's was a federal agent with the ATF whom Frankie loathed. He said that the fed was constantly "on top of his case," always showing up wherever he was in court, and seemed to "want to put me in jail." He spent hours devising an appropriate fate for the agent, telling Wedra that he intended to cut the agent's head off if he ever got the opportunity.

Frankie's lust for murder was disconcerting even to Wedra. According to Harris's report, "Viserto enjoyed killing people. From his conversations with Viserto, Wedra learned that Frankie especially enjoyed torturing techniques such as burning the flesh of victims with lighted cigarettes and playing a Russian roulette game of dry firing his weapon at the head of his victims."

Since Viserto's known associations all seem to have an LCN basis it also appears likely that Paulie Rizzo was associated with the Genovese Purple Gang since the two men kept in close touch while Viserto was in prison. One FDLE investigative report noted that Viserto continued to conduct mob business from prison. (McMahon comments that mob leaders often continue to conduct their business from prison, using lieutenants as their intermediaries. "Going to jail just temporarily disrupts things," he observes.)

McMahon obtains NYPD intelligence profiles on individual members of the Purple Gang for me. We split them and start looking for "Paulie." There is no Rizzo, but one file, on the number two man in the Purple Gang, catches Rory's eye.

"Take a look at Paul Caiano," he says. "Under alias, it says 'Paulie.' He's only got one prior, 1970, a burglary in Manhattan. Subject is president of Paul and Jerry's fruit market. Owns a pizzeria in Mahopac. That's in upstate New York, real close to Brewster. You said Brewster, right?"

"That's where Paulie Rizzo said he lived," I confirm.

Rory points to the page. "Okay, here's his home address, Fairmont Road, Mahopac. Says he specializes in the distribution of cocaine. Cocaine and heroin."

"That would explain his connection with Santo Trafficante III and the Alessi bakery," I note. Tampa FDLE agent Sanz had said that Trafficante Three was "big into coke and heroin."

"He's got a d.o.b. of 12/18/1949," continues Rory. "He's got a baby face and he looks pretty chunky in this photo."

"Right age, too," I respond, reading the report over his shoulder. "He's got a brother Angelo. Could be Alex Rizzo. And this Paulie likes boats. It says in August 1974, 'Subject, Frank Viserto, Richard Rocco, Joseph Solce, Fred Zangaglia, and Angelo Caiano departed Florida and cruised the Bahama Islands aboard Rocco's boat, *Tradewinds III.*' All the Purple Gang bigwigs on a boating vacation."

Later, on the way over to see Jerry Engelman, I check a map of New York State. Mahopac is five miles from Brewster. I show Jerry the photo of Paulie Caiano. Engelman, a former criminal defense attorney, is thoughtful and precise. With his bifocals balanced on the tip of his nose, he examines the mug shot carefully. Then he says it's the man he knows as Paulie Rizzo.

SIXTEEN

Long before the clandestine Blue Thunder–Super Chief South deal with drug kingpin Ben Kramer, Don Aronow was involved in Mafia-sponsored narcotics trafficking. Marijuana smuggling with Joey Ippolito, who brought grass in by the ton; perhaps even heroin trafficking with Frankie Viserto, who dealt with hundreds of pounds of "white" Southeast Asian heroin at a time.

It's apparent that one of Aronow's functions was to meet all the "business and pleasure" boating needs of mob dopers. A trusted mob associate who would build smuggling boats with extra fuel tanks, accept checks made out to aliases and paper bags filled with cash, and not ask any questions. Was he involved in the drug operations because he was the Mafia's private high-performance boatbuilder? Or was there more to it?

Perhaps Aronow's involvement with smuggling wasn't his idea at all. It's clear that Don knew his position in the mob hierarchy—a kind of "indentured servitude" status as former FBI agent Arthur Nehrbass had described the precarious life of a mob associate. While Aronow may have been a "tiger on the open seas," he was a pussycat when it came to his relations with wiseguys.

Young Ben Kramer (though technically not a wiseguy because he isn't Italian, he still held equal rank) simply took whatever he wanted from Aronow. Don meekly and unhesitatingly followed Frankie Viserto's orders for money and favors. Paulie "Rizzo" Caiano treated Aronow condescendingly, demanding special treatment as a boat customer. Aronow, powerless to resist, was left to invent explanations of his impotence to puzzled employees and friends.

Over the years, an endless stream of wiseguys came to Thunderboat Alley to hang out at his factories. Jerry Engelman once called USA Racing and its boats "like a mob Disneyland, a tourist stop for out-of-town wiseguys." He added that Aronow always stopped whatever he was doing and spent hours talking to the mafiosi—even those he just met.

Seeing how subservient Aronow was with wiseguys, it's hard to imagine his becoming involved in any criminal activities when Meyer Lansky was alive unless "the boss" specifically directed him to do so. According to Art Nehrbass, it would be against the mob code for him to do so, and Lansky ran a tight organization. He was never sloppy. If one of his coterie of trusted associates free-lanced in drug smuggling, it could jeopardize the organization. No one needed to free-lance anyway because, as one fed explained, everyone who associated with Lansky made money.

In this vein of thought, I found some interesting parallels between Lansky's business endeavors and those of his protégé Don Aronow. An FDLE "Intelligence Analysis" compiled in the 1970s concluded that many horse-breeding farms in Ocala were in fact secretly owned by Meyer Lansky through fronts. While Aronow's Ocala horse farm was not among those mentioned, it's just another example of Aronow's business activities neatly meshing with the business interests of the "chairman of the board."

There were more overlaps. Lansky owned cattle farms and shrimp boats; so did Aronow. Lansky was involved with oil and gas exploration; Aronow was as well. Lansky held large-scale real estate holdings through fronts; Aronow had considerable holdings and at one time appeared to own most of Thunderboat Alley.

Meyer made himself and the Mafia rich by providing things people wanted and the government wouldn't let them have. Booze during Prohibition. When that ended, he moved into illegal gambling. With the gradual legalization of gambling, especially the state lotteries, which imitate the mob's numbers racket, Lansky sought new ventures.

Marijuana would have been a logical choice for Lansky's attentions. It has a relatively benign, middle-class image and doesn't generate much heat from law enforcement. "It's smart mob thinking," says one OC expert. "With marijuana you can get people to look the other way. You deal heroin and cocaine, everybody is pissed off at you. You can't control the politicians if you're talking cocaine and heroin. But marijuana can engender sympathy because everybody's kids are smoking pot."

The assertion is credible. Most of the government's efforts against drug smuggling have been focused on cocaine and heroin. Too many people are ambivalent about grass to engender stronger law enforcement efforts in that direction. Even presidential contenders have admitted smoking a marijuana cigarette, but none will ever admit "sampling" cocaine or heroin.

Occasionally there is a major marijuana bust, but not often. It isn't a guaranteed headline or top-of-the-news television story. Because it doesn't get that much publicity for the War on Drugs, the government doesn't allocate as much money to catching marijuana smugglers. All of which makes it a perfect choice for a black market activity. It's overshadowed by the harder drugs, there is less public pressure against it, and yet, there's a huge demand for it.

Looking into Florida's smuggling activities, I find that the Lansky name has continued to surface, subtly, tangentially, but always omnipresent. While the godfather has often been linked with gambling and money laundering in the media, he has never publicly been identified with the drug trade. But his presence throughout the Aronow story seems more than coincidence.

Many of the marijuana smugglers, in addition to Aronow, appear to have ties with Lansky. Could he have been involved in the lucrative Florida marijuana operations? Perhaps the more realistic question was: Could he have allowed an astonishingly profitable business to exist in his "domain" and not have a stake in it?

Looking for information on Viserto in old Justice Department reports, I find a "DEA listing of forty-eight significant drug violators, Florida area." Frankie Viserto was on it, along with Santo Trafficante, Jr., and Robert Vesco, another customer of Aronow's.

Meyer Lansky was there on the list as well.

In a separate DEA report, Meyer and his brother, Jake, were listed along with Frankie Viserto as "influential nonmember LCN associates in south Florida—1979" narcotics trafficking.

Florida's marijuana-smuggling industry differs sharply from cocaine and other drugs. While Latinos seem to dominate other drug-smuggling enterprises, the major players in grass have been Anglos. And they all had a connection with Lansky. Since 1973, the six largest marijuana trafficking organizations in Florida were headed by:

Richard "Ricky" Cravero

Joseph "Joey Ip" Ippolito, Jr.

Raymond "Little Ray" Thompson

Donald Steinberg

William "Bill" Whittington (and brother Don)

Benjamin "Darth Vader" Kramer

Rory McMahon personally supervised the paroles of three of the kingpins—Kramer, Steinberg, and Don Whittington—and was involved in formulating the sentencing review on Thompson. He notes many similarities among the smugglers on the list. "They were all gringos or wiseguys," he explains. "Not Hispanic. Young—late twenties, thirties. And they all seemed to come from nowhere and make it to the big time overnight."

As each man fell in turn, another heir seemed groomed and ready to take his place, smoothly and without any interruption of business. Following the kingpin trail, I continue to turn up the Lansky name.

The first of the big-time grass smugglers was wiseguy Ricky Cravero. Around 1973, Cravero first implemented and then perfected the "mother ship, go-fast boat" method of drug smuggling. A large boat, usually a fishing trawler or shrimper, would work its way up from Colombia loaded with dope. In the international waters off the Florida coast, the mother ship would rendezvous with four or five go-fast boats. The powerboats would pick up a share of the large cargo, then sprint the twelve miles into shore.

Cravero's brand of go-fast boats: the Cigarette.

A radar operator for the National Drug Interdiction Program once described how the operation appeared on his equipment. "It looks like half a star exploding on the screen. You'd see the smaller blips streaking out toward the shore. Boom! First one 'star' would 'explode,' then boom, another. Three or four each night." He said that at the time of the mother ship idea, all law enforcement could do was watch, helpless to intervene. "They'd zip into shore and that was it. It was damn near impossible to catch them."

It was a brilliant concept and it revolutionized Florida's drug smuggling. Neither Customs nor the Coast Guard had anything in their fleets then that could hope to keep up with a Cigarette. If by some chance one or two boats were caught, it was considered by the dopers to be an acceptable, even expected, business expense. An idea worthy of Lansky, Inc. especially in light of Aronow's talents and his ability to supply an unlimited quantity of go-fast boats.

But was Lansky associated with Cravero in any direct way?

Cravero's bodyguard and "enforcer" was Gary Bowditch, described in testimony before a 1979 Senate subcommittee on organized crime as a "principal nonmember associate of organized crime." Bowditch was also identified as an associate and bodyguard for Phil "the Stick" Kovolick.

There was the link. The Stick was the lieutenant and lifelong friend of Meyer Lansky.

Bowditch, who became a government witness, testified before that 1979 subcommittee. He said he was a bodyguard for Phil the Stick in 1970 when Anthony Scotto, head of the International Longshoremen's Association, passed $40,000 in cash to Phil "for Meyer." He told the committee that while Scotto didn't actually mention Lansky's last name, "when you hear of the Pope, you don't ask which Pope."

McMahon calls it "a safe bet" that Gary Bowditch was Meyer Lansky's liaison with the Cravero organization. "That's the way the mob works," he explains. "Bowditch's purpose would be to watch over Meyer's interests and keep Ricky [Cavero] in line—make sure Ricky didn't fuck up."

Ricky Cravero eventually wound up on Florida's death row. He became convinced that a man in his organization was an informant. According to Bowditch, Cravero personally "squeezed [the informant's] testicles with a pair of pliers" and then killed him. With Cravero removed from the scene, another kingpin promptly replaced him: Aronow's friend Joey Ippolito, Jr.

Joey Ip also had ties to the "chairman of the board." One of John Sampson's informants, who happened to be Ippolito's brother-in-law, had said that Joey was smuggling grass on one of Lansky's shrimper boats and that Lansky was behind all Ippolito's operations. There was another connection as well. Joseph Ippolito, Sr., was LCN and he reported to Sam the Plumber DeCalvacante. Sam was very close to Lansky; the two men reportedly had held high-level meetings at Al Malnik's The Forge Restaurant on Miami Beach.

Joey Ippolito also used Aronow's Cigarette Racing Team facilities for his off-loading, and Aronow's Cigarettes to rendezvous with his sources' mother ships.

John Steele, the former mayor of Hallandale, was also part of the Ippolito group. He was convicted and served time for his part in Joey's operation. When he was mayor in the 1960s, Steele became close to Lansky, reportedly placing a police substation at Meyer's request at the entrance to the Lansky's subdivision, an area dubbed Lanskyland by local residents. In return, Lansky bought two police cars for the city. In recent years, Steele has bragged to friends that he and Meyer were "great friends" and that Meyer was "the greatest genius of all time."

For his role as a major marijuana smuggler, Joey spent less than five years in prison.

The next kingpin on the list, "Little Ray" Thompson, also lived in Lanskyland, just around the corner from Ben Kramer on Meyer's street in Hallandale. Indicted with Thompson was former Dade County judge Steadman Stahl, a protégé of Richard Gerstein. Stahl was the judge who threw out a 1970 charge against Lansky for having a bottle of ulcer medication without a prescription. Feds also linked Mel Kessler with Thompson's activities. Thompson was later charged with and convicted of a triple murder in connection with a grass-smuggling operation.

Little Ray's preferred brand of go-fast boat: the Cigarette.

Perhaps the most famous of the marijuana kingpins is Donald Steinberg. The DEA estimated that at one point he imported one-sixth of all the marijuana smuggled into the United States. He has never been linked with the mob, but there seem to be some ties there.

"I remember that Steinberg had run into some mob trouble in Boston during his drug operations in the 1970s," McMahon recalls. "They held one of his people for a million-dollar ransom, but it was all smoothed over. Somehow the whole deal with the mob got resolved. I think there was a 'sit-down' somewhere, but no money changed hands."

The incident suggested to McMahon that Steinberg had some "major heavy-duty connections somewhere." He says the Mafia rarely "peace-parlays" with outsiders, and he considers it "fucking amazing that a gringo doper was able to settle things with them without having to pay up."

The Steinberg operation followed the same arc as Kramer's and the other kingpins'. "The guy comes out of a suburb of Chicago," says McMahon. "Ends up in south Florida in the midseventies. Quickly makes some connections in the boating business, and boom! He's bigger than nickel beer. What happened there? How did he go all of a sudden from being a nickel-and-dime marijuana smuggler to buying freighters, running a multimillion-dollar marijuana smuggling organization with Cigarette boats, tankers, even buying land in Africa to cultivate his own crop? He didn't get all that from nickel-and-dime bags of marijuana. Somebody financed him."

McMahon recalls that Steinberg was always complaining to him that "everybody keeps talking about me, like it's my organization, but I'm just running it. I'm not calling the shots." Rory talked to Steinberg often about this, but at the time he believed it was self-serving parolee talk. "I didn't even think. I thought it was his organization, that he did everything. But now looking back on it, he's probably right. The money had to come from somewhere."

Steinberg relied on Cigarette boats as well. He also shared mother ships with the Whittington organization, which operated until the early 1980s. Though not as large as Steinberg's, it was still mammoth. Authorities linked Whittington to Kramer, and many investigators came to regard them as different parts of the same organization. Bill Whittington was also implicated in the narcotics-financed transfer of three parcels of land for Ft. Apache Marina from Don Aronow to Ben Kramer, via a holding company.

During his surveillance of the Ft. Apache Marina, McMahon observed Whittington and Kramer together on several occasions. He suggests that in 1983, the year Lansky died, Ben stepped in and took over Whittington's operation when it became apparent that Whittington was going to be indicted for smuggling.

According to FBI agent Bob Duker, the spring of 1983 marked the beginning of Ben Kramer's meteoric ascendancy to the top of the marijuana smuggling world. The pattern again was the same. Before that date, Kramer had seemed to be nothing more than a small-time doper. Suddenly, just a couple of years out of prison, he was the titular head of an international drug empire with a battery of high-priced lawyers (most of whom had worked for Lansky at one time or another), financial advisors, bankers and money launderers, distributors and suppliers.

Since Kramer—an eleventh-grade dropout with a scholastic average of F—was never known for being bright or organizationally skilled, his sophisticated and far-flung empire doesn't make any sense. Unless one assumes a well-oiled organization was already in place for him to manage. He simply stepped in and took over from the Whittingtons.

"So it's like all these guys were 'general managers' of the Marijuana Division of Lansky, Inc.," I remark to Rory, building on the idea that Lansky was known as the "chairman of the board" of organized crime. "When one of them is 'retired,' the next one steps in and takes over."

"Exactly," Rory responds. "Now that Benny's gone, I'm sure there's somebody out there replacing him right now as we speak."

. . .

Everywhere there are hidden ties between the Mafia, the Lansky organization, and Florida's drug trade. Another name that has surfaced over the years in relation to the people on the doper list is Melvyn Kessler, former attorney for Meyer Lansky.

"That prick," exclaims John Sampson when I ask about Kessler. "During the Ippolito investigation we followed Louie Ippolito to meet with Mel Kessler, in Miami, and I thought it was rather interesting at the time. I didn't know what it meant, because we were on the outside at the time. But the house that they went to was a known doper's. I figured they were some very heavy people."

If the mob was behind the drug business, it seemed natural to assume that Lansky would be the umbrella for all LCN-related trafficking in Florida. Sampson postulates that Kessler could have been the connection between the Cravero and Ippolito marijuana operations. "Ricky was the head of the gang," he notes, "but Mel Kessler was involved with some people at the fringe of that gang." Kessler has also allegedly been linked to "Little Ray" Thompson's activities.

According to 1983 Hollywood Vice records, "Melvyn Kessler is mentioned by U.S. Customs in twenty major drug-smuggling cases. A report by Detective Joseph Nickmeyer revealed that "in May, 1979, Kessler was suspected of arranging the shipment of 200 kilos of cocaine from Bolivia to the United States." Customs case #GFGS-81-4011 alleged that in December 1980 Kessler was suspected of financing a smuggling venture from the Caribbean islands to San Juan, Puerto Rico.

Both Kessler and Thompson, according to federal agents, used Shaun Murphy's "accounting" services in the British Virgin Islands. It was through one of Thompson's associates who went to deposit narcotics cash in a bank on the Isle of Man that New Scotland Yard first learned of the money-laundering operations coordinated by Murphy. That discovery led to Operation Isle of Man and the 1987 indictments of Kessler, Ben and Jack Kramer, and the Gilberts.

Kessler may have been even more powerful than the Hollywood PD records suggest. Telephone pen register evidence collected against Ben Kramer during 1983 shows thousands of calls to Kramer's smuggling and money-laundering associates. But two numbers stand out on those massive logs of his telephone calls: those for Mel Kessler's home and office phones.

The logs show that Ben called Kessler almost daily, sometimes three or four calls in a day. The records don't take into account any calls made by Kessler to Kramer. (A pen register doesn't show incoming calls.) One DEA agent believes that Kessler was "Ben's puppet master, the real brains behind Kramer's operations" and that Ben was simply a spoiled, overgrown kid who wanted to be a "boss." So the organization let him play the role. But when his wild, high-flying ways attracted widespread attention, Ben brought about his own downfall.

McMahon, Ben's probation officer, concurs, saying he understands the frequent phone calls between the two. "I can see Mel telling Benny to do something," he says, laughing. "And Benny gets off the phone and gets confused. So he has to call back: 'What did you want me to do with that two million dollars again, Mel?' I mean it would take two or three calls just to tell Benny how to use a screwdriver. Benny fucked up a lot, and I think Mel had to step in a lot because Benny's such a dumb fuck."

Rory tells me about a "typical Benny fuck-up" that required Kessler's assistance. More and more, Benny seems like the incompetent Danny DeVito character from the movie *Wiseguys*. The story takes on an even quirkier perspective in light of the fact that the incident took place while Kramer was secretly in control of the U.S. government's Blue Thunder boat production.

On October 5,1985, Kramer was stopped by MetroDade police. It was eleven P.M. He had just left Joe Sonken's Gold Coast Restaurant, reportedly a mob hangout, and was speeding down one of Miami's main avenues in his Porsche. The cops stopped him, and when they approached the car, they were enveloped in an overpowering aroma of marijuana. After calling Kessler from his car phone, Benny consented to a car search. In the trunk, the cops found a trash bag with a large amount of cash in it.

Kramer told the police that the money was a down payment for a boat but that he lacked documents to substantiate the claim. Then, according to the report, "Kramer further stated that he knew the money was the proceeds from narcotics sales but that he had to make a living. Kramer also stated that he only counted the stacks of money, not the bills."

Kramer was arrested and taken to the station along with the money. It was more than $100,000 wrapped in small bundles of 10,000 ten-dollar bills. Kessler was waiting at the station for Ben, and he confirmed Kramer's story that the money had been a down payment on a boat. He, too, was unable to produce a receipt.

After the incident, the police notified McMahon as Kramer's probation officer, and he brought the subject up at their next meeting. Rory recalls, "I said, 'Benny, when you have a hundred thousand in a trash bag in the back of your car do you normally stop to have dinner?' He said, 'Oh, it was Joe Sonken's. I knew the parking lot would be secure.' " Kramer was right—nobody tampers with a car at the Gold Coast Restaurant—it's widely acknowledged to be the mob's hangout.

McMahon asked Ben how he came to have so much cash in his car. "Benny said his father took sick and left Ft. Apache in a hurry," McMahon relates. "And he left the money in his office laying around in a trash bag. Benny says his father told him to go pick up the money and deposit it. So Benny picks up the money and then gets hungry—he's in north Miami—so he drives up to Joe Sonken's for dinner, just leaving all the cash in the car."

Long after Kramer was arrested on drug-kingpin charges, I asked a fed involved in the Operation Isle of Man about the money in the trash bag. He explained that the operation used color-coded Glad bags to denote certain amounts of money. The bag found in Benny's car was white, signifying a hundred thousand dollars.

"It was a late payment on a drug deal—you know, after they did the final weighing," the fed says. "And that money was needed to square the account. It was part of a two-million-dollar deal. To him it was chicken feed. Kramer just grabbed the bag and threw it in the trunk, like it was nothing at all."

When I suggest to a fed that the Lansky organization might be behind much of the marijuana-smuggling industry in Florida, it sparks another link between two marijuana kingpins. He says that both Ben Kramer and Bill Whittington were represented by Richard "Bad Eye" Gerstein during their respective legal difficulties.

The fed says that just as Ben Kramer received telegrams of support before his sentencing on drug charges in 1977, impressive support was marshalled for Bill and his brother Don Whittington prior to their sentencing for drug smuggling in 1986.

Famed lawyer F. Lee Bailey wrote to the judge and urged leniency for the Whittingtons. The letter was on the stationery of Gerstein's law firm. (I later learn that Bailey is moving to Florida and setting up shop—a law firm—with Gerstein.)

Another letter in support of the Whittingtons came from a Dade County judge. The fed, like many of his colleagues, is disgusted by what he sees as the pervasive effect of the Mafia's unlimited funds and enormous influence on so-called "respectable" people in the community. He reads the judge's letter for the Whittingtons, whom he calls "a couple of the largest dopers in south Florida history." The fed turns the page so I can see the letterhead. It's from Judge James

Rainwater—"the guy writes this on his official stationery, Dade County Courthouse, Seventy-three West Flagler, Miami, Florida:

" 'I first met Bill and Don Whittington approximately ten years ago when I placed my motor home with their company General RV to sell on a consignment basis. I also purchased another motor home by Bill, calling a dear friend of his in Arizona. I picked up this motor home at the factory. I have always found the Whittingtons to be straightforward and honest in their dealings with me. I can always depend upon what they told me to be the truth. I also believe that they have a fine business reputation in the community in which they do their business. Judge Gonsalves, I would hope and recommend that their lives could be salvaged. If you have any questions, please don't hesitate to advise me.' "

The fed flings the judge's letter on the table. His mood turns dark as he exclaims, "It's unbelievable. No wonder we can't ever get anywhere."

Pete Wagner was an integral part of Donald Steinberg's marijuana-smuggling operation. He was convicted on federal narcotics charges and recently released after ten years in federal prison.

In the 1970s, Wagner was an agent for marijuana purchases in Colombia. He was responsible for the actual smuggling of dope into the United States. "I took care of all the stuff down South [America], riding a burro in the mountains and picking the pot in Colombia," he says. "I did all of Steinberg's off-loading, but once it hit the docks, I had nothing to do with it and I tried not to get involved."

Despite the fact that the Steinberg organization was toppled ten years ago, Wagner doesn't want to talk about it. I ask if his reluctance is because the people Steinberg reported to are still in business. He denies that there was anyone behind "The Company," as Steinberg's group was known.

I mention to Wagner that I've turned up information that suggests 1973 (Lansky's return to Miami after an extended stay in Israel) was the real beginning of marijuana smuggling through Florida. He concurs. When he moved to Fort Lauderdale in 1972 from Chicago and started "doing a little wholesale work," he didn't know anyone who was bringing marijuana into Florida, particularly any sizable amount. He says there were a few small-time independent operators who threw some into a boat and brought it into the country. "Maybe a sailboat with three or four hundred pounds," he says. But there were no major grass smugglers and no organized efforts.

The first major grass smuggler in Florida that Wagner heard of was Ricky Cravero. "They were kind of like the frontier boys," he says. "Ricky Cravero and his partners. And the Whittingtons, they were doing it before anybody. Anybody that I knew that ever smuggled marijuana somehow or another got it from the Whittingtons." He says that Steinberg often shared mother ships with Bill and Don Whittington. "They were big-time boys," he says of the brothers.

"How about Gary Bowditch, he was the Meyer Lansky connection to Cravero?"

The question takes Wagner by surprise. There's a long pause. Then he mumbles, "Um-huh. But I think it was more Stan Harris. I think he was the connection more than anybody." Wagner says he's always made it a practice not to talk about Lansky and the mob. He explains, "When we heard about all those guys, you made a point to stay away from them. They can be vicious."

Mentioning Lansky seems to have an effect on Wagner. It's as if the code of silence still remains—no one talks about him. Even though the chairman has been dead since 1983, the power behind the name is still present.

I ask if Wagner knew Don Aronow. He says sure, everybody did. I mention that I've heard Aronow was the man to see when you needed a boat, no questions asked.

"When Don was in business, he dealt with everybody," Wagner comments. "He knew what was going on, and everybody else knew what was going on. You could pay him with cash money and there wouldn't be any paperwork. You go in and give him cash, take the boat away. He knows the name that you're using is a false name. You don't get all the racehorses he got just by selling boats," he says, laughing.

Wagner bought Steinberg's first Cigarette boat from Aronow in 1976. One of the Company's mother ships enroute from Colombia was off course in the Bahamas. Wagner needed a boat quickly so he could go looking for the missing ship the same afternoon they learned there was a problem. He was directed to Aronow.

"A brand-new thirty-five-footer," he recalls. "I paid seventy grand for it in cash. If I woulda been a legal person, I probably coulda got it for forty-five. I went in there, I needed a boat that day, and the boat was there and he said, 'I got the boat there—you want it? Seventy grand.' I had the money in a briefcase, and Don grabbed it up."

Through business, Aronow and Wagner became fairly friendly. "I bought that boat from Don, then another from Don, then I bought another boat from Don, and went down and bought two boats from him," he says, explaining how the relationship started. "Then I bought some racehorses. I talked to him then about racehorses. He had, like, two hundred thoroughbred horses. This guy had some money tied up in horses."

At one point, Wagner needed to buy a Christmas present for Steinberg. Aronow suggested that he buy some horses from Farnsworth Farms in Ocala. Wagner took his advice. "So I bought three thoroughbred horses, cost a hundred thousand dollars. Cash of course." Wagner was unaware of it, but according to a Florida Department of Law Enforcement report, Farnsworth Farms was allegedly owned by Meyer Lansky through a front.

"So was it commonly known that Aronow was Meyer Lansky's boy?" I ask.

"No."

"Did you know?"

"Yeah, I had a hunch about it," he replies. "Everybody said there was somebody big in Miami behind him. He had a lotta shit. We talked about it a lot in the fed [federal prison]. About it being Lansky. But nobody really knew for sure. That's why nobody ever fucked with Don."

Wagner says that a lot of the dopers who were in prison with him used to talk about Lansky as being the money man behind narcotics smuggling. "Lansky was being talked about a lot then, as a financer [*sic*]," he says with a nervous laugh. "It takes money to smuggle. Anyone who tells you any different is crazy. Before you do anything you gotta get a lot of money so you can get the right things together. You gotta have your shit together."

The employees of the various smuggling ventures believed the only man who could come up with the enormous amount of money needed to fund mega-scale operations was Meyer Lansky.

"Look, when you got a commodity that's against the law, and it's expensive, the first thing you gotta realize is that you gotta front it," Wagner explains. "Shit, say you got ten thousand pounds of pot. That's seven million bucks. Nobody's got that kind of cash. That's [Lansky] who's gonna give it to you."

"So Lansky was the banker for the big-time dopers, and Don was the guy you'd go to for the go-fast boats to meet the mother ships," I conclude. "And it's all part of the same company."

"Right, yassuh," he drawls.

Meyer Lansky had evidently become the biggest drug kingpin of all time. The trails were all around. But few people on either side of the law made the connection—at least publicly.

After his return to the United States in late 1972, the facts suggest that the ever-so-adaptable chairman of the board had diversified once again. This time into Florida's marijuana trade. It's also apparent that loyal Lansky, Inc. employee Donald Aronow had played a vital role in his boss's most profitable business venture ever.

All the major marijuana smugglers used Cigarettes, boats that were virtually uncatchable, and they all knew Don. Since he didn't use dealers to sell his Cigarettes, the only way to get one was to go directly to him. Aronow always had a built-in customer base as soon as he opened up a new company. The new owners of his previous company were stunned to find that most of their customers flocked to Aronow's newest enterprise. Perhaps Lansky realized the value of Aronow's talent in building the fastest boats on the seas. Then he instructed Don to provide his services to a wide range of syndicate-supported smuggling ventures.

The DEA, Broward OCD, and the Miami U.S. Attorney's Office have all tagged Aronow as building boats specially designed to conceal grass. A pivotal role in Lansky-approved drug-smuggling ventures would account for Aronow's unique business success on Performance Alley. With a few exceptions, the other boatbuilders who took over his companies failed. As McMahon puts it, "They didn't have all those mob dopers lined up outside the door waiting to buy whatever's hot off the assembly line."

An IRS agent who keeps close tabs on Thunderboat Alley shares McMahon's view. "The boatbuilding business is inherently unstable and unprofitable," he explains. "And operating a quote racing team is a bottomless pit. The only way to survive on that street is to be crooked. Money laundering, selling boats out the back door to smugglers, you name it. You just have to do something else to survive." He adds that almost every boatbuilding company on the Alley has been under federal investigation at one time or another.

Aronow's go-fast boats revolutionized the powerboating sport and the industry. They also enabled drug smugglers to gain a stronghold in the coastal war against drugs. As a trusted mob associate, Aronow undoubtedly played a major supporting role in the entire Mafia expansion in the drug trade as well.

Interestingly, 1973, the year after Lansky returned to Miami from a two-year respite in Israel, marks the beginning of large-scale marijuana smuggling into Florida. Small wonder that by 1976—with Lansky's financing and connections, and Aronow's boats—more than 80 percent of all the marijuana imported into the United States came through Florida.

BOOK THREE

SEVENTEEN

Aronow's mob connections were coalescing into two general categories: Genovese crime family with its Purple Gang offshoot and the Lansky OC network. The two crime families were often aligned. Lansky, while not Italian, had been a founding member of the Genovese crime family with Lucky Luciano and Bugsy Siegel. It wasn't until the 1960s that the "Luciano" crime family was renamed the "Genovese" crime family.

Into the first group fell Dominic "Swats Mulligan" Ciaffone, Joey Pagano, Paul "Paulie Rizzo" Caiano, and Frankie Viserto, Jr. Joey Ippolito from the Genovese-aligned DeCalvacante family could be included here as well. Into the second, the Kramers, Kessler, Sam Gilbert, Joey Weichselbaum, Alvin Malnik (vociferously denying his involvement—it's all "a myth, my albatross, an incredible, inescapable myth"), and Meyer Lansky himself.

By now there was no longer any doubt in my mind that Aronow had been killed by the mob. Since he continued to be intimate with both the Genovese and the Lansky organizations, his murder had to be a matter of mutual interest. One crime family won't order a hit on anyone affiliated with another family without a consultation. To do otherwise could be considered grounds for retaliation.

Aronow was a highly prized mob associate with a personal relationship with the Vice President of the United States. The reason for the hit had to be strong enough to outweigh the value he offered and the high-profile investigation that would follow. Both families had to agree and each could have had a particular role in the murder.

Genovese personnel may have choreographed the hit, tracking Aronow's moves on the fatal day and intimidating people who might talk. Murder, especially for the Purple Gang, is a routine part of doing business, something at which they excel. The Lansky organization's forte is its influence in the law enforcement system. Their efforts would have focused on damage control, impeding the investigation, and ensuring that the mob not be connected to the murder.

On the day Aronow was murdered, there were many strange phone calls.

In the morning, someone who wielded control over Aronow had called him on the phone, pressuring him to "write letters" apparently similar to the one in which he attempted to spring Frankie Viserto from prison. The call agitated him, and immediately after, he left his estate and headed across the bay to see Jack Kramer at Ft. Apache Marina.

The next curious phone call was to USA Racing, fifteen minutes after the shooting. It was Paulie "Rizzo" Caiano. Rizzo had two boats worth half a million dollars waiting for him in the USA Racing dry dock, including a new one he had been very anxious to get. He had been incommunicado for five months—then he suddenly surfaced the day of the murder.

Patty Lezaca took the call that afternoon, but "she wouldn't talk about it after," Engelman recalls. "Whatever Rizzo said to her—it really blew her mind. And later she changed her story and said she called him. But we didn't have a direct number for him so she couldn't have. And then later still, she denied the call altogether."

A third phone call came just minutes after Aronow arrived at the hospital. The call was routed to Lillian Aronow, who was in the waiting room while the staff was vainly trying to save her husband. When she answered, the man hissed, "Is that son of a bitch Aronow dead yet?" Lillian blanched and dropped the phone. She told a few friends about the call, then later denied that there was one.

A few minutes after the hospital call, Donny Soffer, a good friend of Aronow's and the developer of Turnberry Isle, also received an intimidating phone call. The caller said, "You're next." Soffer immediately hired five bodyguards, threw some belongings onto his boat the *Monkey Business,* and headed out into the Atlantic. He remained at sea for almost a week before he dared to return to Miami.

All four phone calls had a startling effect on the recipients. Was it four different callers? Or were they all from the same person? The first call may have been to locate Don's whereabouts for the hit men, the discussion of "letters" simply a pretense. The others all followed a similar pattern and seemed intent on evoking similar feelings: scaring people into silence.

Patty Lezaca was very close to Aronow. She had worked for him for fifteen years, longer than anyone else at USA Racing, and was an officer in many of his corporations. Among Don's employees, Patty was in a class by herself. "She alone was privy to many of Don's innermost secrets," Engelman says. "Especially those of a business nature." An IRS agent familiar with Aronow's businesses agrees, stating, "She was his alter ego."

Since many of Aronow's dealings were connected to mob business, Patty was in a dangerous position. Engelman maintains she knew many of Don's under-the-table business maneuvers; she was familiar with his wiseguy associations, and she had more than a decade's perspective on how it all meshed.

Steve Parr says that MetroDade Homicide investigators spent a lot of time talking to Patty. She was very reluctant to talk to them, especially in the beginning. It took five days of interviews before they were satisfied with the answers they got from her. But Parr concedes that, like Aronow's attorney, Murray Weil, Patty didn't say much of anything.

"I could've told them that she wouldn't tell them a thing," Jerry Engelman comments: "They were wasting their time with Patty." Old Mike agrees, saying that Patty had even tried to discourage him from talking to the police after the shooting. Mike had been around the street too long for anyone to tell him what to do, so he ignored her.

In the chaos following the hit, Patty, like others close to Don, reacted emotionally. But her actions were contrary to what would have been expected in the situation. She seemed intent upon muddying the circumstances of the incident. Rather than helping the police identify the killers, she apparently attempted to hamper their efforts.

When Engelman mentioned to Patty that he had told DeCora about the strange visitor at the office, he says "she got weird, all bent out of shape and started giving me a lot of shit. She said, 'What are you sticking your two cents in for? You're out of line talking to the police.' She didn't want to tell the cops anything." Jerry still wonders whether anyone would have told the police about the visitor if he hadn't said anything.

Patty's description of the sandy-haired man differed greatly from that given by Engelman and Old Mike. "She said the guy had a mustache, and that he was in his twenties," Engelman notes. "He didn't have a mustache and no way was he in his twenties. That's complete and total bullshit." Jerry's and Old Mike's descriptions, on the other hand, were virtually identical. They both said the man seemed to be in his mid-to-late forties, with a few days' growth of stubble.

As an organized crime specialist, Rory McMahon has spent the last ten years with the U.S. Justice Department supervising wiseguy parolees in New York and Miami. He meets with his parolees at least once a month, sometimes weekly, and often visits their homes unannounced to check up on them. He's heard all their stories, been privy to the gossip of various mob families, and gained a rare perspective on how wiseguys operate, having dealt with "the scumbags close up and personal, eight hours a day, five days a week, for years."

I tell him about the phone call from Rizzo. He says that would be standard mob procedure following a hit. "Paulie knows Don's dead and now there's got to be damage control," McMahon explains. "He's probably known Patty for years. He knows that the cops are going immediately to come to her, which they in fact did. He warns her to keep her mouth shut." Patty, naturally frightened, would quickly try to throw confusion into the investigation to ensure that no one would think she had cooperated with the police.

"That telephone call fits that idea—scaring the shit out of her," Rory concludes. "Her reactions right after the murder were really strange. Unless, of course, you see them as following a 'friendly' call from one of the boys."

Since the murder took place in south Florida, it had to have been discussed, agreed upon, and coordinated from some secure haven in the area. Negotiations with the hit men had to be arranged at some point, as well as their payment.

While there are many mob hangouts in Florida, one stands out above all the rest: Joe Sonken's Gold Coast Restaurant. "Tradition-ally, we've known for years that your top organized crime figures frequent the place," Steve Bertucelli, director of the Organized Crime Division of the Broward County Sheriff's Office, once told the *Miami Herald*.

The Gold Coast is a meeting place for mob people. It's centrally located for them because many wiseguys live in Hollywood, Hallandale, and Golden Beach in north Miami. "It's a nice little jaunt right up to Joe's to get some stone crabs and talk business with the boys," says McMahon, laughing.

It's also considered the mob's message center. McMahon notes that when "wiseguys are coming down here to get some sun or do some business, they tell their people back home, 'If you need to get me, leave a message at Sonken's.' Any wiseguy can go there, but it's really for made members and associates. Not for some fucking punks."

Over the years, various feds and state and local cops have lain in wait on the other side of the waterway that runs behind the restaurant. With their telephoto cameras they occasionally hit pay dirt, the personal appearance of the Mafia's high and mighty. They've seen John Gotti, Carlo Gambino, Meyer Lansky, Sam DeCalvacante, Santo Trafficante, Jr., John Roselli, Sam Giancana, as well as many of the mob's most notorious hit men, plus a stunning variety of wiseguys, half-assed wiseguys, and so-called "respectable" people with hidden ties to the mob.

While he was heading his huge drug empire, Ben Kramer enjoyed the Gold Coast Restaurant. He ate there often (and evidently liked it since his running tab for one month, June 1983, was $5,293), as did another figure whose name has surfaced repeatedly during my investigation of the Aronow story: Richard Gerstein. The man who helped Aronow's widow after the murder and along with the former Miami Beach chief of police, oversaw the PI efforts for the family.

Almost three decades ago, Gerstein was dining at Sonken's, and even then it was mobbed up. In the 1960s, the *Herald*'s "Mafia hunter" Hank Messick went to the Gold Coast Restaurant to pick up secret documents from an undercover agent. He later wrote in his book *Syndicate in the Sun*:

> The dining room was still crowded, but somehow the customers had changed. Whereas before there had been family-type groups, complete even with children, there were now hard-bitten Mafia types with well-painted dolls. . . .
>
> The waiter [who slipped Messick secret documents] brought the check. His face was expressionless. Briefly, I wondered about him. Was he really a waiter first and an undercover agent only by accident?

Or was it the other way around? It was none of my business, of course. He had served me well. . . .

And abruptly I froze. Two couples were being escorted to a nearby table. One of them towered above the rest, his scarred face unmistakable. Bad Eye, they called him. Better known as State Attorney Richard E. Gerstein of Dade County.

Eight years ago Jack Anderson had called this place a message center for the syndicate. . . . Yet here was Gerstein—in a place where the Big Man himself, Meyer Lansky, liked to eat.

Joe "the Blimp" Sonken, eighty-one, the cigar-chomping owner of the Gold Coast Restaurant, has always denied that he is a host to the nation's Mafia elite, despite reports he was very close to Meyer and his wife Thelma "Teddy" Lansky, both of whom ate there often, along with a clientele that was a veritable who's who in the mob.

An investigative TV journalist once charged into the Gold Coast with a camera crew, videotape running. In his best "Mike Wallace– *60 Minutes*" style the reporter marched around the restaurant until he located Sonken—who isn't hard to find, especially with the huge painting of himself, cigar in hand, that dominates one wall. The reporter demanded, "Mr. Sonken, do you have any comments on reports that this restaurant is a message center for the mob?"

Sonken grabbed the microphone from his hand and said, "Yeah, you're right, it is." The reporter's eyes snapped wide open—he had a headline. Then Sonken yelled over his shoulder at his patrons, "Call for Mr. Capone, telephone call on line two for Mr. Al Capone." The wiseguys loved Sonken's joke; the reporter was red-faced.

In the often bizarre world of Miami, Joe Sonken's name now adorns more than his restaurant. It's in the halls of academe. In 1986, Sonken engaged in some philanthropic public relations and gave a large sum of money to Nova University, a local south Florida school. In return they named a building for him, the "Joe Sonken Upper School Building."

"I gave 'em quite a sum," Sonken proudly told a reporter from the *Miami Herald*. "They got whites, they got Jews, they got coloreds. It's only money. Can't take it with you." He was interviewed in his office under a poster with the picture of a bulldog and the caption, "When I want your opinion, I'll beat it out of you."

Sometimes a poster is worth a thousand words.

A few months after the interview, Sonken was in the paper again. Only this time the story had a different "hero." Sonken almost drowned when his car accidently plunged off the restaurant dock into the waterway. As it began to sink, Sonken could be heard screaming, "Get me the fuck outta here. I can't swim. Somebody give me a fucking hand!"

Two men dove into the water and pulled him "out of the car window seconds before the car filled with water and went down," the *Miami Herald* reported, "but it sank too fast for the rescuers to save Sonken's two pet hounds, Tillie and Amos, his longtime pets." One of the rescuers was Ben Kramer.

Benny's heroism did not go unnoticed in high places. Two weeks after the rescue, U.S. Congressman William Lehman wrote to Kramer:

CONGRESS OF THE UNITED STATES

House of Representatives

Dear Ben:

I recently learned of your heroic act of saving an elderly person from his car which plunged into the Intracoastal Waterway.

Your quick thinking and unselfish act in risking your own life to save another person is most commendable.

Best of luck to you and I hope you will be successful in bringing the 17th Congressional District the World Championship for Offshore Power Boat Racing.

With best wishes, I am,

Sincerely,

William Lehman
Member of Congress

The Kramers also had business dealings with Sonken. The huge factory building in Hollywood which housed the Apache boat manufacturing facilities was purchased from the Blimp, according to an IRS agent familiar with the transaction.

Sonken's restaurant is a ten-minute drive from Thunderboat Alley, across the Dade-Broward county line in Hollywood, Florida. Could the Aronow hit have been coordinated from south Florida's most famous mob hangout? With a private and secure second floor that ran the entire length of the restaurant, it was one of the safest places for wiseguys to discuss such mob business.

Over the years, law enforcement had continually attempted to infiltrate the restaurant, and a fed suggests that I try to find out if there were any undercover operations there at the time of Aronow's death. If there were, perhaps some "interesting faces" had shown up there just around the time of the murder. The fed says he has heard that Broward County OCD recently finished a case there, but he doesn't know what was involved.

Broward County's Organized Crime Division is in a new, mirrored high-rise office building in Fort Lauderdale. But the similarity to other office buildings ends there. The first four floors of the structure are for parking, even though there are acres of empty land around it that could be used for vehicles.

The garage floors are heavily barricaded. An electronic gate protects the entrance to the parking area, and cameras constantly monitor the area. The measures are no doubt designed to prevent tampering with agents' cars, perhaps the planting of bugs or bombs. Security in the lobby is tight as well. After a call upstairs, the guard points me toward the elevator.

The organized crime unit is by itself on the tenth floor. In fact, half the floor is unoccupied, and I walk through hundreds of square feet of empty and unfinished office space until I come to an unmarked door. Opening it, I abruptly enter a crowded reception room.

Steve Bertucelli is the director of Broward OCD. Formerly with the MetroDade OC unit, he is considered one of the foremost experts on the Mafia in Florida. We had met a few times in the past, and he had given me some useful background information on the mob, but it is Lt. Dave Green who agrees to meet me. We walk back to his corner office overlooking the runway at Fort Lauderdale Executive Airport. Green, a burly man with sunken eyes and jowly cheeks, has a bad cold and constantly blows his nose throughout the conversation.

We engage in small talk about the photos on his wall. One catches my eye. It's a telephoto shot of John Gotti. The dapper mafioso was exiting the Gold Coast Restaurant flanked by two very big and very mean-looking bodyguards with what must be a standard wiseguy accessory—toothpicks dangling from their mouths.

I bring up the subject of Aronow's murder. Green wants to know who heads the MetroDade Homicide team.

"Huh," he grunts when I mention Mike DeCora. "You know that one of those Dade County detectives made an appointment to come up to talk with me about that murder, but then never showed up. A no-show."

I describe the alleged hit men: a tall, sandy-haired man in his mid-to-late forties wearing shorts and a baseball cap, and a broad-shouldered man with olive skin and dark hair. Has he heard of a mob hit team like that?

"Yeah." He doesn't elaborate.

After what seems to be several minutes of silence, I ask who they are.

"They're friends of Joe Sonken's."

I wait for him to continue but he doesn't. Finally, he picks up the phone and talks to someone. A few moments later, a man brings a folder in. Green opens it and pulls out a photograph. It's a mug shot of a dark-haired man. "Frankie the German," he mutters. "Works with a tall, muscular, sandy-haired man."

"Where are they from?"

"Chicago."

Green gives new meaning to the term "laconic." I wait as he blows his nose again and decides whether to continue or not. "The big guy used to be a football player, six feet four, two hundred thirty pounds," he resumes at last. "Both come down to Florida."

The mug shot bears an uncanny resemblance to the composite drawing of the man who drove the Lincoln and shot Aronow. "How about the football player, what's he look like?"

Green hands me an eight-by-ten blowup of the man, obviously taken from a great distance. "The photo doesn't show it very good," he explains, "but the guy has sandy hair. 'Sandy' is the right word for it."

On the back of the photo a date is marked "3/1/87." The photograph was taken at the Gold Coast Restaurant, twenty-six days after Aronow's murder.

"Who's the Broward guy who was just undercover there?"

"Me."

As I slowly extract bits and pieces of information from Green, he tells me that the hit team was in Miami in the winter of 1987. Although he's not sure if they were sighted in February at the time of Aronow's murder. He says he only saw the tall man during the winter months. The other member of the team, the one called Frankie the German, keeps a very low profile when he's in Florida.

"But I know he was down here then, too," Green says with satisfaction. He's starting to warm up. "You know, the football player always wears shorts and he likes caps," he continues. "I saw him at the Gold Coast a lot that winter, I spent of lot of time there. Operation Cherokee. That was my case and I went undercover to investigate—"

"I think these are the men who killed Aronow," I blurt out. It immediately halts the conversation. We stare at each other for a few more uncomfortable minutes again.

"I think I should call MetroDade Homicide," he finally announces.

It's Friday, March 22, 1988, and I've spent nine months looking into the murder of Don Aronow. MetroDade has all but dropped the case—if Broward OCD contacts them, the investigation will be caught in a vast interagency limbo. I want to get as much information on these hit men as possible before they become "official." More to the point, if Green talks directly to MetroDade, I'll be frozen out of the loop and never get any information.

"Look," I finally declare, "I had an arrangement of confidentiality with Director Bertucelli. I really insist on talking to him first before you do anything."

Green thinks for a moment and then agrees, commenting that he'll be in court most of the following week. He puts me on notice that if I don't do something by the time he's finished with his court appearances, he'll "put the ball in motion" himself.

I decide to drive to MetroDade Homicide. The traffic on I-95 is heavy with rush-hour congestion, and it takes an hour and a half to get there. Before I walk into the building, I realize that in my excitement, I don't have the last names of the hit men or even the football player's first name. I call Broward OCD from a pay phone.

"What did you say their names were?" I ask Green.

"I didn't. Call me next week," he says, and hangs up. We're back to cryptic answers.

At the MetroDade front desk, the guard calls up to the Homicide Division. Steve Parr was on his way home, but when the guard beeps him, gives my name and tells him it's about the Aronow murder, he heads back to the office.

I call my attorney, who was working nearby. Then the three of us meet in the corner interview office. I tell Parr that while pursuing Aronow's mob connections I've seen photographs of two Mafia hit men who fit the description of the killers, adding that they're friends of Joe Sonken, they're from Chicago, and they were in Miami around the time of the murder. But I don't tell him where I saw the photos. Because of my previous "tit-for-tat" conversations with DeCora, I've learned the value of playing my cards one at a time with MetroDade.

We're interrupted by a man who sticks his head in the door and says there's a phone call for Parr. He picks up the extension.

"I'm talking to that writer guy," Parr says. "He says he's seen photos of two men from Chicago who fit the descriptions in the Aronow case. Remember that 'Chicago connection' ?"

Parr listens for a while, then hangs up, explaining that it was DeCora.

Parr is intrigued by the idea that the hit team is from Chicago. He says that the day before the murder two men in a dark Lincoln Town Car pulled alongside a pedestrian and asked for directions to the Alley. The encounter took place two miles south and west of 188th Street in another industrial section of North Miami off Biscayne Boulevard.

"He pointed them in the right direction," Parr explains, "and he heard one of the guys say, 'We drove twelve hundred miles and we came pretty close.' Now, I don't know how far it is from here to Chicago, but I'm guessing it's pretty close to twelve hundred miles."

Parr says that the men who asked for directions and their car fit the descriptions of the suspects in the murder—and that my hit team also matches the descriptions of the men in the car. He says that he and DeCora have come to believe both men were actually there at the time of the shooting. "What happened was a second car with a different description was seen leaving at a high rate of speed, but without a tag number."

Parr is confirming that the second car was a "crash car," a tactic sometimes employed by mob hitters. But his comments contradict his department's public statements on the incident. Their details of the murder pointed to just one man, the man who shot Aronow. And just one vehicle, the dark Lincoln. In talking to the press initially a police spokesperson had even specifically denied there was a crash car seen leaving the scene.

Since Parr is more talkative than DeCora, I ask what he thinks was going on with Aronow the last three weeks. Parr says they speculate that Aronow thought he was in trouble, but not that he was going to be hit. The detectives also knew that he met often with Ben Kramer, although the two men didn't get along. Despite their interviews with the people from USA Racing, they've been unable to pinpoint the reason for the frequent meetings.

He says they discovered the Super Chief South deal during their search of Aronow's company. "We kind of stumbled on it," he says. "We found bits and pieces of it. Behind a drawer. Under some stuff. The deal was for the whole thing—the land, the helicopter, the building, the boats, the company, the [Blue Thunder] contract. Yet I only saw paperwork for seven hundred thousand dollars."

Parr says they finally concluded that Super Chief "was between

Aronow and Ben, with Jack as a nameplate. The whole thing to us, after we got into the other deals he [Aronow] was into, was that it was a money-laundering deal. That's from talking to the family and Michael. He wasn't privy to everything, but he knew that there was money floating around at all times in his father's life."

I decide not to ask Parr how the Super Chief deal could possibly be a money-laundering scheme when Aronow got just $100,000 cash for close to $5 million in assets.

"I think Murray knows what went wrong," Parr continues. "I think that he knew at the beginning or at the end, but he wouldn't say anything. A lot of times he said 'I don't know about this' and 'I don't know about that' because he's deathly afraid of the IRS." When the detectives asked Weil about the Super Chief deal, he claimed he had no paperwork on it. Parr says they had to take their copy over to him.

"I don't know whether this is the deal that took Aronow out or not," Parr muses. But, he says, the Super Chief line of investigation led them nowhere. "Unfortunately, when you run it back, you run into Kramer. It's hard to get around Kramer." But their work hits a brick wall with either of the Kramers, especially Jack.

He shakes his head as he recalls the initial days of the investigation almost fourteen months before. "We really for a solid week had no idea what the reason was for this man's murder," he says. "And then we started looking. Excluding things. Trying to go down these paths of different motives. And always ran into a dead end. So we worked as many motives as you could possibly think of trying to lead some-place, and always ran into a stone wall."

He says that there were a lot of different, possible motives. "We worked on the most obvious," he explains. "Jealousy. That didn't lead us anywhere. Worked with narcotics. That didn't go anywhere. Money laundering. Really, none of those motives led anywhere."

Cops just don't talk to other cops in south Florida.

While MetroDade was left guessing what other agencies knew, I became privy to "inside dirt." After almost a year, I had reliable and trusted contacts in the IRS, DEA, INS, FDLE, the Justice Department, the U.S. Attorney's Office, and the Operation Isle of Man Task Force. In addition to police, I had a source "inside" the Kramer organization.

A DEA agent who wouldn't dream of giving MetroDade "fucking diddly," to use Mike DeCora's analysis of interagency cooperation in south Florida, would regularly order up files on the mob's activities for me. Yet this same man would cut his hand off with a hacksaw before he would pick up the phone and call MetroDade Homicide or the FBI. "I wouldn't walk across the street to spit on the 'I,'" he was fond of saying. The I, as the FBI is not-so-fondly known to other feds, is not popular with its fellow agencies.

With my discovery of Frankie the German and his sandy-haired partner, I was just beginning to learn how bizarre interagency relationships in Florida can be.

EIGHTEEN

The Chicago Police Department can't give me a line on Frankie the German without more specific information, such as a booking number or his last name. One detective suggests I call the Chicago Crime Commission. "Hell, they got better files than we do," he says, laughing.

The Chicago Crime Commission is a privately funded agency of "citizens combating crime in Metropolitan Chicago." One of its directors is Jerry Gladden, a retired OCB detective sergeant from the Intelligence Division of the Chicago PD. I call and ask if he has come across Frankie the German.

"Yeah," he confirms immediately. "Frank Schweihs, a hit guy from Chicago." He adds that Schweihs sometimes goes to Florida and stays in a condo there. He puts the phone down for a minute, then comes back on the line with an address: 328 Georgia Street, Hollywood, Florida. "Runs with a guy named Wayne Bock," he comments. "Great big guy. Used to be a professional football player. He was seen staying there with him last season [1987]."

Though retired, Gladden continues to get reports from the PD Intelligence unit. His records show that Bock was driving Sam Carlisi around the Gold Coast in the winter of '87. Carlisi is the liaison between the Chicago LCN family and the unions. He was attending an AFL-CIO meeting in the Fort Lauderdale area. There's no mention of the date.

Gladden pulls Bock's LCN card. "Yeah, Wayne's a big guy all right, very good shape," he reads. "He's six four, two forty, blue eyes, born 5/28/1935."

Mindful of Jerry Engelman's description of the man who came into the office and talked about "the boss," I ask if Bock could look like the outdoor type. Gladden says definitely, pointing out that Bock runs every morning and looks younger than he is.

"Does he have sandy-colored hair?" I ask.

"Yeah."

Gladden continues to read from his card. The records show that Bock owns a tavern in Illinois called Chester's. But one of his key roles is as a "juice collector" and enforcer for Joe Ferriola—the powerful head of the Chicago crime family. A juice collector in underworld parlance is a mob representative who collects payments on money borrowed from the mob. Juice is the interest.

"And Frankie has dark hair, receding hairline, olive complexion?"

"Yeah," Gladden replies. "He's always got a suntan. Let's see, five eleven, one eighty, gray-black hair."

I mention to Gladden that I saw Frankie's mug shot and ask what he was arrested for in 1981.

"They were trying to burglarize a depository for an armored car company loaded with food stamps," he says, chuckling as one would about the antics of some wayward juvenile delinquents. "Frankie was circumventing the alarm when the man who owned an automobile repair shop next door came back to check on his shop. He spotted these guys at the armored car place and called the police. Schweihs at the time had a bum leg, so he hid under a car, and they caught him, but the case was dismissed."

Gladden explains that Frankie is an electronics specialist and excels at disarming alarms, a talent that carries over into bomb-making. He also likes working construction as a hobby. When he first started doing mob surveillance at Chicago PD Intelligence, Gladden didn't know who Schweihs was and he couldn't understand why so many top-level mafiosi were congregating at construction sites.

"Here I'm looking around at all the big shots and paying no attention to the construction guys," he recalls. "And all the hoods are standing around talking, and I think they're talking to themselves, and I'm thinking to myself, why are these guys always going to construction sites? Well, I think, maybe they're looking to make an investment, checking out property. Maybe buying it, what have you. But no-ooo. They just come over to talk to Frankie, and there he is standing with a jackhammer."

Schweihs is also a very good friend of Chicago capo Joey "the Clown" Lombardo. Lombardo, Schweihs, and Bock were a sadistic and deadly crew. Joey the Clown is in prison. He was sentenced in 1982 along with then Chicago don Joseph "Doves" Aiuppa on Las Vegas skimming charges.

So now it's just Frankie and Wayne. Gladden says he can't see Frankie and Wayne doing a hit in Florida without the permission of the head of the "outfit," as the Chicago La Cosa Nostra family is known.

Since traditionally there have been strong ties between Miami and Chicago mobsters, Gladden says that a hit could have been done by Chicago as a favor to someone in Miami. Dave Green had said the two hit men were close friends of Joe Sonken's, who was originally from Chicago. Sonken of course was close to Lansky and his OC network.

Gladden says he couldn't even begin to determine how many hits Frankie and Wayne were behind. But their names are always popping up. "If it was a good one [an important hit]," he emphasizes, "they would call on them. Like if someone were going to testify against another outfit guy, they'd call on them. They've never been caught."

Gladden laughs when I mention that the hit men were seen by witnesses, noting that Frankie and Wayne are bold enough to do daylight hits. They have no fear of being caught. "A lot of times they've been seen in the vicinity," Gladden says, "and then the guy gets killed, but there's not enough evidence to lock them up. They're always seen prior to the hit going down. They even got pictures of them sometimes. And in a day or two, some guy's blown up."

Talking about their hits reminds Gladden that he thinks the duo has done a job in Florida previously. Wayne was seen by Florida feds with a man who showed up murdered two weeks later.

Gladden says that Chicago OCB refers to the team as Frankie and Wayne because they're a set. "Every time we have them together," he explains, "like standing out on a street corner, like way out in the suburbs, three or four days later somebody gets killed. And then we don't see them again. Each one goes their separate ways. And then all of a sudden we'll put them together again. And they'll be meeting at a bowling alley or a parking lot. And they're talking a lot or looking moody and they're not happy, and they're walking up and down. You can see they have a big weight on their shoulders.

"Then three or four days later," Gladden concludes, "somebody goes!"

The Automobile Association of America maintains detailed maps and regularly updated mileage charts for all of the United States. I obtain their package for a Chicago–Miami road-trip routing.

Steve Parr had said that the men who fit the description of Aronow's assailants had arrived in Miami on Monday, February 2, 1987. If indeed it was Frankie and Wayne who murdered Aronow, they probably left Chicago on Saturday morning.

I unfold the map and charts and imagine what their trip would have been like. On Saturday, Frankie pulls up to Wayne's house in Palos Heights, ten miles south of the center of Chicago. As they back out of the driveway, Frankie zeros the trip mileage counter on his Lincoln Town Car.

They certainly know what most mobsters know: the best way for a wiseguy to get around the country is by car. In fact, Frankie and Wayne rarely fly. Taking airplanes leaves a paper trail even with an alias—and there's the danger of videotaped surveillance at the airport. Besides, the Chicago PD usually keeps detectives at the airport full-time recording the comings and goings of outfit wiseguys and their associates, and how can you risk taking a gun if you fly?

The duo drives east for five miles to pick up the Tristate. From there on it's expressway to Florida. They take turns driving, using the cruise control locked at 55 mph to make sure they don't speed. They can't afford the chance of being stopped with weapons in the car. A traffic citation would prove where they were at a particular time and jeopardize the assignment. The first day they drive the length of Indiana, north to south, and into Kentucky, where they stop for the night outside of Lexington. They've stopped shaving—a little stubble goes a long way to disguise a face.

The next morning they're up early driving on Interstate 75 through Tennessee and into Georgia. They drive all day and with each passing mile Don Aronow is one minute closer to death. That evening they stop south of Atlanta. By Monday morning they're in Florida, and by afternoon they're cruising along north Miami's Biscayne Boulevard. The Alley, a short dead end in a factory section of north Miami, is difficult to find, even for people who have lived in the area. They pull up to a pedestrian on a side street.

"Hey, buddy, how do you get to Gasoline Alley?" Wayne asks.

The spot where they stop to ask directions is twelve miles north of the center of Miami.

In my imaginary trip, Wayne looks down at the Lincoln's trip counter as they pull away from the curb. By my calculations with the AAA charts, it would read exactly 1,206 miles.

"How do you like that?" Wayne then says to Frankie. "We drove twelve hundred miles and we came pretty close."

Francis John Schweihs. DOB 2-7-30. FBI #345162A. A broad-shouldered, dark-haired, olive-skinned hit man who looks remarkably like the MetroDade composite of the man who shot Don Aronow.

Former Florida chief homicide investigator Harold Young views the mug shot and the composite. He doesn't know who the men are, but he's had years of experience matching people from witnesses' descriptions and old mug shots.

"Christ, I'd say you got your man," he says.

"How about the age?" I ask. "The composite looks younger."

"Age is the least reliable witness identification factor," Young says. He suggests the best way to "read" a composite is to compare and match individual features, one at a time. "I'd give it an eight-out-of-ten match," he declares.

Former special agent William Grieves, one of the FBI agents who arrested Ben Kramer, views the pictures. "Let me tell you something," he says. "I've been working with composites for twenty years, and most of the time you're lucky if you get one feature that matches. This composite looks like the police artist sat down and drew it right from the mug photo."

Grieves places the photo over the composite and holds them up to the light. "See, look." There's almost a perfect overlay.

Wayne Bock, Jr. DOB 5-28-35. FBI #267318F.

When the sandy-haired man came into the office the day of the Aronow murder, he and Aronow stood side by side for a few minutes. Both Jerry Engelman and Old Mike had said that the two men were the same height. They had also said the man was solid, muscular, with well-developed legs and shoulders and a small potbelly. Ex-Marine Bock was a former tackle for the University of Illinois and the old Chicago Cardinals football teams. According to his LCN card he is 6'4", 240 pounds. And he favors shorts and baseball caps.

Engelman had said the man had a "ruddy face" and an "outdoorsy" look. Old Mike described it more like a Northerner who had just come down to Florida and stayed in the sun too long on his first day. According to Jerry Gladden, Wayne Bock jogs on the beach every morning when he's in Florida—he has a fitness fetish. Did a few hours in the strong Florida sun jogging on the morning of the hit cause Bock's skin to burn?

Frankie and Wayne, a murderous matched pair, so notorious that their hometown cops joked that when you saw them together, you knew that "somebody was gonna die." They were together in Florida in the winter of 1987. And Don Aronow died. Were they in Miami on February 3, 1987?

The photograph that Broward OCD's Dave Green had shown to me indicated that Wayne Bock was in Florida on March 1, 1987. Green recalls that Frankie was in town, too, though he didn't see him.

Jerry Gladden had said that Frankie and Wayne were both in Florida at the time of an AFL-CIO convention that winter, staying at a condo in Hollywood. A map of the area shows that the condo is just five miles from where Aronow was murdered.

The headquarters of the AFL-CIO is in Washington, D.C. A woman there checks her files and announces that there were no union conventions in Florida in the winter of 1987. She points out that there was an Executive Committee meeting at the Sheraton Bal Harbor in Miami. Formerly, in the Lansky era, the Sheraton Bal Harbor was the Americana Hotel, a favorite wiseguy hangout. The Executive Meeting was February 16–20.

Frankie and Wayne's schedule was getting closer and closer to the date of Aronow's murder.

The hit on Don Aronow was a high-risk proposition, and not simply because of his status. Most Mafia hits are "a piece of cake," as Gladden had described them. The victim is told to come to a meeting in some remote location and then shot a few times in the back of the head. Even if the target suspects he might be killed, he still goes, hoping he's mistaken. If he doesn't go, he's a walking dead man anyway.

The decision to kill Aronow was clearly made at the last minute. The MetroDade story about the two men asking directions indicates that they weren't quite sure where Gasoline Alley (as they called it) was when they arrived in town on the day before the murder. Even brazen and experienced killers such as Frankie and Wayne meticulously plan their jobs—it's just one of the reasons they've never been caught—and as Jerry Gladden had noted, they often took weeks stalking their target before they moved in for the kill.

For some reason, the assassins of Aronow had to move quickly and take risks. They had to have one of the team enter USA Racing to positively identify Aronow (there are a lot of athletic men who could be mistaken for Don on the Alley) then flush him out before the end of the boatbuilding shift when the street would be filled with workers.

Who better then, given the apparent urgency of the assignment, than Frankie and Wayne? They are seasoned, confident, hard-core professional killers who are called on for the really tough jobs; the Mafia's "killer elite." Their resumes read like a who's who of the underworld's "hit" parade.

Eight months before the Aronow hit, mob capo Anthony Spilotro, the outfit's man in Las Vegas, and his brother Michael were murdered. Joe Ferriola ordered the hit in a grab for control of the Chicago LCN family. The two brothers were taken to a rural cornfield and beaten with baseball bats to reveal where they had hidden $10,000,000 in skimmed casino cash.

The brothers had been lured with the promise of a "sit-down" with Ferriola. Evidently they suspected trouble because Michael Spilotro told his wife as he left, "If we're not back by nine o'clock, we're in big trouble, and you might not see us again." Authorities believe the money's hiding place was near the cornfield, and that after the men revealed its location, they were beaten to death and then thrown together into a shallow grave.

Among the suspects: Frankie & Wayne.

In 1984, Chicago dentist Dr. Burton Isaacs was gunned down. The dentist was involved in the mob's thrust into the lucrative Medicaid fraud racket.

Among the suspects: Frankie & Wayne.

In 1983, Allen M. Dorfman, an associate of Tony Spilotro and a top official of the notoriously corrupt Teamsters Central States Pension Fund, was convicted in federal court. While out on bail awaiting sentencing, he was shot to death in an elevator. As a longtime official of the mobbed-up fund, Dorfman was in a position to do considerable damage. Prior to his sentencing, he was no doubt under great pressure from the feds to cut a deal and would have been vulnerable to "rolling over" on his mob backers.

Among the suspects: Frankie & Wayne.

In 1976, Paul Gonsky, the owner of a pornographic movie chain, was shot to death in a parking lot in Chicago. In an interesting parallel to the Aronow hit, Gonsky was shot seven times while sitting in his car, taking bullets in the head, shoulder, and chest. Authorities believe it was a message to other theater owners that the outfit was taking control of the business.

Owner of the parking lot: Frankie.

In 1974, Daniel Seifert, the prime witness in a massive federal case involving Joey the Clown Lombardo and the Teamsters Central States Pension Fund, was cornered by three men in ski masks at his factory. They threw his wife and child into a bathroom, chased Seifert around the building until they cornered him, and blew the back of his head off. He was also shot at point-blank with a shotgun in the front and back of the chest. "They killed him the day before he was to testify," says Gladden. The government's case fell apart.

Among the suspects: Frankie & Wayne & Joey the Clown.

In 1972, Gerald Covelli was killed when a remote-controlled bomb detonated in his car in Los Angeles. Covelli was a half-assed wiseguy turned government informant in a hijacking case involving Chicago LCN members.

Seen in L.A. at the time of the bombing: Bomb expert Frankie & Joey.

The three men have been suspects in literally dozens of murders over a thirty-year period. While Frankie has been arrested sixty times on a wide variety of charges—from suspicion of murder to burglary to hiding outside a hotel with a lead pipe waiting to beat a mob associate—not once has a case against him stuck. Wayne Bock has just one conviction, for a truck hijacking in 1966. Only Lombardo has ever been convicted of any charge carrying major prison time: a federal racketeering case, in 1982.

Chicago police believe that Frankie's first murder took place in 1962. A manicurist whose body was found floating in the Chicago River was identified as his girlfriend. The police crime lab concluded she had been shot in the heart as she was sitting in the right side of an automobile. The dead woman's hairdresser told police that she last saw the victim a few hours before she left to go on a date with Schweihs, who was married at the time. Frankie was questioned by a coroner's jury but no charges were ever filed.

Wayne Bock reportedly started his career with the mob as a torch and a bomber. He was first suspected of murder in a 1965 car bombing that killed the wrong target, a twenty-two-year-old woman. His brother Eugene, a local sheriff, was forced to resign when an investigation revealed he was a close friend of Alberto Capone, Alphonso "Al" Capone's brother.

Bock is said to run a bookmaking operation out of Chester's Tavern in a Chicago suburb. In 1976 the body of an unemployed local man was found covered with blankets in a car behind the tavern. He had been shot in the head and his pockets turned out as though he had been robbed. The case remains open.

Bock's tough ways evidently impressed ex-daredevil Evel Knievel, who once lived in a large motor home parked behind Chester's Tavern. In 1977, in a well-publicized incident that ended his career, Knievel beat with a baseball bat a former associate who wrote an unflattering book about him. He was convicted and sentenced to six months in jail for the assault. In 1982, Wayne Bock reportedly beat Knievel up, causing Evel to be hospitalized.

Their numerous and infamous exploits show that the Chicago hit team was certainly suited to the task of killing the celebrated Don Aronow. As Jerry Gladden once summed up Frankie and Wayne: "Murder. That's their business."

After Gladden filled me in on the deadly duo, my lawyer contacted MetroDade with a request that we meet with a certain captain, whom Edna Buchanan had noted was particularly conscientious. While my attorney negotiates for the meeting to give them the names of the suspects and the location of the photographs, I contact Dave Green and arrange to talk again with him and Bertucelli.

The following day at Broward County OCD headquarters, the three of us adjourn to a conference room next to Bertucelli's office. Steve Bertucelli is in a good mood. Green seems withdrawn. I summarize what I've discovered about Aronow's mob connections and the details of the Super Chief South–USA Racing deal.

Bertucelli, like everyone else in the area, is aware of the problems that plague the Blue Thunder boats. From the time I mentioned that Kramer owned the contract, Bertucelli has been interested in getting the feds to look into the mob's involvement and whether that had anything to do with the boats' disastrous performance. He has a friend in the Washington FBI office whom he would like to get interested "in Kramer and those fucking Blue Thunders." He admits it might be difficult though because of the potential to reflect negatively on Vice President George Bush.

I mention that Ben Kramer probably took over the Blue Thunder company "for his ego and for the fun of humiliating Aronow," although, I add, it could have been strictly business for his father, Jack, and the Lansky OC network.

Bertucelli is particularly interested in the specifics of the Aronow murder, and I map out the details of the hit on the Magic Marker board on the wall, using three different colors to show the movements of the two killers and Aronow on the Alley. I mention that Richard Gerstein and Rocky Pomerance were quick to come to Lillian's assistance after Don's murder.

"The mob's damage-control boys," he says, shaking his head. "It's amazing the places those guys keep showing up." Bertucelli says that when he tried to get the state legislature to pass laws making it easier to get wiretaps on the mob, the two men were there, effectively blocking his efforts. Based on that and other experiences, he sees their involvement as an indication of very high-level mob interest in the Aronow case.

The idea of the damage-control team's "helping" the widow and interviewing the witnesses is, as he puts it, "really typical of the arrogance of Lansky's organization. All those people are our enemies. We've been trying to get them for years with no luck."

Several weeks pass, and still my attorney can't line up a meeting with MetroDade Homicide. Her request that a high-level departmental official be present at the meeting proves to be an insurmountable stumbling block.

In the meantime Chicago Crime Commission's Jerry Gladden gives me several hundred pages of intelligence information on Frankie and Wayne plus some photographs.

By April 16, 1988, my attorney gives up on the idea of a meeting with MetroDade Homicide. She sends registered letters to Mike DeCora and Steve Bertucelli explaining that I've come up with two men who fit the suspects in the Aronow case and suggests they get together. We also arrange for Jerry Gladden to call MetroDade. Gladden contacts Mike Diaz, DeCora's immediate superior, and offers his assistance with the case.

On Thursday, April 21, 1988, DeCora drives to Fort Lauderdale and picks up the photos of Frankie and Wayne from Broward OCD.

Later that same week I mention to Bob Magoon what Steve Bertucelli said about Dick Gerstein and Rocky Pomerance's allegedly being the "mob's damage-control team." We also discuss the Riley, Black private investigation agency that seemed more interested in finding out what the witnesses had told MetroDade than in looking for any leads.

Could the whole PI investigation possibly have been purely "damage control"? It was a macabre notion. The mob reaching out to comfort the grieving widow of one of its own, "helping" her look for her husband's assassins. Even "soaking her," to use Steve Parr's words, in the process.

Yet, if it was true, it was an inspired tactic. Everyone spoke freely to Lillian's private investigators—even the secret eyewitness. The

PIs learned more than enough to keep track of the investigation and monitor where it might lead. More importantly, it would help them determine who constituted a threat.

"These people were picked by Rocky Pomerance," Magoon states. "He came in and he picked these people."

Magoon wants to talk to Lillian about her impressions concerning the PI firm. After he does, we speak again. "She thought about it," he relates, "and she said, 'They really haven't turned up anything. And everything that I tried to think of and tell them, they pooh-poohed.' "

After agonizing over the possibilities, Magoon says he still finds it hard to believe that Pomerance would be involved because "he seems to be such a nice guy. But I can see Gerstein doing it in a minute," he concludes. "Lillian agreed to keep quiet about what I said. We don't want it to get back to them because [if it's true about Pomerance and Gerstein] we could have a problem."

The next day, Magoon says he wants us to show the photographs of Frankie and Wayne to Lillian. We meet at his Sunset Island home, up the street from the house Don was living in when he was killed. Over a Chinese meal in his kitchen we discuss Don. On the wall behind Magoon is a huge painting of a tomato-soup can. The Magoons collect modern art; this appears to be a Warhol. Bob's wife is out, and once the maid leaves, we start talking about the murder.

"You know, I still can't figure out why the police never made any progress on this case," he says. "You know that they never even talked to me?" Homicide's Sergeant Diaz had an appointment to talk with Magoon at noon the day after Don's memorial service, but a policeman called at twelve-thirty P.M. and canceled. "Here I was Don's best friend. Can you explain that to me?"

Magoon mentions George Bush: "How about him? He's the Vice President. Why the hell can't he do something about all this? Maybe we should call him and bypass MetroDade." He emphasizes how close Aronow and Bush were. "They talked all the time. Once when Bush was in town, Don introduced us. And George says, 'Bob Magoon! Wow! We talk about you at the dinner table.' And I was dumbfounded. I said what do you mean by that? And he said, 'You're a champion.' " Bush was referring to Magoon's powerboat racing exploits.

Suddenly Magoon looks at his watch, saying he had told Lillian to expect us at six P.M. We get into his souped-up, classic red Firebird and drive over to the North Bay Road mansion that Lillian had moved into three weeks after Don was killed. We're cleared by intercom at the gate to the estate and drive up to a side entrance. A maid greets us at the door and takes us to the study.

A few minutes later Lillian returns from racewalking. She's tall, striking, thirty-six, with a model's face and figure. She's in a black designer bodysuit with a purple stripe down the side. A Walkman is attached to her belt and earphones are draped around her neck. "Let's go outside," she says curtly. We proceed to a table by the pool on the bay side. "I don't want anyone to hear what we say," she explains when we sit down.

Lillian has been dead set against a book on her husband and considers the press in general and me in particular "the enemy." She's tried to keep people from talking to anyone from the media— at one time even warning USA Racing employees that they'd lose their jobs if they did. We've never met, and while the maid brings out some Coca-Cola for us, she glares at me.

Finally, when the maid has finished serving us, Magoon suggests I show the pictures to Lillian. I hand her a photograph of Wayne Bock and mention that I believe he's the man who came into the office. She looks at it and throws it down on the table. It slides off the glass top and spins onto the ground. "That man is in his forties. The man who came into the office was in his twenties," she announces firmly.

"Come on now, Lillian, please listen," Magoon entreats as he reaches down, picks up the photo, and dusts it off on his shirtsleeve. "Lillian, it's been fourteen months and neither the police or your private investigators have come up with anything, have they? Not one single damn suspect, have they? Well, don't you think it makes sense to listen to what he has to say, and then you can decide?"

Lillian says nothing, but I take her silence as consent and tell her briefly about the two hit men. "Wayne Bock is six four," I point out. "The guy was heavier than Don, a real big guy. How heavy was Don?"

"Two twenty-five," she states.

"Wayne Bock is two forty. An ex–football player in excellent shape for his age. The man in the office was described as having 'sandy-colored' hair with 'salt-and-pepper.' Look at the photo. Now what color hair would you say that Wayne Bock has?"

She doesn't answer but her manner begins to change. I show her Frankie's photo. This time she doesn't argue that there's a striking similarity with the witness description and the composite.

I tell Lillian that the dark Lincoln made a right turn, and then another right turn after leaving the scene. That put it on a direct route to Georgia Street in Hollywood where Frankie and Wayne were seen staying on February 16, 1987.

"It's just five miles away," Magoon points out. "Just think. These are two Chicago hit men who we now know were in town thirteen days later. A coincidence? They always work together, and you know, Lillian, how many times we discussed that the man who came into the office must've been working with the killer."

"Okay, so what do we do next?" Lillian surprises both of us.

I hesitate, and then tell her that I'm going to follow the escape route.

"Okay, good," she says firmly. "What time are you going to pick me up?"

NINETEEN

At nine the next morning, Lillian is standing on the front grounds of the Aronow estate in Miami Beach, drinking coffee and watching her children play nearby with their nanny. She walks over to greet me and sits in the car with the door open. As she finishes her coffee, she tells me about the children.

"Gavin, he's the older one, he just turned eight. He looks like his father," she says, pointing to a young, dark-haired boy who's sitting nearby on the grass. "But Wylie, he's got his father's personality. I can tell. Even now." The blond one-year-old toddler is laughing and running around in circles, stumbles, and plops on his rear end. He hesitates for a moment, then laughs. "See," Lillian says, laughing. Then just as quickly her mood turns serious. "Gavin and Wylie must always think their father was a hero." She motions to the maid, hands her the empty cup, and we leave.

We drive north, then across Biscayne Bay into north Miami, and a few minutes later turn onto Thunderboat Alley. I stop the car at the head of the street. "No." Lillian motions with her hand. "To the exact spot."

I pull up to where the dark Lincoln had stopped next to Don as he backed his Mercedes out of Bobby Saccenti's factory. She looks out the window at the ground. The large dark stain that had seemed to last for months is gone. "You know, Don's car was in neutral when he was shot," she says, looking away. "He always shifted from reverse into neutral then into drive. Like they do on a boat, you know? I used to tease him about that. If Don had just shifted straight into drive, he might have gotten away when the man pulled out the gun. Instead Don floored it but the car was in neutral."

We had decided to recreate the getaway for time and distance readings. I set the mileage and elapsed-time counters on my car to zero. We make a wide turn around the spot where the Mercedes had stopped, cut across the grass, and back onto the street. The Lincoln had accelerated rapidly up the street, so we do the same.

At the beginning of the Alley we turn right, as the killer had. "You know the Lincoln was really moving here," she points out. "There was a boy walking—there. He almost got run over." Lillian has become detached, clinical in her discussion of the events surrounding Don's murder. We're comparing notes as if we're in a classroom seminar. I accelerate to 45 mph down to the end of the cross street and make a right, the tires squealing, onto a blacktop road that cuts across a large expanse of undeveloped wooded field.

"If they had turned left," I note, "they would've run into Biscayne Boulevard, a stoplight, and lots of traffic. This back road was an ideal escape route. No one would see them speeding along here with all these trees."

"They were smart," Lillian agrees.

We're doing 50 mph and could go faster. At 1 minute 15 seconds and 0.7 miles from the murder scene, we roar past a dirt-road cutoff that leads to Turnberry Isle—too obvious a place to dump the car— then onto a causeway and across a bridge to Route A1A. "Notice this is the first traffic light we've encountered so far." Lillian nods.

We make the light, turn left, and almost immediately cross the Dade-Broward county line. We've come 3.2 miles in 5.5 minutes. "This is Broward County, a different jurisdiction, different cops," I mention. "Before anyone up here even gets the word to look for a dark Lincoln—before the ambulance even gets to the Alley—we're in a different county."

We continue north on A1A, observing the speed limit, and then turn onto Georgia Street and pull over. "The place is there," I point down the street. "That's where Frankie and Wayne were seen on February 16, 1987, thirteen days after the murder."

"What are the readings?" Lillian asks.

"Five point four miles in ten point two minutes," I note. Lillian says nothing.

"They could've parked the car and been having a beer before the first MetroDade squad car even arrived on the Alley," I say. "Though I'm sure what they did first was break down the gun and get rid of the parts, dump them in the ocean or melt the barrel down. After that they probably shaved and were, once again, clean-cut."

We drive slowly by the condo, a little way down Georgia Street. Although it's been more than a year, we both half-expect to see a dark Lincoln parked there. The driveway is empty. The windows on the condo have a peculiar coating. It's a gold-tinged two-way mirroring similar to the type used in some jewelry stores. It's not something I've ever seen on a house.

We cruise around the block slowly a few times, wondering whether Frankie or Wayne might be inside, perhaps even looking at us. Then we drive the six-tenths of a mile up A1A to Joe Sonken's Gold Coast Restaurant and park across the street.

"Frankie and Wayne are close friends of Joe Sonken," I tell Lillian. "This is the biggest Mafia hangout in the United States."

"I don't know anything about that stuff," she says in a manner that seems to say, why are we here?

"You know that Joe Sonken sold Jack Kramer the building for Apache Boats in Hollywood," I mention. "And Ben Kramer saved Sonken's life and hung out here all the time."

Lillian becomes excited and launches into a tirade about Kramer. "It was Ben Kramer. I know he was behind the murder. I said to DeCora and those ninnies at MetroDade, 'Arrest him! Why don't you fucking arrest him?' "

"Jack says his son had nothing to do with it," I remark, "and that you're the source of all these negative stories about his boy."

"You've talked to him?" she asks in astonishment. When I nod, she says, "And he thinks I'm responsible for all these rumors?"

I tell her Jack's idea—that a jealous defense attorney hired someone to kill Don over some of his "other activities." She knows I'm referring to Don's highly publicized flings.

There's a long pause. Then she says, "Which isn't to say he may not be very right, you know."

"I doubt it. I think he knows. He's involved somehow and he knows exactly what's up."

"These are nasty people, you know?" she comments. "Which is specifically why I haven't said anything for as long as I have. Think about it. Why do I want the bad guys mad at me? It's a stupid statement on his part. The only thing that was printed about me was that article in the paper and it said nothing about him."

"Don't you see?" I ask. "The people you were dealing with, like Dick Gerstein and the PI, who were supposedly on your side, were listening to all the things you were saying. What if they were telling the bad guys everything you said? I mean, you didn't tell anybody else, but here Jack knows what you've been saying. How does Jack know what you said if you only said it to your PI and Rocky and Dick?"

She says nothing. I decide to pass on some information that Bill Norris, from the U.S. Attorney's Office, had told me about Richard "Bad Eye" Gerstein.

"Gerstein was almost indicted a few years ago as part of a drug-money laundering scheme," I comment, not mentioning Norris's name. "He was supposedly carting cash personally down to a Panamanian bank for a central-Florida drug figure, J. D. Raulerston. Dick Gerstein has also represented Ben Kramer, you know."

That brings a reaction. "How do you know that?"

"He was helping Kramer around the same time he was quote helping you. He showed up at secret negotiations with the U.S. Attorney's Office in Miami on Ben's behalf."

Norris had told me that Gerstein attended a meeting between Norris, and Ben's attorney of record. They discussed what information Ben would have to give up in order to make a deal on the south Florida charges.

We head back to Miami Beach, stopping for lunch at the ritzy Bal Harbor Mall. Ironically, it's right across the street from the Sheraton Bal Harbor, formerly the Americana, where Meyer Lansky daily held court and where Don lived with Shirley and their kids in 1961 when he "retired" to Florida.

As we walk around the mall looking for a restaurant, we continue discussing Rocky Pomerance and "her people," as Lillian still refers to the PIs despite her doubts. "I don't trust anybody," Lillian declares. "I don't trust Gerstein. I don't trust Riley, Black-Kiraly. I don't trust any of them."

She says she can't understand why they weren't able to make any progress. "They never once came up with a lead of their own," she says in disgust. "And whenever I told them to follow some ideas, they blew me off. 'We've already considered that, Lil-li-an,' or 'That makes no sense, Lil-li-an.' Then they said they didn't want to take my money anymore, that I should get on with my life. Anyway, whose money is it, you know?"

Bill Riley did propose a few theories to Lillian. He told her that

Jerry Engelman's story about walking to the canal after the sandy-haired man left the office was suspicious. He also suggested the possibility that Don had been murdered by the CIA or some feds "gone in too deep." His theory was that Don had been killed because he helped spearhead the government's antismuggling efforts. That some CIA agents had eliminated him as a favor to the drug kingpins who were assisting the CIA-backed "freedom fighters" in Nicaragua (It was all the more absurd in light of Blue Thunder's reputation for spending more time on land than in the water.)

Lillian comments that she "was in a fog" right after the murder, but she seems to recall that originally Rocky Pomerance had suggested for her consideration two attorneys to oversee the investigation: James Hogan or Richard Gerstein.

Hogan or Gerstein. What a choice. Somebody certainly had all the bases covered. I don't mention that James Hogan represented Frankie Viserto, the head of the Genovese Purple Gang, and that Richard Gerstein has been repeatedly linked in published reports to Meyer Lansky. Or that it was possible—even probable—that both the Genovese crime family and the Lansky OC network had something to do with Aronow's murder.

Then Lillian tells me that she has no records of Riley, Black's information on the murder investigation. Bill Riley had told her it was better if she didn't keep anything in writing—not even her own notes. He said it was for her own protection—that she was in terrible danger.

"Lillian, look at this objectively," I counter. "This PI took a fortune from you and came up with absolutely nothing. Zip. The firm's not even listed in the yellow pages. He tells you that the CIA or Central American terrorists might have killed Don. And they might come get you. Then when they have you totally confused and scared out of your wits, they tell you to drop the case and get on with your life. You've been gaslighted."

She stops walking. She stares over the rail of the mall, at the well-heeled customers below flitting from Saks to Bonwit's to Neiman's.

"I don't feel so good," she says, grabbing on to the railing. "I think I'm going to be sick."

When Lillian feels better, we have lunch. She picks aimlessly at her chicken sandwich and we eat mostly in silence. I wasn't prepared to like her. I had expected her to be an arrogant, pampered Palm Beach bitch, long past agonizing over a dead husband—especially since he had made her a very wealthy widow.

Instead, she's a bright but surprisingly insecure woman with

Vogue looks, a tendency to curse (no doubt a habit picked up from Don), and an ambivalent feeling, for obvious reasons, about solving her husband's murder. In the past year, she has been violently widowed, manipulated, lied to, and made to fear for her own life and that of her young children.

And she has had to confront the fact that her husband was both more and less than she thought.

We return to the estate. She has hardly spoken. I go to wash my hands, and when I come out of the bathroom, I can't find her. After wandering around the huge home I locate her in the kitchen, talking on the phone.

". . . and you got a good look at the man?" she's asking. "Could he be in his forties?" She listens, then suddenly slams the phone down.

"Ninny!" she yells at the hung-up phone. "You're right, she is a bimbo. That was Patty Lezaca. She says that you can't always tell nowadays how old people are. She now says, 'Well, maybe he could've been in his forties because he was in such good shape.' Idiot!"

After more than a year has passed, Patty is changing her description of the sandy-haired man—an identification that had the cops on a proverbial wild-goose chase.

We move to the pool area. It's a beautiful, sunny day. All of Biscayne Bay is spread out before us, and the Miami skyline sparkles. A Concorde, its nose lowering for landing, seems to hover in the distance on its final approach to Miami International Airport. It's all spectacular, but for Lillian it's a sight that no longer offers any satisfaction.

She's very agitated. "Why didn't MetroDade come up with them?" she says, referring to Frankie and Wayne. I shrug my shoulders. She comments angrily, "Those fuckers couldn't find their way home with a road map."

After a moment she continues voicing the turmoil in her mind. "This is all going to go nowhere," she says, sighing. "I know it, I just know it." She hesitates and then blurts out, "Why don't we take care of it?"

"Take care of what?"

"Kill them," she says emotionally. "Why don't we kill them? Frankie and Wayne. Kill them. Kill them. You know that the cops aren't going to do anything. They wouldn't even come to meet you about Frankie and Wayne. We should kill them ourselves."

Her suggestion stuns me and we both fall silent.

· · ·

Lillian and I spend the next several days together, exploring the wooded areas around the escape route. The undergrowth is dense, the weather is hot and humid. It's an unpleasant, arduous task, but it doesn't deter Lillian. We're hoping for the all-too-slim chance that we'll find a piece of the discarded gun or a Lincoln Town Car concealed and abandoned.

As we pick through the area, we discuss the case and her husband, especially his last three weeks. She says she knew something was wrong, but she has no idea what was bothering him. The motive for Don's murder continues to be elusive.

I convince her to ask Murray Weil to send her all the documents he has on the Super Chief South deal. She calls him, the conversation is brief, and when she gets off the phone, she says he's coming over right away. The subject of Aronow's business dealings evidently spurs Weil into action. "You better leave right now," Lillian announces. "Wait until you see his car leave, then come back."

An hour later I return. She explains, "Murray wanted to know why I was interested after all this time. I said I just wanted to know. He says that he doesn't have any documents on it at all. The police still have all the paperwork. So then I called Patty and she said the same thing."

I dial Steve Parr's line. He still takes my call despite the recent imposition of a freeze on contact with me by MetroDade brass. "Patty and Murray told Lillian that you guys didn't return the records on the Super Chief South deal," I tell him.

"No," he corrects me. "We did. In fact they both kicked and bitched about it. We returned them two or three months after Aronow's death."

When I return to Lillian's later that evening, I'm stopped at the entrance to the estate. She won't buzz me in. "I've been told that I shouldn't be talking to you alone anymore," she says via the intercom at the gate at the front of the estate. "I'm just laying here in bed. I'm burned out, I can't take all of this." She pauses, and then suggests, "Come tomorrow at lunchtime and meet with the family. Michael and his wife, Ellen."

The next morning I drive up to the circle and park. When I walk around to the bay side of the building, only Lillian and Murray are there. They're both seated on stools at the bar next to the Jacuzzi. Lillian introduces us and Murray immediately takes charge.

"As the attorney for Mrs. Aronow and the Aronow estate, I would like to thank you for your contributions to the investigation," he proclaims, his pomposity not quite masking his nervousness. All the time, he scrutinizes my pants. "However, I must insist that you cease all contact with Mrs. Aronow. Please confine your interactions to the appropriate law enforcement authorities."

Lillian avoids looking at me while she speaks. "Look, thank you for your help, but you're the enemy. You're the press. The press is the enemy."

"Thank you," Murray Weil quickly interjects, still fixated on my pants. "Thank you," he repeats, louder, trying to push me out with the force of his voice.

Later, Bob Magoon explains that Lillian's questions about Super Chief greatly alarmed Murray, who suspected something was up. He suggests that Patty's daughter told her that Lillian was secretly meeting with someone. Patty's daughter had become Lillian's personal secretary, and she worked on the estate.

"I don't know about Patty," says Magoon. "But Murray doesn't give a damn about Lillian. He's just scared out of his fucking mind. You know, all the wheeling and dealing Don did. Murray took care of this and that. God knows what else. He's afraid of being pulled into some federal grand jury by the Internal Revenue Service and getting indicted." Everyone in Miami seems to think that Murray is terrified of the IRS.

He explains that Weil thought he saw a tape recorder in my pocket at the meeting by the pool. "Murray's such a weenie. He thought you were wired and went berserk. It took all weekend for him to calm down."

He laughs heartily when I tell him that it was just my Daytimer's notebook.

A week later, I stop by MetroDade headquarters to let DeCora copy my files on Frankie and Wayne. We go over to the copy machine and talk while the machine hums away.

He says that the day after Weil had banished me from Lillian's estate, he was summoned there. Waiting for him were Lillian, Weil, and Michael Aronow.

Lillian Aronow asked him why MetroDade Homicide wasn't doing anything about Frankie and Wayne. He told her that he had obtained photographs of the pair from Broward OCD and that he was going to Chicago to check out the hit men.

"Michael Aronow was upset and demanded that we arrest you for talking to Lillian," DeCora says of the meeting. Michael evidently became even more petulant when DeCora said he couldn't do that.

"That little fucker is such an asshole it's unbelievable," DeCora comments.

Then DeCora changes the subject.

"We checked the tricounty OC logs," he says, "and we came up with a listing for Frankie and Wayne. They were seen sitting in a car in a parking lot in Miami Beach. February twelfth, 1987. Nine days after the murder."

DeCora usually has the demeanor of a war-weary cop, but now he looks excited. Although the detectives who authored the report didn't bother to write down the type of automobile, they did include a license number.

"It was an Illinois plate, and it came back to a 1988 light blue Lincoln Town Car," he explains. "Then we checked with Ford. They said the chassis wasn't even assigned that number in the factory until May of 1987, so we knew that couldn't be right."

DeCora made another request of the Illinois Department of Motor Vehicles, this time trying to find what car the plate was on in February 1987. He smiles like the proverbial cat that just swallowed the canary.

"It came back to a 1985 Lincoln Town Car," he says, grinning. "A dark blue Lincoln Town Car!"

He says he plans to go up to Chicago and look for the car. Jerry Gladden and Johnny Murray of Chicago PD Intelligence have promised to help him out.

"I'd really like to find that car," he emphasizes, adding that one of the cartridges from the .45 was never recovered. "The weapon ejects to the right, so I'm hoping it might have gotten stuck in the window-wiper recesses. And I want to see what kind of wheel covers it has." He reminds me that they had a description of the wheel covers on the Lincoln.

I ask DeCora who the car was registered to, but he says he doesn't want to tell me. "We're trying to figure out who he is. He's outfit connected—that's what they're surmising in Chicago [PD Intelligence]. They're trying to do an active workup on him now." He chuckles, then says, "I caught them with their pants down because they never heard of the guy."

DeCora walks me out the front door. "I'm leaving tomorrow for Chicago," he says. "Give me a call up there at the Intelligence unit next week and I'll let you know what happens." He gives me the thumbs-up sign.

TWENTY

A titillating piece of information had come my way while looking into the Aronow story. Although apparently unrelated to the murder, it reinforced the omnipresence of the mob and its infiltration into all aspects of society. When the feds busted Ben Kramer, they discovered originals of Gary Hart's stump speeches in Ben's Ft. Apache safe. Somehow a Lansky, Inc. drug kingpin had gotten possession of a presidential contender's papers.

At the time that Hart was blown out of the presidential waters, he had been the Democratic front-runner. The rest of the Democratic contenders seemed to have little chance of knocking Hart off the winning path. On the Republican side was George Bush, the heir apparent to the Reagan era. Bush was considered a weak candidate; even Reagan had expressed doubts about his loyal veep's presidential fortitude. It looked as if the Democrats might capture the White House for the first time in eight years.

Suddenly, "Snow White," as Hart was dubbed by the press, was devastatingly and humiliatingly knocked out of contention. With the Democrats' strong front-runner gone, the party was divided among the "Seven Dwarfs," the remaining Democratic candidates. The precarious unity was gone, and a fractious campaign ensued with no one able to amass the strength that Hart once commanded.

Despite Gail Sheehy's famous "psycho-political" article in *Vanity Fair* about Hart, there may be more behind the story than simply the tale of a man whose rigid religious upbringing forced him to punish himself by self-destructing. A closer look at the Hart debacle reveals an interesting panorama played out behind the highly publicized story.

Lynn Armandt, the woman who brought Gary Hart down, had worked for a long time at Turnberry Isle before the infamous *Monkey Business* trip in May 1987. Don Soffer, the developer and manager of the resort, had made her the head of "Donny's party girls"—which some cynics likened to high-priced call girls. He also provided her with free floor space to sell bikinis. (Turnberry's shops are considered some of the most expensive retail space in Miami.) In all, an extremely lucrative position for a woman with her background.

She and Donna Rice, another of Donny's girls, were very good friends. The two women lived in upscale, neighboring condominiums not far from Turnberry and Thunderboat Alley. As Donny's girls, Armandt and Rice made money, "dated" wealthy and famous men, and had entrée to Miami's high-flying lifestyle.

After the incident, Rice supposedly ended her association with Armandt, angered over the "betrayal." Or so she told Barbara Walters in a *20/20* television interview. But people at Turnberry and Rice's Miami condominium saw the two women together often after the Hart affair. A maintenance man at Rice's condo saw them sunbathing at the pool frequently both before and after the *20/20* piece. "They were laughing and joking and were the best of girlfriends," he had said. "Nothing changed."

As the scrutiny of the scandal continued unabated, Armandt moved to New York and then went underground. She was castigated as a money-hungry woman who sold out her friend and brought down a presidential contender for a handful of dollars. But if she had been so inclined, why not blow the cover on some of the other celebrities who cavorted at the resort over the years? The resort's client roster included a long list of powerful and celebrated men. Some whose often compromising activities there would have been ideal fodder for the gossip rags.

A street-smart woman such as Armandt knew she would become a pariah among Turnberry's clientele and her relationship with her boss and benefactor would be severed if she publicized the secret life of any patron. Armandt also knew that some of the Turnberry boys could play a rough game. If it ever slipped her mind, she only had to remember what happened to her drug-smuggling husband. The last trace of him was a bloody bullet-riddled car and a piece of paper containing the telephone number of Turnberry patron Ben Kramer.

Gary Hart had already been to Turnberry before the *Monkey Business* incident, despite his denials. When he returned in May 1987, a "setup" may have been arranged with Armandt being directed at every step of the way.

One fed who has investigated Turnberry (he alleges that the twenty-nine-story condominium is "mobbed-up from the twenty-ninth floor down") agrees with the notion that the Hart affair was masterminded by OC interests. He points out that Armandt went to the *Miami Herald* with her story, where she had no prospect of making any money but the greatest chance of destroying Hart quickly. The key question is, who stands to benefit from destroying Gary Hart? "One thing to always remember is [the mob] they're big business," he reminds me. "As goes the economy, so goes big business. Meyer Lansky was a staunchly conservative Republican, you know."

There could be a deeper motive behind the Hart fiasco than simple partisan preferences. Contemporary organized crime depends on a protective shield of middle-level governmental and law enforcement officials. These are the people who possess valuable information and make decisions that directly affect the mob—selecting which cases to investigate and which to ignore, which drug smugglers to go after, which wiseguy convicts to parole. It's the mob's real muscle and it comes from owning not the president but the appointed politicians and law enforcement management.

After eight years of productive, well-oiled relationships at all levels of the federal government, it's unlikely the mob would look favorably on a completely new administration. With a Democratic win, these relationships would be lost as officials and appointees made way for a new administration. The protective shield would falter—temporarily—as OC bagmen had to start anew finding people willing to take envelopes stuffed with cash in return for favors.

Keeping the same party in power and simply changing the head ensures that the machinery continues to run smoothly. From organized crime's perspective, the "right" people retain their jobs: those not-so-really-new faces who would be expected from the not-so-really-new President Bush.

It is widely acknowledged that the Republicans didn't win the 1988 election so much as the Democrats lost it. Perhaps there was an unseen hand making some adjustments in the direction of the election by strengthening the Republican chances of winning.

The mob had influenced presidential campaigns in the past. It's common knowledge that Lansky, along with mob boss Sam Giancana, had tipped the scales in Jack Kennedy's favor when he delivered the state of Illinois. And if the mob could influence an election, manipulation of a local murder would be a small endeavor. It was all just a matter of "taking care of business" for the world's largest and most powerful "corporation."

On Monday, May 9, 1988, Mike DeCora flew up to Chicago. At the Chicago Crime Commission, he met Jerry Gladden, who had promised DeCora's boss, Mike Diaz, that he would help out on the case. Gladden took DeCora around and introduced him to his close friend Johnny Murray from Chicago PD Intelligence. Murray assigned detective Brian Murphy from his department to help DeCora.

For the first couple of days, DeCora reviewed the department's files on Frankie and Wayne. Then he and Murphy went looking for the car. "They found the 1988 vehicle," Johnny Murray tells me when I call to see how things are going. "They did a drive-by a few times. But my understanding was that they saw the vehicle that has the plate now, not the one at the time of the murder."

In Illinois a license plate remains with the person, not the car, when a vehicle is sold.

At the middle of the week, I talk to DeCora in Murray's office. He says he hopes they'll hear by the next day from the state DMV office on the current owner of the 1985 vehicle. Then they'll go out to take a look at it. He sounds excited and it seems like the investigation is going well.

Back in Miami, Steve Parr is gearing up for a renewed effort on the case. He says he's always believed the Aronow murder could've been a mob hit. "We had looked at the boats and drugs and business, and then we were struck with the possibility that it was Mafia," he tells me.

Despite the difficulties in prosecuting a mob hit, Parr says he's confident that MetroDade will be able to get Frankie and Wayne to reveal the motive for the murder and to roll over on whoever hired them. "We have dealt with contract killings, serial murderers, and when they face the electric chair, they deal," he says. "Once we get them with the photos [photo lineups]—and they do fry them here—they'll deal. If Wayne won't, Frankie will. If Frankie won't, Wayne will."

On Friday, suddenly and without notice, the "born-again" Aronow investigation grinds to a halt. After five days DeCora unexpectedly leaves Chicago without locating the 1985 Lincoln.

John Murray tells me that when DeCora left he didn't say much, he just asked Murray to follow up on the car and take additional surveillance photos of Wayne Bock so MetroDade could do a photo lineup with the witnesses. Murray can't understand that request. "There are excellent surveillance photographs of Bock in existence," he says. "I almost wanted to say to him, 'Jesus Christ, we gave you a beautiful photograph of him. The guy doesn't change. It's a full-on view.'"

Murray says that Chicago PD Intelligence is concerned that if MetroDade doesn't move soon, they and Chicago will once again lose any chance of nailing Frankie and Wayne. "Look at it practically," he explains. "This homicide is getting older and older. The witnesses' recollections are getting older and older. You don't wanna wait until months after the case and show a witness pictures, you know? It's not smart to do that. But everything is on hold until we hear from him again."

I try calling DeCora several times to find out what happened, but he's not in and doesn't return my calls. A few days later I call Murray again to see if they've made any progress on locating the 1985 vehicle. He says they're still looking. He adds that his department has now become especially interested in the Aronow case because of the possible involvement of Frankie and Wayne, and he wants to help all he can. Chicago has been trying for years to get something on the pair.

Although DeCora said he would send the Miami police reports on the murder to Chicago, Gladden says neither he nor Murray have heard back from him. Gladden called a number of times, but De-Cora never returned the calls.

Two months after DeCora left Chicago, John Murray is disgusted that MetroDade has never been in touch. He sends his files on the Lincoln to Gladden, who initiates a trace on the car anyway, still hoping to work something out with MetroDade . Tracking down cars that may have been used in hits by Frankie and Wayne is nothing new for Gladden. He was involved in tracing the getaway car used in the hit on Daniel Seifert in 1974. "We even found Joey's [Joey "the Clown" Lombardo's] fingerprint on the underside of the ashtray —he hadn't wiped it clean there—and on the title papers in the DMV office," Gladden recalls of that investigation. Despite this and other evidence, however, no charges were ever brought against Lombardo, Schweihs, or Bock.

There has been some confusion over the VIN number of the Lincoln. Gladden says he's going to unravel it. He's true to his word. A few weeks later, he explains, "The plate number is Illinois GNZ-987. Belonged to a four-door 1985 Lincoln Town Car, VIN 1LNBP96F6FY606400. It was owned at the time of the murder by Mel Cerovina. I know Mel. He's the guy who owns that condo on Georgia Street in Hollywood. He's a buddy of Frankie."

Gladden continues, "So now, Mel's got an '88 Lincoln, and it has those plates on it. The '85 is sold, to a Jerome Scott, in Wauconda, Illinois. It's a nonpublished number so I couldn't call him. So I guess they didn't chop the car."

Would they actually use a borrowed car for "business"? Apparently so. "They borrow a car," Gladden says, "whack somebody. Throw the body in the trunk and go bury it. Bring it back and say, 'Hey, don't pay any attention to that bleach smell in the trunk. And oh, why don't you sell the car when you get a chance.'" Gladden laughs, "So, I would say no, it's not strange at all."

Gladden's former partner, Ron Kirk, a retired lieutenant from the Chicago PD Intelligence unit, agrees, "Under normal circumstances of a hit they would use a stolen car, some untraceable vehicle. But if the hit needed to be done right away. If they had major time pressure. Yes. It may not be ideal, but I can see them doing that. Certainly."

There's little doubt the hit men in the Aronow murder were under time constraints—they had arrived in town less than twenty-four hours before the murder.

Customer service at Ford Motor Company checks the VIN number that Jerry Gladden has researched. They confirm that it's a 1985 Lincoln Town Car, four doors. Only they say it's not a Signature Series model.

The newspaper accounts of the hit had said that the dark Lincoln was a Signature Series. That's what the "secret witness" had supposedly told the police. This is the first wrinkle in the case against Frankie and Wayne. Everything else fits.

Bob Magoon knows the secret witness. He says he'll ask him the exact description of the car. The next day Magoon has the information. "I asked about the Lincoln," he says. "Now the guy owns a Town Car himself, so he knows the cars. Anyway, I asked him, 'Was it a Signature Series? Did you actually see the Signature logo on the side of the car?' 'No.' The guy said, 'No, it wasn't a Signature Series.'"

. . .

At the time they were caught in the chance surveillance of Miami Beach on February 12, Frankie and Wayne were in the precise type of vehicle used in the hit. The Lincoln Town Car fits the description of the vehicle given by the eyewitnesses at the scene of the murder.

There had been some initial confusion over the color of the car. Witnesses had said it was dark colored and that's how it was described in newspaper accounts. One witness thought it was black or dark blue. Another eyewitness is definite. "Nope, not black, dark blue," insists Mike Harrison. "The car was dark blue. I'm a hunter and my eyesight is excellent. There's no doubt about it. It was dark blue."

Harrison's description is highly credible. He had insisted from the beginning of my discussions with him right after the murder that the weapon was a .45 semiautomatic pistol. The police never released information on the type of gun used, and the talk on the street was that it was a 9mm. Yet Harrison was right. The weapon was a .45, according to DeCora. Certainly the color of the car was easier to spot than the exact make of a gun jutting out of a window for a few seconds.

One last curious detail remained, a puzzling one. Mike Harrison thought he'd seen a green National Car Rental sticker on the rear bumper of the car. Checking NCR rentals was one of the first things MetroDade had done after the murder. But they had come up empty —no listing matched. Since Harrison's information seemed reliable, there had to be some NCR connection to the case. I went back over the files that Gladden had sent. There were a number of surveillance reports on Wayne Bock over the years and listings of Illinois plate numbers with the letters "NCR" before the numbers. In Illinois the plates are recorded with letters signifying a rental company.

I contact Gladden again and mention the glitch of the National sticker. It strikes another nerve. He says that Wayne Bock has a close friend who owns the National Car Rental franchise in Elmhurst, Illinois, and he frequently gets cars from there.

"I can see him getting some green NCR bumper stickers from him [Bock's friend] and plastering Mel's car as a disguise," Gladden says. "What professional—or any person in his right mind—is going to rent a car and then do a hit with it with this big green sticker on it? Heck, what a great trick to throw a monkey wrench into the investigation."

Gladden was right about the NCR sticker's throwing the investigation off. The possibility that the car was a rental from National had sent DeCora all over the state of Florida, even into Georgia in the weeks after the murder.

If Frankie and Wayne had to use a friend's car—perhaps because time was of the essence—the NCR sticker was a clever ploy that definitely had the intended effect. As Jerry Gladden commented about the pair: "They're good and they're smart. They know exactly what to do to get away with murder."

"Johnny Murray never heard back from Mike DeCora," Jerry Gladden tells me some months after DeCora's trip to Chicago. "Never a phone call, never a nothing from Florida after he was here. We treated him well when he came up here, took him out to dinner and things. They're either so busy or just don't give a damn. We've just crossed them [MetroDade] off our list. They'll never get anything from us again, that's for sure."

They weren't the only ones who suddenly ran into a brick wall of silence. Despite numerous calls, I was never able to get in touch with DeCora, either. Perhaps Gladden and Murray wouldn't have been angry if they knew what had happened. DeCora was probably still interested in the Aronow murder and the results of the trace on the Lincoln. Not that it would have mattered, though. He was no longer on the case. He had been taken off it and a lower-level detective had been assigned to it.

Despite the mob's entrenchment along Florida's Gold Coast, and the many mob hits, there has never been one solved. So far the Aronow case appeared to be following a classic pattern.

Rory McMahon suggests that every time the MetroDade Homicide detectives began pursuing promising leads on the Aronow investigation, they were pulled off or told to hold off by someone from "on high."

He elaborates on his own experience. MetroDade detectives had made arrangements to interview him after Don's murder. Then they canceled without explanation. "I mean, I was Ben Kramer's probation officer," Rory says. "I thought he was supposed to be the key suspect, right? Did they even bother to talk to me about him? They know me and they don't even ask me—a guy who knows Benny better than his own mother. What does that tell you?"

Nor did the homicide detectives follow up with a friend of Mc-Mahon's, an LCN specialist in a local intelligence unit. The agent was first approached about a meeting then he was stood up like the others.

"They don't bother to check Aronow's Lansky connections," Rory says, rattling off a list of things the cops didn't do. "They don't bother to find that dark blue '85 Lincoln. They don't bother to show the pictures to the witnesses. They don't roust the guys and do a lineup. As soon as DeCora gets up to Chicago and is close to finding the car, he's yanked back and presto, like magic he's off the case."

McMahon says he believes that Frankie and Wayne and their car fit every detail on the hit. "There isn't one fucking thing that doesn't fit, for Christ's sake," he remarks, "but still they won't even check it out. Eliminate them at least. Why not just show the photos, eh? Fixed? Fixed?! Fuck, yeah, I'd say it's fixed. My guess is there's a lot of envelopes stuffed with cash making the rounds."

Fixing things after a hit is standard operating procedure for the mob. Virtually no mob hit has ever officially been "solved" anywhere. (Although unofficially, the hitters are often known to the police.) The list of murders that Frankie and Wayne are suspected of—and have never been charged with—illustrates the effectiveness of damage control. Mob murders in Miami are no different.

An important mob hit needs more fixing than most LCN homicides since there simply aren't that many people who would qualify to handle a high-profile Mafia murder. There are probably no more than twenty or thirty hitters in the entire country that the mob can call on to handle critical assignments, which means by definition a limited number of suspects.

Since OCD intelligence units are aware of the top mob killers, it makes it imperative from the mob's perspective that local homicide investigations be sidetracked immediately. Before any ambitious detectives get into dangerous areas of inquiry and uncover evidence that can't be ignored—such as a vehicle involved in a hit.

When local detectives do wander into such sensitive avenues, someone from the brass is on hand to "advise" them to focus their efforts on some other "more productive" aspects of the case. "They tell them not to waste their time, that it's a dead end, some bullshit like that," says McMahon. "You know how that shit is, when the big boss makes a quote suggestion. It's all very subtle."

Did some OC figures in the background "manage" the thrust of the investigation via an "in" with the top brass, attempting to make sure that this murder would go the way of other mob murders in Miami? In other words, go nowhere.

As the *Herald*'s crime reporter, Edna Buchanan has seen the inner workings of Miami's law enforcement agencies for two decades. "Richard Gerstein used to be the most powerful man in Dade County, and he's still pretty powerful," she says when I bring up the subject. "Gerstein's always been on the edge, but they never, ever, nailed him. He's always had connections. Connections to somebody.

I assume it was Lansky. And Rocky Pomerance always knows what's going on. He may never tell, but the Fat Man's got his ear to the ground. Always has. And he does have access to everybody and anybody."

Buchanan thinks it's a toss-up regarding the reason behind the stalled police investigation. She says there could be two theories. One is a "conspiracy of silence" with MetroDade detectives being told to back off. Edna believes she knows Rocky's "top brass" contact, the "in" that Parr had mentioned. The Homicide Division is within his reach. "Quite honestly, I can see that guy fixing whatever Rocky wanted fixed," she says. "And doing it in a second." She adds that it might explain why I couldn't get any top MetroDade PD officials to meet with me when I first identified Frankie and Wayne.

On the other hand, she says, the detectives could simply have a lax attitude. "MetroDade and lots of police departments have long had this attitude that if it's an OC hit, it's going to be impossible to prove," she explains. "It's hard—so why not go on to something easier?"

Buchanan also notes that the Aronow family isn't really pushing the police to solve the murder. She points out their dilemma. The family has to push the police if they are to have any chance of nailing the killers—but then everything about Aronow would surface. If MetroDade doesn't pursue the investigation, and the family tries any other law enforcement agency, the first step the outsiders will take is to call MetroDade. "And," she sums up, "Metro'll say, 'Hey, it's our case, forget it.'"

As far as prodding the investigation along, she tells me there's little further that can be done. "In any other case, I'd say take it to the FBI," she comments, "but the FBI's got this Washington connection [George Bush] to worry about. They don't want to rock any boats."

It's an interesting confluence of the interests of the "good guys" and the "bad guys" with the goal being the same: make the Aronow story go away, and most importantly keep the Mafia and the Vice President out of it.

Clearly the mob has the muscle to stop the investigation. For years MetroDade has had a massive Organized Crime Bureau that was well funded with millions of dollars in their budget. And yet, no one can remember if they ever arrested any major organized crime figures.

Talking about OC murders reminds Buchanan of a twenty-year-old mob homicide—one that was never officially solved, although everyone knew who the killer was. She recalls, "You know, one of the first organized crime killings I ever covered was a guy who got killed on St. Patrick's Day on the [Miami] Beach in a parking lot. His name was John Biello, and he was gunned down. He was just getting into his car. It was eleven o'clock in the morning. Broad daylight—but guess what?—nobody saw anything. I was up there photographing the body."

I tell her that Don Aronow knew the day before the murder that Biello was going to be killed.

"Wow," she responds. "You know [at first] it seemed like the cops were gung ho on it, and then it became clear it was an organized crime hit. And I heard later through the department that they knew who did it. Knew the guy's name. He was a hit man out of Boston. But like they just totally backed off. And you know who the chief of police of Miami Beach was then?"

"Who?"

"Rocky Pomerance," she says, laughing. "You know I couldn't figure it out at the time. Like all of a sudden they just totally backed off. And after that, if somebody had walked in and said, 'I know who did it,' they would've kicked him out of the station. They didn't want to hear anything. Miami Beach was always safe, sort of a refuge for them. Gerstein, Goodhart, Lansky, all of them. Maybe that's why so many mob hits have taken place there over the years."

She recalls that in the late 1960s, she had been very interested in Meyer Lansky. She had mentioned it in a conversation with Pomerance. "And Rocky said to me, 'Oh, come on! He's a little old man. He goes to Wolfie's. He has a cup of coffee.' He made fun of it [my interest] saying that Lansky was just this little old Jewish guy. A little harmless guy. That there was this big media hype about him and here he was just walking his dog on Collins Avenue and going to Wolfie's for a bagel." Edna shakes her head in amusement at Pomerance's statements.

"Think about Biello," I suggest. "The word came down from the mob to the cops: this was an officially sanctioned hit, bug off. Sounds incredibly like the Aronow case, doesn't it?"

"Sure does," she agrees. "And lots of others, too."

Buchanan also covered the Miami hit on Johnny Roselli, the Chicago mafioso who was killed after testifying before a Congressional committee investigating the Kennedy assassination. She was at the scene when they found the oil drum floating in Biscayne Bay with his partially dismembered body in it. (Rigor mortis had set in, so his legs had to be hacked off and stuffed in beside him to make the body fit in the drum.) Edna knew it was Roselli before the cops did. She says they were astonished when the fingerprint check came back that night and it turned out she was right.

"The lead detectives, they were just plodding along, like they didn't know what was going on," she recalls. "I had talked to Roselli's lawyer in Washington, and I was eager to help. So I said [to the detectives] come on into the office. I said, 'Look, you need all the help you can get. It's big, the picture is big.' I said, 'This thing could even be linked to the Kennedy assassination.' And they're sort of looking at each other and sort of looking at me. And backed off. They never wanted to find out who killed Roselli. And they never did."

She smiles and remembers, "I'll never forget the looks on their faces. They're rolling their eyes at each other and wanting to be someplace else. So that's how a lot of these guys are. If it looks too hard, or too big, too much shit hitting the fan, they just want to back off and investigate some 'mom-and-pop' shooting. It's a lot simpler."

John Biello was a prominent Miami businessman with hidden Genovese crime family connections. Donald Aronow was a prominent Miami businessman with hidden Genovese and Lansky connections. Was history repeating itself? The 1968 Biello investigation conducted by Pomerance's Miami Beach PD and Gerstein's Dade County State Attorney's Office never went anywhere. The Aronow investigation seemed to be heading in the same direction.

John Sampson had a friend in Miami PD at the time of the Biello hit. "I remember it got fucked up," he says. "Some of the evidence was lost. There was a guy who used to work for Dade County. And he ended up leaving the employ of Dade County and going to work for the State Attorney's Office and [its chief investigator] Martin Dartis. He took evidence out on the murder investigation, the one we're talking about—Johnny Biello—and the information disappeared. Evidence disappeared. And the investigation was ruined by this guy, who at the time was working for the State Attorney's office."

"Dick Gerstein's office?" I ask.

"Yeah, exactly."

Sampson says his friend was always complaining about how the investigation had been botched. "He knew how this guy fucked up the case," Sampson recalls. "He used to complain what a pisser that was. He'd say, 'They had it! They coulda done it!' " Sampson pauses for a moment, then concludes, "It's amazing. Sort of sounds like this case, doesn't it?"

After months of unreturned phone calls from MetroDade, one of my calls gets through to Archie "the Mole" Moore. "Everyone is out on the road," he says. The Aronow team at MetroDade Homicide appears to be constantly on the road. But not investigating the Aronow murder. "We got tons of other cases we're working right now," he says. "It's taking a backseat."

I ask him when they're going to do a photo lineup on Schweihs and Bock. "That's an ongoing investigation," Archie says. "I can't talk about it." The fact that it was an ongoing investigation has never stopped the Mole before from talking at length when we were comparing notes on Aronow's financial transactions. "I can't talk to you anymore," he says before hanging up, "I'm sorry."

It seems like somebody is clamping down hard on MetroDade.

Steve Parr has always been fairly open with me. I phone him at Homicide headquarters late one night, hoping to catch him alone and get some straight answers. Instead we have a peculiar conversation.

"What's happening with Wayne and Frankie?" I ask. "Have you discarded them? Are they still possibilities?"

"They're, eh, they're, they're, eh, well, I really don't know." Parr sounds very uncomfortable. "I really don't know."

"But did Wayne and Frankie pan out at all?"

"That doesn't mean anything," he says in a whisper. I don't understand his answer, but I assume from his manner he's at his desk in the middle of the Homicide squad room where others can hear him.

"Did the people not identify Wayne and Frankie?" I ask, knowing that no one has approached any of the witnesses with their photos.

"We haven't got that far."

"Have you found out that Wayne and Frankie were somewhere else?"

"No," he replies.

"So Wayne and Frankie are still possibilities then."

"Well, nothing has really changed as far as our knowledge. We don't have anything new that's going to change what you think." Parr then uses MetroDade's classic line. "We've been extremely busy here the last months . . ." His voice trails off.

Parr seems to be trying to tell me something without actually saying anything. Are Wayne and Frankie still suspects or not?

"Well, a lot of things fit," Parr whispers.

"So when are you going to do a photo lineup?"

"We will have to wait and see what the witnesses say. We are trying to get good pictures . . ." He stops as it's apparent to both of us he's dishing out bullshit. It's been months since DeCora left Chicago with surveillance photos from Chicago PD Intelligence.

"I hope I've helped you there a little bit," Parr adds suddenly to my surprise. He pauses, then asks, "What will you do if—say, for example, for whatever reason—the witnesses either don't identify these men or won't make an identification? What do you do with the identification in your book then?"

I tell him that since I think Wayne and Frankie fit so much of the witnesses' descriptions, I'll name them as suspects who should have been checked and I'll present the evidence to support my contention. He's stunned.

"You can print that without us doing anything on the case?"

"Yes."

"Oh."

It was the last time I ever spoke to Steve Parr.

I phone the press relations office of the MetroDade Police Department and officially request copies of the composites of the two suspects. The officer says she will call the Homicide detectives and see that they're sent out right away.

When I still haven't received them a month later, I call again. The woman says she passed the request on to Homicide and that I should have received the composites. I follow up with a letter formally requesting the composites. I never hear back from MetroDade Homicide and never receive the composites.

The events surrounding the Aronow murder suggest that it required more damage control than usual. Since the hit apparently had to be accomplished quickly, the killers were forced to take great risks. One went into the USA Racing office to flush Aronow out and the other waited for him outside of Saccenti's factory with his window down, poised to fire. As a result, there were witnesses who got a good look at both men.

It's hard to imagine that there are many 6′4″, 240-pound, sandy-haired Mafia killers who work with broad-shouldered, dark-complected partners and live 1,200 miles from Miami. How difficult would it have been for MetroDade with all their resources to come up with Schweihs and Bock? (All they really had to do was keep their first appointment with Dave Green several weeks after the murder.)

But none of that happened. Instead, they pursued jealous husbands and business deals gone awry. Ignoring the professionalism of the killers, the brazen daylight hit, the superb coordination of events before and especially after the murder. All of which pointed to the mob.

Unlike the Biello investigation, no one had to "lose" evidence to throw the Aronow case off course. By pulling DeCora back from Chicago, someone was effectively playing their strongest card: time. With each passing month the witnesses' memories would fade, and they would be easier to manipulate.

Damage control is working. The mob is apparently getting away with murder. Again.

TWENTY-ONE

By the summer of 1988 Don Aronow's murder was still shrouded in mystery, and yet a sinister picture was emerging. For years he had skillfully walked a fine line. A Mafia-associated drug smuggler who built boats for the Vice Presidential Drug Task Group, talking to narcs about smugglers one minute, and to smugglers about narcs the next. Flying to the Keys to meet with the Vice President, and flying to Leavenworth to talk with the LCN boss of the Purple Gang.

It was a precarious high-wire act pursued without a safety net, and it was a long way to the ground.

Randy Riggs had told me that Aronow was once at a jai alai game and ran into a mob friend. "Next to this Mafia guy is somebody Don knew from the government, a fed," Riggs recounted. The mafioso called Aronow over and they shook hands, and then the wiseguy introduced Aronow to the man next to him.

"Don knew the fed as one name, but the Mafia guy introduced him as another name," Riggs had explained. "And Don, he had a real decision to make, and he just kind of went along with it. But he called the guy up afterwards to find out what was going on." Riggs said he didn't know whether Aronow had called the wiseguy or the fed; all he knew was that Don went back to his office, dialed a number, and said, "What the hell's going on?"

For all Aronow's success over the years managing a double life, his situation seemed to be falling apart in late 1986. By the last three weeks of his life he was wrestling with personal demons. He took walks on the beach with Lillian and talked about what to do "if something should happen to me."

He made his "emergency" list and left it with Patty Lezaca. Number one instruction: CALL GEORGE BUSH. He spoke to his friend Old Mike asking "What's it like to die?"; he reminisced about the "good old days" with other boat racers; he made inquiries about possible hideouts in the Bahamas under the guise of looking for a "place to get away."

Four days before his murder, on Friday, he was nervously standing on Thunderboat Alley having his photo taken by *Miami News* photographer Pat Cordell. By then, events had taken Aronow beyond the point of no return. In all probability it was that same day when it was decided he had to die. But why had Aronow worried for so long if the hit was decided only a few days before the murder?

And why when he was clearly frightened hadn't he done something, anything, to protect himself?

As the Aronow investigation, like the man himself, passed into memory, it seemed that the reason for the murder would also remain one of Miami's enduring mysteries. All of the popular theories had been bruited about for more than a year, and with time they grew less plausible. None seemed to fit. And none explained the peculiar last three weeks of Don's life or the frantic calls and meetings between Aronow and the Kramers. "Something was up for sure," as Jerry Engelman had observed.

Everything keeps coming back to Kramer, Steve Parr had once noted early in the investigation. The Isle of Man federal grand jury had begun hearings on Ben Kramer on June 6, 1986, coinciding with the last difficult half year or so of Aronow's life.

For the last five years of his life, Aronow was involved in a series of increasingly bizarre transactions with the Kramers. As the Isle of Man investigation moved inexorably toward a conclusion, the relationship between Aronow, Ben and Jack had become frenetic. The investigation brought about the downfall of the Kramers. Could it have been deadly for Aronow as well?

Assistant U.S. Attorney Bill Norris, head of the Major Narcotics Unit and the top drug prosecutor in south Florida, supervised the Isle of Man investigations, including the money-laundering case against the Kramers, Kessler, and the Gilberts. He had spoken before about Kramer and Aronow, but we never uncovered a connection with the murder and the Isle of Man during our conversations. Thinking that there may be some overlooked clue to Aronow's death in the Isle of Man, I ask if we can meet again, and he invites me over to his Miami office.

In order to get to Major Narcotics, one has to pass through four security stages. The first checkpoint consists of armed guards and airport-style metal detectors. Next, a call is made verifying the visitor's appointment before a brightly colored pass is issued for the elevator. The elevator, though automatic, is manned by another armed security guard who checks the color of the pass and pushes the appropriate floor button. Finally, the visitor sits in a waiting room while a receptionist, tucked behind thick bulletproof glass, calls ahead to the person to be seen.

Norris personally greets me at the waiting room and we walk to his corner office. When I mention the security procedures, he laughs, commenting, "It's just trappings. If they really wanted to get us, they could." He calls me over to his window and points out an overpass ramp for I-95 a block away. "For a time, we were worried that some Colombians would stop there and fire a grenade launcher or bazooka at the building." In Miami, the possibility is all too real.

It's lunchtime, so we walk across the street to a mini-mall. We each get a superhoagie and sit down to eat as we discuss Kramer. He explains that the Isle of Man investigation had been able to snare Kramer because he was a hands-on drug kingpin. "He wouldn't actually be there throwing bales," Norris says, "but he did deal directly with a large number of people who were throwing bales. He was very much in control. And because of that people were able to identify, 'Oh, yeah, this is Kramer's load. I know this because Kramer sent us up to New York to unload it,' that kind of thing."

Norris is perplexed by Kramer's insinuating himself into the government's Blue Thunder program. He says it had nothing to do with a money-laundering enterprise because they already had a system in place that was working well. So why would Ben take such an unnecessary risk with USA Racing when he had a multimillion-dollar smuggling empire he wanted to conceal?

Norris muses, "I guess there's a certain amount of fun to owning a company that's building boats to sell to Customs to chase boats that you're building with another company to smuggle dope. Would that be his motivation? I don't know the man, although it's a delightfully amusing thought."

We both laugh. The image it conjures up is remarkably absurd yet something that evidently appealed to "Darth Vader" Kramer. Another only-in-Miami story.

I broach a new subject, organized crime. But the names of Frankie Viserto, Joey Weichselbaum, and Paulie Caiano mean nothing to Norris. He is surprised that they are dope smugglers linked with the Lansky and Genovese crime families.

"It seems like all the LCN drug interests are interconnected," I suggest. "I'm thinking that you just chopped off one arm of an enormous octopus with Ben Kramer."

He nods. "That's usually what we do," he says in a somewhat resigned tone. "And it turns out to be more like one arm of a starfish, so it regenerates."

The reality of the marijuana smuggling industry in Florida that had existed since 1973 was obvious. Kramer was no more "the boss" of his own criminal marijuana organization than any of the others had been with theirs before him. Cravero, Steinberg, Joey Ip, Little Ray, and the Whittingtons were just expendable appendages to something that was so mammoth Norris didn't even understand what he was fighting.

Previously, Norris had told me that when the government started demanding Kramer's cooperation in return for a deal, Richard Gerstein had appeared as part of the negotiation team. He didn't participate in the discussions, he was merely a presence. Now I suggest that Gerstein could have made his appearance as a representative of the Lansky organization or of the LCN in general.

Norris concedes the possibility, but explains that he's more interested in dope smugglers and money launderers than in organized crime figures.

I point out that it's inconceivable that Kramer would give up his OC connections. But perhaps he could give up someone who didn't matter. Gerstein might have been at the meeting to make sure Ben's attorney didn't cross the line. It was possible that the organization was allowing Ben to play footsie with Norris and negotiate as long as he didn't roll over on them.

"That's not uncommon," Norris acknowledges. "Say someone has ten compartments of knowledge—and he knows the government has penetrated three compartments. He'll come in and offer to give you everything that you already know, and then maybe adds a fourth compartment. And he's then given you something that you didn't know, and thereby he maintains the watertight integrity of the remaining six compartments and never tells you about those. That's part of the game."

It's an interesting insight into the realities of the criminal justice system, but nothing that Norris has said provides any hint of a connection between the Kramer investigation and Aronow. I try another tack.

"When Aronow was killed in early '87, you had already been investigating Ben and Jack Kramer, and Kessler and the Gilberts for eight months, right?" I ask.

"Yes," Norris says. "They all knew they were targets of the investigation. We had been subpoenaing their documents and records, following a paper trail, for months."

"When we last talked, you said that you weren't doing anything with Don Aronow and the Ben Kramer federal grand jury," I recall.

"Well," Norris wavers. He puts down his hoagie and stares off into the distance for a minute. A troubled look comes over his face. "That's not entirely correct. Actually, that's not correct at all."

He pauses again. Finally he says, "You see, we were going to subpoena him."

"Him? Aronow?" I ask, stunned. "When?"

"You know when Aronow was murdered?" he asks.

"February third, 1987."

"Right," Norris says. "He was killed in the afternoon. Well, he was going to be subpoenaed the next morning."

A federal grand jury subpoena.

Had a piece of paper with Don Aronow's name on it turned out to be as lethal as the .45 slug that severed his aorta? As Norris resumes eating his lunch, my mind shoots into high gear.

When the Isle of Man federal grand jury began moving against Kramer, the Lansky organization, including Aronow, must have gone into a state of heightened alert. With their close ties, the Lansky group no doubt tipped off the Genovese Purple Gang about the investigation. That would explain why Paul "Paulie Rizzo" Caiano suddenly became MIA during the summer of 1986 when the investigation began. Then he surfaced just fifteen minutes after Don was shot. Thunderboat Alley was one place he didn't want to be, at least not while the feds were crawling all over it.

The "boys" couldn't even phone anyone on the street. Frankie Viserto had summoned Aronow to Leavenworth twice for face-to-face consultations in the last half of 1986—no risk of being picked up on a wiretap that way. Probably for the same reason, Aronow made all his important "personal" calls—including those to George Bush—from his mansion rather than from the Sunset Isle home or the USA Racing office.

The timing of the Kramer investigation also coincided with Aronow's strange drill of stopping his car at the top of Thunderboat Alley and calling USA Racing on his car phone to ask, "Anything up? Anyone there?" before driving into the parking lot. At about the same time, he issued instructions to his staff to check the IDs of anyone coming into the office whom they didn't recognize, a peculiar practice for a sales office open to the public.

Aronow's concern about the Kramer grand jury's inquiries was on display one day in the USA Racing office, about six months before the murder. A stranger entered the company, loudly demanding to see Aronow. Don pointed to Jerry Engelman, and said, "That's Don Aronow." The stranger turned on Engelman and launched into a diatribe about his boat. Visible relief swept across Aronow's face, and he interrupted, saying, "No, he's not Aronow, I am." He then ushered the customer into his office. After the man left, Aronow laughed and said to Engelman, "Boy, I thought he wanted to shoot me. Better you than me." Jerry never thought Aronow was joking.

When the Isle of Man feds decided to add Aronow to the list of grand jury witnesses in early 1987, the mob clearly found out. When it was certain that Aronow would be subpoenaed, they ordered the hit. He was gunned down less than eighteen hours before he was to be served. No wonder the killers were on such a tight schedule, and why the hit went down the way it did. The tall hit man had to risk going into USA Racing to "flush" Aronow out of the office. One hour later and Aronow would have been home, safely ensconced behind the manned security gates on Sunset Isle, out of their reach. The next day he would officially be a grand jury witness.

"We were sitting around the office when the word came over the radio," Norris says, breaking my thoughts. "Dan Cassidy, my assistant and the AUSA [assistant U.S. Attorney] on the case, had just signed it. It was in his briefcase when Aronow was killed."

"So that's it," I finally say, recovering from the surprise. "Why Aronow was killed."

Norris shakes his head, saying that his office had considered that but decided there wasn't a connection. "The people who were closest to the investigation really don't feel there was any connection, and—" He sighs. "Besides, there was no indication that Aronow was going to cooperate, was gonna say squat to us. No one outside had any idea he was going to be called. Not him or anyone else."

Norris has clearly considered the stunning coincidence of the subpoena and the murder, but can't accept it. "Look," he explains, "you know in these investigations, if you happen to have an extra half hour of time, you'll fill in something that's a long shot. A shot in the dark.

You don't know what will come out of it. Maybe something, maybe nothing. You see, it's not as if Aronow was out there as a source for us. No one here has ever spoken to him."

"But the mob didn't know that," I respond, thinking that the government's "shot in the dark" may have killed Aronow.

Norris suggests that if some crime family were reacting to the Kramer investigations, they would whack the people who were co-operating in Illinois first—long before Aronow—because of the much more serious nature of the charges up there. He adds that there was no indication that Aronow would cooperate or give some-one up.

"Still the coincidence is compelling, don't you think?" I point out.

"What you've just said to me is why it's a matter for internal discussion," he says. "We simply haven't resolved the matter and put it away. The case obviously can be made for what you say, but my sense of these things—I mean, murder is not something that is very common in the criminal justice system."

Norris's contention that government witnesses are rarely mur-dered has one fatal flaw. If the witnesses are killed before they are subpoenaed—as in Aronow's case—the connection is never made. The victim is not listed as a government witness.

I continue to delve into the link between the subpoena and the murder. "Wasn't there a similar situation with Watergate? It wasn't the break-in that they were concerned about. It was the whole range of Nixon's secret activities that was in jeopardy of exposure."

Norris agrees, "From that point of view, it's entirely possible. What you're saying is that he wasn't killed because of what we were looking for. Rather, he was killed because of what he could have said about other things. Who he could've given up had sufficient pressure been brought to bear on him."

He falls silent. Finally, he says, "Obviously, there are clearly forces at work here of another sort."

After some further discussion, it becomes clear that the real rea-son Norris has a problem accepting the subpoena motive is that he has to accept an idea even more repugnant to him: that the mob knew all along the specific plans of a federal grand jury and his task force. All grand jury proceedings are secret by federal law and the Isle of Man group worked under stringent security precautions. Someone obviously had a pipeline into the system. Into the Isle of Man Task Force, the U.S. Attorney's Office, or the grand jury. Per-haps all three.

Norris has become uncomfortable with the direction of our discussion. The idea of the "bad guys" knowing every move his federal prosecutors made is enough to ruin anyone's digestion. We throw our trash into a bin and walk out of the mall back toward his office.

"Did you or anyone from the federal government ever tell MetroDade Homicide about any of this?" I ask.

"No, we didn't." He doesn't elaborate, but his manner implies that the notion of a security breach causing Aronow's death would be embarrassing to the feds, to say the least.

As we wait at the stoplight immediately across from his office, Norris turns to the man standing next to us and says, "Hi, Dave, how are you?" The man smiles in acknowledgement. The light changes and we continue across the street into his office.

The man at the light looked familiar. Very familiar. I think I've seen his picture in the papers. When I question Norris, he says the man is Dave Goodhart, adding that Goodhart's relative works in the Miami U.S. Attorney's Office.

"Former Judge David Goodhart, the guy who used to work with Richard Gerstein?" I ask. Norris nods. Again, I'm dumbfounded.

David Goodhart is Richard Gerstein's crony, his top aide for ten years until 1972 when he quit to run for circuit judge. The same David Goodhart who was subpoenaed to the 1974 federal grand jury investigating Meyer Lansky's gambling empire. Also subpoenaed: Meyer Lansky, Richard Gerstein. And Don Aronow. Goodhart, like Meyer Lansky, took the Fifth Amendment and refused to testify.

The photograph I recalled had been in the Miami papers. David Goodhart and Richard Gerstein were immortalized on a surveillance film taken by undercover cops and local TV crews at one of Miami Beach's alleged mob hangouts on Lincoln Road. A television reporter said he had witnessed Goodhart meeting on three separate occasions with top Lansky associate Hymie Lazar, a gambling-junket operator.

The video and photographs were a central part of the celebrated "Market Connection"—a scandal involving suspicions that Dade County public officials were on the take from Lansky. Although the notoriety may eventually have convinced Gerstein and Goodhart to retire, the investigation went the way of every other one involving Lansky. Poof!

Now Goodhart's relative was working at the U.S. Attorney's Office at the time of Aronow's subpoena.

Running into David Goodhart in front of the U.S. Attorney's Office just as Bill Norris and I were discussing the possibility of a leak from his office was purely coincidence. Yet at the same time it hinted at the many subtle ties between organized crime, the drug business, and the government.

In the war against the "underground empire," law enforcement efforts are often focused on the people who physically smuggle drugs into the country. There is a built-in *Miami Vice* bias toward Latinos as the key drug smugglers. The high-profile Colombianos—their flashy nouveau riche lifestyles and bloody shootouts—have reinforced the notion that disparate and warring Latin groups are the main source of drugs in this country. So the "war" efforts are focused on fighting the Colombians, the Cubans, the Haitians, the Jamaicans, or whatever new successive group of immigrants enters the fray.

All the while, the LCN-backed drug operations continue unhampered. The feds, fighting the many vying Latino drug factions, have little time to step back and view the bigger picture. The pressure is on to produce some concrete evidence that the country is gaining in the war. The American public and the politicians want immediate action—they want the splashy headlines and the multimedia drug-bust stories: "Two hundred kilos of coke and two million dollars seized, film at eleven." There is no incentive for law enforcement to marshal its efforts on the infrastructure supporting the drug business. It would be far too time consuming and they would be accused of doing nothing.

When on occasion intrepid officials do try to put together a case against OC, they find it goes nowhere. The mob manages a series of checks and balances that ensure the unhindered continuation of their most profitable endeavor, narcotics. Besides dealing with the importation and distribution of drugs, they've infiltrated the government with associates and "clean" front people who occupy positions of power at all levels.

The popular stereotype of organized crime is outdated. The image made famous in movies by Brando, De Niro, and Pacino clearly still exists, as Joe Pistone showed in his book about his undercover activities, *Donnie Brasco*. The old-time mobsters still frequent their dingy, run-down meeting halls and restaurants, spending hours talking about this heist or that shakedown, or how to fence some stolen goods.

They are vestiges of another era, inexorably losing their power and influence. But the passing of the stereotype by no means signals the end of the LCN, despite what some OC watchers predict. Not long ago, one national magazine proclaimed that it was the twilight years for the mob. It was a naive look at organized crime in contemporary America and it couldn't have been more wrong.

The ill-fitting black suits have been cast off for Savile Row styles. The dingy neighborhood bars have lost out to four-star gourmet eateries. The Brooklyn accents have given way to Ivy League tones. Street smarts are being enhanced by law degrees and MBAs. This is today's mob. At its disposal is a sophisticated network of lawyers, bankers, businessmen, and officials who help them manage global operations that are woven into the fabric of legitimate society.

Organized crime has penetrated the system so pervasively that it has become almost invisible. Except that every so often a name pops up in the most unexpected place, and for a brief moment a link between the "respectable world" and the mob is glimpsed. Then the link vanishes, leaving the observer to wonder whether it was all a mirage.

Perhaps it's a state attorney who likes to dine in a Mafia hangout; maybe a U.S. senator who's quick to offer his support to keep a wiseguy doper out of jail; a relative who just happens to get a sensitive job in a federal law enforcement agency; or a state attorney investigator who loses vital evidence in a mob-hit case.

It might even be a famous movie star, such as Jimmy Caan, who likes to socialize with wiseguys. In March 1989 Caan, a close friend of Ben Kramer and Bobby Saccenti, was involved in a headline-making story. Caan, attracted to wiseguys perhaps from his most famous role as mafioso Sonny Corleone in *The Godfather,* wanted to make a movie about the real godfather Meyer Lansky and star in it as well. He met with Meyer's wife, Teddy, who bestowed her blessing. Then Caan heard that a similar movie project was already under way.

According to unsealed federal affidavits, during a dinner with some of the Genovese boys, Caan expressed the wish that the competing movie not be made. More specifically, he allegedly said he would see to it that the other movie "would never be distributed." The Genovese crime family was on Caan's side. Not only is Caan considered a gumba, but they saw a chance to reap some profits.

The FBI says that Vincent "Jimmy Blue Eyes" Alo, a retired Genovese capo and Lansky's closest friend, interceded in the matter. The other movie project has been shelved.

Meyer Lansky had once said about the mob: "We're bigger than U.S. Steel." At the time, U.S. Steel was the largest corporation in the world. Since then, the steel company has gotten smaller. The mob is bigger and more powerful than ever. As the cordial street encounter between the fed Norris and the rumored Lansky associate Goodhart indicates, its presence is nearly imperceptible even to those who wage war with its minions.

The underground empire has become the invisible empire. And no amount of armed security at the gates of government is going to keep it out.

TWENTY-TWO

The Operation Isle of Man Task Force had meticulously followed a paper trail—financial transactions involving hundreds of millions of dollars—from Shaun Murphy to the middlemen lawyers to Ben Kramer, from banks to dummy corporations to investments, from Switzerland to Hong Kong to the U.S. I was now following my own paper trail: the path of the subpoena with Don Aronow's name on it.

"It's a federal crime to reveal details of federal grand jury proceedings," says a fed intimately involved in the Kramer investigation. "Besides, it's highly unlikely there was a leak."

We're meeting in an out-of-the-way conference room that seems to double as a storage area in the basement of the Federal Building in Fort Lauderdale. He has brought a friend along. A muscular "street" fed who looks like a black Bruce Willis. It's his role to bust smugglers on the high seas or kick in a doper's door, yelling, "Federal agents! Freeze! Search warrant!"

All three of us are nervous. They can lose their jobs for talking to me, or worse, they can be prosecuted. I'm concerned about getting whacked for sticking my nose where it doesn't belong—somewhere along this particular paper trail are more OC connections.

The black agent, his thick arms crossed, leans back in his chair, balancing himself against the wall. The outline of a large gun is obvious under his loose-fitting shirt. Another member of the ".357 magnum" club at the Federal Building.

His colleague is slightly built, pale and balding, with horn-rimmed glasses and graying sideburns. He's an "inside man," the person who carefully, quietly, and often monotonously sifts through thousands of pages of documents to solve a case. "You promise not to use our names? I don't want to see our names in a book," he says.

The "inside" agent says the Aronow murder was just a coincidence, or at best, an educated guess on somebody's part.

"Aronow was squirming like a stuck pig for the last three weeks of his life," I respond. "The Thursday before he was killed he was asking a friend to find an out-of-the-way place in the Bahamas. That's not a guess that you guys might be coming for him. So what exactly were you doing from mid-January to February third, 1987, when he was killed?"

"We can't answer that," the black agent says again. "Federal grand jury proceedings are protected by federal law." His chair snaps forward and cracks against the floor.

"Well, let me ask you a hypothetical question. If a guy was going to get a subpoena on February fourth, 1987, what would be the timing considerations?"

"Hypothetically speaking?" responds the "inside" fed, catching on to the semantics charade. "We give subpoenaed witnesses ten to fourteen days prior notice. Especially when they are asked to bring documents." He says a February 4th subpoena would correspond to the February 17, 1987, grand jury session.

The details don't account for Aronow's highly agitated state that began three weeks before his subpoena was prepared. There had to be some explanation that would tie his anxiety into the grand jury proceedings.

"Couldn't it have been more like three weeks for the scheduling to be finalized?" I ask.

The agent states flatly that it couldn't have taken that long. Then he frowns, saying, "Actually, he was first scheduled earlier, and it was postponed. You see, Donald Aronow was scheduled then postponed. There's the three weeks you're looking for."

"So, where could that information have leaked?"

"If it had to leak out—a leak—" the black fed says, then pauses. He looks at his friend, who nods. "You're looking at it, okay? Or, it's down there in the U.S. Attorney's Office. That's the only two places."

"So you guys are the beginning of my paper trail?" I laugh, but they're not amused.

They seem suddenly distracted by the unpleasant implications. Even the clerical staff isn't involved in this highly sensitive part of the process. The feds do all the typing of the subpoenas themselves, and then they bring them to the U.S. Attorney's Office by hand. They tell only those few people who need to know. There just aren't that many suspects for a leak.

The two agents confirm what Norris had previously said. No one on the task force had ever had any contact with Aronow. Yet Norris had been vague about the precise reason for subpoenaing Aronow, suggesting it was because they thought he could shed light on the scope of drug-smuggling activities in the high performance power-boat industry. But there were many others who could have provided such insight and they weren't subpoenaed.

So why Aronow?

The inside fed admits that he's the one who first came up with the idea of calling Aronow before the grand jury. "It was a result of my check of Dade County's records," he says. "We were tracking Jack and Ben's property holdings and we came up with a transaction between them and Aronow."

"You mean the Super Chief South deal?" He nods.

It wasn't enough that for years Ben Kramer had taken from Aronow whatever he wanted, whenever he wanted it. He was driven to humiliate Aronow as well. But by making him give up USA Racing on the record, Kramer had created a permanent linkage between the two men that could never be erased. Despite its obscurity, the August 29, 1985 deed and note had become an indelible part of the public record. For Aronow, it was a ticking bomb.

"You don't kill somebody because they can give up information, correct?" I ask for confirmation of the prevailing wisdom. "You kill them because they can testify, right?"

"That's right," says the inside fed. "A witness who has direct knowledge. Not hearsay."

"So Aronow must've been in a position to put somebody in jail. To testify against someone from his personal knowledge. And it wasn't Ben or Jack or Mel because you already had them by the balls, right?"

"Yeah, by the balls." The big fed laughs. "They were cooked by then."

"You never had the feeling throughout the Kramer investigation that there was a Mr. Big somewhere behind the scenes?" I ask.

"We just knew this—there were a lot of questions we had, why certain people were chosen, why certain things were done," says the inside fed. "And we still can't explain them." He looks over at the other agent and stands up, signaling the end of our talk.

"You understand, of course," the big fed adds as we leave, "this conversation never took place."

After our discussion of a link between the impending federal subpoena and the murder, Norris had said he would take steps that might clear things up one way or the other.

When we meet again, he says he has made some changes in the focus of his office's narcotics investigations. This time they'll be looking for evidence of OC involvement. There are new U.S. Attorneys going on the Isle of Man project, and they are shifting the investigation in the organized crime direction. Norris has added an organized crime assistant U.S. Attorney on the case.

He is hopeful that his decision to link an OC specialist and a narcotics specialist with a major narcotics grand jury will help clarify any LCN-drug links and resolve the Aronow matter. "What you uncover," he comments, "depends so much on what you look for."

The thin federal agent, the inside fed, has been plagued since our last conversation by the possibility of a leak in his task force's operation. Especially if it leads to the mob. Never before has he had reason to question the security of federal investigations.

"That was pretty heavy stuff," he tells me when we meet again. "What you said about Aronow's last three weeks. When you look at something from just one angle, you can sometimes draw a different conclusion than if you see it from more than one angle."

Aronow's name appeared on some scheduling piece of paper for the first time in mid-January. Immediately all the Lansky people, including Aronow, knew about it. It was obvious there was a good pipeline somewhere.

"I'm treading a little lighter now in that building [the U.S. Attorney's Office in Miami]," the fed says. "It's hard to think of any one person who would have access to all that information. There are two possibilities that I'm considering. One, there was some electronic surveillance in some manner, shape, or form. Or, it's a clerical person."

He says he's been checking into the phone systems in the Fort Lauderdale Federal Building and the U.S. Attorney's Office. The Federal Building itself, except for local phones, is really not tap-able because of the way the phone system happens to be set up.

A number of generic trunk lines run into the building and then the computer selects whatever line is open for either outgoing or incoming calls. But the U.S. Attorney's Office in Miami has a different setup, with direct lines for each phone extension. A tap is feasible there, the agent concludes.

"Are you going to work Goodhart or Gerstein and the possibility they had a pipeline into your proceedings?" I ask. "You know Goodhart's relative is supposed to work in the Miami office."

He seems surprised at the question, but shrugs his shoulders, commenting, "I can't say one way or another."

It wasn't just a theory that the Kramer drug operation benefited from a functioning intelligence network. All throughout the summer and fall of 1987, Ben and his Lansky, Inc. superiors were clearly aware of key details in the Southern Florida District investigation of his empire. Even as the Isle of Man grand jury—under the direction of the Miami U.S. Attorney's Office—was moving inexorably toward his indictment, Kramer was systematically dismantling the multimillion-dollar engine shop at Ft. Apache, "selling" it to a business associate in north Florida.

"Sure, Ben Kramer knew when we were getting close," recalls one DEA agent. "Obviously, he had some good intelligence. For example, he had purchased a house in Malta. He was moving things overseas in anticipation. He was even looking for a buyer for Ft. Apache Marina. It looks like he had at least a two-month lead on us here in Florida in us getting him indicted and seizing his assets."

Knowing that all his assets would soon be subject to government seizure, Kramer sold his four-engine corporate jet for half its book value and unloaded several boats. A half-million-dollar racing catamaran was spirited out of the Apache factory late at night and hidden at the Jockey Club to avoid seizure. A tractor trailer was repainted, the Apache logo sprayed over, and the vehicle moved from the premises.

Jack Kramer, evidently alerted as well, was making emergency preparations to flee the country. Two weeks before the unsealing of the supposedly secret south Florida federal indictments, he and his wife, using aliases, allegedly applied for and received false British passports.

The DEA agent says the Kramers' strategy was to stay in business until they got arrested, then bond out and continue operations until the last minute before a trial. Neither Ben nor Jack Kramer ever suspected that bail would be denied. They assumed that with enough lawyers and enough money, they could get out of anything. So they planned to string the proceedings out for another year with motions and appeals. When the heat finally became unbearable, they would just disappear.

The Kramers' behavior was cocky to say the least. Instead of packing their millions and fleeing by private jet at the first sign of trouble, they had played everything right down to the wire. Not only were they apparently aware of the timing of the Florida federal actions (the indictments and seizure of Ft. Apache were originally scheduled for October 1987) but they were also familiar with the limits of the judicial system to restrain them after arrest. It was an arrogance born of supreme confidence—and probably superb inside information.

Their game plan would have worked. Except for two unforeseen events. The DEA agent explains, "Scotland Yard alerted us about Jack's false passport and his bail was revoked. And Benny got fucked up by that Illinois [federal district] indictment. That quickie grand jury with its bullshit two-count indictment was a surprise to him. Let's face it, it was a surprise to us, too. It caught Ben with his pants down, so they obviously didn't have any pipeline up there."

Since the Illinois charges carried a maximum sentence of life imprisonment without chance of parole, the government was able to get the judge to deny Ben's bond.

The Lansky boys had everything under control in Florida. They just hadn't paid any attention to a small-town federal prosecutor's office in southern Illinois. It was the surprising arrival on August 26, 1987, of a federal warrant issued by the Southern District of Illinois that forced the Florida feds to move prematurely on the Kramers. By October—the month the seizure was originally scheduled—Kramer would have had all of his assets liquidated and been waiting for the feds, his lawyer by his side and bond money in his hand.

"In the end, it was some shit-kickers out of God's country that brought Ben Kramer down," the DEA agent admits. "If it was just us [Florida], he'd be out on bail and be gone. I mean, who knows where Malta is? He'd be living it up there with his Swiss bank account, his little honey, and their boxful of sex toys. He'd be happy for the rest of his life. Poor Benny. Now all he has is Carlos Lehder."

If Lansky, Inc. had a line into the Florida feds in mid-1987, it wasn't hard to imagine they were plugged in during the first weeks of 1987, when Aronow's appearance before the grand jury was being contemplated and the deadly subpoena was issued. Actually, as far back as 1970, Meyer Lansky himself saw the value of such inside information. A "friend" in the Justice Department had forewarned him about an impending subpoena and he beat it by leaving the country for Israel.

Bill Norris is somewhat discouraged, a change from his usual upbeat personality. A major case that his office had been working, similar to the Pizza Connection, has just fallen through. It was a heroin ring involving Sicilian Mafia couriers in the U.S., the Zips, so-called because of their fast-paced Sicilian dialect. He's also met resistance on the Aronow investigation.

He comments in a dejected tone that he had a talk with the Bureau. But he had no luck getting them interested in the Aronow case. The FBI told him that Lansky wasn't around anymore. That the story was "ancient history."

"The 1987 murder of a pending federal grand jury witness isn't ancient history," I remind him.

"Right," he concurs. "Well, I'll pass on the more recent information you've given me. We'll see what the Bureau will say about it. Give a call in a couple of weeks."

What a difference a day makes.

Kill Don Aronow the afternoon before he gets a subpoena, and nothing happens. Nobody makes the connection. It's simply an unpleasant coincidence that can easily be dismissed. Washington won't waive grand jury secrecy regulations and allow local feds to inform MetroDade about the impending subpoena. So only a handful of people even know about it—and who would suspect such an egregious leak in the criminal justice system? The result: the head of the Major Narcotics Unit of the Miami U.S. Attorney's Office can't get the FBI interested in what seems to be a local murder.

If Aronow had been killed after receiving the subpoena, everything would have been very different. The "coincidence" would have been impossible to ignore. Since he was to be served at USA Racing on Wednesday morning, his employees would have known. Lillian Aronow would have learned that her husband had been served and then murdered. She would have gone public with the information, attracting local, even national, media coverage.

High-powered officials at the senior levels of the U.S. Justice Department would have been galvanized into action. Killing a person who has just been subpoenaed before a federal grand jury is not something that can be ignored or tolerated. Such an incident jeopardizes the integrity of both the grand jury and the federal court systems. Adding to the impact was the fact that Don Aronow wasn't just any person. He was the Vice President's friend.

Undoubtedly, a special "multiagency task force" would have been formed to investigate the matter, and a federal spotlight would suddenly shine on the darker side of Miami. FBI agents in cars with black-walled tires would descend like a D-day invasion force on the Alley looking for answers: Why was Don Aronow killed? What did he know? What was someone trying to cover up by killing him? Who had him killed?

It would have been a messy hit, reminiscent of the Jimmy Hoffa disappearance, generating heat for those connected to the murder. Lansky, Inc. already had enough problems coping with the Isle of Man investigation, which was throwing a kink into their billion-dollar marijuana operation.

Bill Norris was right when he said that federal witnesses are rarely hit. Perhaps if Aronow had actually been served, he might still be alive. "Murder is not something that is very common in the criminal justice system," Norris was fond of saying. "We don't usually lose witnesses." What he hadn't considered was how many potential witnesses are killed before they are subpoenaed.

The Genovese and Lansky crime organizations were very "lucky," indeed, that Aronow wasn't a subpoenaed federal grand jury witness when he was murdered. He was instead just another homicide victim in a city overrun with homicide victims.

It was, like so many things in life, simply a matter of timing. For Don Aronow, eighteen hours had made all the difference in the world.

Bill Norris keeps striking out in his attempts to get the FBI interested in the Aronow murder. The next time we meet, he tells me that the Bureau remains uninterested, even though he pointed out that the murder of a federal grand jury witness is a federal crime.

He says he'll keep trying.

The possibility of a leak on the Aronow subpoena continues to worry the inside fed. He has become nearly obsessed with reconstructing the fateful subpoena paper trail, which is now more than a year and a half old. We get together in a coffee-shop dive, many miles off the beaten path. The coffee tastes as if it were brewed with water from the Everglades and the doughnuts are stale, but neither of us cares.

The fed gets right down to business. He says, "When we talked last, you told me about Gerstein's aide Goodhart having a relative that worked in the U.S. Attorney's Office. Okay, well, hmmm, yes, in fact he was an assistant [U.S. Attorney]."

The relative worked in the Criminal Division along with Norris and the others who were working on the Aronow subpoena. The fed says that he left for private practice sometime after the murder.

We had been looking for a "pipeline" into the U.S. Attorney's Office. Had we found the Lincoln Tunnel instead?

Norris is perplexed. Despite his best efforts he hasn't been able to interest the FBI in the case. "I don't get it," he comments. "The matter's clearly worth their looking into. I want to see this incident resolved and put away."

He says he's still not giving up—he's going to try again.

The inside fed has been busy.

"The Aronow subpoena was typed the week before the murder in Lauderdale at the Isle of Man office," he tells me excitedly the next time we talk. "Or let me rephrase that: if there was a grand jury subpoena—which I can't really say because that would be a breach of grand jury secrecy—it would've been typed in Lauderdale. Hand-carried to Miami the week before, and left for Cassidy's signature." Scheduling of the witnesses would be done by the AUSA on the case —Dan Cassidy.

If Cassidy wasn't in his office, the inside fed would have left the document on his desk. Cassidy's office was open during the day, whether or not he was there. The office of Goodhart's relative was in the same wing.

It's clear to both of us that soon after the announcement was made to the grand jury members in June 1986 that they would be hearing evidence about Ben Kramer's operations, the Lansky people and the Purple Gang knew all about it. It was also obvious that whoever leaked the plans in early 1987 had to be someone with direct access to Cassidy's office where witness scheduling was planned, recorded, and periodically revised to deal with scheduling conflicts.

"The only thing—" The inside fed shakes his head slowly because he can't quite accept what he's saying. "The only thing I can possibly figure was that it was him [Goodhart's relative].

"Hey, ya hear about Bill Norris?" a DEA agent on the Isle of Man Task Force tells me. "He got demoted. He no longer runs Major Narcotics. He was dropped two levels."

As head of the Major Narcotics Unit of the Miami U.S. Attorney's

Office, Bill Norris had the power to initiate investigations. He was the top drug prosecutor in the Southern District of Florida, with ten years tenure. He was a likable person, and more importantly, he was straightforward, decent, and dedicated. The news is surprising and disappointing. I'm curious about his last attempt to get the FBI on the Aronow case. It was just three weeks before that Bill had said he was going to try again to get the Bureau involved.

"Does that mean he can still start investigations?" I ask naively, hoping that his pursuit of the connection between the Aronow murder and the subpoena won't end.

"Shit, are you kidding?" the DEA agent exclaims. "He's just a grunt now."

I decide to contact Dan Cassidy, one of Norris's men and an experienced career narcotics prosecutor. The Kramer operation was the most important investigation of his career and a significant accomplishment—bagging one of the largest marijuana smugglers in history. He had fought vigorously in the arraignments against the Kramers, Kessler, and Gilbert.

Cassidy had been described as a "real go-getter" and a "hands-on prosecutor." He was also said to be looking forward to the prosecution of the southern Florida case. But when I call the Miami U.S. Attorney's Office, they inform me that Cassidy no longer works for the Southern District of Florida. They refuse to give me any information about his reassignment.

"The guy's in the fucking Denver U.S. Attorney's Office," says Rory McMahon, laughing, when I ask if he knows where Cassidy went. "I mean, what the fuck is a hotshot federal drug prosecutor doing in Denver? Looking for some hippies growing pot in Rocky Mountain National Park? Do you think Rudy Giuliani would go looking for mobsters in Iowa, or Wall Street inside traders in Omaha? Would you go to Milwaukee to get into show business? I mean, you wanna prosecute dopers, you do it in Miami. This is the big leagues."

I call Cassidy in Denver to ask about Aronow and Kramer and why he left Miami. His response is reminiscent of my first interviews when I was exploring Aronow's early New Jersey years.

"I got this thing about talking to reporters and guys who write books," he says. "I mean, I don't know you. It makes it impossible for me to really talk to you. I mean, how can I do that? It's a real problem." Cassidy didn't want to say any more and terminated the conversation.

A few months after his demotion, Bill Norris quit and entered private practice. He was never able to get the Bureau interested in the Aronow case. And I was never able to determine exactly whose idea it was for Dan Cassidy to be transferred to Denver.

All I knew was that the Miami U.S. Attorney's Office was suddenly minus two seasoned, straight-arrow drug prosecutors.

Despite the FBI's repeated rejections of Norris's request to investigate the Aronow murder, the agency hadn't always been indifferent to the Aronow case. At one time they had been extremely interested in it. Their involvement, however, occurred more than a year before Norris had first gone to them.

A few months after the Aronow murder, some FBI agents had come to talk with Mike Brittain. As the owner of Aluminum Marine Products, a custom-metal shop, Brittain maintained good relationships with the powerboat builders on Thunderboat Alley. He was a friend of Don Aronow, and, along with Bobby Saccenti, he was the last person to talk with him moments before the shooting. Brittain also had a fairly friendly, casual business relationship with Ben Kramer and had raced with him.

His association with both Kramer and Aronow briefly made Brittain the focus of both FBI and very high level government interest. In May or June of 1987, Brittain was approached by FBI special agents Joseph Usher and John Donovan from the Miami office. He knew both of them. They had talked to him in the past about fugitive doper Michael "Mickey" Munday, a man Brittain knew because he had raced with him a number of times.

"This time they brought along another FBI guy," Brittain says. "Special Agent Usher said he wanted to introduce me to someone from George Bush's staff, from Washington, on the National Drug Task Force. Usher said the agent was down here at the request of the Vice President of the United States."

Brittain says he was very impressed. He felt it was a good sign that George Bush himself was pushing the Aronow case—now it would be solved. Or so he thought until the questioning began by the Washington FBI agent, who identified himself as Special Agent William Temple.

"He didn't ask about the murder or anything like that," says a still-puzzled Brittain. "All he wanted to know about was the merger. I said, 'What merger do you mean?' He said, 'The merger between Don Aronow and Ben Kramer.' I said, 'What the hell are you talking about?' That's all he kept asking me about."

The FBI agent seemed only interested in the relationship between Ben and Don. "They asked questions in reference to the involvement between the two," Brittain says. "How much I knew. How well were they friends? Did they have dinner? Any business dealings? So on and so forth."

Brittain says he doesn't understand. "Why would George Bush send this guy all the way down from Washington to ask me that?" he asks. "What did that have to do with Don's murder? What the hell do you suppose was going on there?"

Bush's special agent came back to Brittain again just after the '88 presidential election. Once again, the agent interrogated Brittain about Aronow and Kramer. He also wanted to know if Brittain had spoken to anyone else about their previous FBI interview or the Kramer and Aronow relationship. Reassured that nothing had come out, the agent returned to Washington.

The "merger" that so interested the FBI and George Bush's special agent was the linkup between Aronow's USA Racing company and Kramer's dummy corporation Super Chief South. The deal that put the Blue Thunder Customs boats into the hands of the country's biggest grass smuggler.

The first Brittain interrogation took place just about the same time the Vice President encountered Lillian Aronow at a Miami dinner party and sent a Secret Service agent over to convey his regards, rather than speak with her directly. The second occurred as Bush was about to take hold of his lifelong goal, the Oval Office.

"Damage control" seemed to be the modus operandi for all sorts of people when it came to Don Aronow's murder.

The news that an FBI emissary from George Bush had been snooping around the Alley intrigues me, and I contact the inside fed about the implications of the new information. I call his beeper and punch in a number for the pay phone I'm using. Now I know why dopers use pay phones and 800-toll-free-number pagers: they're computerized, untraceable, and can't be wiretapped.

A few minutes later he calls me from another pay phone and listens as I fill him in on what I've found out about Special Agent Temple's peculiar trip to Miami. "I guess you're going to have to tell someone about what we've uncovered about the Aronow subpoena matter," I say. "But to be honest with you, this whole thing with Norris and Cassidy, and then the D.C. FBI agent doing what seems to be containment, gives me the creeps."

He's been silent since I mentioned Bush's name. Finally he says,

"You mean tell someone else?" He sounds shocked. "Are you kidding? With Bush's personal 'I' involved? Listen, as far as I'm concerned, you're an *anonymous* informant. As far as I'm concerned, I'm an *anonymous* source. In fact, everything about this is so fucking *anonymous,* I can't even remember my own name."

TWENTY-THREE

After comparing notes with the inside fed about the Isle of Man task force's activities and Don's last three weeks, we had both come to the same inescapable conclusion: Aronow was killed to keep him from being subpoenaed to appear on February 17, 1987, before Federal Grand Jury Number 86-3, the one investigating the Kramer operation.

Aronow was at the nexus of the drug activities of two great crime families and was in a position to do an incalculable amount of damage. Though the Isle of Man investigators didn't know it, Kramer's smuggling empire was simply the "Marijuana Division" of Lansky, Inc.'s global operations. Quite literally billions of dollars of narcotics and other mob business was in jeopardy because of the task force's shot-in-the-dark subpoena.

Paulie "Rizzo" Caiano's actions around the time of the murder suggest that the Genovese Purple Gang was worried as well. Aronow was a suspected member of the Purple Gang according to federal law enforcement records. Perhaps the Purple Gang, with operations in New York and Florida, was operating a heroin joint-venture with the Lansky organization and utilizing Aronow's boatbuilding facilities as some other wiseguy dopers did.

Still, there was something about the subpoena theory that bothered me. Why wouldn't Aronow just take the Fifth and keep his mouth shut, or lie, like every good mob guy does?

Aronow, of course, had been down the federal grand jury path before. In 1974 he had been subpoenaed to testify at a grand jury investigating Lansky's gambling empire. At risk that time was Lansky's billion-dollar national gambling syndicate. Don invoked his Fifth Amendment rights against self-incrimination, was granted immunity for his gambling indiscretions at Calder Race Track, and testified—without getting shot. Obviously he didn't say anything under oath that would have upset Lansky, yet he was an integral part of Lansky's operation. Presumably he lied.

This time however the feds had more than illegal gambling on Aronow. They were aware of his involvement in Ippolito's smuggling operations in the early eighties. Still, without more evidence they could not have indicted him. "It would've been very difficult for us to make a case that would've stuck so many years later," the inside fed conceded. "It would've been a bluff on our part to scare him if need be. If Aronow told us to go pound sand when we asked about him and Joey—we would've had to pound sand."

Aronow could not be forced to talk. So why kill him? Why eliminate a man who was so valuable to LCN interests? Why take such a huge risk when Aronow could easily have told the grand jury to "pound sand"? No one else connected with the Isle of Man or the Illinois cases had been killed—and many had potentially very damaging information. It didn't make any sense. Unless the mob had reason to believe that Don wasn't going to keep his mouth shut.

Rory McMahon says he has a story that might interest me. About a month after Aronow was killed, a half-assed wiseguy doper named Vincent Fasano was in McMahon's office. Rory was his probation officer. "He said to me, 'Did ya hear about the Aronow thing?' I mean the Aronow thing was big news, that's all anybody was talking about. So I said, yeah. He said, 'You know why he got whacked, don't you? It's all over the fuckin' street. He was subpoenaed and he was gonna be a stool pigeon. He got what he deserved.'"

How did a parolee know about the Aronow subpoena? Aronow's family didn't know about it. Neither did MetroDade Homicide. Only a handful of people in a top-security federal task force knew. But the mob knew—even half-assed wiseguys in Miami were in on the secret.

And the word in the underworld was that Aronow was going to talk.

McMahon's story is reminiscent of Jerry Engelman's "chance" encounter with a wiseguy at the Ft. Apache docks not long after the murder. When Jerry reluctantly conceded that he had worked for Don, the wiseguy had made a shocking remark: "Aronow was a fucking snake in the grass. You oughta forget you ever knew him."

Engelman was surprised by the man's vehemence. All the time Jerry worked at USA Racing, Aronow had been very popular with wiseguys. They dropped by his office to talk or just to meet him. Now, one mobster was calling him a snake in the grass. Others were no longer interested in hanging around USA Racing. And a small-time wiseguy doper was telling McMahon that Aronow was a stool pigeon. In the Mafia, there's nothing lower than somebody who talks to the feds.

When the stranger entered the USA Racing office on the day of the murder, he confronted an extremely nervous Aronow. He gave Don the mob's message: "My boss took me from the gutter and gave me a job. Everything I have I owe to him. I'd never turn my back on my boss." The mob clearly believed that Aronow was going to turn his back on them, after they had taken him from the streets of Brooklyn and made him a wealthy, successful, and influential figure.

A few minutes later Aronow was gunned down. After the first four shots, the shooter had extended his arm further, angled the .45 down, and blasted Aronow's testicles. It was an added touch, the mob's way of showing extreme contempt.

As Aronow was dying in the hospital, a phone call came in demanding, "Is that son of a bitch Aronow dead yet?"

Aronow had suddenly become "the enemy" to all wiseguys, even though for years he was one of them. The mob thinks with one mind. If the bosses said he was a traitor, he was. McMahon's parolee had heard within a few weeks through the wiseguy grapevine that Aronow was murdered because he was a turncoat.

Shortly after the Aronow murder, *Herald* sports writer Eric Sharp was with Bobby Saccenti at a powerboating event when Bobby spotted his brother and some friends from New Jersey. "[Bobby] said I want you to meet my brother Lou," Sharp recalled. "And four of these hoods came over, with their black suits and white shirts, and then they all started kissing each other on the cheeks, like out of a movie." Sharp, sensing an opportunity, asked the wiseguys if they knew why Aronow had been hit. "There was a lot of shrugging and handwaving and avoiding eye contact," Sharp remembered. "But they did look me straight in the eye when they said that no one will ever know about it—except the people who are supposed to know."

It's *omertà*—the Mafia code of silence—the strictest of all mob rules. The punishment is swift and certain and the lesson is not lost on anyone in the organization. Talk and you die.

TWENTY-FOUR

Don Aronow was in turmoil the last three weeks of his life. He couldn't stay still, he had to keep busy. He lost his temper often and seemed to blow up over the slightest things. He was nervous, agitated, and pensive. Other times he looked at his two youngest sons with what Lillian described as the sweetest expression she had ever seen on his ruggedly handsome face. His mind jumped from rehashing past glories to coaxing an old friend into a joint business venture to mad thoughts of fleeing to a deserted island in the Caribbean.

Patricia Cordell, the woman who had photographed Aronow for the *Miami News* on the Friday before the murder, shared the impression others had of his final days. He was wistful, regretful, and desperately trying to recapture the days when he had been a macho charmer, full of confidence, a glorified champion strutting in the world of kings and rock stars and athletes. Over the period of an hour Cordell saw swift and fleeting mood changes, but always he seemed to be burdened with a profound sense of mortality. In those last weeks, Aronow was not the ever-optimistic man described by his good friend Bob Magoon.

An hour before Aronow was gunned down, he was asked by reporter Jim Steinberg a seemingly innocuous question for an article: "Hey, Don, how about a story on a drug smuggler buying a boat from you?" It was unexpected and innocently hit close to home. It was the kind of question Aronow knew he would be asked and expected to answer in detail if he decided to cooperate with the government. Steinberg had always gotten colorful anecdotes from Aronow. This time Don waffled and then talked haltingly about the government and his part in George Bush's War on Drugs. Stilted remarks from one of powerboating's best storytellers.

In those last three weeks, it seems apparent that Aronow had made an agonizing choice. A decision that he knew could kill him. When Cordell saw the champion sweating nervously and looking back and forth around Thunderboat Alley, it was bullets—not government questions—that Aronow feared. He knew if the mob discovered his plans, he was a walking dead man. He always said, "You talk, you lose." And after a lifetime of seeing how the organization worked, he was frighteningly aware of just how much the boys could discover.

"I can guarantee that he didn't talk to anyone in the Isle of Man," says the inside fed in response to my question about Aronow's cooperating with the government. He also rejects the suggestion that Aronow had talked to the Organized Crime Strike Force, noting that his agency would have heard about it.

"How about Bush?" I suggest. When MetroDade Homicide was talking to me, they had told me that Don Aronow made a "surprising number of lengthy calls" to George Bush in the last week of his life.

"Quite possibly," the agent says. "I mean Bush was the leader of the [Florida antidrug] task force. And Don was his friend. If I had a friend who was the vice president of the United States? That's exactly what I would do."

Aronow had emerged unscathed from the 1974 federal investigation of Lansky's gambling empire. But in 1987, everything was different. Too much had changed. Most importantly, Meyer Lansky was gone. When the chairman of the board was alive, Don no doubt felt a great sense of loyalty and obligation to the man who saw his talents and enabled him to fulfill and even exceed his youthful ambitions.

Lansky was unique in the underworld: a man of sensibility, genius, and as many feds concede, he was civilized. He was first and foremost a businessman, with rumored connections to an astonishing list of the most successful people in the world. Even the U.S. government had turned to him on occasion for help. To an ambitious and smart young man from Brooklyn, Lansky must have seemed all-powerful, a kingmaker.

By the time of Lansky's death in 1983, Aronow was a celebrated multimillionaire with impressive clout in Miami and Washington. He had been hustling all his life to leave his Brooklyn background far behind. With his talents and Lansky's mentorship, he had made it. But the new managers of Lansky, Inc. had none of Meyer's remarkable characteristics.

That year was a turning point for Aronow. As far as he was concerned, the debt to Lansky was closed with the godfather's death. His obligations to his mentor had amply been repaid. The story that Bobby Saccenti had told Eric Sharp about Aronow's refusing to pay the widow of a "Mustache Pete" in 1983 was Don's declaration that he wanted to sever his ties with Lansky's successors and his own past.

At the same time, Aronow was moving closer to the government, particularly to George Bush. Their ten-year friendship had solidified, and in 1984, a year after Lansky died, Aronow had taken Bush for a boat ride in his latest creation, his Blue Thunder catamaran.

That short trip from the Keys to Miami led to Aronow's receiving the government contract to build the interdiction boats—after Bush nudged Customs into awarding it to his friend. With that decision, Aronow became an integral part of the government's War on Drugs. He was even envisioning a bigger role for himself—anticipating an ambassadorship when Bush became president.

He was also set on a path that led inexorably to his murder. Had Aronow not become so close to Bush, it's highly unlikely he would have gotten the Blue Thunder contract—a prize that had proved so irresistible to Ben Kramer. And without a close relationship with the Vice President, it was also improbable that Aronow would ever have considered allying himself with the government against the mob.

When Kramer's empire began to topple and the subpoena became imminent, Aronow saw an opportunity to cut himself off from the organization. It was obvious the brash but not-very-bright kingpin was racing to his own destruction. "Darth Vader" Kramer was a self-centered, adolescentlike character who considered Aronow his nemesis, the man he had to dethrone. While the mob looked the other way, Ben stripped virtually everything Don treasured, including his self-respect.

Why not—with the protection that only someone as powerful as George Bush could provide—cross over and join the "good guys"?

Aronow was about to turn sixty, his birthday less than a month away. A time when men begin to review the choices of their youth, the roads not taken. When regrets surface, and goals that had once seemed so important become far less so. There was still time to start over. He had a beautiful and loving wife and had recently become a father again. His youngest son was just a few months old. A huge new home, which he had spent a year renovating, awaited him and his family.

The subpoena was the catalyst. Which side? The government or the Mafia? It was his last best chance to cancel the Faustian pact he had made so many years ago in New Jersey. Finally to cast off the past and become the hero that most people had always believed he was.

No wonder Don made so many phone calls to Bush the last week of his life. He was in the most dangerous race of his life—against a subpoena with his name on it—reaching out to the most powerful connection he had. Once he was served, he knew that everything would change. Too many people would then be involved for Bush or a special envoy to make the kind of delicate arrangements a safe defection demanded.

Anticipating the extreme danger, Aronow put together what he called an emergency list. It was a secret outline for Patty Lezaca specifying what she should do if anything happened to him. The first directive: CALL GEORGE BUSH.

Why leave that instruction? If he intended to stonewall the grand jury he certainly didn't have to fear mob retribution. Nor would he be so naive as to expect any help from the Vice President if he took the Fifth Amendment in a narcotics investigation.

But if Bush knew that Aronow was considering cooperating—and Don's life was in danger as a result—then the message to contact the White House in case of an emergency makes sense. It also could insure protection for Aronow's family if he himself was unable to provide it since Bush would immediately know why Aronow had been killed.

It's unlikely, even under the stress of his predicament, that Aronow told Bush all the details of his life or even his narcotics activities. His story was a rags-to-riches saga lived on both sides of the law. It would be too much for the patrician Bush, raised far from the mean streets of Brooklyn, ever to understand. More likely, Don told him what he thought would guarantee that Bush would stick by him through the crisis.

Once he was subpoenaed, Aronow would face only two choices. Both unacceptable: take the Fifth or perjure himself. If he invoked his right against self-incrimination, he would automatically receive immunity and then be forced to answer questions. If he still refused to testify, he would be jailed for contempt. While grand jury proceedings are secret, his incarceration would be a matter of public record. The papers would carry headlines that the man who built antidrug boats for the government had been jailed for refusing to cooperate with a drug investigation. He would remain in jail until he testified.

If he perjured himself—as he presumably did with the Lansky probe in 1974—he faced the very real possibility this time that he would be indicted for perjury and go down with the already fatally wounded Kramer organization.

There was no way out. Except, perhaps, with the Vice President's help. Bush probably couldn't stop the subpoena, nor would that be desirable. It would prompt too many questions from the mob and arouse suspicions. But with the right influence, the proceedings could be sanitized. Don would emerge from the hearing unscathed after a half hour of innocuous questions.

In return, later, Aronow would give the government valuable information about the real enemy in the War on Drugs. Then he would lie low, perhaps in the hideaway Willie Meyers had suggested in the Bahamas, awaiting the inevitable collapse of Kramer's organization. After that he would have a chance to start living his own life for a change.

It had a chance of succeeding. Aronow always believed he could win in everything whether it was a boat race or a business deal. This would be no different.

During his last weeks as he was contemplating turning his back on the organization, he continued to meet almost daily with the Kramers, and probably others in Lansky, Inc., to discuss the grand jury investigation. The trio of men were in constant contact. The Kramers trying to decide how Aronow should handle the subpoena and what he should say about their drug operation. Aronow weighing his options, trying desperately to decide what to do when the fateful piece of paper was handed to him.

All the while, Aronow was playing along, trying to keep up the front that he was still aligned with the Lansky organization. He had to act as if nothing were up. He couldn't get a gun, buy a bulletproof vest, or hire a bodyguard—it might give a hint of the betrayal he was contemplating. But as the pressure built and became almost intolerable, Aronow may have given out the wrong signals to the boys and their always sensitive OC antennae.

Perhaps his loyalty was questioned and a tap placed on his phone.

It was a logical precaution—the mob had everything else under control with the Florida federal investigation. Aronow had firsthand knowledge about Lansky, Inc., going back to Meyer himself. He was likely familiar with the details of the marijuana and gambling "divisions," the money laundering, and the network of politicians, cops, prosecutors, and judges willing to be influenced by envelopes of money. Some feds believe that he was even a conduit for payoffs, since he could roam unchallenged among the ranks of the "good guys."

At best Aronow was a question mark for the mob, especially in his last years. As his relationship with the Vice President grew, he was being enveloped by the government—from Bush to Customs to federal agents.

It was enough to give any underworld chairman of the board sleepless nights.

Lillian Aronow had told me that when she moved into the mansion on North Bay Road right after the murder, her phone was tapped. She was insistent on that point. It was the same phone line that Don had often used during the ten months when he was renovating the mansion but still living on Sunset Isle. It was also the phone he usually used to talk with George Bush.

He felt it afforded privacy. It was conveniently removed from his family and employees and any federal wiretaps on Thunderboat Alley. For that reason he used it for all his private calls, according to Old Mike. The mob knew about the phone in the mansion—someone had called Don there on the morning of the murder to talk about writing "letters"—presumably letters of recommendations for wiseguy parolees.

A wiretap was a simple task that any PI firm—perhaps one such as Riley, Black—could do in fifteen minutes. If the mob had tapped the line, they may have heard their trusted associate—a man "the boss had taken from the gutter"—plotting with "the enemy." After the initial astonishment, rage would quickly have taken over. When the traitor and his plans were uncovered, a hit was the only answer. It had to be done quickly before the subpoena arrived and made him an "official" federal grand jury witness.

The die would be cast: Aronow had to die immediately.

With so little time they would have reached out to the best hit men in the country. The killer elite: men with the experience, the ability, and the coolness to gun down a friend of the Vice President on a busy street in broad daylight. Mafia killers who, as Jerry Gladden noted, "specialize in killing people who testify against the mob."

When George Bush heard of the murder, he was stunned. He called MetroDade Homicide immediately. For weeks he pushed to have the case solved. No doubt, he suspected that Aronow's plan to help the government was the reason for the murder.

Aware of the immediate reason behind the execution, Bush personally contacted the family to tell them that Aronow had died courageously. A month after the murder, he sent a warm letter to Don's son Gavin. In it, Bush chose to call Aronow "a hero." From Bush's perspective his friend had risked his life, and lost it, to help fight the war against drugs.

Many of the people in the Aronow murder mystery, including Aronow himself, seem to revolve around a central "dark star," acting as if a greater but unseen force was influencing and controlling them. A Mr. Big. The Boss. If Meyer Lansky were still alive, he would be the natural suspect.

If not Lansky, then it had to be his successor. For almost twenty years, Al Malnik was considered by OC watchers to be the heir apparent to the Lansky empire. Then in 1982, Malnik's car was bombed outside Miami's Cricket Club. Malnik, once a flamboyant celebrity-grabbing jet setter, suddenly shunned publicity. A few months later he left the country for several years. When he returned to Miami, OC cops paid no attention. It was assumed that Malnik had been pushed aside.

At the time of the bombing, an article in the *Chicago Sun-Times* reported that "since Malnik is a protégé of longtime Miami crime chief Meyer Lansky, the best guess [as to a motive for the Rolls-Royce bombing] is that young-Turk Miami mobsters were sending a message to the aging Lansky: 'We're taking over.' "

It was an absurd notion.

Meyer Lansky reigned supreme in organized crime to his last breath. He was the man with the golden touch where the mob's money was concerned. Until the end of his life, he walked his dog on the beach in front of his Miami Beach condo without any protection. No bodyguards for Lansky. No armor-protected, bulletproof limousines. No guns. Meyer didn't need them.

Former Miami FBI agent Ken Whittaker tells a story that he believes characterizes Meyer's relationship with the mob. After Lansky moved to south Florida in the 1950s, the New York Mafia bosses asked him to meet with them so that they could present some business ideas. But Meyer liked Florida and he didn't want the hassles involved in traveling. Finally, after months of being coaxed, he consented.

The mob had reserved a floor at the Waldorf-Astoria Hotel in his honor. Whittaker says that when Meyer got off the elevator, a young Italian hood who was standing guard there didn't recognize him and said, "Hey, Jew, what the fuck are you doing here? This ain't your floor."

Lansky turned without saying a word and stepped back into the elevator. He was just getting into a taxi when the Mafia bosses from upstairs came running out and begged him to come back in. He did and never discussed the incident.

The next day the Mafia chieftains escorted Meyer to the train station. No one mentioned the unpleasantness of the previous day, but as Lansky bid farewell, he was handed a newspaper. On the front page was the story of a young Italian hood who had been executed that morning. The corpse was found with its testicles in its mouth. The story noted that the man had been castrated first and then shot in the head. The bosses hoped Lansky would accept their gesture of apology.

What punishment would await someone who tried to send a "message" to Lansky with a bomb?

Since the bombing incident, many OC watchers have been puzzled. Supposedly Malnik was out, but who was taking his place? It was hard to believe that Lansky, who had spent fifty years building a staggering global empire, would die without seeing his organization pass into capable hands. No chairman of the board would simply allow an empire to dissolve.

When I contact a number of feds, I keep encountering the same response. A shrug of the shoulders, hands in the air. No one can offer any answers to my questions: Who succeeded Lansky? Where did the billions go? What happened to the organization?

Then I learned the details about the bomb that exploded at the Cricket Club on March 3, 1982. According to former MetroDade OC head Art Nehrbass, it was a tiny device in the wheelwell that was triggered when the tire rotated a few times. The Rolls, Malnik's fourth, was brand new. In fact Malnik had never even seen it. It was purchased in Canada, driven to Florida from Quebec, and delivered to the Club, where it was parked by a valet in a valet-only parking area. The valet was the only one hurt when the device went off. He received such minor injuries that he didn't require hospitalization.

The man suspected of planting it was an electronics specialist and master bombsmith from Chicago by the name of Frankie "the German" Schweihs.

A puny, firecrackerlike device built by a friend of Joe Sonken's, a close associate of Lansky. An apparent intimidation attempt by a representative of a crime family historically close to Lansky. A surprisingly inept "bombing" by one of the country's top hit men.

No punishment awaited Frankie. Even though he had been publicly identified as the perpetrator by the *Chicago Sun-Times*, he never suffered any retaliation from Lansky or the Mafia. In fact, he continued to be an integral member of the Chicago outfit—which continued its close ties to Lansky and Sonken.

Was Schweihs working against Malnik? Or was there another explanation?

At the time of the Cricket Club incident, Lansky knew he was dying from lung cancer. He had less than a year to live. All the crime families knew it. Rather than a "message" for Lansky and Malnik, the affair could have been a brilliantly conceived "public relations" scheme. One possible goal: to lower Malnik's profile, remove him from the spotlight, so that upon Lansky's demise, he could return to the U.S. and assume control, unhampered by federal interest.

Lansky's terminal diagnosis coincided with a startling change in Don Aronow's situation as well. A week after the Cricket Club explosion, Aronow divested himself of virtually every piece of property on Thunderboat Alley that was in his name. A large portion of the multimillion dollar transfers wound up in the Kramers' hands. The week after the real estate divestitures, Don sold Cigarette Racing Team. By the end of March 1982, Aronow was essentially out of the boat-building business, and the "man who owned the Alley" was left with only one small and relatively undesirable parcel of property next to an abandoned concrete factory.

If the bombing were a ruse to distract attention from large-scale management and financial changes in Lansky, Inc., it was a stunning idea. But typical of Lansky. As Lucky Luciano had said of him: "He could see around corners and knew the barrel of the gun is curved."

During the 1970s, Malnik had suffered significant negative exposure, including the well-publicized videotaping when he was briefly caught in the Abscam web. He was regularly identified in the press and by federal agencies as Lansky's "heir apparent," and because he was surveilled, he was occasionally caught linking up with other Lansky associates. Attracting even more attention, Malnik pursued a jet-set life and partied with such celebrities as Brooke Shields. All this garnered what was anathema to Lansky: public attention.

The bomb essentially wiped the slate clean for Malnik. When he returned to the U.S., he was ignored by law enforcement. If he was still the heir, he was now free to run the global empire of Lansky,

Inc., unhampered by zealous feds or annoying journalists like Hank Messick.

Don Aronow was a friend of Malnik's. The relationship stretched back at least to the early sixties. By the late seventies, Aronow was in constant contact with him, presumably as Lansky's intermediary. The men talked on the phone weekly and met often at Malnik's The Forge Restaurant. They swapped helicopters regularly. Aronow had firsthand information on Malnik. He could testify against him, possibly providing concrete proof of the numerous allegations that linked him incontrovertibly to Lansky and to the continuing existence of the operations of Lansky, Inc.

As a fed had explained, "It's not what you know, but what you can personally testify to that gets you killed."

Pete Wagner emphasized that all the dopers in Miami knew that Aronow had a power behind him. "Nobody fucked with him," he had said. Whoever gave the order to kill Aronow was now that power.

On the day before the murder, a large black limousine with dark-tinted windows had parked opposite the entrance to Aronow's new home. It looked ominous and out of place in the sunny, tropical environs. Don was inside the kitchen of the mansion, taking the first of the many strange phone calls that were made that day. No one was seen emerging from the limousine, and none of the neighbors or workers on the street could explain its presence. After a time, the limousine slid away.

Perhaps the new chairman of the board was taking one last look, still stunned that his associate of many years had turned on him.

It was easy to see why no one wanted Aronow's mob connections revealed. It was a Pandora's box for everyone concerned.

The MetroDade Homicide detectives were clearly under some kind of pressure to ease off that line of investigation, otherwise they could wind up pounding a beat chasing crack dealers in Overtown. Not surprisingly, they were pursuing the Aronow case with the same vigor that Rocky Pomerance's Miami Beach PD had investigated the 1967 Johnny Biello murder.

Lillian Aronow wanted her children to grow up thinking their father was a hero. That meant the real story had to be kept secret. Michael Aronow and Murray Weil had understood this double-edged reality much sooner than Don's widow.

U.S. Customs was no doubt also relieved. They were the ones who had officially awarded Aronow the contract for the Blue Thunder boats, even though everyone knew Bush was behind the selection. If

Don's mob associations and wiseguy-related smuggling activities surfaced, it could be sticky—especially in light of the country's increasing focus on drugs.

More damaging, they apparently knew long before the murder
that Aronow had, to use Special Agent Temple's words, "merged"
his company with Kramer, a drug kingpin.

Both Old Mike Kandrovicz and Bob Magoon say Customs discovered that Kramer had taken over USA Racing and consequently was
in charge of the Blue Thunder production. The agency confronted
Aronow with an ultimatum: take the company back or they would
cancel their order. The situation was corrected, on paper at least,
when the Super Chief $600,000 note was canceled. The Blue Thun-
der contract continued.

The fiasco was hushed up. No investigation was ever launched to
see if the poor performance of the boats—and their tendency to
blow up—had any connection to the fact that the company was in
the hands of the mob and a drug kingpin was overseeing the Blue
Thunder production. Despite the fact that Aronow had given his
government contract to a convicted narcotics trafficker who was the
target of a massive federal drug probe at that time, no one suggested
giving the contract to another boatbuilder.

Nor did anyone bother to see if the security of any of the government's antidrug operations had been compromised because of
Aronow, who continued to have access to a wide range of Interdiction Task Force officials because of his relationship with Bush.

It's unclear whether Bush knew about the Customs coverup when
it took place. His behavior during the last year of Aronow's life
suggests that he did not know about the USA Racing–Super Chief
deal.

While Bush initially seemed to want the murder solved, his actions
a few months after the slaying suggest that he had learned enough
to find the specter of a resolution to the murder disconcerting. At
some point, according to one of his Secret Service agents, Bush
would have learned the astonishing news that Aronow was actually
involved in drug smuggling. The murder and its aftermath coincided
with the start of his run for the presidency.

It was enough to give any presidential candidate sleepless nights.

What would the Democrats have done with the information that
as head of the Vice Presidential Joint Drug Task Group, George
Bush selected a man with links to two major crime families to build
the government's interdiction boats? More ironically, that the man
he chose was himself a drug smuggler (with a liking for hashish)

whose close mob associates ran the biggest heroin and marijuana operations in the country.

And how would Bush have explained that for a time the government's Blue Thunders were being built by the largest marijuana kingpin in history?

Fortunately for the Vice President, no one other than his personal "I" ever explored the Aronow-Kramer "merger." And the two top federal prosecutors who attempted to pursue the Aronow case in the critical last months of the presidential election just happened to get demoted or transferred out of town.

TWENTY-FIVE

A few weeks after George Bush is elected president of the United States, I make dinner plans with Jerry Engelman and his wife Barbara. We meet at a Cuban restaurant in Miami Beach. While we're waiting for our food to arrive, I tell Jerry I'm trying to figure out who "Alex Rizzo" really is. In the pack of wiseguy photos, I've slipped a snapshot of Wayne Bock.

MetroDade Homicide had always insisted that I not show any photographs of Frankie and Wayne to any of the witnesses, so I had held off. Now that months have passed, and with no apparent movement on the case, I feel free to run the pictures by some of the witnesses.

Jerry flips through them casually, laughing about the irony of his job with Don. "Here I leave Connecticut to get away from crime, and I wind up working for a guy who gets gunned down on the street by the mob," he says, chuckling. Suddenly he stops. "This guy—" He adjusts his bifocals. "Is this supposed to be the guy from the office?"

"What do you mean?" I ask, not wanting to sway his reaction. He's looking at Wayne Bock's photo.

"The man who came into the office the day Don was shot."

"You tell me."

Jerry stares at the photo. "I think it might be him. The cheek-bones. There was something about the man's cheekbones. And his nose, too. It was peculiar." He turns the photo toward me and points to Bock's distinctive beaklike nose. "It's certainly the same phy-sique," he continues. "The man was solid, real muscular shoulders and legs."

While Barbara examines the photos, Jerry becomes nervous and jumpy. He pushes back from the table and suddenly stands up. "Hey, look, I'm going," he declares, and abruptly walks out of the restau-rant.

I look at his wife across the table.

"Jerry's having an anxiety attack," she says quietly. "He'll come back when he calms down."

Engelman's reaction to Wayne Bock's photo surprises me at first. But it's normal. Who wants to be a witness to a mob murder? Espe-cially since the mob may be keeping track of more than just MetroDade's activities—they appear to be monitoring the witnesses as well. Since the murder, there have been a few unusual incidents, perhaps tests, to see what kind of witness Engelman would be.

Someone associated with Thunderboat Alley called him and sug-gested that he not speak to the press about Don. The man explained that "some things are best left alone."

Later, a wiseguy Jerry knew only as Frankie stopped by the Ft. Apache Marina. He suggested they go to lunch. A man named Paul Maestri joined them. The lunch seemed low-key and chummy, the men mostly chitchatting about the Alley and talking a bit about Aronow and the murder. But one thing struck Engelman as odd: the men insisted on a booth and they sat flanking him on one side of the booth.

Engelman hadn't known who Maestri was, but a fed recognized the name immediately. Maestri is a private investigator who has often visited Ben Kramer in prison and occasionally shares an office with Ben's attorney Kate Bonner.

The Kramers kept even closer watch on another witness. They hired Old Mike Kandrovicz as an employee and put him to work at the Apache plant in Hollywood.

Only one witness had actually seen the shooter in the Lincoln—the mysterious "secret witness" who saw the killer's face moments be-fore the shooting. The witness agrees to talk if I promise not to identify him. Since the man had already spoken to Lillian's people, it seems to be a meaningless gesture, but I agree.

We meet at the Ft. Apache bar. While we walk out to the murder scene, he describes the Lincoln for me. Previously he had relayed the details to me through Bob Magoon. Now in person he confirms what he had told Magoon: the car was a Lincoln Town Car with a half-coach roof and expensive turbo wheel covers.

We stop on the spot where Aronow died, and the man explains the incident. He was driving his truck out of Bobby Saccenti's parking lot seconds before Aronow. As he turned out of the driveway, he saw the dark Lincoln directly across the street. The window was down and the driver was staring at him. "Our eyes met," he recalls. "He was looking right at me sitting there with his arm hanging out the window. We locked eyes." When he turned onto the street, he looked over again and the man was still staring at him.

The witness says he had an uneasy feeling about the man. As he drove a quarter block up the street toward the Ft. Apache Marina, he looked into his rearview mirror. "I saw the Lincoln pull right next to Don's Mercedes," he remembers. "Then I heard the shots. I pulled into the first parking space. It was too late. By the time I parked and ran out to the street, the Lincoln ripped past me."

He doesn't believe there was time for the man in the Lincoln to have any conversation with Aronow before shooting him, despite what the papers reported. "It was all too fast," he observes, estimating that the entire sequence didn't last more than twenty or thirty seconds. "He didn't have time to say more than a word or two—if that—before shooting him and driving out of there."

We return to the Ft. Apache bar and sit at a table overlooking the waterway. In the twenty-two months since the murder, no one from MetroDade Homicide has ever shown him any photographs. He says he's surprised that nothing was done on the case, especially since Vice President Bush had been pushing to have it solved from the first night of the murder. He knew about Bush's involvement since he was at the police headquarters when the Vice President called.

"I was very dumbfounded," he recalls. "I was down in the MetroDade detective area when George Bush called that night. I was there, and he said that Don was his friend and he was gonna send some people down to help them find out what happened. I figured if anything was going to take precedence over this thing, this case would go places because who [Bush] was behind it. And then nothing happened. The only thing that I ever saw happening was the private investigator hired by Lillian."

I ask him about the composite he prepared the evening of the murder. Each of the witnesses had constructed one composite with the help of a police expert and a kit with different, interchangeable facial features. When the sketch was complete, the witness signed it.

He says the composite that ran in the *Miami Herald* two days after the murder was his. "No other witnesses contributed to that," he hastens to point out. "Each of us worked with the police artist on our own composite. Only mine ran in the paper."

"How accurate is your composite?" I ask.

"It's very close, but the hair isn't quite right. I told the police artist about that. Here, let me show you." He grabs my copy of the composite and changes the hairline slightly. He turns it toward me. Now, it looks even more like the booking picture I have of Frankie Schweihs.

I take out a stack of miscellaneous photos and ask him to tell me if he recognizes anyone. I hand them to him one at a time. He takes each one, examines it, and places it on the table in front of him forming a neat row. When I reach the middle of my packet—Frank Schweihs' mug shot—he freezes. He stares at the picture but he won't take it from my hand.

He has a peculiar look on his face. The same look Jerry Engelman had when he saw Wayne Bock's photo. I lean farther across the table, holding Frankie's picture directly in front of his face, prompting him to take it, but he won't touch it.

He continues staring at the photo without moving. "There are a lot of similarities," he finally says. "The eyes. The eyebrows. The mouth, too. The hairline."

"What are the chances that this is the man who shot Don Aronow?"

"It all happened so fast—" he begins, then falters. He hasn't taken his eyes off the photo yet. It's as if they're riveted to the picture. "The killer was a pretty good-sized gentleman," he continues. Schweihs is five feet eleven and broad shouldered.

My arm is getting tired as I hold the photo in front of him hoping that he'll take it and break the spell the picture has on him. "He had a dark complexion, not necessarily a tan, a dark complexion," he comments. "The complexion is the same. The chin is the same, too."

"What are the chances that he's the man who shot Don Aronow?" I repeat.

He sighs. "Seventy percent." He thinks for a second, then nods his head in confirmation. "I'd say seventy percent."

I ask again if I can use his name. His eyes open wide. "No!"

I explain to him that the bad guys know who he is. So does the *Miami Herald,* even though they've never identified him in print. He's better off being named publicly—that would prevent anyone from doing anything to him. But he won't even discuss the idea. He's adamant. "You can't use my name. No fucking way do I want to be named. I'll take my chances."

Three days after I've shown the photos of Wayne and Frankie to Jerry Engelman and the secret witness, I receive a frantic call from Jerry. He has just returned from MetroDade Homicide. Steve Parr had called and ordered him down to headquarters to look at some photographs. Jerry hadn't heard from MetroDade in eighteen months, and his first reaction to the episode was that he had been set up, that I was an undercover cop.

Steve Parr and Archie Moore took Engelman to a conference room. "They showed me some photos," Jerry tells me. "There were six on each sheet, two sheets. Many looked like Hispanics. I said to them, these guys aren't even close. The man who came into the office wasn't Latino."

Then Parr changed the subject. Had Jerry been talking to anyone about the case?

"Like to reporters?" Jerry asked.

"Yeah," Parr responded.

"Just that guy who's writing a book."

Parr asked Engelman if I had shown him any photos. Jerry nodded. "Was it this one?" he asked, pulling a large color print from a folder. "Yeah, that's the photo," Jerry replied. Parr and Moore looked at each other and fell silent. Finally Jerry asked, "Well, aren't you going to ask me if that's the guy who came into the office?"

"Is it?" Parr asked.

"Could be," Jerry responded. To his surprise, the detectives just thanked him and said he was dismissed.

Engelman wasn't the only one to receive a call from MetroDade Homicide that week. The secret witness got one as well. He's very upset and he, too, is starting to think that I'm working undercover for the police. "No one shows me anything for almost two years," he complains accusingly. "Then you come along, and bam! They're here with photos. What's going on?"

After he calms down, he describes his meeting with the cops, which took place at his office. "It was Mr. Slick with his fancy badge hanging on his belt," he says, referring to the smart-dressing Steve Parr. "And Archie Moore and an FBI agent named John Donovan. They showed me a series of photos. There were a lot of blond guys, but none of them looked like anything I saw. I kept waiting for the one you had shown me, but it wasn't there."

"Anything else happen?" I inquire.

"They wanted to know if I had been talking with anyone," he replies. "I said no. Then they asked me not to speak to anyone, and they left. I don't know what's going on, but I don't like it. Those motherfuckers can go to hell."

When MetroDade Homicide's Mike DeCora abruptly left Chicago in the second week of May 1988, he was hot on the trail of the 1985 Lincoln Town Car that Wayne and Frankie had been spotted in nine days after the Aronow murder. DeCora had said that he wanted to find the car to see if it had a half coach roof and "fancy hubcaps," the so-called turbo wheel covers. These special hubcaps were quite rare, and DeCora seemed to consider them an important detail.

But he left Chicago before tracking down the Lincoln. Shortly after, the Lincoln disappeared from Illinois DMV records once again. The car was covering a lot of territory. Jerry Gladden had vowed to track down its new location for me. It had taken several months, but he was finally successful.

This time the car is registered in Indiana to a John McLeod. I call the new owner. He's not home, but his wife is talkative and agrees to answer some questions about their Lincoln. She says that the car is a 1985 model, "very dark blue, almost black in color."

"What kind of hubcaps does it have?"

"The car's out in front and I'm looking at it," she responds. "It's not like spokes on a bicycle, but bigger, the spokes are big. They're what you call turbo, the heavy-looking things in a circle."

"And does the car have a half or full coach roof?"

"Half."

The car that Wayne and Frankie were in when they were surveilled in Miami Beach on February 12, 1987, just nine days after the murder matched the description of the vehicle used in the hit in every detail. DeCora's sudden callback to Miami kept him from finding another compelling connection between two of the Mafia's top hit men and the murderers of Don Aronow.

DeCora's departure from Chicago marked an abrupt turn in the investigation. MetroDade never followed up on the car with Chicago OCB, and although they had pictures of the Mafia's deadly duo, they never used them in a photo lineup with the witnesses. Clearly, MetroDade Homicide was not pursuing the Frankie-and-Wayne angle anymore.

But something was going on, and the photo lineup they conducted with the witnesses indicated that they had two suspects, a dark-skinned man and a blond suspect. Curiously, they showed the Latino photos to Engelman, who had only seen the sandy-haired man in the office; they showed the blond suspects to the witness who only saw the shooter, a dark-haired, dark-complected man.

The Aronow team still doesn't respond to my calls, so I contact a DEA agent on the Isle of Man Task Force. He has some information on the new course that the Aronow case is taking, and it explains what's been going on. MetroDade has been investigating a lead from a jail house informant named Tommy Teagle.

"We put Teagle away as one part of the Isle of Man investigation," the DEA agent explains. Teagle worked with a group of smugglers and money launderers who, like the Kramers, were exposed when the feds got hold of offshore accountant Shaun Murphy's records. Teagle was convicted on eight counts of drug smuggling and sentenced to three years in prison. "While he was in prison, he contacted us with this story about Aronow being killed by a man named Bobby Young," the DEA agent says. "It was about six months ago, in May [1988]." The timing of the new lead coincides precisely with DeCora's abrupt departure from Chicago.

Teagle had assured the feds that he had everything for them on the Aronow case. He knew where the car was, where the gun was, the reason why Young killed Aronow. He said he even had the shirt the killer was wearing covered with Aronow's blood.

According to Teagle, Robert "Bobby" Young had stolen eighty kilos of cocaine from Colombian drug kingpins. The South American smugglers were going to execute Young. But then they decided to give him a chance to live. The drug lords showed him a list of names and told Bobby that if he killed someone on that list, his debt would be wiped clean.

Don Aronow had been placed on the death list, Teagle told the DEA agents, because he also had welshed on a cocaine debt with the Colombians. According to Teagle, Don Aronow and George Bush's son Jeb were partners in a major cocaine-smuggling operation, and they owed their Colombian suppliers $2.5 million. Jeb and Don had refused to pay.

Bobby Young agreed to kill Aronow. The Colombians flew him to a secret place in the jungles of South America where he underwent rigorous training for the assassination. Then they returned him to Miami. But they didn't provide Young with any weapons, so he borrowed a gun and a dark Lincoln Town Car from a man named "Skip" Walton. Young then killed Aronow, discarded the pistol in a storm sewer near an underpass on Interstate 95, and returned the car to Walton.

Teagle told the feds that murder was easy for Bobby Young. He had killed a lot of other people besides Don Aronow. More than thirty. The bodies were buried on a farm in northern Florida. Teagle also said he knew what had happened to Aronow's prized Rolex championship watch that had mysteriously disappeared from the scene. Young had torn the watch from Aronow's wrist because he liked taking Rolex watches from his victims. That's how Young got Aronow's blood all over his shirt, Tommy said.

Teagle reminded the DEA agents that Young had taken a Rolex from another of his murder victims. In 1985, the body of Young's cocaine-smuggling partner John "Big Red" Panzavecchia was found with four .25-caliber bullets through the skull. Big Red had a solid-gold Rolex, but when his body was fished out of a Broward County canal, it was missing the Rolex. Young was a suspect in that case. Teagle told the agents that Young took the watch from Big Red and he took Aronow's as well.

As he relates Tommy Teagle's tale to me, the DEA agent has been doing his best to contain a persistent smirk. He pauses to get my reaction, then says, "Tommy's a cokehead. Want to hear the rest?" I nod and he continues.

While the DEA agents found the story bizarre, it wasn't until they questioned Tommy about the details of the hit that they began to find irreconcilable discrepancies between Teagle's story and the eye-witness accounts of the murder. Teagle told DEA agents that there were two men in the Lincoln when Aronow was hit. A man named Carl "C.D." Davis was driving. Young was in the passenger seat as the Lincoln pulled alongside the Mercedes, pointing in the same direction as Aronow's vehicle.

The Isle of Man investigators were entertained by Teagle's *Miami Vice*–like story line complete with nefarious Colombian drug lords —everybody's favorite villains in the drug wars. And they didn't miss the fact that Teagle was asking for early release from prison for himself as well as a deal for Walton, his friend. Skip Walton was under federal indictment for "murder on the high seas" and cocaine trafficking in an unrelated case. Since the information contradicted what they knew of the Aronow incident, the feds gave Teagle's story little thought but felt obliged to pass the lead on to MetroDade Homicide anyway. Assistant U.S. Attorney Lothar Genge put Teagle in touch with MetroDade.

Mike DeCora interviewed Teagle. He listened, asked questions about the type of gun, the car, and the way the hit went down. Then he told Teagle that the details didn't fit.

Teagle felt he had important information. Not only would he receive the $100,000 reward that was still offered in the case for a lead to Aronow's murderer, but for a con in prison, information about a major crime was more valuable than money. It could bring a quick end to hard time. Teagle wasn't giving up his story even though both the Isle of Man feds and MetroDade rejected it as being full of holes. He continued talking about it to anyone who would listen.

Finally, Teagle turned to the media. He called a local Miami TV reporter, complaining that he had risked his life in order to bring Robert Young to the attention of authorities, and he was being ignored. He claimed the Aronow case was fixed because of the Jeb Bush connection, and no one would pay any attention to him because George Bush was now the president. The reporter called Metro-Dade.

This call evidently galvanized MetroDade Homicide into action. This time the detectives took the Teagle lead more seriously. Steve Parr and Archie Moore were promptly ordered to conduct a photo lineup with each of the witnesses—a procedure that coincidentally took place just three days after I had shown photos of Frankie and Wayne to Engelman and the secret witness. The target of Metro-Dade's photo lineup was the blond-haired Robert Young; the Hispanic pictures were presumably for the driver of the Lincoln.

None of the witnesses selected the photo of Young or made any other identifications. Since the pictures generated not a spark of recognition, and the Teagle story contradicted so much of the evidence, the detectives decided not to pursue it any further.

But Tommy Teagle found one champion for his story anyway. As a reward for coming forward with the information about Young, he was paroled by Federal judge Edward B. Davis after serving only 10 percent of his sentence.

TWENTY-SIX

On April 26, 1989, President George Bush visits Miami. He is completing his first hundred days in office. In an effort to counter some inevitable negative assessments of his leadership, he has embarked on a whirlwind tour of a handful of states trumpeting his antidrug message.

The day before in California he had stopped at Rancho Del Rio, a huge ranch once owned by a drug kingpin. It was an extravaganza photo op in which the President, standing in front of mounds of confiscated drugs and cash, warned drug smugglers in no uncertain terms that he was coming after them. There would be no respite for the "dealers in death."

In Miami, he speaks to an assembly of Drug Enforcement Administration agents in an attempt to bolster their sagging morale on the front line. The leader is exhorting his weary troops into battle. Not everyone attends. A DEA agent who had investigated Aronow's links to Joey Ippolito's smuggling empire has declined the invitation.

He is instead in his office when I call.

"So how come you're not out there with the President?" I ask.

He emits a sound of disgust. "Hell, I don't want to get anywhere near that guy."

The fed, like many agents in the trenches, is unimpressed by Bush's antidrug pronouncements. He's become cynical about the government's efforts to stem the drug problem, particularly when, as he notes, the President "is the guy who bought interdiction boats from Don Aronow."

In his speech to the agents, the President blames the drug problem on American companies for selling chemicals overseas that are used in the processing of narcotics in South America. Bush also announces his plan to have the International Association of Longshoremen help in the War on Drugs. He wants the union to ask its members to patrol the nation's docks and keep an eye out for suspicious cargo. No doubt IAL head Anthony Scotto and his good friend former marijuana kingpin Joey Ippolito, Jr., plus a lot of other wiseguy dopers are delighted with the suggestion.

During his stop in Miami, the President makes no mention of a headline-making jail-break attempt that had the city abuzz. It had occurred the previous week. Convicted drug kingpin Ben Kramer had tried to escape from the Miami Federal Correctional Facility.

Kramer had evidently realized that he was in one mess that even Lansky, Inc. couldn't handle. He had been sentenced a few months before in Illinois to life imprisonment with no chance of parole. While he was in a Florida prison, waiting to be tried on the Isle of Man indictments, he attempted to escape.

The plan was daring. A small helicopter was to drop into the prison yard at recreation time, pick Ben up, and fly him to a waiting plane in the Everglades. From there it was just a few minutes out of the country. Freedom, money, and an estate in Colombia were waiting for him.

The helicopter appeared. Kramer jumped on the runner. They began lifting off. Abruptly, the tail rotor caught on the barbed wire. The craft was flipped vertical, whipped over the fence, and slammed onto the ground. Kramer was thrown thirty feet. Both he and the pilot were severely injured.

There had been only one hitch in the plan: a small helicopter had been required because of the narrow size of the recreation compound, but Kramer had eaten so much during his months in prison that he had put on fifty pounds. The additional load had thrown the helicopter off balance.

It was, as Miami feds laughed delightedly, "another Benny fuckup."

The story was carried on all the national television networks. Kramer was described as an international powerboating champion who had become a marijuana kingpin. No mention was made of his mob associations, his connection to the President's close friend Aronow, or his involvement in the Blue Thunder program.

George Bush doesn't mention it either when he talks to the Miami DEA agents about stopping the drug kingpins who are destroying American society. He also fails to mention that because of his actions, one of those very kingpins infiltrated his Vice Presidential South Florida Drug Task Force. No doubt those who knew the real story behind Kramer breathed a collective sigh of relief that Ben's role in the government's War on Drugs remained a secret.

After Bush leaves town, the U.S. Marshals Service announces an investigation into the attempted jailbreak. They say there is reason to believe that someone other than Kramer masterminded the escape and they are confident they will be able to determine who was behind the plan. Later they announce that the pilot appears to have some connection to Kramer's younger brother. Subsequently, Mark Kramer, a twenty-nine-year-old California law student, pleads guilty to conceiving and implementing the escape plot all by himself. No further leads are pursued. Like most investigations concerning the real powers behind Lansky, Inc. it comes to naught.

A week after President Bush's speech in Miami, I hear from Bob Magoon. "I have some information that is going to shock you. It's going to shock you like you've never been shocked," he exclaims. "A friend called me and said that a person told him there's going to be an indictment in the Aronow case within the month. Some known murderer, a drug dealer named Robert Young. This friend is a very prominent criminal attorney."

Magoon says the new revelations, particularly those about the motive, are very disturbing to him and to Lillian Aronow, who refuses to believe them. Magoon has heard that Aronow and Jeb Bush owed some Colombian drug lords money on a cocaine deal and wouldn't pay. Young was sent to kill Aronow. So the murder is solved, Magoon says, and any day it's going to be announced in the paper.

Months pass, and no announcements are made. Tommy Teagle, relishing his freedom from prison, goes into high gear telling his story to everyone who will listen. In meetings with his probation officer and various federal agents (he's acting as an informant for the DEA and the FBI on other, unrelated cases), he relays the ongoing developments at MetroDade in the Aronow investigation.

He tells the agents that homicide detectives have told him an indictment is imminent. He's also heard Carl "C.D." Davis, the man Teagle says drove the Lincoln as Young shot Aronow, is going to show police where the gun was dumped and lead them to the car.

Despite the apparent progress, Tommy fears for his life. He's not worried about Young, who's already tucked away in prison serving two concurrent seventeen-year sentences for a 1985 murder and a 1987 attempted murder and kidnapping. Tommy's big fear is the President. He thinks George Bush will have him killed because his information implicates Jeb Bush in cocaine smuggling. His protection, he feels, is in having the press know the full story.

A fed calls to say that Tommy wants to talk to me. When I phone Teagle in the summer of 1989, he's guarded at first. "Are you a probation officer?" he asks suspiciously. Besides George Bush, Teagle worries about probation officers—the people who could put him right back into the penitentiary for parole infractions. Reassured, he recaps his information on the Aronow murder.

"The scoop of it was that I was not involved in it whatsoever," Teagle begins. He says he just told authorities what he had heard, "that's it." In the spring of 1988, while still in federal prison, he had contacted federal authorities and told them that he heard from a friend named Skip Walton that Bobby Young had murdered Aronow. Arrangements were made for Tommy Teagle to talk with Mike DeCora, who told Tommy the information didn't sound right. For one thing, Aronow was shot with a different kind of gun from the one Teagle describes. "But that was just one little detail," Teagle protests. Things didn't go any better when Tommy insisted on another meeting with MetroDade Homicide.

"I told them [about Robert Young] in front of just about everybody and they just like laughed at me," Teagle recalls. "And nothing happened. I went crazy. I thought when I was sitting in jail that there was some kind of government cover-up. It was like, man, I've been telling everybody. And nobody wanted to listen. I called this woman who's on TV and told her what had happened. I said something's wrong here. Something's drastically wrong here."

Tommy says *that* got action, real quick. "All of a sudden they came to me again to talk," he exclaims. "They all flocked to see me." He says that at first Archie Moore was in charge, then Mike DeCora took over. "DeCora was off and then he's back on the case again. I don't know how that happened because he's the one who told me my story didn't sound like, you know—" He laughs.

He tells me that the FBI is also involved in the case. Teagle wants them to arrange a deal for his friend Skip Walton, who is facing prosecution on federal drug charges in an Oklahoma drug case. "I proceeded to get with Skip to work out a deal, but then my probation officer told me not to talk to him," Teagle explains. "But I heard there are some complications with Skip and the FBI. He's stuck up in Oklahoma in some solitary room."

Tommy can't understand the problem and why they're delaying in nailing Young. "I said to them, I can solve this in ten minutes," he points out. "Bring Skip here, put him in a room with C.D. [the alleged driver for Young during the murder], and it's over. Skip already said he's ready to do it."

I tell Teagle that I've learned he heard about Bobby Young's involvement from his friend Skip Walton a year and a half after the murder. That's wrong, he says. "I first heard it through Rick Fidlin; he was Bobby's partner," he corrects me firmly.

Then Teagle proceeds to tell me his current version of the Aronow killing. He says that Bobby Young called Rick Fidlin after the murder and asked him to come meet him and help him to get rid of the car. Fidlin went to Teagle's house the very next day and told him all about the hit.

"You knew about this the day after Aronow was shot?"

"Yeah, the next night. Rick came over and said, 'Hey, Bobby's shot somebody, again.' Rick was all panicky, he thought Bobby was going to kill him because he knew too much." According to Teagle, Bobby Young left Thunderboat Alley after killing Aronow and drove south to the Omni Mall. There Young went into a barbershop, got a haircut, and called Fidlin to come pick him up.

"And Fidlin said that Skip Walton loaned his car to Young?" I ask, remembering the story Teagle first told the DEA agents.

"No, it was a rental car," Teagle corrects me once again. "Budget Rental Car."

I don't have the chance to ask Tommy if Bobby Young walked into the Omni Mall with a shirt covered with blood, because he continues excitedly with his story.

After Young got a haircut, he and Fidlin drove to the Budget Rental office in Ft. Lauderdale to turn the car in. "When they returned the car, the [rental] agent found .45 shells on the floor," Teagle explains. "He said, 'Hey, you guys. You forgot something.' And the rental car guy gave them back the casings."

Teagle's story seems to evolve as he tells it to different people and learns about the discrepancies in his version. When Teagle originally contacted the Isle of Man feds with his information, he had told them the Lincoln used in the hit belonged to Skip Walton's girlfriend. Now he's evidently aware that some people claimed there was a rental-company sticker on it. In his first meeting with DeCora, Teagle claimed Young had used some weapon other than a .45 pistol; now he mentions the correct caliber.

Mike DeCora had told me early in the investigation that all but one spent shell casing was recovered from the murder scene, and that the Lincoln had what appeared to be a National Car Rental sticker on the bumper. Because of the sticker, MetroDade had scoured all kinds of rental car companies throughout Florida even into Georgia.

Yet Teagle was saying the car was rented not thirty miles from the murder scene and returned the afternoon of the murder—with a number of bullet casings on the floor in full view of the car rental agent. His story suggests that despite all the media coverage about Aronow's killer driving away in a Lincoln, no one at the Budget Rental office ever made the connection or contacted the police, although a Lincoln littered with spent shells was returned to them just hours after the well-publicized murder.

Teagle also says that there were two people in the Lincoln. Yet, the secret witness, who had an elevated vantage point in his truck, insists there was only one person in the vehicle. Mike Harrison, who saw the entire incident, also states emphatically there was one person. And that one man, the driver, shot Aronow. Both men maintain that Don's Mercedes and the Lincoln were pointed in opposite directions, not, as Teagle tells me, the same direction.

In later meetings with the feds, Teagle modifies his statements again. He tells the agents that the cars were pointed in opposite directions and that Young in the passenger seat had leaned across the driver, Carl Davis, and fired out the driver's-side window. But Teagle doesn't explain how Young pulled the Rolex from Aronow's wrist or got blood all over his shirt when he's on the opposite side of the car from the Mercedes in this version.

Teagle tells me that Homicide detectives are searching for the Budget Rental customer service agent who spotted the shells and returned them to Bobby Young. He assures me that the man will be located soon. Still, he complains, the case is moving too slowly. "I just called Metro down there this morning," he grumbles. "I asked this one guy, Parr. I said, 'Hey, sit with him [Skip Walton] and Carl ["C.D." Davis] and get it over with. It just doesn't make sense to wait to get them together.'

"So who went into Aronow's office the day of the murder?" I ask Teagle.

"That was Bobby [Young]. He went in and bullshitted Aronow about a boat. That was first before he went over to that Apache place."

"What does Young look like?"

"About five feet nine inches, husky voice," Teagle replies. "Slept on my couch many a night. I did many deals with him. I know him real well. He's a scumbag. He's a mental case."

Teagle says he goes back a long way with Bobby Young. Their relationship began many years ago when Young was kidnapped in Colombia for ripping off the Colombians in a coke deal. "The way that whole thing [our relationship] started," Teagle recalls, "is Bobby was kidnapped down in Colombia and I had this dancer come to me and say they were going to kill him down there. She said we had to come up with eighty thousand dollars. So I got the money together [to pay off the Colombians for the stolen cocaine] and brought him up here [to Miami], and then he rips me off. He becomes a madman. Get's a load of coke in here, starts killing people."

The story is getting quite confusing. Teagle is now saying that Young has come close to being killed twice by the Colombians for stealing cocaine from them. The first time Teagle raised $80,000 and saved him. The second time, Young agreed to kill Aronow in return for his life, or at least that's what Teagle had told the Isle of Man feds.

"So why did Young kill Aronow?" I ask, expecting to hear about eighty missing kilos of cocaine and the death list with Don Aronow's name on it.

"That's the fishy part." Teagle hesitates. "I think it was some old vendetta." Jeb Bush has been dropped from his story.

Then Tommy quickly changes the subject, brightening up as he promises me, "You know, Young's going to go to the electric chair on this one."

"But nobody identified him as the killer," I point out.

"What do you mean nobody?" He sounds surprised.

"The witnesses in the Aronow case."

"That's fine," he says cavalierly.

"Has MetroDade told you that somebody had identified the pictures?"

"Noooo." Teagle pauses. "I don't know who you are anymore, you know what I mean? I don't want to get into any of this anymore. I'm on probation, I don't need all these problems. It's a very touchy situation." With that, he hangs up.

Florida Department of Law Enforcement files indicate that Young was thirty-eight years old when Aronow was murdered. He has blond hair, blue eyes, stands 5′ 10″, and weighs 180 pounds.

No photo lineup was required to realize that Young wasn't the hulking sandy-haired man who walked into the USA Racing office minutes before the murder. That man was as big and imposing as Don Aronow. He was the same height, 6′ 4″, and even more muscular, his weight surpassing Aronow's 225 pounds by at least ten or fifteen pounds. Robert Young, who is six inches shorter and forty-five pounds lighter than Aronow, would've been dwarfed standing next to Don that day.

Young doesn't fit the description of the olive-complexioned, dark-haired shooter. Nor does his photo resemble the composite the secret witness had prepared of the man in the Lincoln Town Car.

It was clear why none of the Aronow witnesses identified Young's photo.

I try calling Teagle a few weeks later to discuss these discrepancies, but I learn he's back in prison. His probation officer had been monitoring him for drug use, and in surprise urine tests, Tommy had repeatedly tested positive for cocaine. He was deemed in violation of his parole and a warrant was issued for his arrest.

Even though the U.S. Probation Commission was adamant about putting him back in prison, Teagle almost got out of it. Dade County Assistant State Attorney Gary Rosenberg, head of the county's Homicide Prosecution Unit, fought vigorously on his behalf at a federal hearing, asking that the feds give Teagle another chance. The plea failed, and Teagle was ordered back to the federal penitentiary.

While MetroDade's top homicide prosecutor, Gary Rosenberg, wanted Teagle on the outside, it seems more than likely MetroDade Homicide detectives were relieved to have him out of their hair. Teagle had told me that they were getting very aggravated with his constant calling.

Teagle's motivation in so persistently pushing Robert Young as a suspect in Aronow's murder is a mystery to the federal agents who have dealt with him for years. His single-minded devotion is out of character, they say. Despite being brushed off repeatedly by the Homicide detectives and facing the ridicule of Isle of Man federal agents, he ardently pushed his story. As he told me, he called "every prosecutor in town, every detective I could think of" and even turned to the media to generate pressure on MetroDade to pursue Robert Young as Aronow's killer.

He was "possessed," as one federal agent put it. Yet Teagle, who had told me he knew about the murder the day after it occurred, spent more than six months in prison for his 1987 Isle of Man narcotics conviction before approaching authorities with his story. It was a long time to sit on information that could, and subsequently did, get him out of jail early.

The Teagle story surfaced just as DeCora was about to find a Lincoln that matched the eyewitnesses' descriptions perfectly. Was it simply coincidence or was some power behind the scenes once again steering the investigation away from potentially explosive territory? In either case, the timing was remarkable.

Teagle contacted authorities the week after Mike DeCora was recalled from Chicago where he was on the verge of finding Wayne and Frankie's Lincoln. Instead of looking for a dark blue Town Car with turbo wheel covers and a half coach roof, the Aronow investigators were back at the "Colombian drug lord" theory of the murder.

Federal files on Teagle reveal that he was once a codefendant in a smuggling case with Randy Lanier. Former Indy 500 winner Lanier was a partner in Ben Kramer's drug-smuggling operation, and like Kramer he was sentenced to life imprisonment as a drug kingpin. Yet Teagle, associated with Lanier in several large dope deals, denies knowing Kramer or anyone else in his organization.

Edward B. Davis is the judge who had paroled Teagle in 1988 as a reward for coming forward with the information that Young killed Aronow. He once chastised a federal law enforcement officer for writing in a report that Joe Sonken's Gold Coast Restaurant was a mob hangout. Davis ordered the fed to remove the reference, adding that he ate at the restaurant often and the food was great. Judge Davis is a friend of former Gerstein aide David Goodhart.

It is a small world after all.

When Tommy Teagle told me his story, there was something he didn't know. His efforts on behalf of his friend William "Skip" Walton had already paid off. On June 13, 1989, Walton signed a plea bargain agreement. In return for testifying that Robert Young murdered Don Aronow, Oklahoma federal prosecutors and the Dade County State's Attorney's Office guaranteed that Walton would serve no more than five years in prison on a variety of drug-trafficking charges. Without the deal, these convictions would have put Walton in jail for several decades.

Not everyone was happy about the plea bargain with Walton. Miami FBI special agent Nicky Deary had vigorously opposed it. She didn't think Teagle and Walton's story made any sense. No one paid attention to her objections when the deal was being hammered out. Still she persisted in fighting it every step of the way. Ms. Deary is no longer important. She has become suddenly unemployed.

Shortly after New Year's, 1990, the Florida federal money-laundering case against the Kramers, Mel Kessler, and Michael Gilbert begins in the federal courthouse in Ft. Lauderdale, Florida.

Representing Jack Kramer is Meyer Lansky's attorney E. David Rosen. Rosen's son Lawrence assists Kate Bonner and noted attorney Albert Krieger in Benny's defense. Former federal prosecutor Michael Pasano represents Michael Gilbert. Michael's father, Sam, the noted Los Angeles "philanthropist," is deceased.

For the government, it has been a long process that has involved the efforts of many people over six years. It first began in 1983 with Jo Ann Pepper's investigations of Benny's extravagant $10,000 weekends in New York City. Rory McMahon restarted the stalled Kramer investigation in 1985, and the Isle of Man investigators picked up the ball soon after, aided by Shaun Murphy's accounting records.

Along the way the feds had prepared the fateful February 1987 subpoena—the one with Donald Aronow's name on it. But by the time the trial actually begins, Aronow has been dead for almost three years and he no longer casts a potential threat over the proceedings. His absence from the story seems to be welcomed. Certainly the prosecution team, lead by Assistant U.S. Attorney Bob Bondi, makes no reference to him, despite Aronow's entanglement with the Kramers.

The proceedings are slow and tedious, unlike Ben Kramer's fiery and bitter Illinois federal trial. In those 1988 proceedings, the most damaging testimony came from convicted members of Ben's smuggling operation. Krieger, nicknamed the "dean of defense attorneys," represented Ben in that trial as well, and he savaged the government's "stoolie" witnesses. But in Florida, the most incriminating testimony is financial in nature—complete with complex charts, graphs, and international-banking and wire-transfer statements that would give a CPA a headache. Almost six thousand documents are introduced into evidence.

When a Liechtenstein banking official refuses to come to the United States to testify for the government about the Kramer accounts there, the prosecution and defense teams fly to Europe to interview him. A court reporter goes along and takes down the proceedings. Then transcripts are prepared, and back in the Florida courtroom the judge and the attorneys role play, reenacting the banker's four days of testimony for the benefit of an increasingly restless jury. The judge gets to play the local magistrate who presided over the Liechtenstein sessions, and the attorneys take turns playing the banker and themselves.

Bit by bit, the Isle of Man prosecutors reconstruct the vast money-laundering side of the Kramer drug empire. Halfway through the eleven-week trial it becomes apparent that the tide is turning against the defendants.

Jack Kramer shows the strain first. U.S. marshals report that he cries when he's returned to his cell at night. Kessler is looking haggard and spends much of his time picking his fingernails. Only Benny seems to be holding up. He smiles and waves to people he recognizes in the gallery and writes a lot of notes to his attorney Kate Bonner. The Florida trial is a welcome relief for Ben. His last few years have been a bleak existence in the hellhole known as the Marion, Illinois, Federal Penitentiary. Federal agents say Benny enjoys working closely with Bonner. They emphasize the word "closely." Once, while Kramer was still in the hospital recuperating from his failed escape attempt, the two were indelicately interrupted by a visit from a guard.

When the jury finally begins its deliberations, the Isle of Man feds are exuberant. In the beginning their case had not gone well, and many of their witnesses, particularly against Mel Kessler, had been disallowed. But then the overwhelming evidence against the defendants became obvious, and by the end the prosecutors are confident of success.

The jurors take more than a week to make up their minds. They return their verdicts on March 28, 1990, and it's a clean sweep for the government. All four defendants are convicted.

Ben is found guilty of twenty-eight of thirty-two charges. His father catches twenty of twenty-three charges. Mel Kessler garners twenty-one of the twenty-six charges against him. All three are found guilty on two racketeering counts. The fourth defendant, Michael Gilbert, is found guilty of lesser charges.

After the verdict, Judge Norman Roettger, not-so-affectionately known as "the hanging judge," asks the prosecution to confirm his recollection that each of the most serious counts, the racketeering charges, carry up to a twenty-year prison sentence on each count. Assistant U.S. Attorney Bob Bondi enthusiastically confirms that the judge is correct. Two counts means forty years, but Bondi hastens to add, that's before adding additional time for the other charges. With those included, the sentences could total over a hundred years for each of the three major defendants.

Benny prides himself on his tough-guy image. His life has been marked by life-threatening escapades, tough physical adventure, and a proclivity for the rough and tumble. He was a hands-on smuggler, racing the boats, making the mad dashes to shore with drug caches. He's already serving life imprisonment without chance of parole; this latest conviction changes nothing. And he's young, still convinced that he won't spend his life in prison.

But his father, Jack, sixty, is quite different. Jack's a schmoozer, a talker, who likes the good life, a little fun, and doesn't mind playing on the wrong side of the law as long as it's not violent, demanding, or uncomfortable. He was the paper man, the man who made the phone calls, moved some of the money, and took trips to the exotic offshore locations. He's found life in jail for even a few months almost unbearable. Now he's facing the very real prospect of growing old and dying in prison.

When the verdict is announced, it's likely his thoughts turn to the possibility of making a deal with the government. Giving up someone in return for a lighter sentence could have a chance of getting himself and his son out of prison after serving some time.

Jack knows that he has to offer important information. The government has the Kramer case locked up and they aren't interested in any little tidbits. Both Jack and Ben know the full story of Thunderboat Alley. They know about the subpoena and the murder of Don Aronow. They know the "big boss," the man behind Lansky, Inc., and the man who gave the order to kill Aronow before he received the subpoena. They know the decision to talk is usually answered with a bullet.

Still, facing life in prison, and worse, knowing his son is facing the same fate, maybe Jack, like Aronow, considers talking, taking the chance. Perhaps he even contemplates testifying against the man who ordered the hit on a friend of the President of the United States. How is he to know that the last thing the government wants is for the real story to come out?

While Jack's mind is in turmoil, he is unaware that the people behind him are leaving nothing to chance. Especially now that the convictions are in. And if Jack thinks about trading information, a powerful hand is already closing the window of opportunity for a deal. In less than six hours, the opportunity to "offer" Don Aronow's murderer to the feds will be gone forever.

Later that same day, in a courtroom thirty miles south in Dade County, a secret state grand jury is listening to the testimony of three informants. Skip Walton, Carl "C.D." Davis, and Rick Fidlin are brought in one by one. When they are finished, Assistant State Attorney Gary Rosenberg asks the panel to indict Robert "Bobby" Young for the murder of Donald Aronow.

The indictment is sealed. No announcements are made, and the jurors are sworn to secrecy.

Two weeks after the secret Young indictment, the *Miami Herald* runs a front-page story on the Aronow case. There is no suggestion of an indictment. The story says only that Young is a suspect.

No mention is made either of Teagle's tale about Jeb Bush and Don Aronow owing money to the Colombians. Instead, the article suggests that investigators now believe that Ben Kramer may have ordered the murder. The business-deal-gone-sour-with-Aronow-as-hard-as-nails motive has evidently been revived. It's likely Jack and Ben read between the lines and saw another message—the logical conclusion of this theme is the electric chair for Benny.

Speedboat King's Death Still a Puzzle

Robert S. Young, a self-described mercenary with a fondness for call girls, guns, and mean dogs, is the hit man who gunned down Donald Aronow, the legendary speedboat demon, investigators suspect.

And Benjamin Barry Kramer, the world champion fast-boat millionaire, could have ordered the daytime ambush after he and Aronow squabbled over a shady business deal, some investigators surmise.

The murder of Aronow, shot to death three years ago, seems to be unraveling as one of the most sensational chapters in the nation's drug story. . . . No one has been charged. Investigators don't have the proof. Maybe they never will.

Miami Herald assistant managing editor Gene Miller is said to have been very uncomfortable about the story. He insisted reporter Sydney Freedberg include in her article that Robert Young "does not match a composite drawing of the Lincoln's driver made from eyewitness accounts." Some people thought the paper was being used, that the whole affair was simply a "trial balloon" by Dade County State Attorney Janet Reno to see what would happen when Young's name was mentioned as the murderer.

Janet Reno is a protégé of Richard Gerstein. She got her start in government in the early 1970s when she accepted a position as personal aide to Gerstein, then state attorney. She took the post despite the fact that her late father, *Herald* police reporter Henry O. Reno, had made allegations that Richard Gerstein was on the take. Years later when Gerstein stepped down as state attorney, Janet Reno became his successor.

Finally, two months after Freedberg's *Herald* article appears and more than two years after Tommy Teagle first told MetroDade Homicide his story, the Dade County State Attorney's Office announces the murder indictment of Robert Young. Young's lawyer, Virgil C. Black, tells the *Herald* that his client was aware for some time that he was a suspect in the murder.

Black also tells the paper that he just recently took Young on as a client. Previously, Robert Young had another lawyer, who had to stop representing Young when he himself was convicted of criminal charges in another case. That attorney used to work for Meyer Lansky. His name: Mel Kessler.

In the years since Don Aronow was murdered, the same faces keep flitting about in the background. It is happening again. Mel Kessler, one of Lansky, Inc.'s top people, had represented the man who was now wearing the mantle of Don Aronow's killer. For Young, the newest charge should rest lightly on his shoulders. He's a convict who is already serving so much time for his other murder, attempted murder, and narcotics convictions that he could easily plead guilty to the slaying and not spend any extra time in jail. Curiously, the murder conviction could make life even better for Young.

A deal between Young and the state means that no real evidence would be required linking him to the murder. For Young, it could mean a more comfortable cell in a nicer prison than his present digs at Florida's nightmarish Raiford State Correctional Facility.

The sinister circle is closing in upon itself.

Despite the fact that Robert Young has been in custody on one charge or another since June 1988, no one has ever put him in a lineup. With the unsealing of the first-degree murder indictment, it can be postponed no longer.

All the witnesses except one are called to MetroDade on June 14, 1990. For some reason, the stubborn (and uncontrollable) "Old Mike" Kandrovicz, isn't invited. When the witnesses arrive at headquarters, they are overwhelmed by their reception. Heavily armed police are everywhere; the halls are bristling with activity.

The witnesses are told there will be a delay before the lineup and they are brought into a room together to sit and wait. Patty Lezaca announces to the witnesses that she has seen photographs and knows that Robert Young is the man who killed Aronow. She says she has come to the conclusion that there was actually only one man involved in Aronow's murder after all—not two as they had thought.

Patty also says she has some good news for everybody. Don was killed by the Colombians because he was helping the United States government fight the War on Drugs. She says police now say that Don was a hero who died for his country.

Jerry Engelman doesn't say much. He finds it odd that they should all be permitted to talk together before going into the lineup. As a lawyer, he thinks it isn't the best way to conduct a lineup. And he isn't happy that Patty is taking charge, trying to influence everyone just as she had on the day of the murder. But he decides not to say anything.

The Homicide staff is fully represented by Mike DeCora, Archie Moore, Steve Parr, Mike Diaz. Gary Rosenberg as the state prosecutor on the case is there, too. Dade Country State Attorney Janet Reno insists on personally supervising the lineup herself.

Finally, the witnesses are called into the lineup one by one. The room is crowded with Reno, Rosenberg, Young's lawyer, a stenographer, and the four detectives. Everyone faces the huge one-way window to see the six men on the stage. They are all dressed in red jumpsuits, the official garment of the Dade County jail. One is Bobby Young, the others are police officers.

The witnesses are given all the time they want to look at the men on the platform. They are told to make a selection when they're sure.

Despite the dramatic buildup—an impressive show with thirty armed guards watching over the witnesses—the lineup is a complete bust. Not one of the witnesses, including Patty Lezaca, is sure enough to make a positive identification. When Jerry Engelman can't pick anyone out, he's told to look again and select the man who most closely resembles the visitor to the office on the day of the murder. Reluctantly, Jerry points to one man who is tall and muscular with light hair. It's one of the cops. When pressed to select anyone who looks close, another witness also picks a cop.

Two weeks later the state arraigns Young and announces plans to bring the case to trial, but the ultimate conclusion is apparent. Whether the case goes to trial or Young makes a deal, Robert Young will be the official murderer of Don Aronow. Case closed.

EPILOGUE

In a city where truth and reality aren't always the same, where light doesn't always illuminate and shadows don't always obscure, where the impossible is always possible, a most fitting solution to the murder has been found.

Donald Aronow.was killed by Robert Young, who chose his victim from a death list prepared by Colombian drug lords. Aronow's name was there because he built drug-interceptor boats. This infuriated the Colombians. His murder was a bloody return salvo in the War on Drugs, a brutal message to George Bush and to anyone who tries to stand in the way of the South American "dealers in death."

So the "bad guys" turn out to be anonymous (and untouchable) South American drug lords and their triggerman, an already convicted killer. There is no mob connection. No subpoena probing the drug-smuggling activities of the two men who built Blue Thunder. No conspiracy that put Customs' interceptor contract into the hands of the nation's largest marijuana smuggler. And no cover-up when the scandal was discovered.

Instead, Lillian Aronow has her fervent wish: that her children would grow up believing their father was a hero.

The FBI can rest easier. The President won't be dragged into the story about his friend's Mafia and drug-smuggling associations. Customs doesn't have to worry any longer about the true story of "Blue Blunder" surfacing. MetroDade Homicide and Dade County prosecutor Gary Rosenberg bask in the glory of having solved their toughest and most celebrated case, and State Attorney Janet Reno gets a big boost in her upcoming reelection bid.

Tommy Teagle and his buddy Skip Walton are awarded two "Get Out of Jail Free" cards. Teagle promptly cashes his in, gets a new identity courtesy of the FBI, and disappears into the Federal Witness Protection Program. Walton gets a dramatic reduction in his sentences on drug convictions and could be out in three years.

The Mafia and the Purple Gang continue their drug operations without the scrutiny that the investigation of Don Aronow might have brought about. Meyer Lansky's successor, whoever he may be, goes on silently about the business of supervising Ben Kramer's replacement as head of Lansky, Inc.'s ongoing marijuana operations.

Wayne Bock is happy. He's now a top aide to Sam Carlisi, allegedly the new head of the Chicago Mafia crime family. Things aren't going as well for Frankie Schweihs, however. He finally got caught by Chicago-area FBI agents. They sent one of the nation's most feared hit men to jail not for murder, but for extorting $1,200 a month from a porno-theater operator. While in prison, Frankie learns he has cancer. Still, he gets regular and free medical treatment, courtesy of the U.S. government.

Robert Young coasts along waiting to hear what progress his newest lawyer has made on his behalf. Miami's federal prison is a lot nicer (and safer) than Raiford, and the prospects of a deal look good. He has a lot of confidence in his new lawyer William H. Thomas, who's a friend and ardent supporter of Mel Kessler. And if things don't go as planned for Bobby? Well, who's really going to care or listen?

After all, he is on the record as a murderer, attempted murderer, drug smuggler, pimp, and a kidnapper. No citizens' group is going to be outraged that perhaps the murder case against him this time seems questionable. Or that the witnesses couldn't pick him out of a lineup—even though three of them had been less than four feet away when he allegedly confronted Don Aronow in the USA Racing office.

No one is going to ask questions about the two different men that the eyewitnesses talked about in the first few years after the murder —the tall, sandy-haired man who entered the office, and his accomplice, the big, dark man who pulled the trigger. The new version is that it was just one man who went into the office and later pulled the trigger. And anyone who does question the circumstances of the investigation has only to remember what happened to others who tried to probe too deeply or didn't want to go along with the direction the case was heading.

Bill Norris had wanted the FBI to look into the fact that Aronow was killed the day before he was subpoenaed as a government witness. When he persisted in bringing up the subject, he was demoted and soon left the U.S. Attorney's Office. The man who actually signed the Aronow subpoena, Dan Cassidy, was gung ho to tear the Kramers apart in the Florida federal money-laundering trial. Instead, he was shipped out to Denver. Nicky Deary, the FBI agent who fought the MetroDade deal with Skip Walton, was suddenly out of a job.

The official version of the murder is the only one that matters, and it says that Robert "Bobby" Young is the killer. It is an inspired denouement to the life and death of Don Aronow.

A few days after Robert Young is arraigned for murder, I drive by Thunderboat Alley. It seems different now. Perhaps it's my imagination. The days when legendary figures controlled the street are gone. Probably forever.

The mood is far less carefree as people go about their business. An era has ended. Everyone on the street knew that Don Aronow had been an extraordinary figure. He was responsible for the street, for the industry, and for the fame focused on that tiny parcel of land. As Ted Theodile had remarked, "Whether you liked him or not, everyone knows that we're here because of Don Aronow, that people all over the world know the names he created: Magnum. Cigarette. Donzi. Without him, this street would still be a plot of weeds."

There was a time not long ago on the Alley when drug smuggling seemed acceptable. A part of the wild, cavalier world inhabited by men who made powerfully fast boats and felt alive only when they were taking great risks. Money was made fast, and spent fast. It was a curious type of innocence. The rules didn't apply in Miami, particularly on the Alley, and there was no retribution for those who broke them. Aronow's murder and Kramer's downfall had removed that aura.

A fed who has spent a great deal of time surveilling the street recently told me that they now have their eye on another powerboat builder, a man involved in supplying boats to mob dopers and whom the agent calls "the new Genovese crime family presence on the street." He thinks it won't be long until he takes the fall as well.

Thunderboat Alley will never be the same.

. . .

Don Aronow was a real-life Great Gatsby. Like the Jay Gatsby of F. Scott Fitzgerald's novel, he set out as a young man to remake himself. He found a mentor, a clever New Yorker of Jewish descent with links to the underworld who recognized his talent and guided him. For Jay Gatsby it was a man named Meyer Wolfsheim; for Don Aronow it was Meyer Lansky.

Wolfsheim said of Gatsby, "Start him! I made him. . . . I raised him up out of nothing, right out of the gutter. I saw right away he was a fine-appearing, gentlemanly young man, and when he told me he was an Oggsford I knew I could use him good."

Through his association with Wolfsheim and his underworld activities, Gatsby became fabulously wealthy. He bought an elaborate mansion, a symbol of the life he had devoted himself to attaining. He rewrote his past and filled it with more myth than truth: fortunes lost in the panic, money made in a variety of businesses. There were few people he could confide in completely, few who knew the truth. Gatsby never questioned how he made his fortune. The brightness of his dream obscured everything else for him.

The narrator in Fitzgerald's book said: "I thought of Gatsby's wonder when he first picked out the green light at the end of Daisy's dock. He had come a long way to this blue lawn, and his dream must have seemed so close that he could hardly fail to grasp it. He did not know that it was already behind him, somewhere back in that vast obscurity beyond the city, where the dark fields of the republic rolled on under the night." Gatsby was gunned down as he came close to realizing his lifelong dream.

Like Jay Gatsby, Don Aronow must have stood on the grounds of his elaborate estate in Miami Beach and looked across the bay to Miami, the city of the future. His future. He must have marveled at how very far he had come, propelled ever forward, always believing that everything would work out right for him, that he could achieve whatever he set out to do. Racing, just as he did in his boats, toward his goal. The path he took simply a passing blur.

Mike Brittain had been one of the first people to reach Aronow seconds after the shots were fired. He found his friend slumped back in the seat of his Mercedes, dying. "He was bleeding all over," Brittain recalls. "His foot was on the pedal and the motor was roaring. And I looked at his face. He had the strangest expression I've ever seen. It was a look of complete and total surprise." Perhaps Aronow was seeing his greatest dream slip away from his fingertips.

Fate had made the journey with him from Brooklyn to Miami, bringing him a message from a long time ago.

INDEX